A Theory of Communication

Other books by Philip Hobsbaum

POEMS

The Place's Fault

In Retreat

Coming Out Fighting

ANTHOLOGIES (editor)

A Group Anthology (with Edward Lucie-Smith)

Ten Elizabethan Poets

A THEORY OF
COMMUNICATION

PHILIP HOBSBAUM

MACMILLAN

First published 1970 by
MACMILLAN AND CO LTD
London and Basingstoke
Associated companies in New York Toronto
Dublin Melbourne Johannesburg and Madras

SBN (boards) 333 11026 9

Printed in Great Britain by
WESTERN PRINTING SERVICES LTD
Bristol

FOR MARK ROBERTS

Contents

What would be highly ambiguous by itself becomes definite in a suitable context.

I. A. RICHARDS

A Theory of Communication

Demaine, unfortunately, was born dumb,
All senses else alert, speech organs numb.
His conversation was to sit or stand,
His argument a shy jerk of the hand.
Of what he missed (we said) he had no sense,
Expecting only from experience;
Yet compromise, as in colloquial prose,
Need never mask the happy thought he chose;
Animals view in silent consternation
Our fluent and vociferous conversation;
Perhaps Demaine, as we in jest, would balk
In earnest at our heedless, ceaseless talk;
As a lapsed poet thinks, had he the time,
He'd thunder out potential thought in rhyme,
But when the time is come he may be taught
That silence has decayed potential thought;
For in some idle moments he would seem
To lose himself in an unrealised dream,
And maybe would have, given but the gift,
Denied such diagnosis, healed the rift:
What heart-arousing songs might he have sung
Could he but have controlled his torpid tongue;
What tones of voice to sound, what notes to reach,
Had he the unheeded faculty of speech;
What unimparted truth, gone dead inside,
Means of communication atrophied;
What might-have-beens of vision, hoped-for light,
What cris-des-cœurs, what gestures in the night!

Preface

The fact that all existing theories of art are fallacious does not mean that it is impossible to voice one that would be valid. Rather it suggests that the methods of argument adopted by aesthetic philosophers are imprecise.

Aesthetic discourse pivots on one idea. Roughly it can be said that theories of the arts differ according to the degree of subjectivity they attribute to the response of the percipient. Or, what comes to the same thing, they differ according to the extent of the objectivity they attribute to the work of art. Thus the gamut of theory stretches from Subjectivism, where it is felt that each person will recreate the work in his own private way, to Absolutism, where it is felt that an ideal standard has been revealed to which each work of art should conform.

As it exists, aesthetic theory rests upon a paradox. It is impossible to suggest a Subjectivist theory which does not bring in the concept of a shared satisfaction and so imply some general standard: 'the greatest good of the greatest number' is one such example. Equally, it is impossible to suggest an Absolutist theory which is truly objective: the 'standard' necessarily is one envisaged by an individual sensibility.

It would be true to say that the old Subjective–Objective paradox is, and always has been, irrelevant to the arts. Clearly each and every response to a work of art is personal. However, since we live in Western Civilisation and are biologically similar, it is equally clear that in certain circumstances one individual's reaction will very much resemble that of another. The key circumstance is that of quality in the work in question. A powerful work of art is liable to induce a powerful response in its percipient. My contention would be that an individual's response to such a work would not be eccentrically different from that of his fellows. It is up to the critical theorist to explain how a work of art can have this effect and how it works upon the interested percipient. Such is the purpose of this book.

But it is beyond any theorist at present to propound a theory that would do for all the arts. The media vary so widely that there is no rationale capable of covering them all. Any such undertaking would be so inclusive as to be useless for purposes of discussion, unless it were to leave out a great many manifestations of art altogether. It will be time enough to attempt an aesthetic fitting all the arts when we have worked out the theory of any one of them.

Therefore my present purpose is to demonstrate a theory of literature. Any such theory, to be complete, must take in the nature of value in literature and, arising out of this, the means and efficacy of linguistic communication. My basic procedure has been to locate a text that has caused a fair amount of dissension; to locate within that text the main points of divergence among the critics; and, at each point, to map out a pattern of variation. The next task was to ascertain the cause of variation, and, from each cause, to draw out a point of critical theory. It was only necessary to analyse sufficient groups of dissensions in sufficient detail to produce a composite theory of effect in literature; and, hence, of value. Since the effect of a work of literature depends very much upon the words in which that effect is conveyed, it therefore follows that any theory of value in literature must necessarily entail a theory of language. And, because language is by a long way the most efficacious method we have of recalling, judging and conveying experience, a composite theory of literature-value-language is best described as a theory of communication.

So it may be said that this book seeks to answer the following questions. Why do the critics disagree? What makes one work of literature good and another bad? How does an effective work of literature communicate with its readers?

The preliminary fanfare to my book may be found in a paper I wrote for the *British Journal of Aesthetics* of April 1967. It was called 'Current Aesthetic Fallacies' and consisted of a classification and critique of the existing range of aesthetic theory. The book itself begins with a consideration of the personal responses of individual critics. It moves on through a discussion of the effects and conditions necessary to increase availability and diminish resistance both in the reader and in the work. These effects and conditions are described in the final chapters in terms of a theory of language which is also a theory of communication in literature.

The book itself may be read at either of two levels. The intelligent layman may well choose to ignore the numbers that spangle the text: they are no more than references to the notes at the back which will supply further evidence. But the specialist – critic, philosopher, linguist, psychologist – will probably need those numbers as a guide to the tissue of allusion that underpins my text. The book works through the exploration of critical divergence. Though I have done my best to represent fairly those whose views are pictured within, nevertheless it seemed right to let the specialist have every opportunity to check my accuracy and information.

Sections of this book have appeared in *Arrows*, the *British Journal of Aesthetics*, the *Bulletin of the British Association for American Studies*, *Essays in Criticism*, the *Keats-Shelley Memorial Association Bulletin*, *Neophilologus*, the *Poetry Review*, *Studia Neophilologica* and *The Use of English*.

My debts are few, but crucial. To the staff of the British Museum Reading Room, North Library and Newspaper Library who bore with my demands over nine years of research. To the work of I. A. Richards, founder of modern critical theory, whose influence is immanent throughout. To my great teacher F. R. Leavis, who set an example his students can never equal but must try to emulate. To William Empson, who read over a million words of this book's raw material and who paid me the highest compliment an older critic can a younger: reasoned disagreement. To my friend and departmental head, Peter Butter, who allowed me the facilities to pursue research. To my old friends of the Group, especially Martin Bell and Edward Lucie-Smith, for years of encouragement and advice. To Ruth Pepper, Vernon Napier, Liz Annand and Pam Rennie for help in preparing the last of many drafts for publication. To my former wife, Hannah, without whose undeviating belief in my work, it would never have been carried out. And to Mark Roberts, who campaigned tirelessly for me during a dark period. To him, therefore, this book is given.

Sheffield–Belfast–Glasgow
1959–1968

CHAPTER ONE

The Personal Response

If all responses to literature are personal, why should we not hold a subjective theory of art? After all, there is a very great variety of response to works of literature among the critics. True, it does not seem to trouble Critic A that Critic B disagrees with him; he is always at liberty to denigrate his colleague's taste, understanding or knowledge. Yet such disagreement opens extraordinary fields to conjecture. Is it possible that *both* critics are right? or neither? or that rightness is a goal impossible to critics at large? in which latter case, criticism as an activity would be invalidated altogether.

If we are not to believe this, it might be worth our while to consider what happens when critics disagree. Such a consideration may throw light on more than the critics; it may tell us something about the work which has occasioned this disagreement.

My own belief is that even the most active disagreement is anything but arbitrary; that there is always a pattern in diverse reactions to specific authors. And this is true even when the reactions come from critics who have very little in common.

For example, no two critics could be less alike than R. P. Blackmur and Yvor Winters. Blackmur is characteristically urbane, interested in aesthetic problems, committed to an exploration of linguistic texture – almost, it would seem, for its own sake. For Winters, on the other hand, language is an instrument of moral directive: he is interested in themes, not words, and the tone in which he discusses them is discriminatory, assertive, not to say moralistic.

Certainly Blackmur discriminates; but he does so in terms such as these. 'Merely because Crane is imperfect in his kind is no reason to give him up; there is no plethora of perfection, and the imperfect beauty, like life, retains its fascination.'[1] And certainly Winters is appreciative, but his manner is that of a prescriptive critic. 'Crane possessed great energy, but his faculties functioned clearly only within a limited range of experience.'[2] Who, from the tone of these remarks, would have deduced that Winters thinks more highly of Crane than does Blackmur? The contrast we see in little here is that between the

1

work of these critics as a whole. It is a contrast between the aesthete and the moralist. And yet there is a relationship between the views of these radically differing critics.

If we keep to their discussion of Hart Crane for the moment, we shall see how these differences act out a pattern. Blackmur does not concern himself with what is valuable in Crane's poetry, merely with what is characteristic of it. Because of this, he goes into considerable detail in analysing a poem called *Wine Menagerie*, which is more remarkable for its typicality than its merit. Personally I find this poem very obscure; much of Blackmur's account is an attempt to justify the texture of the verse – claiming, for instance, that the words are not referential but have a life of their own.

> . . . *New thresholds, new anatomies! Wine talons*
> *Build freedom up about me and distil*
> *This competence – to travel in a tear*
> *Sparkling alone within another's will* . . .[3]

It is difficult to give an interpretation of this poem that would be more than tautological. Blackmur avoids this necessity by discussing Crane's use of language, and so seems to derive from *Wine Menagerie* mainly a sense of fresh adventure. For him, the phrase 'new thresholds, new anatomies' is wholly natural and alive.[4] Unfortunately for Blackmur's case, this phrase will bear a considerable range of possible constructions. For example, it may mean that the thresholds are themselves anatomies; that the anatomies are beyond the thresholds; that, once over the threshold, experience is re-ordered into new forms; that the beginnings of new experience are consolidated into actuality; that the horizon of sensation is in fact a barrier preventing further extension of the senses – and these by no means exhaust the possibilities. What is more to the point, these possibilities flatly contradict one another. Any two or three interpretations may be compatible once taken into relation with the text, for the individual sense of any given reading may be included in some composite linguistic creation: it is in this way that a poem replaces the prosaic meaning of individual phrases. But there is no interaction among the words here – wine talons are made to 'build' freedom and to 'distil' competence – actions that are disparate in themselves and inappropriate to the organism motivating them.

How, then, is it possible for Blackmur to speak up for this poem? Simply by positing a special approach to the problem: he is compelled to enlist the reader's good-will by maintaining that Crane was employing in this poem an extreme mode of free association; in short, a flux of intoxicated sense.[5] This certainly gives rise to verbal effects, themselves susceptible to exegesis, if not to admiration. But the whole is of interest only to those who seek what is characteristic of Crane's poetry; it will not encourage the reader to discriminate among the various poems.

The approach of Yvor Winters is very different. He makes a major – and necessary – concession; that Crane's style is seldom at its best.[6] Therefore it behoves him to make a canon of those poems which are comprehensible wholes. The poems which he chooses for discussion are quite different from those chosen by Blackmur; and readers may feel the choice to be equally personal. Nevertheless, it cannot be denied that Winters's canon, notably three lyrics from *The Bridge*, requires much less exegesis than *Wine Menagerie*; and certainly it demands no special sort of reading method whatsoever. For instance, the River, in the poem of that name, symbolically depicts the folk of America flowing towards the gulf of eternity. Nevertheless, says Winters, this river is described as if it were the real Mississippi.[7]

> *. . . You will not hear it as the sea; even stone*
> *Is not more hushed by gravity . . . But slow*
> *As loth to take more tribute – sliding prone*
> *Like one whose eyes were buried long ago*
>
> *The River, spreading, flows – and spends your dream.*
> *What are you, lost within this tideless spell?*
> *You are your father's father, and the stream*
> *A liquid theme that floating niggers swell.*
>
> *Damp tonnage and alluvial march of days –*
> *Nights turbid, vascular with silted shell*
> *And roots surrendered down of moraine clays:*
> *The Mississippi drinks the farthest dale . . .*[8]

There are no glittering effects and far-fetched word connotations here; to that extent it is uncharacteristic of Crane. What is remarkable in this passage is its inevitability of language, movement, thought, feeling. These component parts work together because of the realism with which the symbol of the folk as a river is developed. As Winters says, this is no ideal river but the Mississippi.[9] The irresistible and ever-changing tide of the human race is imaginatively fused with that of the great stream. And the rhythm acts out that flow – itself the movement of the river it describes. For example: the first stanza I have quoted is

3

fairly regular, but, after this, the rhythm slows down and broadens out, as the River does –

The River, spreading, flows – and spends your dream.

This slowing down of a movement already none too fast is achieved in this line by a plethora of pauses, by the syntax with its tenuously attached present participle and by the lip-movements required to enunciate the juxtaposed 'spr . . . fl . . . sp' sounds.

This may not constitute an unarguable evaluation, but it does suggest that more is available to common experience than in *The Wine Menagerie* – where every effect has a range of significance whose relevant sectors are so hard to determine that each reader takes away with him his own poem.

For Blackmur, this is a matter of textural explication. He suggests, in effect, that the poems cannot be interpreted without undergoing a special reorientation of understanding.[10] In practice, this seems to mean considering verbal effects out of thematic context. Granted Blackmur's premises, disagreement would be difficult: his approach inclines the reader to consider parts, not wholes. Blackmur's divergence from Winters is not, then, so much a matter of finally placing Crane as of deciding how to read him. Both critics may be accused of approaches personal to themselves; but I should be prepared to argue that Blackmur's approach is less relevant to the work as a whole than that of Winters.

Still keeping to the same critics, let us see what happens when they concur as to a poet's 'greatness'. That much-abused word might be expected to mean something very different to Blackmur from what it does to Winters. Both think very highly of Emily Dickinson: for Blackmur, the charm lies in potentiality; for Winters, in achievement.

Once more, we find Blackmur discussing language in virtual isolation from meaning. 'The greatness of Emily Dickinson . . . is going to be found in the words she used and in the way she put these together.'[11] And he cites the following.

> *Renunciation*
> *Is a piercing virtue*
> *The letting go*
> *A presence for an expectation –*
> *Not now . . .* [12]

It may be felt that this is elliptical; but Blackmur takes it upon himself to supply the logical links. For example, he defines the word 'renunciation' in terms not determined by the poem: as heroism, hypocrisy or sentimentality, mostly kept in abeyance.[13] And he talks about the word 'piercing' as though it were directly physical and so able to precipitate a relation between renunciation and virtue.[14]

But surely we should need to know more about 'piercing' for this to be true? As it stands, the word seems a counter for some situation not given to us in the poem. Blackmur calls the effect one of shock;[15] but, even to a sympathetic reader, 'renunciation is a piercing virtue' seems rather an effect of mild paradox. The critic has been impelled to make specific what the poet left general; to supply his own referent.

Again, Blackmur identifies the final phrase of this poem, 'Not now', with some moment an infinite amount of time away.[16] But it could equally well mean 'never' or 'any time but the present' or 'the inability of the poet to renounce'. All these are as logical as Blackmur's gloss; and none of them are imposed as a necessary reading by the poem on the reader. In other words, the poem is bizarre enough to appear to have a meaning, cryptic enough to leave it to be supplied by the more logical reader.

Yet there is something in Emily Dickinson which induces this over-personal sort of reading – a reading which relates to the critic rather than the poem. There is an excitement which suggests feeling, but which does not define it. Possibly the words are misused enough to make for speculation, but not enough to make for bewilderment. Or it may be that Emily Dickinson's poetry does not do enough, that the critic is started off by its initial brief impact on his own course of emotions – which, in rationalisation, he attributes entirely to the poet. A poem by Marvell is completed; one by Emily Dickinson simply stops.[17] This is an insecure basis for her great reputation.

It is those poems of hers which do not go on that seem to be the ones most likely to interest the critics. Mostly, Yvor Winters discusses Emily Dickinson in terms of theme, and finds fault with her personal shorthand and loose and indefinable manner.[18] But these remarks refer to poems that seek to complete their statement, such as *Farther in summer* and *Because I could not stop for death*. Winters remarks of the latter that it is only successful in so far as it evokes the life being left behind; in so far as it attempts to experience the death to come, it is fraudulent.[19] In other words, when Emily Dickinson 'goes on' she has to eke out her theme. This is not the way of a great poet; and it is noticeable that, to substantiate a view of Emily Dickinson's greatness, Winters has to abandon his characteristic, thematic, approach and to discuss the poem, like Blackmur, in terms of potential. Once more we see the poet inviting the reader to fill in his own details, to supply his own data. Winters does this in terms of rhythm; and sees subtleties which – until he has pointed them out – another reader might take to be no more than mild irregularities.[20]

> *There's a certain slant of light*
> *On winter afternoons*
> *That oppresses, like the weight*
> *Of cathedral tunes.*
>
> *Heavenly hurt it gives us;*
> *We can find no scar*
> *But internal difference*
> *Where the meanings are.*[21]

We can imagine what a consideration of theme would do to this poem: it would be impossible, for instance, to pass evasions like '*a certain* slant of light' or '*internal* difference' or '*the* meanings'. But Winters, for once, does not relate his analysis to the sense conveyed. And, without such a relation, it is difficult to see how the variations of metre described by Winters can be of very much interest. In fact, the reader might question how far any useful discussion of verse-movement can take place separately from language, sense and feeling.

For example, Winters praises the line 'Heavenly hurt it gives us' because it has only five metrical syllables, the initial one having been dropped in the interests of variety.[22] To this one could reply that the line is no more than tripping and bright; it certainly does not convey the effect of hurt, heavenly or otherwise. Winters claims that the *us* at the end is carried over into the second line.[23] But the stress with which 'We can find no scar' begins emphasises the 'we' and this cannot be felt as a felicity since there is no reason for it to be emphasised; no one other than 'we' is in question. Like Blackmur, Winters has been led by something in the poem to read into it his own preoccupation. There is little in this poem to justify Winters's tone of pleased surprise at discovering what are undoubtedly rhythmic variations, but hardly rhythmic effects.

This would suggest that even the most acute critics fall prey to their private interests in dealing with Emily Dickinson; and should be enough to show that her reputation is vastly inflated and that her talent is that of a minor poet. Blackmur, who does not find Emily Dickinson rhythmically interesting, discusses her in terms of his own

6

Specialised view of language; Winters, on the other hand, sees that poem which he most elaborately discusses largely in rhythmic terms. So far the responses would seem to be not only personal but highly subjective.

But what happens when the critics come to discuss one who really is a great poet? Is there a greater measure of agreement? Certainly the areas of disagreement are far more clearly defined. In even the worse poems, there is an extraordinary amount to disagree about.

For one thing, the critics appear to be more certain of the poems which deserve discussion. Take Wallace Stevens, for instance: a comparison of Blackmur's canon with that of Winters shows that they both comment upon *The Comedian as the Letter C, A High-Toned Old Christian Woman, On the Manner of Addressing Clouds, The Man Whose Pharynx was Bad, Le Monocle de Mon Oncle, The Snow Man, The Death of a Soldier, Sea Surface Full of Clouds* and *Sunday Morning*. Needless to say, they do not agree on the value of all these poems; though here, again, the area of agreement is greater than might have been expected. Let us, however, see first of all what happens by way of disagreement.

Blackmur, as usual, adopts a textural approach, and is concerned mainly with Stevens's language; this he characteristically discusses in terms of vocabulary. His essay on Stevens begins by citing what is probably the most uncommon word in *Harmonium* – 'funest'. It occurs in a poem called *On the Manner of Addressing Clouds*.

> *Gloomy grammarians in golden gowns,*
> *Meekly you keep the mortal rendezvous,*
> *Eliciting the still sustaining pomps*
> *Of speech which are like music so profound*
> *They seem an exaltation without sound.*
> *Funest philosophers and ponderers . . .*[24]

Blackmur concedes that the word is odd, but attempts to elucidate the obscurity by relating it to another hardly less obscure. In this case, his explanation of 'funest' leans heavily on one of another word, 'pomps'; but this, in its turn, is used in several senses – 'ceremonial', for instance, and 'funeral processsion'. We cannot therefore feel very happy about Blackmur's summing up of the meaning: 'The pomps of the clouds suggest the funeral in funest.'[25] The gloss seems, on the whole, rather harder than the poem.

This is a personal interpretation, no doubt, but one which is unlikely to be widely shared. Another reader might not care to detach the words from the phrases in which they are used: not 'pomps' in isolation, that is to say, but, 'pomps *of speech*'. And if the phrases are put together rather than taken apart, the passage as a whole will seem rather more clear than Blackmur makes it. Thus: '(Gloomy grammarians) Eliciting the still sustaining pomps / Of speech which are like music so profound / They seem an exaltation without sound' can then be paraphrased in this way: '(The clouds) drawing forth rhetoric so dignified that, like great music, they seem to be an emotion one feels rather than a sound one hears.'

Unfortunately for my case, the latter part of this paraphrase relies on ideas embodied in other poems by Stevens. *Peter Quince at the Clavier*, for instance, has

> *Music is feeling, then, not sound.*[26]

And in *Notes Towards a Supreme Fiction* we find

> *Music falls on the silence like a sense,*
> *A passion that we feel, not understand.*[27]

This sort of dependence of one poem upon another indicates that *On the Manner of Addressing Clouds* does not really stand on its own feet. After all, the analogy between 'pomps of speech' and 'music so profound' in *this* poem requires far more elucidation than the music analogies of the others. It is, perhaps, rather too elaborate to be convincing.

In any case, it is difficult to see how the analogy could be justified by the approach chosen by Blackmur: the discussion, that is to say, of a poem in terms of its vocabulary. One could certainly concede that the choice of vocabulary in this poem goes well with the attitude it takes towards its subject-matter; but, in order to make this concession, we should have to consider what that subject-matter is. In other words, the poem demands a more thematic consideration than that given by Blackmur: the personal response, in his case, can be shown to have left out much of the meaning. Stevens's view of clouds is harder to accept than Blackmur seems to realise; and a consideration of its theme leads us to question how far the poem is being proffered seriously.

The thematic approach is the other chief way of reading poetry, and its prime exponent with regard to Stevens is Yvor Winters. If, in this case, it exposes weaknesses in the poem, it may be that the weaknesses were there to be exposed anyway, and that they can be seen most clearly when language is related to subject. In Winter's words:

'Mr Stevens's commonest method of ironic comment is to parody his own style, with respect to its slight affectation of elegance; or perhaps it were more accurate to say that this affectation itself is a parody, however slight, of the purity of his style in its best moments. The parody frequently involves an excess of alliteration . . .'[28]

This last sentence suggests one of the ways in which the style of the poem draws an excessive amount of attention to itself. Instead of the eccentric 'funest' being conditioned by its context into seeming inevitability, it merely passes unnoticed among the poem's other eccentricities.

But, unlike Winters, Blackmur's approach allows him to accommodate these eccentricities, and even to regard them as being felicitous. He is, however, limited by this approach: it is noticeable that he does not say what he thinks the poem is about. The words engage his attention to an extent that excludes any concern with a larger context. 'Mr Stevens has created a surface, a texture, a rhetoric in which his feelings and thoughts are preserved in what amounts to a new sensibility . . . Nature becomes nothing but words and to a poet words are everything.'[29]

This occurs at the end of an essay, and so may be taken as a summary of Stevens's procedure throughout *Harmonium*; but it also refers specifically to *The Comedian as the Letter C*. For Blackmur, who bases his appreciation of the poem on its language, this is one of Stevens's most important works;[30] for Winters, who criticises the poem in terms of its theme, it is no more than crude comedy.[31]

The difference between the critics is not only one of valuation: they do not even agree on what the action of the poem conveys to the reader. For Blackmur the central persona, Crispin, is a kind of Everyman,[32] but for Winters the poem is autobiographical.[33] The point at issue between the critics is this: How far is Crispin to be regarded as a universal type?

The evidence as to how far the poem is autobiographical can hardly be derived from its text. It is true that the critics do not dispute the general direction of the plot: it is agreed that Crispin voyages to Yucatan, returns to North Carolina, projects a colony which fails, and, after its failure, settles down as a family man. But an agreement about the main shifts in action can hardly seem important when we consider that at no point are the critics in accord about what that action signifies.

The nature of Crispin's development remains unclear. An examination of the verse at any given point would show a measure of

9

evasiveness; but the failure is not a local one. Rather it may be considered that something has gone wrong with the action as a whole.

Why, after all, should Crispin acquire a family? For Blackmur, this is a return to social nature, a resolution of the sensual confusion of man;[34] and it is noticeable that he refers to man generally rather than one particular man. As with *On the Manner of Addressing Clouds*, he takes the poem at its face value – completely unironically. He is certainly aware not only that it differs from most poems that have been written in the past but also from most of those in *Harmonium*. But he ascribes this to the inadequacy of the simple statement – of which, he concedes, Stevens is a master – to meet the dimensions of the subject. And so Blackmur finds it necessary to maintain that Stevens invented a new form – rhetoric, language used for its own sake, persuasively to the extreme.[35]

But surely, in the creation of this new category, the issue has been evaded? Blackmur applauds the poem's 'extraordinary luxuriance of rhetoric and image'[36] without once indicating to what uses he thinks this undoubted luxuriance is being put.

> *Was he to bray this in profoundest brass*
> *Arointing gleams with fugal requiems?*
> *Was he to company vastest things defunct*
> *With a blubber of tom-toms harrowing the sky?*
> *Scrawl a tragedian's testament? Prolong*
> *His active force in an inactive dirge,*
> *Which, let the tall musicians call and call*
> *Should nearly call him dead? Pronounce amen*
> *Through choirs infolded to the outmost clouds?*
> *Because he built a cabin who once planned*
> *Loquacious columns by the ructive sea?*
> *Because he turned to salad-beds again?*[37]

Winters regards this as the crux of the poem, and calls it a renunciation of Crispin's art; unequivocally, he identifies Crispin with Stevens himself. He says that Crispin loses interest in his art because it is without an adequate moral basis and cannot proceed to more complex subjects. This is, in fact, the old – and false – antithesis: Crispin abandons 'art' in favour of 'life'. Winters goes on, 'What I wish the reader to note is this: that the passage describes Crispin's taking leave of his art, and describes also his refusal to use his art in process of leave-taking, because the art is, after all, futile and contemptible. Yet for Stevens himself the entire poem is a kind of tentative leave-taking; he has not the courage to act as his hero acts and be done with it, so he practises the art which he cannot justify and describes it in terms of contempt.'[38] The mode of this passage, and of the poem generally, is for Winters a parody, often crude and tawdry, of the refined and inimitable style of Stevens at his best.

Now this is severe – possibly too much so – but nearer to an understanding of the poem than the view of Blackmur, for whom Stevens is no more than a creator of the beautiful and a purveyor of rhetoric.[39] One might say that this is a personal viewpoint, and that Blackmur is entitled to it. But to take this line as a general approach is to ignore the bulk of Stevens's work where he is concerned to put forward a vision – perhaps, as the poet himself would have said, a philosophy. His poems are usually about something: one key theme is the barrenness of the world without the colouring power of imagination. Another is the impossibility of any permanence in a life limited to a brief mortality among the transient beauty of our physical surroundings. This should do something to show that Stevens's poems do not exist merely as word-collocations, texture to be enjoyed for texture's sake.

Yet, in practice, when a poem offers more than this, the critics – even those concerned with texture – can be seen to have responded to it. Much of the effect of Stevens's 'philosophy' is to be found in the illustrations and examples in his longer works and in his many small meditative/descriptive poems. His 'system' is emotionally convincing as the testimony of one man's reactions to the world, rather than intellectually acceptable as a general philosophy; and it ought not to be divorced from his poetic practice. But, in fact, the finest poems of Stevens do not permit such a divorce: they are poetry, not ideas abstracted from poetry. Take *Sunday Morning*, for instance: Winters summarises the poem in order to show its trend of thought, while Blackmur, as ever, is keenly aware of its texture. But in this case texture and theme are not so easily separated; and it is noticeable that there is a much greater consensus between the critics than hitherto. They are, to begin with, completely in accord about the initial situation in the poem. Winters says: 'The first stanza sets the stage and identifies the protagonist. We are given a woman, at home on a Sunday morning, meditating on the meaning of death.'[40] And in Blackmur's summary, too, we are given this tension between physical ease and serious meditation. 'Visually, we have a woman enjoying her Sunday morning breakfast in a sunny room with a green rug. The image is secured . . . [not] in directly visual terms, but by the almost casual combination of visual images with such phrases as "*complacencies* of the

11

peignoir", and the "green *freedom* of the cockatoo", when the italicised words are abstract in essence but rendered concrete in combination.'[41] And Blackmur goes on to suggest that the purpose of the images is to show how they dissipate the 'holy hush of ancient sacrifice'; the body is aware, but mostly unheeding, that Sunday is the Lord's Day and that it commemorates the Crucifixion. (Strictly speaking, Blackmur is misleading here: the Crucifixion was on a Friday.)

> Complacencies of the peignoir, and late
> Coffee and oranges in a sunny chair,
> And the green freedom of the cockatoo
> Upon a rug mingle to dissipate
> The holy hush of ancient sacrifice.
> She dreams a little, and she feels the dark
> Encroachment of that old catastrophe,
> As a calm darkens among water-lights
> The pungent oranges and bright, green wings
> Seem things in some procession of the dead
> Wandering across wide water without sound.
> The day is like wide water without sound,
> Stilled for the passing of her dreaming feet
> Over the seas, to silent Palestine,
> Dominion of the blood and sepulchre . . .[42]

Both the critics agree not only about the meaning but the value of the poem. For Winters, *Sunday Morning* is certainly one of the greatest contemplative poems in English 'in a blank verse which differs, in its firmness of structure and incalculable sensitivity of detail, from all other blank verse of our time'.[43] For all their differences about other poems, Blackmur's reaction to the verse is similar in its appreciation to that of Winters. Commenting in greatest detail, as Winters does, on the first stanza, he says, 'A great deal of ground is covered in this fifteen lines, and the more the slow ease and conversational elegance of the verse are observed, the more wonder it seems that so much could have been indicated without strain.'[44]

Even particulars of interpretation find the critics in accord. Both Blackmur and Winters point out the way in which the water images are used. Blackmur demonstrates their use as transition, taking the place of explicit logic to bring into contact contrasting elements: how, for instance, the images act as a junction between the complacencies of the peignoir and the Christian feeling appropriate to the day.[45] While Winters shows how the image of is used in the last stanza as well as the first.[46] And both critics comment upon the content of this image:

> She dreams a little, and she feels the dark
> Encroachment of that old catastrophe,
> As a calm darkens among water-lights.

'From her half-awareness she feels the more keenly the "old catastrophe" merging in the surroundings, subtly but deeply, changing them as a "calm darkens among water-lights". The feeling is dark in her mind, darkness, changing the whole day. The oranges and the rug and the day all have this quality of "wide water without sound" and all her thoughts, so loaded, turn on the Crucifixion.'[47]

(The water image) 'is not only an image representing infinite space ... [but] ... a state of mind, a kind of bright and empty beatitude, over which the thought of death may darken suddenly and without warning.'[48]

Although both critics comment on the water-imagery from different standpoints, there is no disparity: they are recognisably reading the same poem. Whereas *The Comedian as the Letter C* bore contradictory interpretations, *Sunday Morning* is so subtle a complex that any critique is likely to be only a selection of what there is to appreciate in the poem. Therefore the critic will make a selection, according to his interests; but the different selections, as we have seen here, will not amount to different readings of the poems.

And the acceptance of *Sunday Morning* seems to be general. Randall Jarrell says of it that it is the last purity and refinement of the grand style: as perfect, in its transparency, as the best of Wordsworth.[49] And A. Alvarez unequivocally calls it a great poem.[50] It would seem that personal predilections do not stand in the way of appreciating poems like *Sunday Morning*. And indeed it would be ludicrous to suppose that a fine poem could be understood only by a fine critic; or that only one critical approach is viable. In the cases we have considered, it seems that each critic has his personal responses, whether the poems were widely intelligible or not. The respones to *Sunday Morning* were markedly similar; not so those to *The Comedian as the Letter C*. It is reasonable, then, to suggest that *Sunday Morning* is more intelligible, or more effective in conditioning critical response, than *The Comedian as the Letter C*. Or, to put it more tersely, *Sunday Morning* is the better poem; since two critics as different from each other as Blackmur and Winters come out decisively in its favour.

Therefore it may be said at once that a response *is* personal and that it *may be* shared. Every critic has his predilections, but only some poems can overcome these. But the poems that succeed in this have broken down psychological barriers; bridged the gulf between human beings; asserted that no man is an island. They have governed idiosyncrasies and private characteristics, and have compelled those who can make contact in no other way to share in the response to a great work of art. It is obvious that the critics will continue to disagree about most literature, since there may not be very much in the literature for them to agree about. What is far more rare and wonderful is when a work of art manifests itself so tangibly and forcefully that they have no other recourse but to agree.

The Appreciation of Minor Art

All responses to literature, then, are personal. The cause of any difference among the critics is to be found not in the psychology of individuals but in the work to which they are reacting.

This issue is blurred by the confused way in which critics rationalise their reaction. For instance, we are likely to find even the most acute among them apparently speaking of a book's stylistic qualities when in fact they make judgements which are demonstrably moral ones.

Discussion of texture is less useful in prose fiction than in poetry. Even for the purposes of criticism, it is rarely possible to abstract stylistic effects from a novel. Such effects, in practice, serve some moral end. Thus a Conservative would have a hard time discussing the prose of *Studs Lonigan*, let alone more overtly political writings, such as those of Robert Tressell or Len Doherty. It is those who regard *1984* as a parody of Communism, and so mistake its theme, that find its style lacking in vigour.

Such tendencies to abstract are by no means confined to doctrinaire critics or to philistines. A divergence between two critics of indisputable ability is just as likely; and will often be found to stem from a moral or political bias which will prevent a full response to the novel. However, it must be suggested that, if a novel is sufficiently impressive, it is likely to exert a counter-influence of its own. Therefore, when we find two of our finest critics of prose fiction diverging in their assessment of James Gould Cozzens, it is reasonable to believe that some of the fault may be found in *By Love Possessed*. At the same time, their mode of discussion may not adequately reflect the nature of their experience.

D. W. Harding and Angus Wilson are the critics in question;[1] and they discuss *By Love Possessed* largely in terms of its texture. They agree on certain factual points: for example, that the novel depends heavily on technical terms mostly of a legal nature. Harding, however, sees these terms as symbolising the non-rationality of 'love' and the intense, sustained discipline of rationality undertaken especially in the legal professions. Wilson, on the other hand, does not feel that the

15

technical terms are digested into the book as a whole: Cozzens delights too much in words seldom seen outside a dictionary.

This would seem to be a question of how far one is justified in finding a positive in the disciplines invoked by Cozzens as an ideal. The vocabulary and style, both critics seem to agree, have a relevance to the book, whether they are digested into it or not. Harding sees the routines of the law as being too stiff for human nature; and hence, for him, the stiff vocabulary has a moral application. It is a way of showing the complexities that make moral codes inadequate as guides to moral action: the book, says Harding, is a serious examination of crime and moral debility.

But Wilson does not sympathise with the morality of the book at all; therefore, for him, the technical terms seem otiose. In his own words, 'Mr Cozzens is as impatient of modern language as he is of modern life and ideas.' He feels, for instance, that Cozzens gives undue weight to the wisdom of the years. The novel, it is true, is full of reminiscences of Brocton's past, before it was industrialised; and the aged attorneys, Willard Lowe and Noah Tuttle, are somewhat idealised. Tuttle's views on law have long since passed into statute, and therefore his utterance is – to say the least – dogmatic.

> Shall a justice of the peace arrogate to himself the right to refuse bail; at his whim or discretion to refuse what the highest court in the state is not permitted to refuse? There would be misfeasance, if you want. Consider the status of the accused! Even if the strongest sort of case had been laid out against him, his right to bail would be unaffected! On application, the court of oyer and terminer and general jail delivery would fix bail immediately. Here, no case at all's made out! Lodged against him is a mere information, for all the magistrate or anyone else knows, malicious, wild, groundless, false.[2]

Wilson does not object to the authority with which Tuttle is allowed to speak, or even the exaltation of the past, so much as its concomitant: denigration of the present. One sees something of this in Cozzens's references to the golden past of Brocton, before 'the influx of labour, so much of it foreign'. The reader would not have to be unduly sensitive to such matters to be aware of a deprecating note in that 'so much of it'. Wilson is unhappy about Cozzens's range of indictments, his attribution of causes. He aims most erratically, says Wilson: 'Cosmopolitans, metropolitans, Jews, Roman Catholics, foreign immigrants of all kinds, delinquent youth, neurotics of all sorts are lumped together as the enemy eroding by their lack of principle, their emotionalism and their basic inferiority the good old American way of life as represented by Brocton.' For Wilson, then, Cozzens's morality is a neo-Conservatism with more sinister overtones of prejudice.

It is, therefore, not surprising that Harding, a favourable advocate, concentrates on what Cozzens stands for. Brocton itself is a standard: 'a civilised small town'. Cozzens himself is civilised, well-read, ironic. However, much of what Harding attributes to Cozzens is an exclusion of what Harding himself would seem to dislike. 'He waved none of the right flags for attention in the Thirties and early Forties. He is not convinced that being oppressed ensures true worth, he cannot have needed to explain that he was never a Communist, knows that brutality and cruelty are not the expression of toughness, does not take copulation to be a touchstone of value, does not believe that "reality" is to be found exclusively in wretchedness.'

But this is, at best, negative. What Harding admires and Wilson objects to – the neo-Conservatism and extreme provincialism – is not defined by Cozzens in positive terms. Our concern ought to be with what Cozzens puts forward for our approbation; but the particularities, so precisely evoked in themselves, amount to no total world picture. Instead, we are faced with questions which Harding makes no attempt to resolve and which Wilson – because of his distaste for the author's politics – does not get as far as asking. Those who are unsympathetic to particular attitudes in a novel will, like Wilson, balk at social criticisms with which they cannot agree and will be annoyed by Cozzens's stylistic traits.

The critics agree on the factual point that the sentences used by Cozzens are lengthy and interspersed with parentheses. But Harding says that the parentheses suggest the rapid tangential surveys that may occur in a thought sequence without disrupting it, while Wilson find them involuted and curiously stilted. Harding applauds the style for departing from the spoken language with its irrelevant associations; but for Wilson the innumerable modifying sentences blur the outlines of what is said and account for the lack of immediacy which distinguishes By Love Possessed from its nineteenth-century predecessors.

How can this issue be resolved? Since Harding is more in the position of an advocate for the book than Wilson, we would do well to see what he himself puts forward as one of its 'better parts'. He comments especially favourably upon the last scene of the book, when the respectable lawyer, Arthur Winner, 'walks distraught and appalled through the town, in the morning-coat of an usher in his prosperous

Episcopalian church, saluted by the police, on his way to the first practical step in his new programme of abetting an embezzlement by the senior partner of his firm'. This comment of Harding's puts clearly in his critical prose moral implications which are less clearly managed in Cozzens's own writings; and it suggests, moreover, that the writing has a vivacity which the reader may find it cannot pretend to.

> . . . Federal Street, the shops all closed. On this side, on the whole stretch of pavement up to Court Street, to the bank at the corner, not a person was to be seen; though quick in the Sunday stillness, one or two cars had passed. Not improbably, those in the cars would know him, might see something strange, something odd – *wasn't that Mr Winner* – in his rapid walking all alone along the glass-faced line of closed shops; the straight tall solitary figure, his clothes of a kind which most of those who saw him would have seen in advertisements only, not in life. What phenomenon, what portent, they might ask, was this? Arthur Winner thought: If I'm to be at mother's at four, I haven't time to go out to Roylan and change.
>
> In its wisdom, the law said: *No man shall be judge of his own cause.* Descending Federal Street, two troopers in a state police patrol car slowly drew near. The one not driving, who wore corporal's stripes, gave Arthur Winner a glance, plainly, from appearance in court, identified him; informally respectful, brought his hand to his hat brim saluting as he passed. To return! *no man shall be judge* – yes, the law; the work of his life. The law, nothing but reason, took judicial notice of man's nature, of how far his conscience could guide him against his interest. For the sake of others, for his own sake, the law would not let him be led into temptation. In its wisdom, the law only aimed at certainty, could not, did not, really hope to get there. This science, as inexact as medicine, must do its justice with the imprecision of wisdom, the pragmatism of a long, a mighty experience. Those balances were to weigh, not what was just in general, but might be just between these actual adversaries. (Judge Lowe said: *Caroline, you have done something very wrong and very serious . . .*)[3]

Professor Harding in his comment has supplied the view by which Arthur Winner is seen from the outside. In the passage itself, all is internal monologue and recollection; appearance can only be inferred and is therefore actually less vivid than in Harding's comment. In much the same way, the irony, rather diffuse in Cozzens's account, of the meeting between Winner and the police, is made much more clear by being summarised by Harding. The effect of the passage is that of a reprise: the events of the book are put into perspective, into Arthur Winner's new perspective. That being so, the praise one would accord this passage would hardly be attached to its stylistic properties, especially since it is unlikely that the passage would mean much to a reader not previously acquainted with the book. The emotional qualities which Harding finds in this passage are there only by virtue of its connection with preceding events. Thus effects that Harding discusses as matters of style are, in fact, solidly technical matters. Such merit as the passage has is a question of construction rather than of texture, although one would have to concede that its texture is highly characteristic of the book, and, if anything, superior to most of it.

Harding's acceptance of the prose, then, is an acceptance of the morality of the novel itself. Yet when he goes into detail, he indicates that the novel is less positive than his generalisations would suggest. The action of *By Love Possessed*, according to Harding, is a way of teaching Winner (and the reader) the necessity that may somewhere be lurking for a really decent man to sacrifice the conventionally clear conscience that has formed the mainstay of his life in the community. The codes of reason and law by which Winner has previously lived are too rigid to allow for his attachment to other people. 'By love possessed he finds the price of a clear conscience too high.' And so we see Winner abetting the embezzlement of Tuttle, his senior partner, itself a step taken as a result of attachment to others, or, as Harding puts it, his 'deep concern for the people he lets down'.

But there is some doubt as to the meaning of this change in Winner's course. 'Possessed' is hardly a word expressive of respect, or even sympathy. According to Harding, Cozzens's use of it conveys 'the disturbance of all rational codes and calculations by the influence of one or the other of the states of mind labelled "love" '. Are we then to put Tuttle's heroic deception and Winner's concern for others on the same level as the brat Ralph's lust for the Kovacs girl? Harding does not seem to be quite sure. 'The short, but perhaps not quite sufficient answer is that in ordinary speech, too, "love" covers both social attachments and sexual appetites, and that the contrast between them creates in itself relation enough for the purpose of a novel.'

But the problem is more than a verbal one. Some of these varieties of affection are offered to us for our detestation. Others we are (according to Harding) supposed to respect. How are we to make the distinction if the author does not? The answer may be that Cozzens is trying to deflate Winner and make him aware of his share in the weaknesses of common humanity. This is borne out by the treatment of Winner's seduction of his best friend's wife – a seduction that he chooses not to remember and of which the reader is not aware until it is forcibly brought to Winner's attention by an outsider.

But the morality covers a void. Although Winner's defection is admitted, Winner himself remains wholly estimable: he struggles to rectify what is wrong, he feels unselfish affections, etc. He remains the mouthpiece of much of the author's philosophy. There is no such qualification in the treatment of Ralph. His consistency is only in reckless misbehaviour and evasion of any consequences that misbehaviour may bring about – such as his skipping bail when under a charge of rape – 'rape' that was no better or worse than Winner's own lapse in the same direction. We are not expected to assess Ralph in the same terms as Winner, evidently; there are no extenuating circumstances for him, even though he, like Winner, is 'by love possessed'.

Is, then, Winner's 'sympathy' of the same kind as Ralph's 'lust'? The effect on the reader, no doubt, is different. This is because Winner is seen from within, while Ralph is full of self-justification – maudlin, because heard by us with the ears of the unsympathetic Winner. But possibly Winner's internal monologues would assume the same character if heard by an unsympathetic Ralph.

Is Winner's 'sympathy' meant to show he's just as bad as Ralph? Or just as good? Or does the correlation of Winner and Ralph indict us all as imperfect? A critic advancing claims for Cozzens as a moralist ought to be able to tell us what the end of the book, when Winner shares in his partner's crime, is supposed to mean. Harding feels that this is a sacrifice of laws, codes and reason for people, and feels sympathy for the desperate gamble on which Winner is entering. But Wilson feels mainly pleasure that Winner is brought down from his hitherto lofty sphere.

The ambivalence of the novel as a whole can, in fact, be shown in the critics' extremely different views of Winner himself – views which vary according to their political instincts. Thus, for Harding, Winner is 'really decent', a 'man of feeling', a 'percipient of almost Jamesian subtlety', while for Wilson he is 'a know-all and a prig'. Both seem, in spite of this, to agree that the novel largely depends on Winner's viewpoint; therefore their divergence on this issue is extremely damaging to the novel as a whole. Through Winner's judgement many of the values of the modern world are assessed. This being so, we would be expected to sympathise with Winner's final plight. But the action of the book, summarised, would be so unfavourable to Winner as to cast doubt on his identification, as dramatic character, with Cozzens himself. It is only when Winner reflects generally that he carries the weight of the author's approbation; though he is at other times protected from taking the full consequences of the reader's distaste for his lapses; as in the delayed revelation of his adultery.

This is only a partial concealment. But the author withholds so much of the pattern through this device of a dramatised consciousness that the emphasis of his approbation, like so much else in the novel, remains unclear. It is not being naïve to ask for a moral differentiation between characters. This is not a matter of insisting on characters who are either black or white; it is rather a demand for organisation, for pattern. Without a very high definition of either, a novel is likely to communicate only to those already in sympathy with what is being communicated.

Our habits of reading are such that critics seldom find a novel obscure. On the contrary, they are often too ready to supply, in their summaries of the action, the links which the author has omitted. But the critic who does not sympathise with those omitted links will often be found objecting to details which the sympathetic critic will regard as grateful and germane to the purpose. This divergence between critics may often take the form of a debate on style. But it will take place because of a different view of the total pattern: as a man who is colour-blind will not see a number patterned out upon a test-card but may comment upon the odd dots that help to comprise it. The difference between the two halves of this analogy is that the critic may not be at fault in his colour-blindness. It is a function of the novel, as of any work of literature, to make us see.

The reverse procedure is hardly less common: the effects of style may be all too readily erected into moral enactments. The critic may be led to eke out in terms of his own vision a moral pattern left incompletely sketched by the novelist. At worst, this can lead to a distortion of values when the critic is out of sympathy with the novel he is discussing. At best, the divergence may take the form of a debate on incidental moral propositions.

I think it can often be shown that there is a difference between what a novelist writes and what his critics say that he writes. Take, for example, Scott Fitzgerald: characteristically, the critics can manage to agree on matters of stylistic detail, but differ hopelessly when they come to consider Fitzgerald as a moralist.

Fitzgerald, I feel, seldom shows any insight into society. But if he ever does, it surely is in the first part of *Tender is the Night*; that is, in its original version. Such, at least, is Arthur Mizener's view: 'Detail by detail, the sterility and deadness of his chosen world is established.'[4]

And he instances such scenes as the homosexuals chaffing each other, or the futile attempt of the unpublished novelist to explain his decadent book. 'Portraits, acrid and mephitic'[5] agrees Maxwell Geismar. And J. W. Aldridge says that Fitzgerald has scattered evidence of a general decay on all sides of the principal characters.[6]

This, perhaps, is the trouble. Even the most favourable critics feel that there is some uncertainty about the central situation in *Tender is the Night*. Specific details, everyone agrees, are accurate and vivid. Dan Jacobson finds much to admire in the particulars of Dr Diver's breakup. At the same time, however, he considers that it is inadequately motivated.[7] John Farrelly, too, seems to have difficulty in believing in the personality thus surrendered. He suggests that Fitzgerald was too close to the situation: a statement of the facts will not, in itself, compel the emotional assent of the reader.[8]

Other critics consider the motivation entirely satisfactory. I find it curious, though, that the motives they cite all contradict one another. John Chamberlain believes that Diver breaks up because his marriage to a rich woman cuts him off from his work as a doctor.[9] Andrews Wanning, however, considers that it is because of his work as a doctor that he breaks up: he is exhausted by trying to cure his wife of her neurosis.[10] A third possibility is the one put forward by Mizener – it is because Diver succeeds in curing Nicole that her love for him declines.[11]

Three motives are too many for one break-up. In any case, as Harding points out, Diver stands up very well to the 'ordeal' of his marriage, but seems to collapse almost as a result.[12] In fact, the more we are told of what happens, the more questions seem to be raised. We can, for example, never be sure how far the Divers' relationship is a 'professional situation'. Nicole's abandonment of Diver is interpreted as an emergence from her fixation. And yet much of the misery of Diver's collapse springs from Nicole's departure wrecking what has, earlier, been made to seem a genuine and complete marriage. Moreover, as Farrelly says, Nicole abandons her husband only after he has cracked up and turned against her: she is at once a convalescing neurotic and an embodiment of the Fitzgerald glamour.[13]

There is, in other words, some doubt as to how far Nicole is to be condemned. It may be that she appears to fluctuate as a character because she is not seen from a sufficiently positive standpoint. We are told that Nicole lived again because Diver succeeded 'in restating the universe for her'.[14] But this is never shown in the action. The result is that each critic will interpret *Tender is the Night* in whichever way he likes. The novel lacks a decisive norm; and Diver's charm is not really sufficient to provide one. What, asks Jacobson, is Diver supposed to be declining *from*?[15]

Such a concern never troubled the author, though it does some of his didactically inclined critics. The dichotomy can be seen in the severe critiques drawn by this rather attractive passage.

> Simultaneously the whole party moved towards the water, super-ready from the long, forced inaction, passing from the heat to the cool with a gourmandise of a tingling curry eaten with chilled white wine. The Divers' day was spaced like the day of the older civilisations to yield the utmost from the materials at hand, and to give all the transitions their full value.[16]

Jacobson points out that nothing has been said or done by anyone on the beach to warrant phrases like 'the day of the older civilisations'.[17] And Farrelly says that the nature of the experience seems to be contradicted by the solemn and inflated language.[18]

Is, then, the scene a failure? One argument in its favour could be that all is perceived through the consciousness of Rosemary Hoyt, a film starlet only too eager to be dazzled by the Divers and their set. This has been hailed by more favourable critics as a dramatic device. Geismar says that what seem to Rosemary glamorous aristocrats are, in fact, idle and unhappy expatriates.[19] According to Mizener, the deadness of their world is never understood by Rosemary, and is, therefore, established dramatically.[20]

Jacobson calls Rosemary an evasion of the author's responsibilities. 'Why should we take *her* word for anything?' he asks.[21] We could answer him by saying that the qualities attributed to the scene are there only for Rosemary; that we need Rosemary as an observer because a more sophisticated consciousness would not be taken in. This, I think, establishes a limited sort of success for scenes like those on the beach. But, in spite of this, a good many critics have felt that an uncomfortable amount of approval is being exacted for the Divers. However the passages they adduce in support of this seem to be of a different kind.

> Rosemary's naiveté responded full-heartedly to the expensive simplicity of the Divers, unaware of its complexity and its lack of innocence, unaware that it was all a selection of quality rather than quantity from the run of the world's bazaar; and that the simplicity of the behaviour also, the nursery-like peace and good will, the emphasis on the simpler virtues, were part of a desperate

bargain with the gods and had been attained through struggles she could not have guessed at.[22]

Jacobson is on surer ground when he says that we are embarrassed by the fervour of *this* passage.[23] But, as he himself recognises, this is not Rosemary but the author's supposedly undeceived and discerning voice. In the first passage, also, there was an undue vibrance, but it was placed dramatically in the mouth of a persona. In the second, it is left to stand by itself; and, of course, falls heavily beneath the weight of its own portentousness.

This wouldn't matter so much if it was merely a particular passage or scene that had failed. But *Tender is the Night* does not rest with Rosemary's first impression of the Divers. And, as Jacobson says,[24] unless we believe in their initial grace and brilliance, we are unlikely to find their story as significant as Fitzgerald seems to have wanted it to be.

The sense of the falsity in the better scenes, however, is used dramatically – though what Geismar calls 'glamorous'[25] is, for Farrelly, 'portentous'.[26] But exactly what the drama is about – *that* is blurred by the absence of any sense of what the falsity is false to!

Yet the book succeeds in its incidentals – the characters on the fringe of the situation, for example. It is interesting that Jacobson and Farrelly, who dislike the book as a whole, do not object to the 'mephitic portraits' which more favourable critics have instanced as being successful. While, on the other hand, these critics – Geismar, Aldridge, Mizener – in their turn say very little about the 'grace' whose absence so much troubles Jacobson and Farrelly. It would be a mistake, however, to read too much into the satiric incidentals. They hardly amount to 'a general decay', 'a whole society's disintegration'.[27] The truth may be rather with Hartley Grattan, who, in a most perceptive review of the book when it first came out, found the Diver set 'insidiously beguiling'.[28]

In much the same way, too many big guns have been brought up in the battle to decide whether *The Great Gatsby* is a satire or a myth. A more useful question would be to ask whether it can relevantly be called either.

There isn't, it seems to me, much to support Harding's belief that a perfectly sure condemnation of Daisy Buchanan and her set runs throughout the book.[29] Of course, as in *Tender is the Night*, it is possible to point to isolated insights. For example, right at the end we find 'They were careless people, Tom and Daisy – they smashed up things and creatures and then retreated back into their money or their vast carelessness, or whatever it was that kept them together and let other people clear up the mess they had made.'[30] Mizener quotes this as an ironic summing-up.[31] But Farrelly says that it should have pervaded the book rather than serving as an anti-climax to Gatsby's death.[32] What comes over is not a satire on the rich but rather the fascination that their life has for Gatsby.

This, after all, need't be such a bad thing. Passages such as Daisy's first appearance, 'buoyed up as though upon an anchored balloon',[33] are manifestly successful in such terms. Too much weight can be put on the brief statements of intention that occasionally follow them. 'The instant her voice broke off, ceasing to compel my attention, my belief, I felt the basic insincerity of what she had said.'[34] Such statements have an effect only if we have actually been shown scenes that justify them – that act them out, so to speak. But, in this case, nothing has been done to show that Daisy is anything other than the fascinating creature Gatsby takes her to be. On the contrary, 'her eyes flashed . . . she laughed with thrilling scorn'.[35]

Of course, she is speaking not to Gatsby but to Carraway – the narrator who (some critics say) was devised to prevent any confusion arising in the book. William Troy and Arthur Mizener have both argued that Carraway's judgements place the people of the book in a satirical light.[36] However, if this in fact is the function of Carraway, all that can be said is that he seldom fulfils it. Consider this passage, for instance:

'She has got an indiscreet voice,' I remarked. 'It's full of –' I hesitated.
'Her voice is full of money,' he said suddenly.
That was it. I'd never understood before. It was full of money – that was the inexhaustible charm that rose and fell in it, the jingle of it, the cymbal's song of it . . . High in a white palace the king's daughter, the golden girl . . .[37]

Mizener believes that, in contrast with Daisy's world, Gatsby is ludicrous.[38] Marius Bewley, however, feels that it is Daisy who falls short – of Gatsby's dream: 'the value lies not in the gold but in something beyond'.[39] Alfred Kazin does something to show the limitations of this view when he suggests that Fitzgerald himself is fascinated, and so had to create a cool narrator in order to place the indefensible world of Daisy.[40] But there is clearly no agreement about what we are to think of Daisy, or of Gatsby either. This whole mode of reading has been discredited by John Farrelly, who points out that it is not only

Gatsby, the admiring and *nouveau riche* farm boy, who is enthralled by Daisy's voice. The words are those of Carraway, the supposedly detached narrator.[41]

There is, it seems, some difficulty in separating Gatsby's fascination from that of the author. Because of this, a school of thought has grown up which would erect this fascination into some kind of myth. Lionel Trilling and Marius Bewley, for instance, both regard Gatsby as an embodiment of America.[42] But the symbolism is hardly coherent enough for that. One of the key images occurs on Gatsby's first appearance – in characteristic attitude.

> He stretched out his arms toward the dark water in a curious way, and, far as I was from him, I could have sworn he was trembling. Involuntarily I glanced seaward – and distinguished nothing except a single green light, minute and far away, that might have been the end of a dock . . .

This light recurs through the course of the novel. In chapter 5 Gatsby refers to it explicitly.

> 'If it wasn't for the mist we could see your home across the bay . . . You always have a green light that burns all night at the end of your dock.'
> Daisy put her arm through his abruptly, but he seemed absorbed in what he had just said. Possibly it had occurred to him that the colossal significance of that light had now vanished forever. Compared to the great distance that had separated him from Daisy it had seemed very near to her, almost touching her. It had seemed as close as a star to the moon. Now it was again a green light on a dock. His count of enchanted objects had diminished by one.

At the end of the book, however, the light is still there – invested with even more weight of 'significance'.

> Gatsby believed in the green light, the orgiastic future that year by year recedes before us. It eluded us then, but that's no matter – to-morrow we will run faster, stretch out our arms farther . . . And one fine morning –
> So we beat on, boats against the current, borne back ceaselessly into the past.[43]

Of course, we can never do much more than point towards the meaning of a symbol. But, in this case, the critics seem to be pointing a little uncertainly, and mostly in different directions.

Bewley says that the green light embodies Gatsby's sense of the future.[44] For Kazin it has no such universal application; it merely suggests the glamour that Gatsby had, by ill chance, missed.[45] Aldridge sees this as the great American success dream, and calls Gatsby's attitude towards the green light a parody.[46] While Mizener agrees that it is a dream, but regards it as a serious one – the only positive good in a world of foul dust.[47]

If these differences are anything to go by, the green light seems to be not so much meaningful as portentous. Moreover, the critics read so much significance into the symbol that its success for them negatives the rest of the book. For example, Bewley goes on to say that the green light signals Gatsby into the future away from the cheapness of his affair with Daisy.[48] If this were true, it would seem to be a mistake on the part of the author to attach the light so firmly to the end of Daisy's dock. Possibly Bewley senses the case that could be made against him, for he says that some might object to the symbolism on the grounds that it is easily vulgarised.[49]

John Farrelly has objected to the whole Gatsby attitude on these very grounds. Gatsby's 'incorruptible dream' is, he feels, only too corruptible. He makes this the central issue of his attack on Fitzgerald's uncompromising romanticism 'for which the value of life is in the illusion and in the falsifying glamour'.[50]

Well, at least the romanticism is uncompromising, and even that may be a virtue. Farrelly appears to be taking for total disablement what is no more than limitation. It may, however, be agreed that it puts Fitzgerald beyond the pale of the great writers. We are told of Gatsby's 'heightened sensibility to the promises of life',[51] but we are shown it as fantasy – pink suits, lavish parties and a desire to impress a rich man's wife. Harding says that Fitzgerald seems to have had no expectations which could be disappointed by the rich;[52] and this remains true whether they are called an ideal aristocracy by Trilling[53] or the Big Spenders by Farrelly.[54] One could say that the fascination is conveyed far more clearly than any reason why it should be shared by the reader. But it is conveyed. The achievement may not be a great one; but it is an achievement.

The critics who believe that Gatsby is a fully dramatised and morally placed character are reading in much of their interpretation. In order to make Gatsby acceptable as a character, they have to read the narrator, Carraway, as an ironic observer. They also have to follow Bewley and Jacobson in emphasising a contrast between Gatsby and the rich Buchanans. Neither of these modes of interpretation is really acceptable. Andrews Wanning may be nearer the truth when he says that the feeling of the novel owes a good deal to the author's identity with his subject.[55] At times, indeed, it is difficult to determine from the syntax alone whether a critic is speaking of Gatsby or his creator. This identity can, however, be an embarrassment. Gatsby's fantasy is so central to the book that it assumes the wrong sort of authority. And yet, as Wanning says, this gives the portrait of Gatsby its warmth and compassion.[56] Kazin, too, has said that to have approached Gatsby from the outside would be to have sacrificed a tragedy of 'pure confession'.[57] It all sounds rather like Othello writing *Othello*! But Kazin admits that the book is in no sense a major tragedy.[58] And, in Aldridge's damaging words, Fitzgerald's closeness to Gatsby makes the book not tragic so much as pathetic.[59] Farrelly agrees that he wrote not so much about the rich as about his own dazzled impressions of them.[60]

The book, in other words, exists on the level of one man's fantasy. Its personal lyricism is at once a characteristic and a limitation. The central persona may be lyrical, imperfectly placed and without an adequate dramatic context. And yet *The Great Gatsby* has an attitude which, as the consensus of agreement shows, has unquestionably communicated itself to the critics concerned. Even the minority who appear to differ will be seen to have read into the 'grace' a weight of moral indignation which is all their own.

By entering so wholeheartedly into his dream, Fitzgerald makes his narrative, on one level at any rate, convincing. A discerning commentary would have accorded ill with this autobiographic projection. Such a commentary, however, has been supplied by some of Fitzgerald's critics. Admittedly, this would not have been possible if Fitzgerald had himself possessed an overall grasp of social values. For example, we find Geismar asking sceptically whether in fact Gatsby's parties are an appalling display of 'a vast, vulgar and meretricious beauty'.[61] They are not that, though that is what some critics believe them to be. One can quote, almost at random.

> There was music from my neighbour's house through the summer nights. In his blue gardens men and girls came and went like moths among the whisperings and the champagne and the stars. At high tide in the afternoon I watched his guests diving from the tower of his raft, or taking the sun on the hot sand of his beach, while his two motor-boats slit the waters of the Sound, drawing aquaplanes over cataracts of foam. On week-ends his Rolls-Royce became an omnibus, bearing parties to and from the city between nine in the morning and long past midnight, while his station wagon scampered like a brisk yellow bug to meet all trains. And on Mondays eight servants, including an extra gardener, toiled all day with mops and

scrubbing-brushes and hammers and garden-shears, repairing the ravages of the night before.[62].

This, on the level of fantasy, can hardly be faulted. However pretentious it would all be in real life, it's made magical by Fitzgerald's dream-world style. Of course, such transmutation takes away from any moral point that could have been made. Fitzgerald is, therefore, liable to be misread by critics taking him too solemnly. Marius Bewley, for instance, writing of this passage, says: 'It possesses an ironic nuance that rises towards the tragic. And how fine that touch of the extra gardener is – as if Gatsby's guests had made a breach in nature.'[63] Such a reading is rather heavy-weight for anything the passage can be shown to be doing. The details may be at times humorous, at times quite beautiful, but they are always fantastic and decorative, the qualities instinct in Fitzgerald's style. When *The Great Gatsby* first came out in 1925, Mencken put his finger on what made it an exceptional book. Not, he insisted, the action as such, but the charm and beauty of the writing.[64] Charles Weir agrees that Fitzgerald can do brilliant set-pieces, but qualifies this by saying that he never attempts an evaluation of society in larger terms.[65] Trilling, for all his talk about Fitzgerald's ideal aristocracy, would, it seems, agree with this – 'the voice of his prose is the essence of his success'.[66] Even so predominantly hostile a critic as John Farrelly concedes that Fitzgerald's gift for the quasi-poetical evocation of atmosphere achieved a real, if limited, success; the more certainly since illusion itself was the subject of his book.[67]

When the critics try to claim much more for Fitzgerald than this, they tend to write in their own moral preconceptions. Hence, I feel, the apparent variety of response to *The Great Gatsby* and *Tender is the Night*. It's no use drawing for moral justification on a text which offers no more than a nice pattern of imagery, or the equivalent. Fitzgerald's work is charming, attractive, evocative, but essentially of the surface. We do no service to his readers in trying to find a deeper seriousness in his work. The most anti-social actions, the worst characters, are sweetened out of satire into his fantastic prose. When the critics attempt to discuss Fitzgerald in terms of 'satire' or 'myth', over and over again it can be demonstrated that they are talking only in terms of style.

But the style could hardly have an effect unless it suggested something, however mysterious. The answer would seem to be that such books as this work piecemeal; are better appreciated in isolated passages than as wholes. The analogy perhaps is with lyric poems; except that a lyric needs to be a self-sufficient whole while it is difficult to see how even the most purple of prose passages can be entirely divorced from its context.

The extent to which the context is found satisfactory will probably depend on an affinity between the mind of the writer and that of his reader. It may be taken as axiomatic that minor writing appeals most to the like-minded. Such authors as Cozzens and Fitzgerald invite the reader to fill in preconceptions that the author omitted; in reading, the partial critic recreates a little avidly; creates, in fact, some of what the author should have created for him.

Thus it can be seen that though all response to literature must be personal, all literature is not equally there to be responded to. We appreciate most works in part, some in so far as they correspond to our own predilections, others to the extent that we can recreate them in our own terms. But this is not the way in which we appreciate a masterpiece.

The Concept of Availability

All works of literature are not equally present to the interested reader. A given text may convey different things to different people. In such a case, it would be unwise to assume that any of the readings are necessarily 'wrong'. What should be said is that the work is not completely available.

Certain works do not awaken in one reader much that corresponds with the experience of another. To interpret these works as wholes seems to be a venture doomed to fail. Critics who make the attempt do much of the author's work for him: their effort at understanding is not recreative but, in a bad sense of the word, creative. They rely, in fact, upon a mode of reading which to those who do not share the same predilections may seem nothing short of wilful. There is always a temptation to turn the author's inconsistencies or failures into strokes of ingenuity miraculously uncovered by percipience on the part of the critic.

This is very marked in the body of criticism that has grown up around John Milton. In the last thirty years, critics have been urgently concerned to tie up conflicts of sympathy and lapses in tone into a cohesive whole that they could confidently call *Paradise Lost*. But different critics with different preoccupations find different faults to discount and virtues to praise.

The critics would no doubt reply to all this that there has never been a time when Milton was regarded as other than a major poet.[1] This is true, and seems to me a strong argument that he is one. Nevertheless, the history of Milton criticism has not been one of unalloyed appreciation. Even in the days when Milton's theology could be accepted, many critics were worried by the language in which it was couched. Dryden complained of the flats among Milton's elevations,[2] and Dennis ascribed this flatness to the poverty of his ideas, especially in the last two books of *Paradise Lost*.[3] While Addison, in his turn, suggested that the poet gave so much attention to his theology that he neglected his poetry.[4] All three were troubled by Milton's antiquated vocabulary and forced constructions; and these were actually altered by Bentley under pretence of emending the text.[5] Bentley's emendations were less salutary than his objections, and Johnson followed him in some of the latter when he blamed Milton's diction for being harsh and barbarous.[6]

Now this consensus of opinion surely points to a defect in the verse. Even Coleridge, who revered Milton, jibbed at some of the points that had thrown the Augustans;[7] while Keats's criticism of the Greek and Latin inversions in the poem is well known. 'The Paradise Lost though so fine in itself is a corruption of our language', he wrote.[8] And it was in this way that the young poets of the twentieth century, a hundred years later, were to come out against Milton. For Eliot and Pound *Paradise Lost* was an enduring argument against their attempt to use in poetry the inflections of the speaking voice.[9]

But these are not the most damaging criticisms that have been brought to bear upon the poem. Far more serious is the fact that, over the years, *Paradise Lost* has become demonstrably less available to its readers. For Milton's contemporaries, *Paradise Lost* was an epic on the greatest of all subjects; until well on in the eighteenth century, it expressed a theology to which everyone more or less subscribed. Even Johnson, for all his strictures upon the language of the poem, took it to have fulfilled the moral intentions of its author.[10] Only eleven years separate Johnson's remarks on Milton from those of Blake. Yet Blake seems a contemporary of our own in the problems he raises. For the first time, a dichotomy is found between Milton's intention and his performance. Blake said that Milton was free only when writing of Satan because he was 'of the Devil's party without knowing it'.[11] That this was no individual quirk of Blake's is shown by the independent testimony of Shelley who proclaimed Milton's Devil as a moral being far superior to his God.[12] The change had come with the coming of Romanticism, and throughout the nineteenth century most of the criticism attracted by *Paradise Lost* had to do with the apparent conflict between the sympathy aroused by Satan and the action of the poem as a whole.[13] Critics were at last able to look upon Milton's figures as characters, and the poem as a work of literature. This has not proved to be to the poem's advantage.

The moral problems were argued out to the bitter end by Walter Bagehot. He said that Milton could hardly have anticipated the effect of his teaching in an age of scepticism: the author of evil in his universe now seems to be the most attractive being in it.[14] Already Bagehot has the idea – which was to be heard with increasing frequency – that a work of art can fade along with the beliefs that conditioned it. The sympathies which Addison and Johnson found clear-cut now seemed to be disturbingly distributed among the various groups of characters. Pattison and Arnold felt, in their different ways, that the story of *Paradise Lost* could no longer be taken literally and that therefore it was losing its hold over the imagination.[15] The demonology had passed from fact to fiction: critics at the turn of the century found little interest in the temptation of Man and took the poem rather to centre upon the fall of Satan.

It is true that, in our own time, academic critics have found ways of explaining, and even justifying, the moral ambivalences that disturbed Bagehot, Pattison and Arnold. There can be no doubt that many of them are able to read *Paradise Lost* as a whole. But it is open to question how far a critic's own personality is involved in such a reading. Certainly no two critics have re-created *Paradise Lost* in the same way.

The understanding of *Paradise Lost* does not seem to be an easy matter. If the idea and action of the poem were unified and defined, it would be difficult to see how the dissension concerning their nature and efficacy could have arisen.

A. J. A. Waldock has pointed out the difficulty different critics have had in determining what the theme of *Paradise Lost* really is.[16] Some critics have a fairly clear-cut moral interpretation; others simplify the theme down to a single word or phrase; and yet others elaborate the theme until it becomes something more pertaining to themselves than to the poem.

The first group differ from each other mainly in the emphasis they place on Milton's explicit avowals of intention. C. S. Lewis, for example, believes that Sin itself is at the heart of the poem,[17] and B. Rajan sees the fall of Adam and Eve as the victory of darkness.[18] But for J. M. Murry[19] and Douglas Bush[20] the fall marks the possibility of regeneration. The divergence would seem to turn upon the Atonement; but this is presented so perfunctorily in the poem[21] that agreement upon the subject seems hardly possible, even among this moralistic group of critics.

A great gap separates these from the second group of critics – those who seek to characterise the theme briefly. Their tendency is to oversimplify: Raleigh[22] and Muir[23] see the poem as a tension between the forces of puritanism and humanism, and for David Daiches,[24] too, the subject is the tragic ambiguity of the human animal. But how far is this ambiguity, how far inconsistency? Edwin Greenlaw, at the other extreme, considers the poem to be 'about' temperance.[25] A far less elaborate structure than *Paradise Lost* could hardly be interpreted in such ways. The attempt to summarise is one that may leave the critic only with a private version of the poem. This may be because he has particularised a generality too indefinite in the poem to shape his interpretation into anything that would be relevant to the reaction of another reader.

However, when the critics of our third group expound their interpretation on a scale worthy of a complex work of art, it cannot be said that they accord any more closely with one another. Bush feels that the 'real theme' is the war between good and evil in the soul of man:[26] a fascinating idea, except that Milton takes pains to make Eve's temptation external. E. M. W. Tillyard believes that *Paradise Lost* is about the true state of Milton's mind when he wrote it,[27] but fails to show how the poet's achievement matched up to what the critic can surmise of his intention. A later interpretation of Tillyard's suggests that the poem treats of abundance,[28] but he stops short of relating this to the main action. Such a loose relation of matter to theme reflects a quality in Milton's poem that undoubtedly permits interpretations more remarkable for their ingenuity than for their application. Cleanth Brooks, for instance, discovers city–garden imagery; pastoral elements in relation to the heroic; the theme of imperialism and colonialism.[29] It should be enough to say that these are in the poem as much as Tillyard's abundance and Greenlaw's temperance.[30] That is to say, they are there for the critic who wants to find them, but need not be apparent to another reader, one who is less committed.

Enough has been said to indicate the difficulty of proposing an interpretation which will be acceptable to a nucleus of readers. A form that is not self-evident has been imposed on the poem by each individual critic. And some such process seems to be inherent in any attempt to interpret *Paradise Lost* as a whole. This may account for the endless discussions as to who the hero is; and the very different conclusions reached. For Raleigh, the hero is Satan;[31] for Lewis, God;[32] for Addison, it was the Messiah;[33] for Landor, Adam;[34] for Bowra, Abdiel;[35] for Saurat, Milton himself.[36] Daiches, in trying to decide whether Messiah or Adam is more central to the poem, indicates how the doubt arises; the plot has Christ as hero and Adam as the object of conflict, but the poetic meaning contradicts this at every point.[37] It does not matter that Daiches eventually pitches on Adam as the hero; he has already shown the impossibility of answering the question. The overt intention is pulling one way; the poetic realisation is pulling another. This all seems to indicate that there is something unsatisfactory in the form of the poem, and therefore it is surely relevant to examine some of the claims that have been made for this.

According to C. S. Lewis, *Paradise Lost* is meant to be an epic;[38] but critics who consider achievement rather than intention have come to other conclusions. H. J. C. Grierson holds that the pressure of Milton's metaphysics turns the epic into a didactic work,[39] and John Diekhoff makes great play with the doctrinal side of the poem.[40] This aspect is unimportant to E. E. Stoll, who says that epic grandeur gives place to drama in such scenes as the temptation of Eve.[41] And some critics emphasise the dramatic aspect more, even, than that. Arnold Stein, like Lewis, insists that the critic must accept Milton's terms, but cannot agree with Lewis on what they are, since he considers that the poet plainly conceived of his epic as a great drama.[42]

There are, then, these three views of the poem's form: is it an epic, an argument or a drama? One way out of the impasse is to suggest that the poem partakes in character of all three. It does, in a sense, of course. In external form it is a classical epic; since its dogma is stated as well as demonstrated, it is a didactic poem; and scenes such as the temptation of Eve are undoubtedly dramatic. But only to a limited extent can these characteristics of form be reconciled, one with another. Dramatic as the great scenes are, even Stein admits that they are not typical of the whole poem:[43] the drama, in other words, is intermittent. Stein approves of this, saying that immediacy must be sacrificed in the interests of total structure.[44] But the total structure will indeed have to be impressive if we are to be vouchsafed so few glimpses of drama in comparison with the bulk taken up by the larger considerations of perspective; which is what Stein puts forward as a consolation.[45]

It is a fact that the majority of critics have not felt happy about the way in which the parts of the poem contribute to the whole. Half the poem is concerned with matter that takes place before or after the central event: a short story is eked out to a long poem by means of episodes. No doubt these could be defended if they were intrinsically interesting. But Lewis calls the Michael episode of the last two books an untransmuted lump of futurity,[46] while Kenneth Muir complains of its excessive condensation.[47] And even those who defend the episode are half-hearted: Bush concedes that this outline of Hebrew history is long and dull, but sanctions it by reference to epic precedent.[48] Tillyard considers it to be a hasty scramble through the ages, but suggests it is well-placed at a point of rest and so prevents the interest flagging.[49] This, if true, would be a sad comment on Milton's management of the action to date. Only F. T. Prince has attempted to justify in detail the last two books as contributing to the poem, claiming that the imaginative intensity is to be found in the vibration of the story in Adam's reacting consciousness.[50] But there are only three examples in 1500 lines of Adam reacting to the events he is shown, and these are all by way of being public utterance – *O goodness infinite, goodness immense*, for example.[51] We do Milton no service in claiming for this outline of history effects possible only in the complex later development of the novel.[52]

The Raphael episode is more plainly functional: it is a way of narrating events prior to the angels' fall. How far this is really essential is another matter; enough should have been understood from books I and II to make it clear what has previously happened. Moreover the War is an astonishingly confused piece of narrative: why, for example, do the angels put on armour? Lewis says it is to make themselves stronger;[53] Stein says it is to make themselves weaker;[54] and Muir says that it is a convention – the battle is conceived in Homeric terms.[55]

These three answers to what, after all, is a simple question all contradict one another. More than that, not one of them applies to the text. Lewis's point is settled by Waldock when he points out that the angelic substance is shown to be subtle enough to resist the wounds of arms.[56] And Stein can be confuted from his own interpretation: the identical action, the assumption of arms, is regarded as a stroke of genius on God's part and at the same time as an act of folly on Satan's.[57] While Muir confutes himself by admitting that Milton has attempted to merge two incompatible conventions, scientific 'angelology' and Homeric epic.[58]

But Stein has kept a theory in reserve for just such an emergency as this. He sees the War in Heaven as a huge joke, implicating even the good angels. 'Surely it is naïve to think Milton straining for grandeur in this passage . . .'[59] Well, a good number of critics must be considered as being more naïve than Professor Stein. Grierson stresses the motivation of the War;[60] Tillyard bows to its sublimity;[61] J. H. Hanford sees it as the overturning of order.[62] The 'sense of strain' observed by Stein is less likely to be a comic effect than a result of Milton's battle with the disparities of his subject-matter. Moreover, it is surprising that such an effect, if it really existed, should have remained unrecognised for so long. Not a very good joke, one would imagine, since so few have laughed at it.

Only a failure to operate decisively on the reader could have produced the diverse interpretations which we have been considering. It is easy enough to argue with the theories of Lewis and Stein, and in one's turn to say what the War in Heaven is not; it is much more difficult to say exactly what it is. This may be a fault not so much in the critic as in the inconclusive nature of the work he is seeking to interpret.

Milton's verse will not bear this kind of reading. The description of Paradise, especially, has suffered from over-interpretation. There is no consensus of opinion about what the Garden is supposed to be. The chief point at issue is how far Paradise can be termed a happy place.

Lewis talks about the garden as though it were the Never-Never Land;[63] Stein suggests it is a sensuous and wanton pastoral scene;[64] for Bush it is equally an earthly Paradise, but the evocation is not sensuous and wanton but controlled and literary.[65]

There is quite a gap between these views and those of Tillyard and Diekhoff, who think that Adam and Eve could not *really* have been happy, living this sort of life.[66] Basil Willey and John Erskine feel, in their turn, that Paradise was meant to be rejected in favour of a more active existence.[67]

Again, a gap separates this group of views from those of Daiches and Paul Elmer More who believe that Milton suggests all human longings for an ideal Garden.[68] William Empson finds here a rich nostalgia,[69] and Cleanth Brooks and J. E. Hardy feel the melancholy in Eden as a yearning for a past Golden Age.[70] This is, in the words of R. M. Adams, an inclusive melancholy for a lost synthesis of virtue and grace.[71]

How can these three groups of views be deemed compatible? There can be little doubt that the feeling in the verse is ambivalent: the explicit presence of happiness is contradicted by the poet's own nostalgia. But these exist as elements side by side; and even when they seem to come together, the imagery is so generalised, not to say stock, as to allow a wide range of possible interpretation.

F. R. Leavis points out that the medium calls for a kind of attention that is incompatible with sharp realisation;[72] and instances

> All amid them stood the Tree of Life
> High eminent, blooming Ambrosial fruit
> Of vegetable gold.[73]

This final phrase has, indeed, been defended, but in widely divergent ways. Daiches claims it as a description perfect in its generalised suggestion of natural beauty;[74] but for Bush it is particular – the rich natural life implied in 'vegetable' gives pliant form and vitality to the hardness of 'gold'.[75] This latter interpretation, however, would seem to be a reading-in of a set of arbitrary personal associations. One could equally well say that 'vegetable' conveys an idea of non-reacting immobility; and it would then be up to Bush to show why his association of pliancy and vitality is to be preferred. In fact, of course, either association could be conveyed by the word 'vegetable'; and a good many other associations as well, if there were any point in listing them. A word by itself is anyone's property; and Milton's context does little to determine its implication here. Therefore the generalisation praised by Daiches[76] is a defect in the verse. If any further proof were needed, one could say that Lewis and Empson have brought away from the passage very different ideas of the paradisal fruit: for Lewis, it is the satisfaction of an ideal,[77] for Empson the sorrow for a lost paradise.[78] The description, then, is defensively stylised; it is an evasion of the issues raised by the very conception of Paradise.

Critics have certainly been prone to fill in the suggestions Milton provided. Consider, for instance, the first appearance of Adam and Eve.

> *Two of far nobler shape erect and tall,*
> *Godlike erect with native honour clad*
> *In naked majestie seemed lords of all . . .*[79]

Raleigh says, almost as though it were a virtue, that the portraiture is left to be filled in by the imagination.[80] Each imagination, however, is likely to fill in something different; the reader will get very little out of this passage unless he has a gift for fiction. Lewis fills in the description thus: we 'meet at last the white, severe, voluptuous forms of our first parents'.[81] 'White', 'severe' and voluptuous' are all telling words, especially in combination, but they are supplied by the critic not the poet. A less sympathetic reader will supply less. Leavis sees only 'conscious and characteristic moral solemnity' and 'poetic decorum'.[82] This may not be so; but the poet should have made it harder for the critic to be wrong by imposing some of his own idea on us, and so obviating the need for excessive sympathy with his aims.

In much the same way, the defence of Milton's Hell falls into three groups of propositions. (i) Hell is a fully realised place of torture; (ii) Hell is symbolic of something else; (iii) Hell is not what Satan thinks it is.

The first aspect can hardly stand up against the particular points raised by Waldock,[83] among others. For example, we are told of tortures, but they do not seem to impede the fallen angels going in for planning and building. Waldock may be at fault in requiring Hell to be primarily a place of torment, but there is some point in enquiring what else it is supposed to be. Muir, indeed, suggests that the inconsistencies give Hell a nightmare quality;[84] but surely this is present as unevenness in realisation rather than as dramatic embodiment. What Eliot notes as lack of focus[85] is much more than a defect in visualisation. How does one imagine a burning lake when there is only darkness visible? Perhaps Leavis was right when he said that we are not bothered by the absence of visual consistency in Milton's world because our criteria of relevance have become unexacting.[86]

To reply, as David Daiches and J. B. Broadbent do,[87] that Milton's Hell is symbolic is not sufficient to answer such points as these. This is no abstract or symbolic hell: Milton every now and again takes some pains to put a physical semblance before us –

> There stood a hill not far whose griesly top
> Belch'd fire and rowling smoak; the rest entire
> Shon with a glossie scurff . . .[88]

The trouble is that in between such passages action takes place that contradicts the physical torment they describe. Milton's concept of Hell does not seem to impose itself on the reader at any level.

A third possible defence could be that the horrors of Hell are real enough and that Satan is wrong in thinking he can embark on further operations. Stein argues that very little is done towards an invasion of Heaven and that therefore Satan's followers are unofficially carrying out a policy of their own.[89] In fact, however, it is Satan himself who advised his followers to render Hell more tolerable.[90] So much for an unofficial policy!

To such contortions of ingenuity does the compromise nature of Milton's Hell drive the critic who would seek to justify it. An overall interpretation of Hell is impossible because it is inconsistent with itself; its nature varies from page to page.

The disability can be localised in Milton's style, whose most disturbing feature is not obscurity but what may be called indeterminacy. Lewis has noted that to a great extent the poem requires co-operation from the reader in rendering its statements with any degree of definition. He is, in fact, arguing in favour of stock responses – those habits of mind 'on the maintenance of which depend both our virtues and our pleasures, and even, perhaps, the survival of our species'.[91] But what is stock cannot be akin to virtue or pleasure because it is not alive enough to be akin to anything. However, many critics have, quite independently, carried out in practice Lewis's theories. They import into the text highly personal interpretations and therefore diverge from other critics who have read in interpretations of their own. There is a fault in the work which will accommodate such disparate readings: the personal response should be determined by an external stimulus.

This fault, which I have called indeterminacy, is often found in the similes. De Quincey was the first critic to point out the way in which these work[92] – usually by bringing in associations that contrast with what appears to be described. The local associations of action or scene, as Rajan says,[93] are often extended cosmically. But the extension of the sense, rather than its definition, may bring in its wake misunderstanding; at the best, it may give rise to considerable variety of interpretation. So many associations may be awakened that the reader is likely to select a few, and those not necessarily very relevant to the subject of the simile. Eliot quotes a simile from Book I.

> *Thus Satan talking to his neerest Mate*
> *With Head up-lift above the wave, and Eyes*
> *That sparkling blaz'd, his other parts besides*
> *Prone on the Flood, extended long and large*
> *Lay floating many a rood, in bulk as huge*
> *As whom the Fables name of monstrous size,*
> Titanian, *or* Earth-born, *that warr'd on Jove,*
> Briareos *or* Typhon, *whom the Den*
> *By ancient* Tarsus *held, or that Sea-beast*
> Leviathan, *which God of all his works*
> *Created hugest that swim th' Ocean stream:*
> *Him haply slumbering on the* Norway *foam*
> *The Pilot of some small night-founder'd Skiff,*
> *Deeming some Island, oft, as Sea-men tell,*
> *With fixed Anchor in his skaly rind*
> *Moors by his side under the Lee, while Night*
> *Invests the Sea, and wished Morn delayes:*
> *So stretcht out huge in length the Arch-fiend lay*
> *Chain'd on the burning lake . . .*[94]

The verse allows us to lose ourselves, and it is the reader, not the poet, who exercises control to prevent this from happening. Eliot says that we nearly forget Satan in attending to the whale, and draws from this the conclusion that the simile therefore strengthens the passage.[95] Leavis says, at least as justifiably, that this is a weakness – 'we are happy about the introduction of so much extraneous matter because the "Miltonic music" weakens our sense of relevance, just as it relaxes our grasp of sense'.[96] Eliot commends this musical mastery as evidence of control,[97] but, as Leavis points out,[98] one of his own footnotes indicates that the versification may induce a relaxed concern with meaning: a *foundered* skiff could not be moored, to a whale or to anything else.[99]

Eliot's excuse for the digressive nature of this simile seems, in the light of this, unconvincing. The reader is expected to bear in mind the way in which Satan was extended on the flood through a list of synonyms for Leviathan and an incident concerning a boat anchored to the beast. It may be held that the names and the general idea of size are more or less relevant; but what purpose does the story serve? There is no equivalent in Satan's predicament to the story of the skiff. Reading, in such a case, is likely to turn into involved rationalisation. The critic is driven to state what the passage could conceivably mean rather than what it is.[100]

All digressive similes need not be as confusing as this one. Some, as James Whaler has observed, are proleptic in character and appear to relate to the action as a whole.[101] Read with regard only to their immediate context they can be enjoyed as separate poems and prized for their pictorial qualities. But it is contended that they will yield far more to the reader if they are read as an allegory in little.

> Mean while the Adversary of God and Man,
> Satan *with thoughts inflam'd of highest design,*
> *Puts on swift wings, and toward the Gates of Hell*
> *Explores his solitary flight; som times*
> *He scours the right hand coast, som times the left,*
> *Now shaves with level wing the Deep, then soares*
> *Up to the fiery concave touring high.*
> *As when farr off at Sea a Fleet descri'd*
> *Hangs in the Clouds by* Aequinoctial *Winds*
> *Close sailing from* Bengala, *or the Iles*
> *Of* Ternate *and* Tidore, *whence Merchants bring*
> *Thir spicie Drugs: they on the Trading Flood*
> *Through the wide* Ethopian *to the Cape*
> *Ply stemming nightly toward the Pole. So seem'd*
> *Farr off the flying Fiend . . .*[102]

This can, of course, be defended as an independent poem. What is more difficult to show is how it relates to the context of *Paradise Lost*.

This mode of simile has been characterised by Empson as working through implied comparisons relevant to the main impulse of the poem.[103] We can take some of the resemblances that he points out – the night, the flying – but what about the more circumstantial details? What, for example, have the spices that are said to be on the ships to do with Satan? Empson's suggestion is that the ships are carrying spices because they stand for paganism and earthly glory – those goods for which Eve is to exchange her innocence.[104]

This solution has been widely disputed. Adams says that a fleet would rather bring to mind the spice and gold convoys of the rich and wicked empires of Spain and Portugal.[105] Whaler treats the ships as a digression within the simile – they are there because their purposes are *different* from those of Satan.[106] And Waldock takes the simile as no more than literal description.[107]

One can certainly agree with Waldock that the simile is pictorially apt on the scenic level of the immediate narration. But he does not go on to show any justification for the presence of spices in the passage. If the spices do not represent paganism, then what do they represent? Waldock should either have told us what they are doing in the poem or have indicated that they are irrelevant.

Empson's reading may be disputable, but not on the grounds of going against Milton's intention. After all, the passage affords very little evidence of what that intention was. So much is included in the simile that we have a choice either of disputing its relevance or interpreting it into a coherent pattern – by main force, as it were. It is notable that all the critics agree as to the value of the simile as an independent poem; where they differ is in their discussion of the way in which it is linked up with the rest of the action.

All digressive similes are not as successful in themselves as this one. In certain cases, the simile itself is indeterminable, and so provides an inadequate launching-pad for interpretation, valid or disputable.

> While thus he spake, th' Angelic Squadron bright
> Turn'd fierie red, sharpning in mooned hornes
> Thir Phalanx, and began to hemm him round
> With ported Spears, as thick as when a field
> Of Ceres ripe for harvest waving bends
> Her bearded Grove of ears, which way the wind
> Swayes them; the careful Plowman doubting stands
> Least on the threshing floor his hopeful sheaves
> Prove chaff. On th' other side Satan allarm'd
> Collecting all his might dilated stood,
> Like Teneriff or Atlas unremov'd . . .[108]

The self-disruptive nature of this simile may be seen in the differences among critical opinions as to the function of the Plowman. According to Tillyard, because the Plowman comes between the description of the angelic guard and that of Satan, he is the focus of the power of Heaven and Hell and thus resembles Adam and Eve.[109] But there is nothing in the simile to suggest a reference to Adam and Eve: the conflict is between Satan and Gabriel, with God interposing on Gabriel's side. This would seem to lend weight to Empson's suggestion that the Plowman can be associated with one or the other of the contending parties. But he admits that this interpretation has its difficulties: if the Plowman is God, he should not be anxious, and if he is Satan, then he is the natural owner of the good angels.[110]

What is happening here is that the ambivalence which is Satan's through most of the first two books has got out of control. The plot would appear to require that Satan be a cowardly thing beside the angelic guard, but the poetic sympathies are driving the other way. The confusion is faithfully reproduced in the verse.

It is therefore reflected in the critics' divergences. Geoffrey Hartman is in favour of God as the Plowman;[111] John Peter prefers to identify him with Satan.[112] Either view could be supported with an equal weight of evidence. Some critics, like Whaler, feel that the Plowman is no more than a point of balance through whose eyes we see the action.[113] Others, like Waldock, regard the Plowman as being no more than himself – a pictorial detail having a relation neither with the immediate context (Satan) nor with the larger action (God, Adam and Eve).[114]

As one might have expected, the critics differ about the effect this simile is likely to have on the reader. Waldock says that it turns his mind away from the imminent fight to make him think only of the 'Plowman'.[115] Tillyard, on the other hand, considers that the simile focuses on the immediate context to attach the gigantic action to earth.[116] Empson seems to have something of the same impression, but limits it to Satan and puts it the other way round – 'the homely idea is put before Satan to make him grander by contrast'.[117]

Now either Tillyard or Empson could be 'right': the simile may make Satan homely because it compares him with the Plowman, or it may make him grand because it contrasts him with the Plowman. The reader may be puzzled, however, to see in what way it could do both, at least for any single reader. It would seem, then, that two different readers would experience different, and opposed, effects as a result of reading the simile.

We have to ask ourselves what the simile has achieved. It does not comment on the general action of the poem because it has not order within its own framework. By the same token, it is unable to define the immediate context. And yet we cannot follow Zachary Pearce,[118] as Waldock seems to,[119] in believing that Milton merely took the liberty of wandering into some unresembling circumstance. Which of these views is correct is a matter impossible to demonstrate. The degree of confusion exhibited by the verse at this point allows, as we have seen, for an anarchic diversity of response.

And yet it is uncritical to discuss Milton's similes as thought they were all of a kind. Self-disruptive similes, like the ones we have just discussed, cannot be understood even when read in isolation from their subjects; while digressive similes, like that of the Merchant, at least exist as self-consistent poems.

There are, however, similes which are integral to the action, serving to focus more sharply their immediate context; and these represent the most coherent writing in Milton. One of the earliest of the epic similes that occur in *Paradise Lost* is a notable exception to any unwary generalisation about the digressive character of the genre. It at once provides the range and amplitude that Rajan admires in Milton,[120] makes the telling comparison that both Empson and Tillyard require,[121] and focuses the scene out of which it arises all the more compellingly because of its own local vitality.

> *Nathless he so endur'd, till on the Beach*
> *Of that inflamed Sea, he stood and call'd*
> *His Legions, Angel Forms, who lay intrans't*
> *Thick as Autumnal Leaves that strow the Brooks*
> *In* Vallombrosa *where th' Etrurian shades*
> *High overarch't inbowr or scattered sedge*
> *Afloat, when with fierce winds Orion arm'd*
> *Hath vext the Red-Sea Coast whose waves orethrew*
> Burisis *and his* Memphian *chivalrie*
> *While with perfidious hatred they pursu'd*
> *The Sojourners of* Goshen, *who beheld*
> *From the safe shore their floating carkases*
> *And broken Chariot Wheels, so thick bestrown*
> *Abject and lost lay these, covering the Flood,*
> *Under amazement of their hideous change.*[122]

If we begin by considering the details of this simile, we shall see that the critics agree as to their function and appear to be reacting similarly to their effect. Each interpretation differs slightly, but only because each brings out a different aspect of the image. However, there is nothing like the divergence which was produced by the last simile we considered. The prose in which a critic conveys his reaction is fairly certain to be less precise than the use of language by a creative writer. Yet we can deduce from the commentaries on the Vallombrosa simile that all its aspects work on one another to produce a totality and tend, therefore, to a common end.

This can be demonstrated from the text itself. Peter has noted the relevance of the image to its immediate context: the angels are scattered as well as numerous, as fallen leaves are.[123] Broadbent suggests another, but not disparate, reason why the angels are like leaves: because once they shone on high and now they are brought low.[124] They are, as Daiches says, reduced in significance,[125] and, as Muir says, have lost vitality.[126] Here, again, the same critique could include both readings. So we could say that the angels are like dead leaves because of their physical change; their moral downfall; their present degradation; and their loss of function.

The second part of the simile is equally alive in itself and relevant to the context. For strict purposes of comparison, Milton need only have said that the hosts of fallen angels were as thick as autumnal leaves or floating sedge. But there is a wider implication here. Muir comments that the Red Sea reference reminds us that the Rebel Angels are evil and God is omnipotent – both they and Pharaoh's troops have been overthrown by God's intervention.[127] Broadbent shows that the link is more than a moral one: the scattered sedge, an image for the devils still more degrading than fallen leaves, introduces the host of Pharaoh by means of a highly serious pun on the Red Sea; this is playing on the colour of fire.[128] Broadbent points out that the sedge was thought to give the sea its colour and this indicates another link between the sedge and the Red Sea – for, as Daiches tells us, its Hebrew name is, in fact, Yam Suph, 'Sea of Sedge'.[129] In a fine analysis,[130] John Peter demonstrates that the core of the simile is a leaf image which, in moving from the surface of a river to that of a sea, leaves us back where we started; with the picture of myriads of soldier-like forms stretched out in defeat on the sea of fire.

This is how comprehensiveness of experience may be included in a simile without disruption. Each critic has been worked upon by this simile, and has, in rationalising its effect upon him, brought out of it a salient aspect of the whole. In considering other similes, we saw how the various commentaries diverged from each other at crucial points; in the case of the Plowman, they diverged, also, from the text. Since this Vallombrosa simile appears not to allow such divergences of reading, it would appear that it communicates in a way very different from that of the other similes. The virtue in being 'right' may not lie in the critics who have commented so aptly on Vallombrosa and the Red Sea. Their agreement is a result of the passage communicating with precision sufficient to make agreement possible. The distinction to be made among Milton's similes is not, then, one simply of kind but also of value.

What is so disconcerting about the attempts to interpret *Paradise Lost* as a whole or in large stretches is that in bulk the poem demonstrably means different things to different people. It has incompletely absorbed its theology into its action; there is no possibility of agreement concerning its theme; its structure is so episodic as to be self-disruptive; it lacks internal self-consistency; and its extreme poetic inequality renders it still further fragmented. Nevertheless, there would be no need to reiterate with such emphasis these strictures and qualifications if they were the whole truth about *Paradise Lost*. To provoke such discussion as has been examined here, something must have been communicated. The parts of *Paradise Lost,* though they may not stand in any organic relation to each other, cannot, therefore, be assumed to be inorganic in themselves. Some of these parts, such as the Vallombrosa simile, command a genuine attention; and it may be that the excessive claims that have been made for *Paradise Lost* as a whole have obscured the brilliant, though fragmentary, nature of Milton's achievement.

The kind of appreciation that Milton has won from many modern critics seems most to flourish where there is a divergence of opinion, and where, therefore, the appreciation may have to be on the defensive. The result has been that the parts of the poem which have been most sharply attacked tend to bulk largest in the commentaries: the History of Mankind, the War in Heaven. Nobody would suggest that these are the strongest sections of *Paradise Lost*: if they were they would hardly have been attacked so sharply in the first place. It is not surprising that the Milton criticism one would most wholeheartedly recommend concerns itself with what would be agreed to be the better passages.

I am thinking particularly of Williams,[131] Lewis[132] and Cormican[133] on the invocation to book I; of Daiches,[134] Lewis[135] and Bush[136] on Satan's first speech, 'If thou be'est he . . .'; of Stoll,[137] Muir[138] and Leavis[139] on the Great Consult; Leavis[140] and Empson[141] on the Mulciber and Prosperin passages; Waldock[142] on the Temptation scene in book IX; Brooks and Hardy[143] on the simile which precedes it, 'As one who long in populous city pent . . .'; and almost anyone you like to mention on the incomparable end of the poem[144] – where, and only where, the explicit theme is embodied in dramatic poetry and all Milton's overt intentions seem to be realised.

Passages of this quality are pretty well bound to stimulate a critic into his best writing, and even the weaker critics of Milton have given good accounts of some of them. But to interpret *Paradise Lost* as a whole is an impossibility so far as any general acceptance of the interpretation is concerned. The 'Milton Controversy' is more complicated than most summaries of it would suggest. There is just as much a clash between the Miltonists Grierson and Lewis in their conception of the poet's God[145] as there is between Lewis and the 'detractor' Waldock.[146] And Lewis's account of the verse is a good deal nearer to that of Leavis than it is to that of Bush.[147] The critics that are likely to be found most helpful,[148] all, in their diverse ways, seem to be anthologising the poem. They may be accused of ignoring the whole and concentrating on the parts. But, if the conclusions implied by this enquiry are not erroneous, it would seem the poet had done just that before them.

This is a phenomenon more common than would be gathered from the critical commentaries. It is a commonplace, indeed, to say that the longer the work the less chance there is of its being flawless. But there is a tendency among critics to patch up flaws, to make connections which may not be there for other readers; and this is, no doubt, a result of the very exigency of criticism and the paradox contained within it. For were the work of art wholly coherent, wholly precise in its communication, what need would there be for the critic? Similarly, given an interested and alert reading public, why should it need an intermediary? But we know all too well that the public is anything but alert, and therefore the works set before it require an exposition. And we also know that many of those works have in-built difficulties; what we are not prepared to admit is the extent to which they disable a totality of appreciation.

There is no way of deciding at what point a work of art ceases to be completely available. A long poem, a full-length novel, can bear many lapses and lacunae; occasionally, as in *Bleak House* and *Daniel Deronda*, it is possible to detach a very sizeable portion of the anatomy and yet leave a recognisable torso – truncated, indeed, but unmistakably living. With other works, the disability is more insidious and wide- spread. The procedure I have followed with *Paradise Lost* could profitably be carried out in regard to other works, most of which have similarly inflated reputations. If we consider the disputes about the allegory in the *Faerie Queene*,[149] for instance, or those concerning the plot of *Tom Jones*,[150] we shall see that we are dealing with works which cannot be read as wholes. Incidentals they have, indeed, and it is these incidentals that account for their continued currency: the procession of the seasons in Spenser, the Molly Seagrim episode in Fielding – these are certainly alive and effective. But it is a hypocrisy to pretend that this life is spread throughout the work in question. That is why the general run of Milton's verse has been found to be unimpressive: the general run of Spenser's verse or of Fielding's prose would afford similar grounds for dissatisfaction. What we go to these authors for is their work at its best; we must take coherence in literature where we can find it.

The problem, as I see it, is that, in order to keep the work in his mind as anything more than detached fragments, the critic has to make some effort at interpretation, no matter how private, how personal, the result may be. The temptation then is to pass on that result *in toto* to the reading public, expressing indignation, as often as not, at the disagreement such a proceeding will inevitably arouse. Surely it is more graceful, as well as more honest, to concede that, however unified a work may be in intention, it is sadly fragmented in effect? That, in fact, all works of art are not equally capable of being read; and would not be, even in the happy event of all critics being capable of reading?

This is what I have called the concept of availability: just as all of his experience is not available even to the most gifted creative writer, so all of a writer's work is not available to even the most interested reader. There is one qualification here: critics have shown extra-ordinary powers of surmising an author's intention when they chance to possess something of a similarity of mind. We saw in our second chapter how easy it was for Harding to fill in the lacunae of *By Love Possessed*; a similar procedure happened when the author of *Perelandra* seized hold of Milton's Paradise. But there is no cachet in appealing to the like-minded; it is the author's job to bridge the gulf which makes us islands, to overcome the prejudices of those who dissent from him.

The extent to which this is done is the extent to which a work may be termed available; and there is a gamut of availability, ranging down from works which are ever-present classics, part of our life stream, to those which cannot, properly speaking, be read at all. There is not the same distinction to be made among reactions of individual readers; each is personal to himself, and differs from that of another only to the extent that it relates to the work that stimulated it. A mistake in the past has been to discuss divergences of opinion away from the text. Obviously there is an element of re-creation in any response to literature; what varies is the amount of personality involved, the amount of work, that is to say, done by the reader. And this, in its turn, derives from the quality or completeness of the stimulus. There is a distinction to be made between responding to a pattern and filling it in from the proffered outlines. In the former case the work is available; responses are similar among different readers because their reaction has been determined by what has been communicated. But work that is incompletely available will not determine reaction at all, except among those who happen to share the author's sympathies and prejudices. And in such a case it will be possible to show from the text in question that a critic is doing more than his fair share of the work. The response, then, is always personal; all works, however, are not equally able to condition it.

CHAPTER FOUR

Misreadable Poems and Misread Poems

Some poems are misread; but there are many poems which cannot be read at all. They communicate nothing with any degree of precision, and so fail to impose a similar reading on different readers. In such cases, divergences will occur which nobody could resolve. Interpretation gives place to endless misreading – endless, because the text is incapable of providing any check against them. Works such as these I call misreadable.

One characteristic of the misreadable poem is private allusion, use of experience which is unavailable to the reader. The difficulties this gives rise to can be localised in the vagaries of memory which afflict those who would comment on the poetry of Edith Sitwell. There was a controversy some years ago about her use of 'Emily-coloured hands'; but this does not, as a deliberately composed phrase, exist. And yet for many people it is among the best-known quotations from modern poetry. One reader *knew* what the colour of the hands was – yellowish and faintly freckled.[1] Another not only defended the apocryphal phrase but provided a ghost-context for it – Emily-coloured hands raising the blinds in a child's bedroom.[2] Evidently something existed, if only in the reader's mind. In this case, the association can be traced back to the first use of this misquotation, in John Sparrow's *Sense and Poetry*: 'If Miss Sitwell speaks of "Emily-coloured hands", a reader will be in the dark unless, perhaps, he knows that Miss Sitwell had a nurse called Emily.'[3] Sparrow's phrase, 'in the dark', coupled with the ascription of the name Emily to a nurse, may have been enough to spark off a reader into a realm of private re-creation in which blinds are raised in a child's room.

This phrase was indignantly repudiated by the author herself: 'it conveys no impression excepting one of ugliness'.[4] Nevertheless, it has had an extraordinary circulation. Sparrow's misquotation was taken up, and no doubt popularised, in a sixth-form anthology of modern poetry edited by Maurice Wollman.[5] This would certainly explain the affection with which so many readers cling to the phrase: they are likely to have come across it at an impressionable period of their lives, and in a book conned with some application. Philip Toyn-bee, for instance, took it as a prime example of obscurity in contemporary verse;[6] and there can be no doubt that 'Emily-coloured hands' has enjoyed a wider currency than its unfortunate original.

This latter, 'Emily-coloured primulas', would seem to be eminently forgettable. It has cropped up in at least two other formulations: 'Isabella-coloured *dress*',[7] a possible mis-recollection of a phrase from another poem,[8] and 'Emily-coloured *auriculas*',[9] a lumping together of two lines in the original poem. A phrase which was wholly satisfactory would be unlikely to have set up such sympathies of misquotation.

Kingsley Amis reduces the argument to two bare questions: 'Why *Emily*-coloured?' and 'Why Emily-*coloured*?'[10] Even when applied to 'primulas', the associations for different readers vary between mauve,[11] green,[12] peaches-and-cream,[13] flowery,[14] black.[15] This depends on whether one is influenced by the syllable 'prim-' to think of old ladies in old-fashioned clothes;[16] by the association of the name with Chaucer's Emily;[17] with the supposed (and erroneous) derivation of the word from *emiellé* (milk-washed);[18] the correct derivation, from *émaillé* (enamelled);[19] or whether one just happens to have known an Emily of that particular colour.[20]

Edith Sitwell herself, in various contexts, maintained that the phrase was meant to convey the pink cheeks of a young country girl;[21] but there is no warrant for this in the text. She may have assumed that her readers would understand 'cheeks', but the majority of those in our sample do not seem to have done so. The noun which is qualified, 'primulas', does not help us very much, for Amis tells us,[22] on the authority of *The Complete Gardener*,[23] that primulas exist in a wide variety of colours, including white, yellow, yellowish-green, apricot-yellow, buff-orange, pink, red, rose, blue, mauve, lilac, purple and crimson. Clearly 'primulas' are a variable as much as 'Emily'. Since the phrase 'Emily-coloured' is used to describe 'primulas', there would be little point in using 'primulas' as a means of defining 'Emily-coloured'. But those determined to read in a sense will read it in, whatever the association, real or illusory. Just what colour the phrase suggests is, as we have seen, a question to which different readers will give very different answers.

The context ought to define the phrase. But – we should ask – how *defining* is the context? Nobody at all, not even Geoffrey Nokes who has given the poem most attention,[24] has mentioned that it has a plot. King Midas is warned that the spring is merely a semblance, and that therefore he must die. He decides to woo eternity with a banquet; and, when the gardener's daughter brings the precious viands – spring winds and waterfalls – to him on a golden dish, he feels that he could conquer eternity if she was his Eve. But she runs away and escapes him.

The poem, then, would seem to be a kind of fairy-tale; and this is borne out by the *simplesse* of the writing – deliberately forced rhymes, innocent bits of descriptive detail. The effects are deft, and, within their narrow limits, well-executed: 'a maiden fair as an almond tree', 'the tulips as bright as the showers'.[25] There is no attempt at definition here, merely a general impression of freshness and pleasantness. The poem departs from this mode only in one particular: the phrase we have just been discussing. Into a background suitable for a fairy-tale comes the unwelcome touch of smartness.

> . . . *the tulips are as bright as the showers,*
>
> *For spring is here; the auriculas,*
> *And the Emily-coloured primulas*
>
> *Bob in their pinafores on the grass*
> *As they watch the gardener's daughter pass.*[26]

So far from being defined by the context, the phrase rather fights against it. Both Nokes and Amis associate the 'gardener's daughter' with 'Emily-coloured',[27] but in what way this can be demonstrated from the poem is more than either of them can tell us. The reason they assume this association is to have some chance of reacting to the text. Experienced readers of modern poetry are adept at doing this; but those less able to read arbitrary details as part of a pattern are liable to find themselves perplexed.

Unfortunately, it is not the practice for people to juxtapose, as we have done here, different interpretations of the same poem. If it were, the reader would see clearly that his own version need not be the same as that of someone else. More, he would become aware of a baseless certainty in all the voices crying up their readings as the only possible ones. If one reads into a poem a set of associations of one's own, the reading thereby produced will be satisfactory only until one tries to compare it with that of somebody else.

There are many arguments against the practice of reading-in; more particularly that, in time, it impedes understanding of poems which do not require this sort of treatment. In our time, a great deal of attention is given by poetry-lovers to comparatively minor verse, and the classics are neglected. The problem of poetry, as of all art, is a problem of communication. If an image conveys an impression to its creator, something quite different to one or two other people, and precisely nothing to anyone else, is there not a failure of communication somewhere? And does it follow that it is the reader who has failed?[28]

Faced with an obscure text, however, it is natural for the reader to supply its deficiencies. An extraordinary example of this occurred a few years ago when an incomprehensible poem by Sidney Keyes was set, as a comprehension test, in a G.C.E. examination for the Advanced Level.[29] 118 scripts came my way, and there were as many as 32 distinct interpretations among them. One would hardly have thought that these 25 undistinguished lines would have given rise to such disparity.

> *Now it is time to remember the winter festivals*
> *Of the old world, and see their raftered halls*
> *Hung with hard holly; tongues' confusion; slow*
> *Beat of the heated blood in those great palaces*
> *Decked with the pale and sickled mistletoe;*
> *And voices dying when the blind bard rises*
> *Robed in his servitude, and the high harp*
> *Of sorrow sounding, stills those upturned faces.*
>
> *O it is such long learning, loneliness*
> *And dark despite to master*
> *The bard's blind craft; in bitterness*
> *Of heart to strike the strings and muster*
> *The shards of pain to harmony, not sharp*
> *With anger to insult the merry guest.*
> *O it is glory for the old man singing*
> *Dead valour and his own days coldly cursed.*
>
> *How ten men fell by one heroic sword*
> *And of fierce foray by the unwatched ford,*
> *Sing, blinded face; quick hands in darkness groping*
> *Pluck the sad harp; sad heart forever hoping*
> *Valhalla may be songless, enter*
> *The moment of your glory, out of clamour*
> *Moulding your vision to such harmony*
> *That drunken heroes cannot choose but honour*
> *Your stubborn, blinded pride, your inward winter.*[30]

At one extreme were those candidates who found the poem totally obscure or took it as literal description. At the other extreme were those with really wild interpretations – the Bard as a clergyman, for example, 'robed in his servitude'; or as Hoder, the blind god who threw the mistletoe at Balder; or as Death, speaking to the upturned faces. Typical of this fictional sort of re-creation is the following: 'Could it be that it is a decorated way of describing a hut during the war, where many soldiers have come to hear two blind veterans play and sing to them?' One can only regret the circumstances that led to such an ecstasy of over-interpretation.

But even if we pick out the more restrained readings, the range of understanding is very wide. Different candidates take the poem to be praise for the honourable craft of the Bard; admiration, and, in some cases, regret, for his suffering; belief that he is a symbol of old age, a pitiful result of war, that he is frustrated because he can no longer perform the deeds about which he sings. Some candidates say that he is clinging to a heroic past when war was a great and triumphant thing; others say that he is disgusted by the immature trash – legends of bravery – which he has to chant. A number of candidates suggest that the Bard is being attacked by Keyes for idealising war – one calls the old man 'pompous', another suggests that he is 'blinded with pride'. Related to this is a view that would take the poem to be contrasting the romantic fictions of the Bard with Keyes's actual war experiences. Quite a number of candidates, however, reversed this process: they do not contrast the Bard with Keyes, they go so far as to identify them. This can be done in various ways; by relating their respective regrets about the war, by relating their respective sufferings and also their respective roles in society. Some readers believe the poem to be mainly about the perils of war, though others take it as a patriotic poem longing for home, or possibly as a plea for wounded ex-servicemen.

One question that seems basic to any consideration of the poem is: who is the Bard? It is difficult to see how he can be a symbol of old age in the earlier interpretations I have cited and yet at the same time be identified with the young soldier-poet, as in the later ones. One could ask, too, how far we are expected to sympathise with the Bard: he cannot be at once a splendid survival from a past age and an unfeeling cynic talking about experiences he never had. The poem that could include all these interpretations would be amorphous. And the range of interpretation would have been even wider if the examination paper had not inserted a note on Keyes's identity. The fact that this note was thought necessary suggests that the examiner had some doubt as to the intelligibility of the poem. And, supposing the note had been omitted, would the candidate have gathered from the poem itself any connection between the Bard and soldier-poet?

An analysis of the poem would, no doubt, draw attention to the remote, unrealised quality of the verse. Commentary, of a generalised kind, bulks much larger than actual description; there is no dramatic content to speak of. Almost the only phrase that comes through with any clarity is 'not sharp / With anger to insult the merry guest'; and it is no accident that this phrase draws by far the largest single group of interpretations; no less than twelve people were able to agree that the Bard was degraded by playing for these drunken heroes.

Certainly any attempt to interpret poems such as these will expose the reader to wild subjectivism. The poem, in such a case, is liable to be a do-it-yourself kit for the construction of private fantasies; as has been the case with these examination candidates. At best, the maturer critic will understand an obscure text only by drawing upon his own experience. Now it is obviously useful to have experience which will help one to understand what is in a poem, but experience can be of little use if the poem is inexplicable. Yet, when faced with obscurity, critics are tempted to refer to such experience as a means of elucidation; therefore, nine times out of ten, they find themselves elucidating what isn't there at all. The 'elucidation' becomes something very like a private poem. What is elucidated will remain personal to the interpreter, since his experience isn't likely to resemble with the requisite degree of closeness that of anyone else.

Perhaps the high-water-mark of obscurity in English verse was reached with W. S. Graham's poem, *The Nightfishing*. Roy Fuller commented that it was roughly about writing a poem about fishing at night, but went on to say that – with some descriptive exceptions – the verse was tortuous, solemn and portentous.[31]

> *So I have been called by my name and*
> *It was not sound. It is me named upon*
> *The space which I continually move across*
> *Bearing between my courage and my lack*
> *The constant I bleed on. And, put to stillness,*
> *Fixed in this metal and its cutting salts,*
> *It is this instant to exact degree,*
> *And for whose sake?*
>
> *It is this instant written dead. This instant,*
> *Bounded by its own grace and all Time's grace,*
> *Masters me into its measurement so that*
> *My ghostly constant is articulated.*

55

Then suddenly like a struck rock all points unfix.
The whole east breaks and leans at last to us,
Ancient overhead.[32]

This is typical of Graham's writing – the clotted occasion (to use the words of Roy Fuller)[33] which comes to every poet when he has not been able to find the proper equivalent for a complex experience. But G. S. Fraser asks, 'Does Roy Fuller remember what it was like when suddenly as a small boy – a similar thing happened to myself, I think, at the age of seven – he became aware of himself as self-conscious, as at once a spectator and a participant: when he said to himself, with a slightly dazed or giddy feeling, "I am Roy Fuller"?'[34] On the other hand, J. A. Stephens relates the whole passage to a statement by Sartre, about a man making himself feel essential to the objective world by re-ordering it in his own subjective terms.[35]

It will be seen that the interpretations of Fraser and Stephens have little in common with each other. Stephens finds it necessary to cite Sartre in order to provide an adequate context, which would suggest that we could have the context without reading the poem.[36] While Fraser takes these generalising and obscure lines and supplies them with a context of his own – in this case, from his personal experience.[37] For there is nothing in *The Nightfishing* about recognising one's own separateness of identity. If we need Mr Fraser's autobiography in order to understand this passage from *The Nightfishing*, then perhaps we don't need the passage.

But it is possible to clinch matters more definitely even than this. Both Stephens and Fraser claim to understand the poem and advance interpretations with a fair measure of confidence. But Stephens regards this passage as a plea for subjectivity,[38] while Fraser regards it as a recognition of objectivity.[39] How is it that their interpretations, both of the whole and of a representative passage such as this one, differ so completely?

I should say that it is because the poem is so obscure that one must, in order to arrive at a coherent reading, supply a good deal of context – of meaning – from oneself. According to different temperaments among readers, the context they supply will be different.

Stephens is evidently interested in philosophy, so his method of talking about Graham's poetry is to diagrammatise its 'thought', often well away from the words in which it is expressed. So therefore, in order to explicate the poem, he calls in additional philosophers to serve as parallels, or even glosses. Fraser, on the other hand, is a poet, and one particularly effective in the realm of personal experience. So naturally he falls back on anecdote and supplies from his varied experience the context which the poem does not itself embody.

To phrase it differently, the interpretations differ because the poem does not adequately communicate its sense. If Graham conveys something like 30 per cent of an experience, then the critic can either (like Fuller) find the poem obscure and give up the puzzle or (like Fraser and Stephens) supply the other 70 per cent. Since we're all individuals, no person's 70 per cent is going to be like that of anybody else. For interpretations to have much in common, far more would have to be conveyed by the poet. And so we have the spectacle of Fraser and Stephens each claiming to understand the poem, yet understanding it differently – and irreconcilably.

An analysis would show that one difficulty is the confidence with which the author puts forward abstractions, as though he expects them to be made concrete by the reader. How, for example, could one gloss the word 'constant'? I should imagine that it has to do with endurance, but would not defend my reading against someone who suggested as an alternative possibility 'norm', let us say, or 'routine'. What, indeed, is to prevent it from assuming a totally private referent, such as 'the human soul' or 'Christ's cross'? And before these possibilities are rejected as being unlikely, perhaps I should say that they have, in my experience, been quite seriously put forward.[40]

If analysis were to be taken further, one could point to the syntax which is liable to suggest two contradictory senses at one and the same time; often as a result of undue emphasis given to minor parts of speech. One could also go on to indicate the burden of dead metaphor which works against the explicit meaning and confuses the action of the poem for the reader.

One could go on, indeed; but there is a point when analysis becomes a species of mockery. The worse the poem, the more it is necessary for a critic to move from interpretation to analysis. And a poem such as The Nightfishing, which is virtually a failure, may drive us into analysing representative passages in order to show how the failure takes place. Any more general procedure would be highly conjectural.

Basically, the plot seems to be at fault. The whole conception of the poem, as far as we can read it through the words, seems to be flawed. I should, myself, say that the poem is an attempt to discuss writing poetry in terms of fishing at night. My interpretation cannot be right, since the poem is linguistically incoherent, and it cannot be wrong, for the same reason. But, for the purposes of argument, let this interpretation – one of intention rather than effect – stand for the moment. In that case, we have an attempt to identify with each other two activities which are fundamentally incompatible. This attempt to unite disparities by force, as it were, leads to a good deal of violence being done to the language in which the poem is couched. In fact, the poem is talking about too many things at once. Mr Fuller points out felicitous descriptions of fishing –

> *We came in riding steady in the bay water,*
> *A sailing pillar of gulls, past the cockle strand.*
> *And springing teal came out off the long sand . . .*[41]

But I don't think I could say what this has to do with the writing of poetry. The desperation of writing poetry is in these lines which Mr Fraser quotes –

> *Each word is but a longing*
> *Set out to break from a difficult home. Yet in*
> *Its meaning I am.*[42]

But this has nothing to do with fishing. There are, indeed, passages such as the first one quoted from this poem[43] which seem to include both activities. But they are, probably because of this, incoherent, and lend themselves only, as we have seen, to wildly subjective modes of reading.

One's approach to a poem must necessarily be governed by what is available to the reader. It seems to me that Mr Fraser has been applying to *The Nightfishing* something of the approach which Wilson Knight makes to *Measure for Measure*.[44] It won't, of course, work; the 'right' approach, but the wrong poem. There is not enough given in this poem to bear interpretation.

This, for me, defines the misreadable poem. There is a sense in which any interpretation of whatever kind will be unfair to such a work. A close reading will involve the attempt to realise metaphors which are unrealisable; and this will lead to over-reading – either a heavy emphasis placed on stock properties, or else a subjective reading-in of private associations.

This may be seen in the discussion of any of Shelley's weaker poems. For instance –

> *When the lamp is shattered*
> *The light in the dust lies dead . . .*[45]

F. R. Leavis[46] and Allen Tate[47] call this a cliché; they read the lines as saying that light cannot long survive its source. Milton Wilson seeks to redeem the lines by reading in a logical figure – where the 'container' is shattered, the 'contained' lies in the dust.[48] But another critic who would defend the lines, F. A. Pottle, insists that 'in the dust' modifies not 'lies' (as Wilson and the others suggest) but 'light'.[49] In which case, Shelley would seem to be talking about reflected light; saying that, when the lamp goes out, the walls and floor of the room don't go on shining with a luminescence of their own.

Clearly, these two defences of the poem are irreconcilable. If 'in the dust' modifies 'lies' (Wilson), then the important thing is that the light *now* lies in the dust dead. If 'in the dust' modifies 'light' (Pottle), then the important thing is that the light which *was* in the dust is now dead. To reconcile these two readings in the poem would be to read it simultaneously as referring to light which is still in the dust but which, nevertheless, is no longer in the dust. An ambiguity, perhaps, but a disruptive one.

Analysis would show that the plot demands at key points the assertion of certain secondary meanings and the suppression of primary ones. But, because these secondary meanings are so clumsily expressed, they fail to condition the primary meanings into silence. And so the expression fights at every point against what can be deduced of the plot. For example

> When the cloud is scattered
> The rainbow's glory is shed . . .[50]

As Leavis remarks, the context would seem to require the secondary meaning to assert itself; 'shed', in that case, would take on the sense of 'dropped', of light *fallen*.[51] But the association of 'shed' with rainbow, and with, moreover, the lamp in the previous lines, means that the primary meaning is predominant; that is to say, the giving of light, light still *falling*. In other words, according to the plot Shelley ought to have been saying that, when the cloud is scattered, the rainbow is destroyed; but succeeds in saying the exact opposite – that, when the cloud is scattered, the rainbow continues to give light.

It cannot be argued that the intention is forced upon the reader by the structure of analogy in the poem, for local obscurities blur any logical pattern that may have been sought after.

> When hearts have once mingled
> Love first leaves the well-built nest;
> The weak one is singled
> To endure what it once possessed . . .[52]

There are at least six possible interpretations of the last two lines. To concentrate on the chief point of divergence: the 'weak one' may be the weaker of the two lovers either (1) on his (her) own or (2) deserted by love; it may be (3) Woman; it may be (4) the less well-built of the nests in which (the god of) Love has found a home; it may be the human heart – weak either because (5) it is too frail to hold love or (6) because it would seek happiness in oblivion. Interpretations 1, 2 and 3 derive from Leavis;[53] no. 4 from Pottle;[54] no. 5 from Wilson[55] and no. 6 from René Wellek.[56] And I have no doubt that, if I could proffer the poem for comment to a whole conference of critics, I should receive at least as many interpretations more.

The last stanza is generally agreed to be the best of the four; but its relative directness can hardly overcome the previous confusion. By this time, there is little chance of the plot recovering itself. And so we find many different combinations of possibilities will fit so apparently straightforward a line as

Its passions will rock thee.[57]

Thus:

Love's passions will rock the weak one. (Leavis)[58]
The passions of the heart will rock love. (Wellek)[59]
The passions of the frailer of the two hearts will rock love. (Pottle)[60]
The passions (or passion itself) will rock love. (Wilson)[61]
Lust will rock the lovers. (Tate)[62]

The variety of response here results from Shelley's use of two imponderables to qualify each other: 'passions' and 'thee'. Opinions about the latter will depend on whether or not the critic believes the apostrophe to be carried on from the previous stanza. And of the former, it should be enough to say that 'passions' is merely a counter; neither an image nor a personification, and not capable of being looked at as closely as such terms would suggest. Only by sliding comfortably past these familiar signals can the poem be 'appreciated'; and this is a way of reading which would invalidate all our great poetry, including Shelley's own.

I am not saying anything so naïve as that disagreement proves disruption, or consensus gives consent. The distinction is rather in the quality of the disagreements voiced about given poems. Those who disagree about misreadable poems can be shown to be producing private fictions; clearly these will not relate to each other, but neither will they relate to the text. The ambiguity is uncontrolled: when a poem will bear two meanings which are irreconcilable, it is obscure –

by definition, can bear no interpretation capable of finding public assent.

A word may, in itself, bear several disparate meanings. But it is possible to fine down the area of connotation if that word is placed in a context which will allow only meanings relevant to it to assert themselves. Definition in language is a matter of limiting the possibilities of words by placing them in a context which, being formed by them, is itself limited by them.

Needless to say, this need not resolve itself to one simple meaning. It is possible to use different meanings as one does the spotlights in a theatre: two meanings may converge to define more precisely a particular attitude. This could be called controlled ambiguity, in the sense that control is exerted to reconcile apparent opposites; as the engineer focuses diversely sourced points of light on to a single area of the stage. If two senses of a word can be reconciled into relevance to the context, then the context bears to some extent the reference of both of them.

Such a reconciliation need not bring about a consensus. There is often a strong temptation on the part of the critic to take a single aspect of the poem and reject the rest. This will in itself produce a simplified reading; it will also produce a disagreement with the critic who is taking another single aspect and, in his turn, rejecting what the first critic responded to. But, in practice, it is possible to locate both aspects in the text; and also in the interpretation of any critic alive to both aspects. In other words, a poem which will bear two or more readings will not be obscure if those readings are reconcilable.

It may be, of course, that the individual critic will be aware of disparity: the aspects that he ignores may not be so easily subdued; may, in fact, fight against the aspect that he recognises. This often happens when a critic is out of sympathy with the ideology of the poem he is discussing. In such a case, it should be possible to show that he is ignoring a relevant sector of the poem; that the disparity he has noted is, in fact, part of a complex that he will not admit as a whole.

All our theorising will not prevent a bad critic from misreading a good poem. But, again, it should be possible even in such a case to show where the reading departs from the text; where the critic is fastening private associations on to a public poem, or ignoring aspects which can be shown to exist.

This, ultimately, is our distinction: between uncontrolled and controlled ambiguity in language; between the interpretations which are irreconcilable and those which merely differ; between the poem which is misreadable and which cannot therefore be understood at all, and that which is misread and yet affords enough critical purchase to allow misreadings to be demonstrated from its text.

Often the distinction is a matter of plot. The technique and even the raw material that would be weakness in one context is virtue in another. The disembodied 'passions' of *When the Lamp is Shattered* may or may not be congenial attitudes; but the fault is in the gap between the stated emotion and its evanescent object. Acted out in terms of plot and context, these 'passions' might be comprehended quite readily. So there may not, after all, be an unbridgeable gulf between misreadable poems and misread poems; often they are produced by one and the same man using similar means. And considerations of tactics prompt us to choose our first example of the misread poem, like our last example of the misreadable poem, from the works of Shelley.

Many of the different readings sparked off by the *Ode to the West Wind* are, in fact, reconcilable. They may be simple aspects of a complex attitude, or recognition that there is a disparity in the material which is resolved in the poem. The poem is, I should say, a balance; often, a subtle deployment of opposites. The resultant ambiguity is not disruptive, but defining.

A relatively uncomplicated example of this is found in lines 2–4 of the poem:

> *Thou, from whose unseen presence the leaves dead*
> *Are driven, like ghosts from an enchanter fleeing,*
> *Yellow, and black, and pale, and hectic red . . .*[63]

F. W. Bateson comments that the *ghosts* in the poem are not properly visualised – ghosts, he says, are essentially colourless.[64] Supposing we grant Bateson's contention; the point of the poem is that the leaves are Shelley's words:

> *Drive my dead thoughts over the universe*
> *Like withered leaves to quicken a new birth . . .*[65]

And, for all the explicit statement of death, the imagery is of a quickening kind. One could say, Shelley's thoughts appear to be dead, but that, in fact, he's pretty sure that they're not. And, by the same token, he produces a poem which in itself *shows* they aren't.

Neville Rogers appositely reminds us that the decaying leaves are regenerated by the seasons.[66] It is true that, as Wilson Knight says,[67] the opening is crammed with deathly impressions; ghosts, pestilences, corpses, graves and the like. And yet the impressions are not equally

deathly: even the ghosts are coloured and animated by the wind. F. A.
Lea has pointed out that, though in the first sentence the leaves are

Pestilence-stricken multitudes,

in the second the wind becomes, as well as an enchanter, a charioteer;
bearing seeds not to a grave but to a bed.[68] Moreover, when one regards the context, the sleep is only apparently death-like.

> *O thou,*
> *Who chariotest to their dark wintry bed*
> *The winged seeds, where they lie cold and low,*
> *Each like a corpse within its grave, until . . .*[69]

As Ralph Houston has pointed out, this is not a true burial.[70] The
metaphor isn't, either, so mixed as Bateson would have us believe.[71]
The seeds are winged; they are going to a bed, but they are charioted
thither; they are going to lie 'like' corpses, but they are going to arise –
here, again, we have the paradox of the poem made dramatic: explicit
despair, actual hope. 'Chariotest' and 'winged' work against 'dark',
'wintry', 'cold' and 'low'. The 'grave' which is permanent is likened
to a 'bed', which is not. The fact that the seeds are *seeds* makes it less
likely that they are what they seem, i.e. *corpses*. And if it seems unlikely
that corpses will rise again, we have to remember that the wind is
first enounced to us as an enchanter. The Calderón reminiscence, a
disruptive ambiguity in the other Shelley poem we discussed –

> *Your cradle, your home and your bier*[72]

– now emerges as a fresh apprehension of that paradox recognised by
the Spanish poet, that buds can be at once a sepulchre and a cradle. In
any case, the sentence is conditional. The seeds only resemble corpses
until

> *Thine azure sister of the Spring shall blow*
> *Her clarion o'er the dreaming earth, and fill*
> *(Driving sweet buds like flocks to feed in air)*
> *With living hues and odours plain and hill . . .*[73]

Houston says, rightly, that Shelley has telescoped the idea of the spring
wind driving the flock out to feed together with the idea of new buds
opening on the spring air; but feels that the association is a forced one.[74]
So does Mr Bateson. The simile is comparing the shepherd driving his
sheep (a horizontal process) with the opening of the buds (a vertical

63

process).[75] But, as W. Milgate has written,[76] the spring calls forth irresistibly ('driving') both buds and flocks; and both are symbols of life and increase ('living', 'fill'). And he goes on to say that, in fact, Spring really does blow: the ambiguity he points to is true of buds opening out and of horns driving out the flock; and both are true of spring. All are blowing. That growth and movement are responding to the spring would argue against Bateson's original contention, that Shelley is comparing horizontal to vertical processes; growth is not limited to one direction.

That the adverse critics have reason for their strictures I would certainly allow. The reconciliation of such opposites – 'destroyer and preserver' – is not to be achieved without considerable plasticity of language. The weight placed on 'blow', for example, may be more than it can bear, although in context it seems to work all right. What I would say, however, is that Messrs Bateson and Houston have to some extent misread the poem, and can be shown to have done so. They tend to see the aspects of death and life, on which, respectively, they comment, as some sort of mistake on the poet's part, but just as the ghosts are colourful because they aren't – in spite of the poet's *statement* – dead, so the revival of spring is one process (not necessarily horizontal or vertical). It is Shelley's peculiar problem to express the negative – in this case, death – in terms positive enough to suggest the opposite; and so, to some extent, to effect a reconciliation.

One need not share in the difficulties critics have discovered to concede that they are legitimate ones. What can be done is to show misreadings: readings, that is to say, that ignore aspects which can be shown to be reconcilable with those that the critic has already isolated.

> *Thou on whose stream, mid the steep sky's commotion,*
> *Loose clouds like earth's decaying leaves are shed . . .*[77]

F. R. Leavis asks in what respects the 'loose clouds' are like 'decaying leaves'.[78] Some critics who would defend the poem might agree with him that no more than a sense of windy tumult is intended.[79] However, such a sense would be an over-simplification of what the poem can be shown to offer: in order to suggest tumult, a poem cannot itself be merely tumultuous. This would produce an effect only of incoherence and fragmentation – which is all Dr Leavis seems to see in this context. A good deal, however, depends on what one makes of the stream –

> *Thou on whose stream, mid the steep sky's commotion . . .*[80]

We can discount Wellek's fantasy about Shelley and his boat on the

64

Arno;[81] if we have to rely on some pseudo-biographical footnote in order to justify the imagery, the poem would seem to be very confused indeed. D. W. Harding, a critic trained in the same school as Leavis, has no need to lean on such extrapolations; nor does he find such confusion in the passage as Leavis does. He points out that the clouds are swept along by the wind, just as the leaves were in the first section;[82] as R. H. Fogle maintains, the wind is the power behind them both.[83] The poem, in other words, assimilates disparate material and reconciles it into a whole. Here as well (as Rogers reminds us)[84] is the sense of regeneration. The very unlikeness of the clouds *in themselves* to decaying leaves tells us that the poem is neither about clouds nor about leaves but about a new birth. Any likeness of clouds to leaves consists largely in the conditions to which they are both submitted – they are being irresistibly swept along. And the connection which links all disparates in the poem is here made clear: for they are being swept along *by the wind*.

This is where the meaning of 'stream' in the poem is so important. It seems to me that Leavis has misread the lines here. 'The appropriateness of the metaphor "stream" in the first line is not that it suggests a surface on which, like leaves, the clouds might be "shed", but that it contributes to the general "streaming" effect in which the inappropriateness of "shed" passes unnoticed.'[85] Dr Leavis appears to be considering 'stream' as a background against which the clouds are moving. In fact, of course, it is the wind.

Once this is recognised, all becomes clear. 'Stream' does not fail because it does not suggest a metaphor. 'Stream' could, by itself, mean either a surface (of a body of liquid) or a motion – streaming. Both have a certain appositeness to the context. But the latter meaning is more present to the reader; and the idea of the stream as river is only present in close association with the idea of such a river in rapid motion. Thus one sense not only predominates over another but conditions it in such a way as to bring out its secondary connotation. The poem is full of motion, is, in a sense, *about* motion –

Wild Spirit, which art moving everywhere . . .[86]

This is a stream which is associated with 'the steep sky's commotion', with the shedding of clouds as easily as leaves, with an aëry *surge*. In other words, the wind is apprehended as being a stream of air.

This is why one can have no time for Professor Wellek's 'poetic' picture of Shelley and his boat.[87] The Arno has only the place in the poem which Shelley gives it: anything else is an intrusion which may lead to misreading. Harding is much nearer the mark when he emphasises that the earlier part of the section is concerned wholly with the horizontal stream of wind.[88]

The poem will not seem obscure if the reader remembers that he is reading a poem addressed to the West Wind. It is no doubt possible to suggest a storm literally by means less complicated than those Shelley has used. Indeed, his own early drafts might be held to succeed on that one level more completely. But they seem oddly thin when compared with the finished poem, and this is because an extra dimension of experience has been included. The wind isn't just a wind. If it were, Shelley might deserve the strictures of Yvor Winters, who feels that no landscape can be an adequate symbol for strong feelings.[89] But, naturally, to make the wind *more* than a wind at all levels, is to make it, at any given level, less than one.

The words that are used have to be at once realistic and symbolic. If it were wholly symbolic, the poetry would be that of vague statement and mythical pretensions, like *The Bards* – where there was so little grasp on the actual that nothing of what was symbolised was conveyed. If it were wholly realistic, it would be literal prose, robbed of Shelley's symbolic intellectualisation.

And so the wind is more than a literal wind – it is a life force, the breath of Autumn's being, the breath of universal being; it is a symbol of resurrection, of poetic inspiration, of the force of progress, even. These interpretations have been put forward, respectively, by Rogers,[90] Lea,[91] Pottle,[92] Wilson Knight,[93] F. W. Bateson;[94] all different critics with different predilections, and yet their interpretations are reconcilable with each other within the framework of the poem. What is held in common in all these interpretations is the poem as an attempt to relate man to the forces of inspiration and life; the wind as an agnostic definition of spirit. There are notable absences from this consensus; but these are critics who do not discuss the poem in terms of its theme at all; who are, it may be surmised, ideologically opposed to it. Yet the theme is plainly there; otherwise no consensus would be possible.

However, even for a sympathetic reader, the poem carries a considerable weight of pessimism to allay its hopeful burden. Shelley's is an exploratory, not a positive, vision. And of course we must remember that, like so many romantic poems, the *Ode to the West Wind* ends on a question.

Such a weight of negation, of questioning, must necessarily give rise to misreading, especially on the part of critics unsympathetic to the moral content of a given work. But it is usually a simple matter to demonstrate the extent of a particular critical deflection; partly from comparison with the views of other critics, partly by relating it to the text. Often a misreading comes about simply through the exigencies of criticism: the critic is driven to rationalise what the poet has dramatised; to rush in with an explanation where the poet has deliberately not ventured to propound one. This may be a fault of the critic for being over-eager, or of the poet for not doing enough; or both.

The Tyger is, in Kathleen Raine's felicitous phrase, a grand incantation of rhetorical questions.[95] By definition, and in common English usage, rhetorical questions are those which do not demand an answer – or, at least, which do not expect one. But, in the case of Blake's poem, several attempts have been made to supply answers; such attempts have resulted in interpretations which, in effect, seek to rewrite the poem. Thus it may be suggested that here we have a poem that has been universally misread. The main difficulties that have been found can be reduced to a single question: Who Made the Tiger? The answers to this are very various indeed; we shall take them in increasing degrees of antipathy to the Creator – whoever he was.

Stanley Gardner is the critic most favourably inclined towards him. He finds parallels between the creation of the Tiger and the compulsion by Los of the invisible spectre in *Jerusalem*; also with his riveting of Urizen's chains in the *Book of Urizen*. Gardner's arguments are based on the prevalent forge-imagery of all three passages, and lead him to the conclusion that the power who has dared grasp the deadly terrors of the Tiger in the night is – Innocence.[96] There are, however, two main objections to this identification. Gardner has neither shown us why we should equate Los with Innocence nor why we should equate Innocence with the Creator. Too many steps are left out of his argument.

Hazard Adams has said that man's imagination created the Tiger and that this imagination, in its turn, was created by Prometheus. It was Prometheus, he says, who brought knowledge to man; it is the Tiger who represents such knowledge. According to Adams, the subsequent images tell us that the Creator is a blacksmith, and therefore, like Gardner, he equates him with the Los of the Prophetic Books.[97] But Adams does not really agree with his fellow-critic, since Gardner sees Los as Innocence, not as Prometheus. Adams's reading is otherwise similar to that of Gardner, and may be faulted in the same terms: the links between the rationalisation and the poem will probably seem arbitrary to the reader. At least they appear to have been forged by the imagination of the critic rather than that of the poet.

Unlike Gardner and Adams, David Erdman is not only conscious of the Creator's softer qualities, but also of his wrath. He feels that the creative blacksmith who shaped such terror into living form must have employed not only daring but also dread power – 'but the dread, Blake hopes, will be sufficient unto the day'. Therefore, for Erdman, the Creator of the Tiger is necessarily a fierce God, but only until the battles are won; and then the foes will co-exist with the Lamb, the wrath of the Tiger having done its work.[98] Here Erdman is assuming a sequence that cannot be shown to exist; where is the development in the argument of the poem that would support this idea of ultimate reconciliation?

F. W. Bateson agrees with Erdman that the Creator of the Tiger is a god not only of Mercy but of Wrath; however, he does not see these states as succeeding each other, as Erdman does, but rather as being co-existent. He feels the poem is not a commitment to one view of God or another, Mercy *or* Wrath, but rather a demonstration of God's duality – Mercy *and* Wrath.[99]

Like Bateson, S. Foster Damon has split the Creator into duality, but in more familiar terms, since he speaks of God the Father and of Christ. He quotes Blake as saying that Christ was the only God and 'God out of Christ is a consuming fire'.[100] From this he deduces that God the Father created the Tiger as an instrument for the punishment of sins.[101]

Certainly Damon has a strong case – strong from within the poem. The Creator is said to be immortal; and one indisputable idea of the poem is that he has made a creature of infinite savagery. But that is as far as an identification will go; and such an identification as Damon's must necessarily rest on a preconceived idea of God the Father. The reader who conceives of him as a Judge rather than as a Tyrant will not find the identification so readily acceptable as Damon does. It may be argued that Blake made some such identification himself in the conversation quoted by Damon. But we require the poem, not Blake's comment, to make what for many must be a difficult judgement. And the remarkable characteristic of the poem is that it makes no judgement at all – whether of Mercy or Wrath – upon what was involved in this creation of the Tiger. It does no more than imply, through its chain of rhetorical questions, that a judgement needs to be made.

Margaret Rudd says that the poet is unsure himself as to who made the Tiger. Despite his firm stand on the Lamb of Christ, she says that Blake is bewitched by the burning energy of evil that is contained in the Tiger.[102] But there is no wavering between poles of good and evil in the poem. The questions all follow one pattern – asking, in their different ways, who the Creator was. There is no choice implied in the questions. The assumption is, perhaps, that the Creator of the Tiger will either be good or evil; but this does not mean that the poet is deciding himself. The decision has been taken already, and the questions are designed to find out what it is – and, at the same time, by their questioning, to present the difficulty involved in making a judgement. Miss Rudd raises the question of whether the abstract laws of Urizen will call this impulse of destruction, the Tiger, evil.[103] But the point is irrelevant once we realise that neither the Tiger nor his Creator are, in the poem, *called* evil. Basically, of course, this problem is much the same as that involved in *Hear the Voice of the Bard*. In neither of these poems can the Creator be easily typified; and Blake does not make the mistake of wanting to try.

Kathleen Raine, falling into this error, draws the conclusion that the Creator of the Tiger must be evil (because the Tiger is). She agrees with Damon that the Son of God made the Lamb; but she deduces this from the poem, *The Lamb*, itself. 'Blake is making a specific theological statement, that the Lamb and the child are made by God the Son who became incarnate as Jesus.'[104]

> *Little Lamb, I'll tell thee,*
> *Little Lamb, I'll tell thee:*
> *He is called by thy name,*
> *For he calls himself a Lamb.*[105]

Helped by the circumstance of the second stanza answering the first, Miss Raine is able to make her point in a brief paragraph. *The Tyger*, however, is a series of questions; none of which is answered. In the remaining four thousand words of her essay, Miss Raine quotes Mosheim, the Gnostics, Paracelsus, Robert Fludd, Hermes Trismegistus and Berkeley, among many others – all as a way of demonstrating what could, if at all, be inferred only from the poem: the identity of the Creator. In her opinion, it is Urizen.[106]

Miss Raine finds in Hermes' book, *The Divine Pymander*, a passage which certainly parallels in its repeated questions the form of *The Tyger*;[107] but this is not a very unusual form, particularly in hortatory literature. Even so, Hermes, after all his questions concerning the creation of man, is not himself clear as to who the Creator was – just as *The Tyger* itself leaves us in a state of 'sublime doubt'.[108] And all Miss Raine's quotations from sources other than the poem, from Blake and those who supposedly influenced Blake, cannot assure us of Blake's intention. Only the poem can do that; and then, only if its intention is inescapably realised. But, when Miss Raine refers to the poem, it is in highly symbolic terms. 'Never, to the best of my belief, is the word "forest" used by Blake in any context in which it does not refer to the natural "fallen" world.'[109] This statement could be taken in itself as being no more than an indication that the critic finds the background given by Blake to the Tiger reasonably appropriate. But Miss Raine goes on from this to an identification of the forest trees with the Tree of Life, and to an association of this with Urizen, and therefore, by analogy, with the Tiger itself.[110] Such a conclusion is far-fetched: the links in the chain of association do not seem to have been observed by anyone other than Miss Raine herself. What is disturbing in Miss Raine's procedure is that it is too laborious to do much to prove her point. A statement like 'Lamb and Tiger inhabit different worlds and are made by different creators',[111] however backed up, must, for its acceptance, rest on the poem. And the poem never commits itself as definitely as that. In answering the poem's questions, Miss Raine is seeking to resolve 'the state of sublime doubt' in which it leaves us.

But Miss Raine is by no means alone in this. Consider the answers that have already been put forward. Some critics say that the Tiger was made by Los. But which Los – the Spirit of Innocence, the Spirit of Prophecy, Prometheus? Others say it was made by God the Father – but which God the Father? a God of Mercy, a God of Wrath, or, as some say, both? And, in the last instance, are the states of Mercy and Wrath co-existent or successive? Was the poet himself uncertain of his aim? – hardly, the poem is manifestly not a failure. Yet these interpretations do not merely vary; they flatly contradict one another.

It is quite evident that the critics are not trying to understand the poem at all. If they were, they would not attempt to answer its questions. The questions are there because the poet does not know the answer. In a sense, that is what the poem is about. It may be that there is no answer; or that the answer is only to be implied by the questions which are asked. But whatever the answer is to the question, 'Who Made the Tiger?', it is, by the terms in which the poem is couched, going outside relevant enquiry. The kind of answer the critics seem to be looking for could be another poem, a mystical treatise, a philosophical dissertation. It cannot be a critique.

70

It is possible to sum up by saying that, with very few exceptions, all critiques of this poem begin with a demonstrably just reaction to it; and this could be shown by pointing to the general consensus of opinion about the Creator's courage and strength. Where the critics differ is when they come to rationalise the poem; to find reasons for what is enacted in the poem. Their attempt to answer Blake's rhetorical questions is a tribute to the force with which those questions are put. Blake gives us no chance to admire his 'beauty' or 'technique' as less urgent poets do. There is nothing luxuriant about the poetry of Blake; for him it is, as it never is for the mere litterateur, a means of communication. We must applaud Blake for having drawn his critics into reply rather than exegesis. However, one cannot help inferring that, in many instances, this eagerness to reply conceals disagreement which the critic is reluctant to admit, even to himself.

Poems vary according to the check they provide against misreading. Clearly there can be no iron curtain between a misreadable poem and one, like *The Tyger*, that is misread; nevertheless, some works are far more available for criticism than others. What, in fact, I am saying is that criticism of a misreadable poem is an illusion; even adverse criticism. We think we dislike what, in practice, we have failed to understand. My contention would be that, in many poems, there is nothing particularly there to be understood – or misunderstood, either, which is why so many defences of a misreadable poem run into private fantasy.

We think we dislike what, in practice, we have failed to understand – this dictum holds, too, for 'good' poems, those which offer some purchase to the critic even if they have been misread. For the fact that one can point to a misreading, can test it against the reactions of other critics and against the text itself, is surely a point in a poem's favour.

I am, therefore, not advocating anything so simple as a *necessary* equation between consensus and value. Before assenting to any such proposition, one would have to know who was agreeing about what. Criticism cannot be got rid of so readily: not agreement alone, or disagreement either, but the *quality* of agreement or disagreement must be our concern. There can be no doubt that consensus, when it occurs among reasonably literate readers, is impressive. But any critic may have his off-day; no critic can be presumed to react to the entire spectrum of literature; therefore he may chance to misread even a good work. And any work may stop something short of total attainment; explore, rather than discover; put forward, with whatever degree of precision, a view unacceptable to some reader or other; can, in fact, be misread. It cannot be too often emphasised, however, that a good poem can be read badly, but a bad poem cannot be read at all; this, after all, is what makes it a bad poem.

The Principle of the Roving Criterion

Even the greatest work can lend itself to misreading if there is some uncertainty in its execution. The misreading may, however, be considerably in excess of the uncertainty. How can we guard against mistakes of this kind?

Every critic has it in his power to decide on the approach he makes to a literary work. Supposing the work not to be utterly misreadable, some approaches are bound to be more relevant than others. It is the critic's duty to choose the most relevant of them all. The analogy I would draw is that of a pattern: one can turn it about in all directions but should stop at that which makes most sense. This process of circling about in quest of a critical approach I call the principle of the roving criterion.

It is useless to catechise a literary work for one quality if it plainly exhibits another. For example, at least two distinct forms of writing shelter under the blanket denomination of the novel. The highly organised prose of the novel-as-dramatic-poem will not yield much to the reader who is looking for the analytical detail of the novel-as-experiment-in-applied-psychology.

The fault in most critics is a certain inflexibility of approach. This is one reason why criticism lags so far behind creative work: the critic bases his approach on past experience and only reluctantly extends himself to accommodate unexpected demands on his sensibility. Such demands, however, are made by any genuinely great work; and the fact that they are seldom met is clearly seen in the neglect encountered in their own time by many who are now accredited classics.

The critic must be prepared for outrage. The affront may be legitimate on the part of the work; it is only legitimate on the part of the critic if he has tried each and every approach and found that none of them makes sense.

In his own time, the author cannot rely on critical flexibility: the criterion is all too often set hard, immovable; judging the right work in the wrong way. But, it is said, time puts all right, and, sooner or later, appreciation matches merit. Often, however, the appreciation is on the part of readers at large rather than critics; that is to say, response often outruns rationalisation. So that we can have the odd spectacle of a writer first entrenched in public acceptance, later in critical opinion, with neither the critic nor, certainly, the public able to give an adequate reason for their favour.

This has certainly been the case with Dickens, whom nobody at first loved but the people. The critics had their own criteria which they vainly attempted to impose upon this colossal artist. They could see everything that he was not doing; but they refused to turn the pattern about and discover what it is that he did.

For example, the young Henry James came out decisively against *Our Mutual Friend* when it first appeared, regarding it as an unsuccessful attempt on Dickens's part to carry on his earlier, comic, vein.[1] The view of Dickens as an instinctive eccentric was one characteristically found among Victorian highbrows: Taine,[2] Bagehot,[3] Lewes[4] and the George Eliot circle in general.

It is a view which, with less excuse, has its counterpart in serious critics of our own time. Santayana's slighting description of Dickens as the great entertainer[5] has been given a fresh currency in the strictures of Dr Leavis.[6] Another *Scrutiny* critic, R. C. Churchill, suggests that the characters in the book would be more convincing if they had not already occurred, far better done, in earlier works.[7]

This preoccupation with character is a major cause of critical deflection in the reading of Dickens. The tracing of parallels between his various personae may blind us to their effect in their given dramatic context. It may also prevent our comprehending the total effect of a particular novel.

Hence, perhaps, the remarkable range of valuation of *Our Mutual Friend*, even in modern times: all the way from K. J. Fielding, who finds it incoherent,[8] to Jack Lindsay, who regards it as one of the greatest prose works ever written.[9]

The difference between these critics is one of the criteria that they apply; some will be more relevant to the work than others.

Much, no doubt, depends on the expectations with which one approaches the book. Henry James particularly objects to the fine gentleman's pursuit of the boatman's daughter. He says that this gentleman, Wrayburn, is no more than a stock cigar-smoking type.[10] And if Dr Fielding is more conscious than James that Wrayburn is a new departure, for him it is only one which anticipates the dandies of Oscar Wilde.[11]

And yet, other critics have seen more in Wrayburn than this. Although, like James, George Orwell regarded *Our Mutual Friend* as an extension of Dickens's earlier manner, he concedes that the episode of Wrayburn and Lizzie is treated very realistically.[12] Wrayburn has too much decency to attempt seducing Lizzie, but not enough to jettison his family by marrying her.[13] G. K. Chesterton went so far as to say that, in Wrayburn's pursuit of Lizzie, Dickens had marvellously realised the empty obstinacy that drove the whims and pleasures of a leisured class.[14]

Even if one plays the game of comparing Wrayburn with earlier creations of Dickens, he will be seen to be more than an imitation. Edmund Wilson finds him more sympathetic than Harthouse in *Hard Times* or Gowan in *Little Dorrit*;[15] Humphry House, more interesting than Steerforth in *David Copperfield*.[16] Monroe Engel, in a recent study, has said that, with this character, Dickens added a new dimension to the consideration of class in English fiction: Wrayburn is too careless even to protect himself.[17] This state of mind has been ably analysed by another recent critic, J. Hillis Miller: the character feels that life is altogether ridiculous because every move in it has been decided beforehand.[18]

But the realistic presentation of ennui would hardly in itself be impressive if it was not part of a developing moral pattern. Edmund Wilson, among others, has shown how this is so. The conjunction of the upper with the lower class, is, in his view, a criticism of the middle-class society satirised elsewhere in the book – this has become dissociated from everything that is admirable in English life.[19] Edgar Johnson has suggested that Wrayburn's scepticism for received values made him an effective instrument for Dickens's criticism of society. And, in his final denial of society, Wrayburn has learned how to act positively: in deserving Lizzie's love, he has achieved purpose and self-respect.[20]

Both Engel[21] and Miller[22] emphasise the importance of the river in this regeneration. Wrayburn's disfigurement and immersion render it possible for him to cast off his old life and begin anew. This enactment may be seen to take place on several planes. For, as Jack Lindsay points out,[23] Dickens never loses hold of the social aspects of this marriage: it transcends the bonds of the society in which Wrayburn has been imprisoned.

This is only one example of the way in which the consideration of a Dickens 'character' will often prove to be far more than that. Here, for instance, it is a way into the symbolic drama of the book.

But there is always some reason for a divergence of opinion. James's strictures on Wrayburn as an original character and on the book's norm of conduct are not without foundation. Wrayburn's moral position may seem equivocal if only because Lizzie, the character with whom he is most closely associated, is (as James said) a conventional figure. Few critics have come to her defence. Wilson and Lindsay may have accurately diagnosed a social intention on the part of Dickens when he took his heroine from the lowest and most illiterate classes. But they do not seem to see that the moral would have more point if her behaviour and accent were less resolutely that of a middle-class heroine. 'Think of me as belonging to another station and quite cut off from you in honour . . . if you feel towards me, in one particular, as you might if I was a lady, give me the full claim of a lady upon your generous behaviour.'[24]

Lizzie's moral position is also rather equivocal. Chesterton found her too romantic to be pathetic,[25] and House charges her with being coy – enhancing her attractiveness as well as her virtue by running away.[26] Engel[27] and Miller[28] do well to stress that part Lizzie plays in the regeneration of Wrayburn, but both note how powerfully this is reinforced by the river as a motivating symbol.

It is true that the scheme of *Our Mutual Friend* does not depend for its success on the 'realism' of an individual character. In this sense, the book may be said to carry Lizzie. Nevertheless, she cannot be termed a satisfactory dramatic creation. And her social and moral indeterminacy may well, for some readers, put Wrayburn, with whom she is so closely associated, in an equivocal light. This does not justify James's opinion that Wrayburn is a character out of stock. But it may go far towards explaining it.

The extent to which a dramatic weakness in a work deflects a critic may depend upon the rigidity of his criteria. Nobody is asking for indulgence here; but it seems senseless to condemn a work because of a local error. Such condemnation takes place when the critic is not aware of a total pattern: the individual strands will then take on an unwarranted significance. Turn the pattern about and they will fall into their own, more subsidiary, place.

The unwillingness to opt for the most relevant of all possible approaches may make for misreading or ignoring the dramatic core of a work. Preconceptions similar to those which led James to identify the eccentric characters of *Our Mutual Friend* with earlier efforts in a purely comic vein led him also to the judgement that even so central a character as the dustman, Boffin, is lifeless, forced, mechanical – 'the letter of his old humour without the spirit . . . Humanity is nearer home than the Boffins.'[29]

Once more, we may deduce that 'character' is being considered in isolation. James gives something of his case away by recognising that a distinction, if only of value, must be made between Boffin and other 'comic' characters.[30] Orwell, however, draws no such distinction: for him, Boffin is just the same as other 'good rich men' such as the Cheerybles in *Nicholas Nickleby*.[31] This can, fortunately, be shown to be a misreading not only of the apparent intention of the book but of the effect that it is likely to have on readers who come to it without these preoccupations.

For, on inheriting his mounds of dust, Boffin deteriorates into a miser. Fielding has called this a fantastic pretence,[32] but, as Gissing pointed out,[33] in fact the dramatic presentation of Boffin's miserdom is most convincing.

> 'What!' said Mr Boffin, gathering himself together in his most suspicious attitude, and wrinkling his face into a very map of curves and corners. 'Don't I know what grabs are made at a man with money? If I didn't keep my eyes open, and my pockets buttoned, shouldn't I be in the workhouse before I knew where I was?'[34]

Miller has pointed out that this is no sudden change.[35] We find the Boffins early on in the book planning to leave their Bower and take a new mansion. 'Our old selves weren't people of fortune; our new selves are', says Mr Boffin in explanation of his changed way of life.[36] His predecessor as custodian of the Mounds was Harmon, also proprietor of 'Harmony' Gaol: 'A tremendous old rascal who . . . grew rich as a Dust Contractor, and lived in a hollow in a hilly country entirely composed of Dust.'[37] It seems that Boffin inherits something of Harmon's temperament along with his Mounds. Lindsay says that fortune perverts Boffin's whole character.[38] House relates, as one should, the degeneration in Boffin to the development of the action – 'everything is corrupted and distorted by money'.[39]

James and Orwell may have been misled by the benevolent aspect Boffin wears in the earlier part of the book. Yet there is more than a hint of criticism in the author's presentation of this. He is shown to be a very odd-looking fellow altogether. 'Morning, sir! Morning! Morning! Morning, morning, morning!'[40] Almost insistently odd, we may feel. He is revealed as being sentimental and tough at the same time in I, viii, snobbish in I, ix; and, in I, xv, the beginnings of real miserdom come.

'Well, it ain't that I'm in a mortal hurry,' said Mr Boffin, 'only when you *do* pay people for looking alive, it's as well to know that they are looking alive.'[41]

This is not the benevolence of the characters in the earlier Dickens. However, since Boffin eventually reverts to something like his initial aspect, and the action is, correspondingly, not worked out to its logical conclusion, James and Orwell may have some *reason* for their belief that Boffin is little more than a lesser Cheeryble; though this certainly does not *justify* their opinion.

A number of critics – Gissing,[42] Chesterton[43] and House[44] among them – believe that Dickens changed his plot in mid-novel. After nine-tenths of an action showing the corrupting influence of wealth – symbolised by the mounds of dust – the good people of the beginning of the novel end up rich as well.

There have been attempts to justify this change in the action. Miller, for instance, suggests that, in acting the role of a miser, Boffin was defining himself as the refusal to be his situation and appearance.[45] This seems rather far-fetched. Lindsay has a better point when he says that we fail to believe Boffin's miserdom is assumed.[46] There is, indeed, little play-acting in the savage attack on Rokesmith – 'I know this young lady, and we all three know that it's Money she makes a stand for – money, money, money – and that you and your affections and hearts are a Lie, sir!'[47]

The scene is at once consonant with the general pattern of the book and, in itself, a powerful projection of greed and suspicion. The fact that Boffin turns out to be a faithful custodian after all does not remove the impression it leaves. And it most certainly does not make the book an imitation *Nicholas Nickleby* or Boffin another Cheeryble. What we most clearly remember in *Our Mutual Friend* is not the universal panacea of individual kindliness but the corruption of Boffin and the relentless struggle for possession of the mounds of dust.

This symbol in action is a moral condemnation. It attracts to itself the anti-social attitudes criticised in the book. That is why it is not germane to say, as Fielding does,[48] that the symbol is used inconsistently. The only deduction he draws from the Mounds is 'that there is no objection to inheriting wealth without working for it, and that it is only wrong for a man like Harmon to build it up by providing an honest service to the community'.[49] Even as a political point this is debatable, since Harmon is represented as a capitalist and a hoarder. And, in any case, it is contradicted by Fielding's own account of the plot: he says that it is the 'golden-hearted Boffin' who has built up the Mounds.[50]

Yet it cannot be denied that the ending of the book permits such misreading. Dickens was not the thoroughgoing socialist that Lindsay, for example, would have us believe.[51] Orwell makes a good point about his liberal idealism: 'Dickens's criticism of society is almost exclusively moral.' He attacks, not the existence of private property, but some of the uses to which it is put.[52]

However, this very idealism saves the end of the book from being the failure it might have been. Miller has called it a fable: when one has recognised that gold is dust, one can go on to make gold of dust.[53] Bella's rejection of her old self and of Boffin's miserdom makes the Harmon gold, in Dickens's own words, 'turn bright again, after a long, long rust in the dark'.[54] This is not the stern resolution that might have been desired, but neither is it a gross inconsistency.

Neither is it true to say that the dust-heaps themselves are inconclusive as a symbol. Yet one can see how such a judgement could come about. The position of Dickens with regard to criticism has been very similar to that of Shakespeare before the work of Wilson Knight. Many of Dickens's earlier critics have abstracted the characters from the total pattern of the book. There is a poetic application of symbolism in Dickens's greatest novels which would do much to explain the currency he has had in spite of the very incomplete attempts to explicate his work. For explication is not the same as appreciation, and it may be that critics have not chosen the right tools with which to approach the problems raised by the reading of Dickens. After all, it is more than a coincidence that the critics who have a low opinion of *Our Mutual Friend* – James, Gissing, Chesterton, Orwell – do not seem to be aware of it offering anything more than the plot-and-character appeal with which the minor Victorian novel has so familiarised us. It was in these terms that G. H. Lewes attacked Dickens[55] and in these same terms that Gissing replied to him.[56] Naturally the reply was inadequate. George H. Ford, comparing the two, said 'The effort of late nineteenth century moral critics to set up criteria which would consistently differentiate the novel from poetry was a necessary effort but one which has now spent its force.'[57]

It is not impertinent to say that by such criteria many of these adverse critics were judging Dickens's work. And with them one may link Dr Fielding, who has attempted to hold their position against the more radical interpretation of Dickens initiated by Edmund Wilson and carried on largely by American critics. We can point to no such landmark of Dickens criticism as Wilson Knight's discussion of *Measure for Measure* which began a new phase in the reading of Shakespeare. Nevertheless, a good deal can be shown to be going on in *Our Mutual Friend* which was not accounted for in the aesthetic of Henry James, or even of George Orwell. And it can be done through a consideration of the striking consensus of views among critics who regard the novel as a dramatic poem.

One of the points Engel and Miller make is about the predominance of dust in *Our Mutual Friend* – it blows through the book, in Dickens's own phrase, like some mysterious paper currency.[58] Humphry House has shown how the dust collected from the streets came to have great value.[59] The dust-heaps may be filth, but, as Engel says,[60] they are also money. And, from this recognition, it is a short step to the working out of a metaphor in which dust and money are equated. Money, the ascription of nominal value to what has no value in itself, is, as Miller says,[61] the central symbol in *Our Mutual Friend* of the successful humanisation of the world. Johnson has shown how society in relation to Boffin is compared with the buzzing and creeping creatures attracted by a dung-hill,[62] and Lindsay, too, links the image with political values: the dust-heap is the one great prize for which everyone is fighting.[63]

The Mounds are also the debris of history. In Miller's sense of the ruins of an ancient city,[64] certainly, but also in the sense of the past. John Rokesmith, in his sleepless nights, buries his old identity deeper and deeper beneath imaginary piles of dust.[65]

The objects are dead, but still have power to dominate the lives that are lived in their midst. So Miller says;[66] and, indeed, the struggle for the dust shows that they do.

The action of the Mounds is to decay and corrupt. Engel has shown how Harmon is the ruined victim of his own money and how it begins to corrupt Boffin and his ward, Bella.[67] In other words, the symbolism is integral to the action of the book, and can no more be separated from it than can the characters. Thus, the weight of matter in the Mounds is related to the world of the Podsnaps and the Veneerings. Miller reminds us of the scene where the heavy articles of Podsnap's table are weighed and assessed, like so much scrap.[68]

In the discussion of the dust symbolism, there is, as we have seen, a remarkable consensus of opinion among the critics, although there have been some notable absences from the discussion. Clearly, something of the same experience has been shared by a number of different readers. Those who do not share it can be shown to have been looking elsewhere for the merits of the book: to its plot, its characters, its realism. In doing so, they have ignored what it does offer: poetry, drama, the authoritative working out of a central symbolism.

It may be that a critical explication of the book can best be managed through a consideration of its central images. As Miller has pointed out,[69] the drama of the novel derives from the central opposition between the death that is represented by the Harmon Mounds and death by water.

The river cannot, any more than the Mounds, be equated with a simple property. If it could, there would be little point in using it as a symbol at all. It includes far more than any one summary of its effect can convey. One needs, to suggest its complexity, to aggregate the accounts critics have given. The river regenerates the good and drags down those who are evil (Wilson).[70] Immersion can be drowning, but also spiritual rebirth (Wilson,[71] Johnson[72]) and the re-affirmation of life (Miller).[73] The river is an agent of retribution in the deaths of Radfoot, Hexam, Riderhood and Headstone, and of regeneration for Harmon, Wrayburn and Lizzie (Engel).[74] It cuts through social distinctions (Engel)[75] and is the great stream of life (Lindsay)[76] as well as the waters of suffering (Johnson).[77] It is the otherness of nature, a more intense reality (Miller,[78] Engel[79]).

It would be easy to demonstrate the variation in these accounts taken individually. But they do not contradict one another. Each fills in a necessary aspect of the whole; each can be related to the text and found relevant to it. Drowned corpses, struggling bodies, float through the book: the symbolism *is* the action, not a convenient summary of it.

> Thus, like the tides on which it had been borne to the knowledge of men, the Harmon Murder – as it came to be popularly called – went up and down, and ebbed and flowed, now in the town, now in the country, now among palaces, now among hovels, now among lords and ladies and gentlefolk, now among labourers and hammerers and ballast-heavers, until at last, after a long interval of slack water it got out to sea and drifted away.[80]

Enough has been said to indicate that *Our Mutual Friend* will yield little to a reader who sees it only as the sum of its disparate characters. It is true that the novel has not the formal perfection of, say, *Emma* or *Victory*. Its weaknesses may give rise to misunderstandings: the eccentricities of Wegg, the wanderings of Betty Higden, the indeterminate dialect of Lizzie, the rather too liberal conclusion. Around such weaknesses all of the basic divergences of opinion have occurred.[81] But only in the case of the critics who expected a plot-and-character novel have they given rise to a low valuation of the book as a whole.

And, since the publication of Edmund Wilson's pioneer essay, there has been an increasing recognition of the novel's strength. The exceptions have been K. J. Fielding, who is an apologist for Dickens, and the *Scrutiny* critics, who are not. That the latter should give so severe an account of Dickens is a matter for some surprise. For to them we owe the critical concept of the Novel as Dramatic Poem.[82] And more than any other work in the language, except perhaps *Wuthering Heights*, *Moby-Dick* and *The Rainbow*, does *Our Mutual Friend* live up to and justify this concept.

It is clear, then, that we shall get nowhere by considering one work in terms which, properly speaking, belong to another. The critic has a duty to make the work seem as good as it can: this is not a matter of reading in his own attitudes but finding out those that are there in the work. The process is one, as I have said, of choosing a criterion: of letting one's mind explore the work from different angles in the hope of finding a viable approach – of finding, one hopes, *the* most viable approach. If *Our Mutual Friend* makes no sense looked at as a realistic novel and a good deal of sense looked at as a dramatic poem, then the latter must be our approach. It will not blind us to the faults of a given work; it may, however, put them in perspective.

Most misreadings of valuable works are failures of criteria. The failure is most evident in the writer's own time: the great writer, it seems, has always to create his own audience. The critics could help here more than they have done; indeed, their record over the past 170 years has been poor. One would not wish them to invent a new genre to fit each work: there have been plenty of experiments that failed. But the value of a work apparent to later generations must have been, at least potentially, discernible in its own time. And on all too many occasions the criteria applied by those who should have been most qualified to judge have proved too inflexible. I shall devote the latter part of this chapter to a number of occasions on which the critics have had their eyes resolutely fixed on some aspect that was not offered to them and were as resolutely blind to that which was staring them in the face.

There is a tendency now to suggest that Wordsworth's roots were in the eighteenth century. This may be so; but such a belief would not explain the genuine horror with which *Lyrical Ballads* was received by the critics. It was in the course of a review of Crabbe – very acceptable to his Augustan ear – that Jeffrey turned aside to deal with Wordsworth and Coleridge. 'The gentlemen of the new school, on the other hand scarcely ever condescend to take their subjects from any description of any persons at all known to the common inhabitants of the world; but invent for themselves certain whimsical and unheard-of beings, to whom they impute some fantastical combination of feelings, and then labour to excite our sympathy for them, either by placing them in incredible situations, or by some strained and exaggerated moralization of a vague and tragical description.'[83] Of course, *Lyrical Ballads*, as the Advertisement to the first edition suggests,[84] was conceived as something of a pioneering enterprise, and there are poems as exaggerated as the show-pieces of any other new school of poetry; *Simon Lee* and the Matthew poems among them. But the piece upon which Jeffrey particularly turns his outraged attention has far more tenacious claims on our sympathy.

> *There was a Boy, ye knew him well, ye Cliffs*
> *And Islands of Winander! many a time,*
> *At evening, when the stars had just begun*
> *To move along the edges of the hills,*
> *Rising or setting, would he stand alone,*
> *Beneath the trees, or by the glimmering lake,*
> *And there, with fingers interwoven, both hands*
> *Press'd closely palm to palm and to his mouth*
> *Uplifted, he, as through an instrument,*
> *Blew mimic hootings to the silent owls*
> *That they might answer him. And they would shout*
> *Across the wat'ry vale, and shout again*
> *Responsive to his call, with quivering peals,*
> *And long halloos, and screams . . .*[85]

What impresses us about this passage is its rightness, its inevitability. It is therefore hard to remember that, in 1808, poetry such as this could upset a critic so badly. Jeffrey's expectations are outraged; and, in commenting upon the poem, he seems to be looking everywhere but in the right direction. In particular, he is obsessed by a passage I have not quoted, the death of the child. 'The sports of childhood, and the untimely death of promising youth, is also a common topic for poetry. Mr Wordsworth has made some blank verse about it; but instead of the delightful and picturesque sketches with which so many authors of moderate talent have presented us on this inviting subject, all that he is pleased to communicate of *his* rustic child, is, that he used to amuse himself with shouting to the owls, and hearing them answer. To make amends for this brevity, the process of his mimicry is most accurately described . . . This is all we hear of him; and for the sake of this one accomplishment, we are told, that the author has frequently stood mute and gazed on his grave for half an hour together!'[86]

After the conventional accounts of eighteenth-century youth, sketched plainly enough in Jeffrey's expectations, this piece evidently seemed *outré*, even arbitrary. But possibly there is an explanation for its failure to make him look in the right direction. Jeffrey is, for instance, badly worried by the way in which the description of the bird-calls leads on to the boy's death. But, though this connection is made in the version that he was reading, and that is usually published, the first draft of the poem shows that the death is extraneous.[87] In its original version, the poem is autobiographical – a straight recollection of Wordsworth's own childhood. The account of the child's death is therefore an addendum. A case could be made out for it: the boy is, after all, received into the nature which he was imitating.

But, as Jeffrey's adverse reaction shows, the end of the poem has been a source of critical deflection, and certainly has no deep-rooted organic connection with the rest of it. It is just possible that, confronted with the original draft, Jeffrey would have had less to say about the piece's tendency towards dramatic inflation; though there is no evidence that he could have responded to its originality. This is clear from his comments on Crabbe as well – a succession of events can have, for him, no more than its literal significance. To do Jeffrey justice, he concedes that the mimicry is 'accurately described'; but he does not see that there is more to it than that. Wordsworth is depicting a boy who is willing himself into the woodland, into the life of the trees; no accident that he is not merely disturbing the owls but actively – and successfully – imitating them, recreating something of their nature in himself. And, in the passage which Jeffrey ignores –

> *a gentle shock of mild surprize*
> *Has carried far into his heart the voice*
> *Of mountain torrents, or the visible scene*
> *Would enter unawares into his mind . . .*[88]

– the boy becomes part of the lake and the woodlands with which he is communing.

Even as it stands, the poem shows the astonishing originality of Wordsworth when he began to write, as well as indicating the direction in which his greatness lies. No wonder that, in his own lifetime, the public preferred Helen Maria Williams, Samuel Rogers, Thomas Campbell – to say nothing of Byron, Scott and Moore. Only Coleridge held out against the general consensus; recognising, as great poets do their peers, the master-spirit of the age.

It is in areas such as these that misreadings have occurred: existing criteria prove unworkable when confronted with a new departure or mixed genre. The romantics outraged the ideas of literary decorum instinct in those whose taste was formed in the eighteenth century. The upshot was that narrative of the highest order, that of the *Prelude*, was lost to writers of the time. A vital link was thereby missing, and the weight of narrative henceforward rested on prose.

Those who wanted to write dramatic poetry did so in the form of the novel; but, because of this, their efforts were often misunderstood. Just as their predecessors in verse outraged literary decorum, so the nineteenth-century novelists outraged the moral decorum of the Victorians. It is rather as though the inability to understand the artistic pattern of a book threw into strong relief the morality of individual characters. In real life your villain may be disgusting; in literature he may be a strand in an overall pattern. The mistake on the part of reviewers is to imagine that they are experiencing a piece of raw life: the structure, the very meaning of the incidents, is hidden from them. Take *Wuthering Heights*, for instance. 'Whether it is right or advisable to create beings like Heathcliff,' wrote one contemporary of its author, 'I do not know: I scarcely think it is.'[89] The doubt comes not from a reviewer, but from a person who might have been thought more sympathetic – Charlotte Brontë in an introduction to her sister's book. One could hardly expect the critics themselves to be more discerning; nor were they. The *Atlas*[90] and the *Examiner*[91] both found Heathcliff unrealistically ferocious, while the *Quarterly Review*[92] said that he was too odiously and abominably pagan to be palatable even to the most vitiated taste of English readers. Denunciations of the brutality and wickedness of the main characters continued far into the century, culminating in William W. Kinsley's confident pronouncement that Heathcliff was incurably mad.[93]

It was beyond these critics to put Heathcliff into the context of the book; to see him as an embodiment of sexual force brought up sharply against the constricting bonds of the social organism. Yet once the book is seen as conflict rather than assertion, some elements of its dramatic pattern fall into place.

The mistake that the critics made was to view the whole novel realistically, to take the characters on the terms that would be adopted in real life. *Tait's* reviewer objects to the book on the grounds that no effective moral was taught;[94] by which he appears to mean that no single character is put forward as an ideal. And, in spite of Charlotte Brontë's desperate attempts to rescue from the general condemnation Edgar Linton and Ellen Dean,[95] this is substantially true. But what of it? The sum of the novel is greater than its individual characters, and it is a misreading to look at any one of these – as the reviewers did – in isolation.

Yet this was a characteristic vice among Victorian reviewers. The mode of approach that would have done very well for Trollope failed disastrously when applied to works that were more highly organised. It seems more than the critic can do to envisage that events in a fiction can have a meaning beyond the mere fact of their occurrence; or that the pattern can emerge from the sum of events taken as a whole, rather than from the stance of a single persona. A strikingly similar misapplication of criteria took place with regard to *Moby-Dick*. Psycho-analysed, Captain Ahab, like Heathcliff, is mad. *The Spectator* took the presentation to be realistic: 'the author attempts delineating the wild imaginings of monomania';[96] the *Albion* condemned the stuff and non-sense spouted forth by the crazy Captain,[97] while the *New Monthly Magazine* declared that the hero raved by the hour in a lingo at once transcendental and transatlantic.[98] In so far as reviewers could see more in *Moby-Dick* than the realistic presentation of character, they felt that the result was a failed sea-story. 'The whole scheme mars, as we have said, the nautical continuity of the story . . .' (*Spectator*);[99] the *Atlas* thought that Melville's rhapsodies and extravagance impaired his descriptive powers;[100] while the *Examiner* took what was to be the most popular line of all and condemned *Moby-Dick* because it failed to measure up to the standards of Melville's earlier simple tales of adventure.[101] And for the next half-century books by Melville were advertised as being by the author of *Typee* and *Omoo*;[102] about *Moby-Dick* a strategic silence was maintained.

Clearly the critics were disappointed because Melville was not re-peating himself. More specifically, they looked for a straightforward story of the sea and found instead 'transcendental ravings'. It is in-teresting to see that even the most adverse reviewers managed to put in a good word for the description of seafaring and whaling matters: graphic 'sketches of scenes at sea',[103] 'descriptive powers',[104] 'interest in cetology',[105] etc. And even the most favourable reviewers felt that the whaling scenes were a necessary ballast to the book's speculative flights of imagination.[106]

Yet suppose we take two modern interpretations of *Moby-Dick*, those of Winters and of Lawrence. At first sight they appear to differ radically. Winters sees the Whale as the spirit of evil;[107] Lawrence as animal blood-nature.[108] Both, however, condemn Ahab: Winters, for taking upon himself the work of God in a blasphemous act of vengeance,[109] and Lawrence for being a civilised mental consciousness hunting down his blood-being.[110] Neither of them takes exception to Ahab's monomania as such; rather, they place it in the developing moral pattern of the book. Whether one approves or disapproves of the Whale, it is certainly a barbaric force; whether one approves of civilised consciousness or not, clearly Ahab's hunt is a perversion of the will. In terms such as these the book makes sense; the early critics only found it nonsensical because they read it as a literal sea-story in the line of *Typee*.

The deflection is in the direction of character considered in its most naturalistic aspect, and away from drama. It is singular how frequently critics at the first publication of a work seek to bind it to some intentionalist fallacy: the work as bodying forth its author's life, for example. Just as Heathcliff and Ahab were treated as mouth-pieces for their respective creators, so the 'I' of *Leaves of Grass* was identified completely with Walt Whitman. Thus *Putnam's Monthly*: 'That he was one of the roughs was . . . tolerably plain; but that he was a kosmos is a piece of news we were hardly prepared for.'[111] Emerson had commended the book,[112] and according to the *Criterion*[113] this has procured the admittance of a scurvy fellow into good society, while the *Boston Intelligencer* felt that the author should be kicked from all decent society as below the level of the brute. ('He must be some escaped lunatic raving in pitiable delirium.'[114])

The main burden of these diatribes is the obscenity of the contents of the book. 'The depth of his indecencies will be the grave of his fame', wrote the *Critic*,[115] and 'a mass of sentimental filth', agreed the *Criterion*,[116] while the *New York Times* said that the author roamed like a drunken satyr with inflamed blood through every field of lascivious thought.[117]

It must be remembered that the text under review differs substantially from later revisions, though in my judgement it is far superior to them in concreteness and directness. Thus the central persona is at once a particularised being, an American working-man, but also the voice of America, indeed, of humanity at large. Therefore the celebration of the body – to which most reviewers objected – is not that of the poet, exactly; rather it is that of the working-man persona, and, through him, every living person. This puts the apparent egoism into a context. The *Critic* said that Whitman should be whipped for the description of sexual intercourse in the section eventually entitled 'I sing the Body Electric'.[118] To us it seems tender, reverent in the extreme –

> *Hair, bosom, lips, bend of legs, negligent falling hands –*
> *all diffused . . . mine too diffused,*
> *Ebb stung by the flow, and flow stung by the ebb . . .*
> *loveflesh swelling and deliciously aching,*
> *Limitless limpid jets of love hot and enormous . . .*
> *quivering jelly of love . . . white-blow and delirious juice,*
> *Bridegroom-night of love working surely and softly into*
> *the prostrate dawn . . .*[119]

The *Criterion* felt that this was too vile to quote.[120] It is ironic that Whitman, who said that those who degraded the body were cursed, should have come in for such attack. The connection with Lawrence is obvious: the more recent author picked up the phrase 'bath of birth' from this poem and applied it with splendid effect to the Ursula of *Women in Love*.[121]

But, like Lawrence, Whitman suffered because his form was misunderstood. The critics detected no pattern in his poetry, and so reacted to events out of dramatic context. It is noticeable that they nearly all complain of the metric: 'his poems are innocent of rhythm' (*Critic*),[122] 'the poem is written in wild, irregular, unrhymed, almost unmetrical "length" ' (*Leader*),[123] 'a sort of excited prose' (*Putnam's Monthly*).[124]

The ear that was accustomed to Longfellow, Holmes and J. R. Lowell might well be outraged by the flexibility and subtlety of rhythm manifest in the passage quoted. The range of mimetic reference is great: the ecstasy of 'limitless limpid jets of love', rammed home in the alliteration, dies down to the slowing, and more lightly touched, rhythms of the last line cited –

> *Bridegroom-night of love working surely and softly into*
> *the prostrate dawn*[125]

Compared with this, Longfellow *et al.* seem very flat; but flatness was what the reviewers had trained on, and for them Whitman's variety of impulse was mere anarchy.

In practice, though, one can never separate rhythm from theme and theme from mode of presentation. The 'Walt Whitman' of *Leaves of Grass* is not a lyrical 'I' but a dramatised symbol. In failing to identify the speaker of the sentiments to which they object, the critics fail to put those sentiments into perspective.

Examples could be multiplied. The nineteenth-century critics were prone to read dramatic monologue as personal utterance, and this certainly delayed the recognition of Browning.[126] The Georgian ear, brought up on Masefield, sought in vain for continuity of narrative in Eliot, and was deaf to the impact of his dramatic juxtapositions of detail.[127] An incipient revival in poetic drama as recently as the 1950s was scotched because the critics looked for cocktail-party dalliance in the plays of John Whiting and found something more akin to Jacobean tragedy.[128] Even when the critics grounded their expectations on the previous work of a great writer, they were left far behind by his capacity for self-renewal: how many reviewers found the speech rhythms of Lowell's *Life Studies* a falling away from the rhetoric of *Lord Weary's Castle*?[129]

Over and over again, it seems, new work is being produced which cannot be gauged by the criteria at the disposal of the critics. Without doubt the greatest extent of deflection takes place in that area where poetry and drama meet. It is no accident that narrative poets, whether in prose or verse, have attracted the worst press: Dickens, Wordsworth, Emily Brontë, Melville and Whitman have at least that in common. The humbler spirits survive – writers of realistic novels, of lyric poems; as though the critics are attuned to the low in pressure and the undemanding. But what is the use of recognising Thackeray and Trollope, even Tennyson and George Eliot, if Dickens and Melville are allowed to go unappreciated? Out of George Eliot came the sociological analysis that has done so much to humanise our statistical studies. But out of Dickens might have come a new poetic drama.

Needless to say, Dickens was not a poetic dramatist, in spite of all his gifts in that direction; hence, perhaps, the difficulty in settling on an approach to his work. Mixture in the genre begets, not complexity of criteria, but confusion, and it takes time, not criticism, to sort out the muddle. But we have no room for congratulation if our methods work only retrospectively; if in our own period we are able to recognise only the second-rate, the readily-explicable, the already-expected. It seems as though literature is bound, not upon a wheel of fire, but within a vicious circle. If the work offers resistance to the critic, then the critic may be depended upon to offer resistance to the work.

Resistance

Resistance is a quality in the work: it may take the shape of complexity, concentration, development upon an existing tradition, mixture of genre. Resistance is also a quality on the part of the reader: it may emerge as puzzlement, boredom, bewilderment or active hostility.

If a modern equivalent of *King Lear* were to be produced tomorrow, we could rely upon the critics to damn it conclusively. The twentieth century's record in such matters is a bad one. Those writers who conform to an existing preconception are lauded to the skies. Those who have produced original works of art are at best neglected, at worst banned and condemned.

The ready recognition of new writers in itself means very little: what is more to the point is whether they were worth recognising in the first place. Here it is useless to talk of minor writers. It is heartening that Iris Murdoch is well spoken of, that Angus Wilson has a secure place in the contemporary pantheon. But if neither had written it would not matter very much. They have their individual notes, and fortunately the reviewers attuned to them happened to be listening. What, however, happens when something completely unexpected occurs – such as the advent of a great writer?

This happens infrequently enough to defy documentation in general. One could hazard a guess and say that, since the eighteenth century, no writer of real genius has been recognised in terms relevant to his success. Wordsworth, Emily Brontë, Melville and Whitman were enigmas to their contemporaries. And even if these writers were caviare to the general, their real qualities ought not to have been missed by critics. The nearest equivalent before this period was Pope, who certainly had an audience wider than a personal circle of admirers; and who seems to have been understood and appreciated for respectable reasons, even if they are not precisely the ones we should choose now. It may seem a little perverse of the neo-Augustans to celebrate *The Essay on Man* and *The Iliad* as being Pope's greatest masterpieces,[1] but at least these are impressive works. And, not so long afterwards, Dr Johnson was to play Leavis to Pope's Lawrence and extensively revalue his œuvre in terms that still seem unanswerable.[2] The difference between these two critics, however, is that the earlier of them was refining an already existing consensus of opinion, while the later critic was practically creating it. And there was certainly nothing in the history of Pope's critical reception to parallel the writing-off of *The Excursion* and consequent suppression of *The Prelude*. But even these latter appalling blunders are tame indeed when compared with the early reception of *The Rainbow*; arguably the greatest novel to appear for half a century before its time, and without parallel since.

Like *Moby-Dick*, *The Rainbow* was greeted with rage and bafflement; like this great novel, and like *The Excursion, Wuthering Heights, Leaves of Grass* and, to a lesser extent, *Our Mutual Friend*. The neglect of experimentalists such as Browning and T. S. Eliot was inexcusable, but, at the same time, understandable; not, I think, the critical attitude towards such works as those I have named. And there has been no conclusive overhaul of our aesthetic presumptions since the time of *The Rainbow*; basically, for instance, we are still talking about large-scale works of literature as if they were something else entirely.

The Rainbow presented a critical problem that, in a way, was more extraordinary than that which was to be exposed by *The Waste Land*. At least one could carp at certain technicalities in the latter work: its freedom of versification, its cinematic progression. But there were no such easy handles with which to seize *The Rainbow*. Its experimentalism was not of the surface. Obviously it was shocking: morally so to the crowd, aesthetically to the intellectuals and literati. It is a sad comment on Lawrence's period, and ours, that so great a work could command no sort of audience at all.

And this was in marked contradistinction to Lawrence's earlier works. Lawrence was so much an established figure by the time of *The Rainbow* that his work was accepted for publication without question; without even (if we are to believe evidence given by the publisher at the 'trial') close reading. In public estimation Lawrence was a pleasantly 'poetic' and fairly innocuous regional writer in the tradition of George Eliot and Thomas Hardy: it seems to have been accepted that he would never be anything more.

It was, in fact, the regionalism in Lawrence's early novels that most struck reviewers. Because of this regionalism – an accepted mode of the time – they were inclined to excuse what they (often correctly)

91

regarded as technical deficiencies; in, for example, the management of the plot.

In particular, there is a striking consensus of opinion about *The White Peacock*. Those who found the terrain of the novel unusual were most inclined to excuse its lacunae in narration. For instance, the *Observer*[3] found the Lawrence countryside primitive and subtle, if also strange and incongruous; and the *Saturday Review*[4] decided that the technique of the book was rough because the locality was.

Other critics found the locale less peculiar and therefore were less inclined to accept what, if true, would have been something of a pathetic fallacy. Frederic Tabor Cooper in the *Bookman*[5] and Henry Savage in the *Academy*[6] were both quite typical when they discounted the plot of *The White Peacock* in favour of its numerous descriptive passages. Hueffer, too, in the *English Review*, celebrated Lawrence's skill in description rather than his craft as a narrator.[7]

But for some reviewers, this power of description failed to save the book as a whole. For instance, the *Athenaeum* reviewer felt that it was wrong to sacrifice traditional structure even for pictures of cinematic vividness;[8] and both the *Yorkshire Post*[9] and the *Times Literary Supplement*[10] considered Lawrence's neglect of plot was hardly compensated for by picturesque passages about nature.

However, it must be said that *The White Peacock* received only one review that was altogether unfavourable, and that was from Robert Lynd, who pursued Lawrence with such malevolence throughout his literary career. Under the title, 'Clever Brutality', Lynd in the *Daily News*[11] argued that this 'tale of country life' was as incoherent as the life it portrayed; and that the book, so far from being redeemed by its descriptions, in fact forced them on us.

This, as I have indicated, was an isolated view of *The White Peacock*. If we look at more considered comments in the works of criticism that came out in the author's lifetime, we shall find them very much an expansion upon the attitudes taken up by the original reviewers. Stuart Sherman,[12] like F. R. Leavis in his early pamphlet,[13] commented upon Lawrence's marvellous awareness of life in nature; Edward Shanks was astonished to find how warmly the descriptions glowed with life,[14] while Bonamy Dobrée suggested that they became poetic objects in themselves.[15]

The latter two critics particularly instanced the keeper's funeral with its evocation of the thrush – perhaps the best single thing in the book.[16] But it is clear that the critics were responding to the passage in question as a prose poem. The thrush is not there to enhance its context; rather the richness of texture takes on an independence and plasticity that prose can't afford unless it is to turn into something quite different. Even the sharpness with which the thrush is visualised mars itself by a certain repetition and insistence – 'blue, blue, bluest of eggs', for example.[17] It is as though Lawrence's perceptions at this time were stronger than any mould he could channel them into. It is clear that the book was appreciated in parts rather than as a whole. The scything episode,[18] which was favourably touched upon by the *Times Literary Supplement*[19] and the *Saturday Review*,[20] moved J. W. Cunliffe[21] into comment and quotation. 'The earth is like a woman married and fading . . . the regular breathing hush of the scythe . . .'[22] So it was possible for the beauty of Lawrence's descriptions to overcome a natural prejudice on the part of some critics in favour of plot and structure.[23]

The general consensus among favourable and unfavourable critics alike was that the author needed to improve his technique. But there was no agreement as to the direction in which improvement should take place. The standpoint of the critics is clear enough if one considers the authors whom they invoke by way of comparison: de Maupassant, Zola, Chekhov, Wells, Hardy. They were able to point out lapses in this book as they were not able to, with any degree of accuracy, in *The Rainbow*, because these were lapses from a kind of fiction they understood, the kind they expected when they opened a novel. The approach was familiar; only the location was new. A certain meekness, a coming to terms with existing convention, is discernible in Lawrence's first novel, and probably helps to explain the relatively favourable press it received. Perhaps the critics had a point they were not equipped to deal with when they faulted the structure of the novel while at the same time conceding the 'poetry'.[24] Poetry, of a sort, was what Lawrence was after; though it emerges eventually as a less lyrical-descriptive entity than could have been foreseen from the early work.

One could sum up by saying that the reviews were the less inclined to judge the book harshly because of a defect – its conventionality of genre – and also because of an asset – its lyrical-descriptive passages. After this book, Lawrence was reasonably well established in the public eye as a minor regional novelist of the school of Hardy. And so *The Trespasser* came as something of a disappointment.

Some of the reviewers were rather disturbed by a sort of lyricism whereby the characters became extensions of the author's personality. Helena, for example, is a musician who goes off for an illicit holiday with her music-master, a married man; but her situation is seen very much from the inside. The one review which took Helena to be a self-sufficient character was that which appeared in the *New York Times*;[25] it was also the most favourable. The *Evening Standard* was more typical in responding to the emotions of the characters rather than to them as separate entities,[26] while the *Morning Post*[27] and the *Sheffield Daily Telegraph*[28] alike responded mainly to the purple passages which unreservedly described physical rapture at high pressure; conceding, however, that they read the novel mainly as isolated fragments.[29]

The only two adverse reviews appeared in the *Nottingham Guardian*[30] and, inevitably, in the *Daily News*.[31] Both deplored the amount of time Lawrence spent in recording 'passionate ecstasies' and 'sensibilities of the flesh'. It is true that these have little to do with the main theme of the novel; the intensity and passion is not that of Helena and Siegmund but of the young Lawrence, as is clearly shown by the letters of this period. The reader need not be troubled by thoughts of inconsistency in the characters, but he is certainly entitled to question the direction in which their ecstasies are taking him, at least in relation to the rest of the book.

If we look at the more considered reports that came out in the form of articles and books in the years after the novel was published, we shall find a similar uneasiness as to the author's powers of dramatising his feelings.[32] F. R. Leavis felt that the novel made for oppressive reading – smothered in a riot of adolescent experience.[33] In the end the characters prove to be at once particular and evanescent: W. L. George held that the psychological perceptions were so minutely observed that Lawrence's persons were too much persons and not enough recognisable characters.[34]

Each of us is liable to regard himself as Everyman, but it is our limitations that make us what we are. Yet in *The Trespasser* we are proffered Siegmund as though all his feelings were necessarily our own. So that one gets the sense of particularity without any real grasp of it. John Arrow localised this in the diffuseness of the prose – evidence of ideas undergoing formation;[35] and Murry said that the book was written out of a turmoil of unresolved experience.[36] The chronicling of emotional fluctuations can have, at best, a psychological interest, unless these fluctuations are dramatised; and dramatised, I would suggest, towards some social end. *The Trespasser* fails because its psychological minutiae have no relation to a central group of attitudes or coherent body of emotion. The detail, instead of tending to the definition of personality, extends it into limitless possibilities of fluctuation. The moral attitudes deployed in *The Trespasser* are not sufficiently integral to the plot to justify the emphasis which the author puts on them; and the plot itself is not remarkable enough to redeem the novel as a whole from the charge of incoherence.

The fact is that these early and relatively simple novels were received rather more kindly than their defects deserved. But this was not so much owing to generosity on the part of the critics as to their recognition of these novels as belonging to a clearly defined genre. The odd thing is that few of the critics found in the novels the merits of the genre: they speak of Lawrence's inconsequential plots, disjointed action and commonplace characters. They would not have spoken so harshly about Hardy; it seems strange that they judge his obvious successor in this way. However, when pushed to declare Lawrence's merits, it was not the action of the book that interested them. More usually, they fell back on the prose – and by this they meant the prose poems, connected to the action by tenuous threads, which break up the plot of *The Trespasser* and have a life of their own.[37] Some of these are very fine; and Siegmund's suicide, in particular, shows a realism which Lawrence was to leave behind him. He was, after all, not that sort of novelist.

But Lawrence took some time to find his *métier*. He wrote a number of short stories which are excellent studies in realism and which have been very influential:[38] stories such as *The White Stocking, A Sick Collier* and *Daughters of the Vicar*. This is not the essential Lawrence, perhaps, though the last-named looks forward to his best work, but it is an engaging part of his output. And he also produced a novel remarkable for its surface realism, though even at the time of its publication some reviewers were uneasy as to how well it fitted into that category. In appearance it resembled a novel of the traditional kind, and it exhibited similar virtues. *Sons and Lovers* was the best reviewed of all Lawrence's novels – contrary to received opinion, it had a wider and more enthusiastic press than *The White Peacock*, even though the latter got into Everyman's Library. For the most part, as in discussion of the earlier novels, we shall take critical opinion in descending order of enthusiasm.

The publishers themselves in one of their advertisements recommended the book as being powerful, human, true, and this is certainly the note struck in the most favourable reviews. Catherine Carswell in the *Glasgow Herald* discussed the book as a realistic novel, a far more successful venture along the lines of the earlier books: 'this tale of a collier and his wife and four children is written from the heart and goes to the heart. It ranks as a story with Mr Bennett's *Old Wives' Tale* and with Mr Phillpotts's epic of maternal passion, *Demeter's Daughter*.'[39] The latter, at least, is not so convenient a reference for value as once it might have been. But it is clear that we have not travelled far from the idea of Lawrence as a regional novelist. What is new is that we can now see more clearly that this characterisation won't fit – *Sons and Lovers* is rather more than a tale of a collier and his wife, etc. Mrs Carswell's view, however, was the current one for years, and probably still has its exponents. 'Some of the truly squalid realism will offend the delicate people who like their squalor pretty,' wrote the *Evening Standard*, and added that those who did not believe in the authenticity of the book were probably those who would misunderstand its characters 'in actuality'.[40] The *New York Times* described the book as 'a human document', 'an admirable account of a mismated couple',[41] while the *Independent*, another American paper, took it as a forceful experiment in applied eugenics.[42] The *Sunday Times* admired the 'strength and realism' of a narrative which brought to light the infinite miseries of human existence;[43] Hugh Walpole, in the *Blue Review*, praised its hard realism and passional colour;[44] which, as the *Saturday Review* said,[45] made the narrative pass from fiction into glowing reality. These were the most favourable reviews; their plaudits are re-echoed in the work of critics writing through the next few years.

Douglas Goldring, for instance, said that the novel showed us the very heart of 'the real England';[46] and Edward Garnett called it at once 'a piece of social history' and 'an epic of family life'.[47] A. R. Marble wrote, 'The earlier scenes among Nottingham villagers, with native dialect and elemental interests, are drawn with sympathy.'[48] Here the graphic metaphor gives us an indication of the critic's standpoint. The book was for Mrs Marble a picture of some kind – indeed, since she was an American, an essay in the picturesque. J. W. Cunliffe, also writing a general book on 'modern' literature, took much the same view. 'The dialogue, now chiefly dialect, reproduces with astonishing verve and colour the forthright colloquialism of the collier folk.'[49] 'Drawn', 'reproduces' – it was not surprising that even the qualifying remarks of these commentators would criticise the book for failing in probability (rather, than, say, shape or moral standpoint). But critics who were sold on the concept of realism were hardly going to provide an exacting criterion: Brewster and Burrell, eleven years after the novel came out, wrote that *Sons and Lovers* was a book essentially from the thick of life – 'life literally picked up and put in the pages, life just as it is lived'.[50]

What is being registered by all these critics is the novel's plethora of detail, lack of selectivity. We are bludgeoned into a belief in its reality by the sheer weight of circumstance. But where the critics may be felt to go astray is when they consider the novel to be life in the raw, 'as it is lived'. There *is* a principle in the book, though not one that is readily ascertainable in the book's own terms. A clue was given by Manly and Rickert in their once popular primer of contemporary English literature – Lawrence, they suggested, was at his best when closest to experience.[51] The problem raised here is '*Whose* experience?' And the answer was given by Paul Rosenfeld in an early and very sympathetic critique. 'The comparatively early *Sons and Lovers* remains one of the most completely successful of Lawrence's novel-forms. *The autobiographic material treated therein relieved the author of the necessity of inventing his characters*'[52] (my italics). It seems to me that the most favourable contemporary reviews and near-contemporary critiques were quite logical in regarding the novel as a realistic (or regional) work, but were, perhaps, not quick enough to see that the events and characters are rather arbitrary, and the whole rather hard to grasp – just like, in fact, autobiography. And, taken as autobiography, *Sons and Lovers* is pretty nearly a masterpiece; with all its fictionalising and prejudice, it no more distorts the truth than many similar works and has the merits of its author's early prose – immediacy, sensuous awareness, exuberant energy.

This certainly commended it to those among the critics who might be termed Lawrence's early disciples. Stephen Potter treated the book as a record of the author's own past dissatisfactions and failures;[53] H. J. Seligmann as a pilgrimage of Lawrence's soul through the world of childhood and young manhood;[54] Murry[55] and Leavis[56] as the intimate life-history of the youth of a genius. But there were critics – reviewers in particular – who could see round the autobiographic projection.

Hubert Bland, for instance, in the *New Statesman*, suggested that the novelist could have been more selective – no need for a novelist to include all the details, however clearly he was able to visualise them.[57] This is an aesthetic rather than a simply moral point: the same note was struck by Hueffer in the *English Review* when he said that the book was truthful but a little meticulous in unnecessary detail.[58] Bland also pointed out a certain arbitrariness in the action;[59] a point which was developed by Darrell Figgis in the *Nineteenth Century* – Lawrence knew, but did not understand; he stood perplexed in his own, indisputably accurate, scene.[60]

Perhaps the most discerning review of all appeared in the *Athenaeum*.

Here the reviewer was keenly aware of the distorting capabilities of an autobiographical narrative. 'The pronoun "I" is not, indeed, employed for him, but the author has lived so completely within his creation that the narrative reads like an autobiography – and, as discerning readers know, autobiographies are less likely than biographies to produce a lifelike portrait.'[61] The fact that the central character would not have understood his predicament in real life hardly absolves the novelist from the necessity of making his readers understand it. And so, as Harold Massingham pointed out in the *Daily Chronicle*,[62] the book ignored the obvious attraction of the novel-form, plot-architecture, continuity, balance and the like – in favour of ruthless fidelity in presenting an objective record of a collier's life in the Midlands.

A good many reviewers[63] felt that this lack of selectivity was unacceptable on the grounds of taste and morality. Phrases like 'lack of reticence', 'brutal realism', 'microscopic detail' were repeated throughout their reviews and serve to give an idea of their tone; conceding the book's power, deprecating its explicitness.

But, in practice, it would be difficult to separate the 'aesthetic' from the 'moral' deficiencies of the book. While allowing Lawrence's 'sincerity', the *Nation* felt that this was the 'observation' of a 'helpless realist' who mistook the Everything for the All.[64] The *Manchester Guardian* complained that the book had no particular shape or recognisable plot;[65] the *Westminster Gazette* that this meant more emphasis was placed on feeling than on action, and this gave the book's moral standpoint its evasive quality.[66] And it must be agreed that, if everything is presented 'as it was', certain necessary emphases are lost, and a good deal of matter extraneous to any pattern is included. Henry Savage said in the *Academy* that Lawrence 'strips everything naked; there is no delicacy nor reticence about his work, but he probes and searches and analyses in ruthless surgical fashion'.[67] Savage was probably objecting to over-explicitness, but this has a deeper relevance to the book as a work of art than he seemed to realise.

Sons and Lovers is an attempt to come to grips with a section of its author's experience; and often we are aware of the struggle almost on the page. It is impossible to feel that a good deal of the material offered, even when finely presented in itself, is necessary for the reader's understanding of the book, though it may have been necessary to the author's understanding of his experience. It is questionable, though, how far this was achieved; the discussion of character-relationships shows, as we shall see, that a good many contemporary reviewers found the action of *Sons and Lovers* elusive, for all its splendidly realised detail. Like most of the reviewers, Savage found the merits of the book in its particularities, the life of Morel and Paul himself, together with their humble circumstances – 'the author records these things with such clearness that we believe in them and feel the characters of the book as real persons'.[68] 'Real' rather than, shall we say, morally significant or artistically relevant.

A good deal depends on what one expects from a novel; and one reason why a more recent reader is liable to be critical of this book, for all its undoubted excellences, is that Lawrence himself was later to do much to transform the solid Victorian conception of the novel as plot and character. But at the time of publication of this comparatively early book, and for some years after it, *Sons and Lovers* was praised for its reliance on conventional means. Edward Shanks said that it was good and normal and written in the ordinary tradition of the novel; though he seemed to realise what was left out of this criterion when he qualified this by suggesting that one usually remembered Lawrence's characters out of context.[69] Bonamy Dobrée, too, said that *Sons and Lovers* was traditional;[70] but it is obvious that the book is both less and more than a conventional novel. It has, indeed, the superficial form, but a greater degree of inconsequence – which nevertheless goes along with a greater degree of immediacy. John Macy, at least in part, approved of Lawrence's abandonment of the sequences of external events which artificially patterned novels of the past;[71] but it may be felt that Lawrence did not replace them with anything sufficiently decisive. Certainly W. L. George[72] and Joseph Collins[73] criticised the autobiographical element for putting forward highly individual circumstances as though they were normal; Lawrence's vision was true but not general.

The most adverse review – which came, predictably enough, from Robert Lynd in the *Daily News* – found the book 'vivid' without being 'real';[74] a view which had its counterpart in Harvey Wickham, who wrote the most severe of the considered critiques which appeared in Lawrence's own lifetime, saying that the facts of normal life were too much for Lawrence to stomach.[75]

However harsh these last two comments are, they do show a disability in the general shape of the book. Of course, it could be argued that the autobiographical novel has possibilities, whether Lawrence made use of them or not; but, without some external determining factor, the novel may well seem amorphous – a species of hold-all for the emotions that the author happened to be undergoing at the time. And, without suggesting that this is all that *Sons and Lovers* amounts to, one must register a certain disquiet at the universality of Paul's characterisation: his distinguishing traits seem to occur arbitrarily, without the concurrence or (it would seem) even the knowledge of his creator.

Certainly the reviewers were impressed by the vividness of individual scenes, particularly in the first part of the book, but they seem very cagey when it comes to evaluating the action of the book as a whole. It is as though the autobiographical element had confused the issues, or the amorphous central character had blurred the moral core of the book. The divergence can be roughly phrased, 'Is Paul's domination by his mother an evil thing?' – and the answers vary surprisingly.

Hitherto the pattern of variation has been taken in descending order of the extent to which the critics enjoyed the book as a whole. There is, however, no relation between the interpretation of the plot and the value put upon the book as a literary work. For instance, Murry[76] and Collins[77] took an extremely unfavourable view of Mrs Morel's part in the action, even though Murry thought highly of the book and Collins disliked it. This should be enough to demonstrate that, for all its surface realism and undeniable authenticity of emotion, the book is arbitrary in its organisation, and even obscure. One could go further and say that it is a long step from Mrs Morel's 'absolute devotion', as recognised by J. W. Cunliffe,[78] to what Murry found – a tie that was strangling her son.[79] Too long a step, perhaps, for us to credit the coherence of the stimulus that provoked such differing reactions.

The most favourable clutch of reviewers found the mother, in the words of the *Daily Telegraph*,[80] 'strong and admirable', and tended to agree that Mrs Morel was a refined woman unhappily married to a clod.[81] But other reviewers held that her very refinement was in part responsible for her husband's degeneration; she could, after all, have been a more understanding wife.[82]

There were even critics who took a wholly adverse view of Mrs Morel, largely on Paul's account and on psychological grounds. In fact Joseph Collins, who *was* a psychologist, interpreted the book as a conflict between mother-love and sexual desire which prevented the young man from fulfilling himself.[83] He was unable to give himself in love either to Miriam or Clara, said Edward Shanks, because he was unbreakably bound to his mother;[84] and both Murry[85] and Seligmann[86] saw the book as Paul's struggle to break away from the mother who had unconciously aroused in him the emotion he should have felt for the girl of his choice.

If only the issues were really as clear-cut as that! But the differences of view show us that they are not; and the only correlation I can make between the critical views is that, generally speaking, those who have a low opinion of Paul Morel – Savage, Wickham, Collins – have a low opinion of the book as a whole. But this is not to defend Paul, merely to suggest that in his conception much of the weakness of the book lies. And it is essentially a weakness of dramatisation. Individual scenes ring true, in the way a good realistic novel does, and with more than a realistic novel's poignancy and immediacy; but they do not, as the critics seem to have felt, add up.

The story, as it stands, is a very bad one for Mrs Morel; yet her part is constantly taken against her husband and also against Miriam. Moreover, Miriam is condemned for many of the traits which are applauded in Mrs Morel; and, though Miriam is represented as being frigid, no blame seems to attach to Paul for being unable to wake her up.

If Lawrence had gone no further than *Sons and Lovers*, we should remember him as an essentially lyrical novelist: with the virtues and faults of a very imperfect genre. If he had gone no further than *The White Peacock*, he would be remembered as a minor regionalist; without the weight of Hardy, but also without the sentimentality of Winifred Holtby; somewhere in talent between Richard Jefferies and Adrian Bell.

As it is, Lawrence's reputation now chiefly depends on two great novels, *The Rainbow* and *Women in Love*, and on the short stories that succeeded them. One might have expected that the critics of the time would have recognised how great a step forward was the first of these: a chronicle of the generations, using the pattern of heredity as a constant with which to illumine the decay of a society; a poem containing at once its own vision of the world as it was and a trenchant dramatisation of the world as it was becoming, even in Lawrence's time. The economy of its means, despite its length, ought to have been remarked: the absence of merely decorative descriptions, or scenes included for their sensuous charm or because they happened to happen. The certainty of effect should have been applauded – scene after scene, alive in itself, and advancing the total drama. Above all, the sheer precision of the work; nothing elusive or incoherent, none of the moral evasions of the earlier novels. All this ought to have been seen at the time, and praised.

But this is to overestimate the possibilities of contemporary reaction. There can be no sadder case of critical imperception than the contemporary reputation of *The Rainbow*. Perhaps, as Douglas Goldring suggested, Lawrence's earlier critics had been rather lavish in their praise for the coming young regionalist. But when he applied the 'acid test' of publishing a manifestly original work, 'not one of Mr Lawrence's fervent boosters ventured into print to defend him'.[87]

For *The Rainbow* offers resistance. In this case, it is the resistance of a dramatic poem in the form of a novel – the latter form then, as now, maintained by floods of 'light reading'. If it took the greatest English critic a quarter of a century of writing and nearly half a century of reading to produce the first adequate study of Lawrence, and if the reviews of other critics are vague and stumbling in expression even when most perceptive, what are we to make of the ordinary reader's task of appreciation?

We have, as it happens, two eloquent testimonies of this nature in the form of statements by Sir John Dickinson, the magistrate of the police court which ordered the book's withdrawal, and Mr Herbert Muskett, the prosecuting solicitor. They were not ordinary readers in the sense of being semi-literate, but, obviously, they were totally unprepared for a work of this nature, and didn't like what they could understand of it. Sir Algernon Methuen himself was, or claimed to be, in something of the same position. He added, however, that three people apart from himself had read a 'disgraceful' chapter without being able to find anything suggestive in it.[88] 'They cannot have read it very intelligently,' replied Dickinson. 'It is headed, *Shame*.'[89]

Quite clearly, Dickinson's way of reading the book was different from that of the publishers' readers, or, indeed, such early critics of Lawrence as Muir, Davis and Leavis. Dickinson seemed, from the words he used, to have been influenced by the Press reviews, especially that of Shorter, who was shocked by the Lesbian episode in the book. He showed a certain naïvety by suggesting that these reviews alone should have been sufficient to cause the book to be withdrawn by the publishers.[90] In fact, there is every evidence that the ordinary 'culti-vated' reader would grasp so little of the book that the more explicit scenes would stand out as being flagrantly obscene: there would be nothing seen in the action to justify them. This would perhaps explain why Dickinson described the book as 'utter filth' and said that he had never read anything more disgusting.[91]

It would also explain the line of prosecution adopted by Herbert Muskett. He called *The Rainbow* 'this bawdy volume' and added: 'There may not be an obscene word in it, but it is, in fact, a mass of obscenity of thought, idea and action throughout, wrapped up in language which he supposed would be regarded in some quarters as an artistic and intellectual effort.[92] Well, even if Muskett was being sarcastic, he was certainly right about the 'certain quarters'. His argument seems especially relevant to a consideration of the book's originality. The only question that is not answered in the various reports of the trial is whether anyone suggested that the difficult nature of the book would render it unlikely to be widely read as pornography. In the meantime, these reports serve to show something of the bewilderment of the common reader. Where one cannot help criticising such readers is in their resenting the effect of bewilderment rather than trying to ascertain its cause. The 'quarters' to which Muskett referred quite evidently saw more in the book than he did; but, no doubt, he would regard them as recipients of high-class pornography.

Through the plethora of adverse comment from every conceivable angle, there can be detected a deep undercurrent of resentment at the originality of the book. James Douglas, whose review helped to bring about the police prosecution, and whose tone is nearest to that of Dickinson and Muskett, insisted repeatedly that the artist was not his own law-giver and must conform to the laws that govern society. He attacked what he called Lawrence's 'dull monotonous tune of spiritless sensuality . . . things that ought to be left unthought, let alone unsaid. It is doubtful whether decadence could further go.'[93] What, one would like to ask, had Douglas in mind? Such commentary as this makes one wonder whether the authorities and the journalists read into *The Rainbow* their own prurience.

James Douglas, however, was writing in a popular evening paper. But Clement Shorter, who seems to have influenced the court most of all, was supposed to be writing a literary letter for cultivated people. Unlike the court and Douglas, Shorter explicitly disclaimed that he was charging Lawrence with a deliberate attempt to produce nastiness for commercial purposes. But, like Douglas, he found the book decadent: 'There is no form of viciousness, of suggestiveness, that is not reflected in these pages.' And he instanced the chapter 'Shame' as being about Lesbianism and so unfit for family reading.[94] This was the chapter alluded to by Methuen himself as being disgraceful and it was explicitly censured by the magistrate.

But it should have been obvious that whatever was enacted in this chapter was unequivocally condemned by Lawrence himself. Its truth is impressive – the story of a 'pash' of a younger woman for an older one which went further than a good many, but which, in its feeling, is probably characteristic of most. In theory, there would be no need for overt Lesbian encounter; as, in fact, it is generally agreed that this is by no means universal in such cases. But, in the practice of fiction, it is difficult to make any feeling clear unless it is acted out. However, the offending passages – until recently cut in all texts but the Penguin – really are devoid of physiological detail. And, in any case, Lawrence takes some pains to judge and evaluate the experience. Miss Inger speaks of sex rather sourly – tells stories of friends dead in childbirth, of prostitutes. There is a dichotomy between what Ursula sees of her mistress and what we see. On the one hand, we have the deliberately near-comic 'Ah, Miss Inger, how straight and fine was her back, how strong her loins, how calm and free her limbs',[95] and, on the other hand, 'a rather beautiful woman of twenty-eight, a fearless-seeming, clean type of modern girl whose very independence betrays her sorrow'.[96] It is quite clear that Ursula's consciousness is not to be confused with the narrative it intersperses. Throughout, there is held an equipoise between the Greek goddess Ursula sees and the masculine, rather horsey, wench that Miss Inger appears, in fact, to be. This view is finally grown into by Ursula – from seeing Miss Inger's body as 'defined, firm and magnificent',[97] she begins to criticise her 'earthy' hips and thick arms and ankles.[98] One could go on to contrast Ursula's admiration for the intellectual attainments of Miss Inger with the new-woman claptrap that lady habitually talks;[99] or comment on the implication of Miss Inger's attractiveness to Ursula's uncle, who sees in her a kinship with 'his own dark corruption'.[100] But the case is clear enough. Lawrence, if anything, seems rather Victorian in his views: there is not thrust at us the psychiatric or even the physical evidence that would support his moral certainty that this perversion deserves its name. It is quite evident that the chapter is about a stage in adolescent development, parallel with Ursula's abortive affair with the narcissistic Skrebensky, and, like much else of the book, a comment on society – in this case, the urge which beset so many women of Lawrence's day to turn themselves, in attitude or career, into imitation men.

This was not seen at the time. The adolescence assessed and found wanting by Lawrence was taken at its face value: Lynd, for example, identified the attitude of the author with that of his characters – whom he found 'as lacking in the inhibitions of ordinary civilised life as savages . . . It is the sort of book which many an artistic schoolboy desires to write, but, on growing to maturity, he refrains.'[101] It would have been truer to say that adolescent encounters in sex are something one develops out of, and that the two examples of this in *The Rainbow* are placed by the manner in which they are narrated and in the total framework of the book – as the experience of a lost girl, without the sexual certainties of her ancestors.

Some critics found this a psychologically unhealthy point of view – G. W. de Tunzelmann felt that the Freudian hypothesis had so grown upon Lawrence that he had allowed himself to treat its most repulsive consequences with 'loving appreciation' and so to be led into salaciousness – the stimulus of legitimate sexual impulse into excess.[102] Like the lawyers, de Tunzelmann must be convicted not only of obtuseness but of resentment at originality; in this case, the new theories of psychology that here found their first complete dramatisation in fiction.

As might have been expected, this was the stand taken up by Joseph Collins, in *The Doctor Looks at Literature*, with a good deal more knowledge of abnormality than de Tunzelmann seems to have possessed. He, too, attacks the 'theory' of the book as being morbid and untenable, and implies that Lawrence was so obsessed with sex as to appear to be sexually sub-normal.[103] It would have been better if he had explained where Lawrence's 'theories' were mistaken. If sex is not the determining factor of adult life, what is? For all his scientifically judicial tone, Dr Collins was very near the hysterical denunciations of James Douglas and the philistine obtuseness of the court – both equally unbacked by argument.

This, however, is a common device in literary, as in other, debate. There seems to be difficulty in registering disagreement in a sensible manner; instead, one denigrates the author in such a way as to cast doubt upon his sanity or moral stability. This is especially suspicious in a book of such stature as *The Rainbow*. One is compelled to believe that to meet this work on its own terms would be to be altered by it, and that such an alteration is what these pretexts are shuffled together to resist. Even a fairly friendly account, by W. L. George, followed Lynd in saying that the book is about people so excessive sexually as to seem repulsive; and almost, like Collins, warned Lawrence against sinking into a literary neurasthenia.[104]

Other critics disliked the representations as such, but registered only their 'unpleasantness' – not trying to justify themselves by attacking the author. J. W. Cunliffe, for example, felt that Lawrence used the 'physical aspect of passion' for artistic purposes, although, in his opinion, it was 'developed to excess'.[105] Certainly the book should not have been banned; a view which was shared by the *Nation*, even though that magazine found the book 'entirely repellent'.[106]

This was the view taken up by the serious literati of the time. A letter by John Galsworthy about *The Rainbow* tells how revolted he was by its 'perfervid futuristic style' and its 'reiterations'. It was, he went on, 'a paean of the undisciplined shallow fervour that passes with the young these days for art'.[107] In a sense, of course, it *was* 'undisciplined'. *The Rainbow* represents a revolution in fiction that makes it difficult to take the 'realism' of Galsworthy's own work very seriously: one remembers Lawrence's own essay on the subject. What is more important is that Lawrence's novel is also profoundly traditional, in a tradition that was disregarded by the successful novelists of the time: *The Rainbow* is a development of the form of the dramatic poem as seen in *Wuthering Heights*, itself the successor in form to the tragedies of Shakespeare. One would not expect a writer of Galsworthy's type to understand anything of this. And even Arnold Bennett, a far more intelligent man, wrote in Lawrence's obituary that he had lacked the power to discipline and control his faculties.[108]

Their rejection of Lawrence was understandable enough: what is revealing was the work they put forward. Sir Ernest Hodder-Williams, for instance, denied that Lawrence was a potent force in modern literature, and claimed that his effect was only on the younger and more superficial critics. The 'solid British reading public' was scarcely aware of him; in Sir Ernest's opinion, and that of the more conservative critics, the dominating figures in the English literary field were Frank Swinnerton, whose novel *Nocturne* was sponsored by H. G. Wells, and J. C. Squire, the literary critic of the *New Statesman*.[109] It is not surprising, therefore, to find the latter speaking of *The Rainbow* as a 'dull and monotonous book which broods gloomily over the physical reactions to sex'.[110] This squares with J. B. Priestley's complaint, in the *London Mercury*, that Lawrence's failures were far away from 'real life'.[111] What appears to be resented is the dethronement of a false convention.

It would be too much to expect Lawrence's fellow-writers to understand the form of his novel. Yet another representative litterateur, Edward Shanks, thought that Lawrence was making it all up as he went along. Admittedly a writer can be *too* exploratory in the use of his medium, but it would take more analysis than Shanks was prepared to undertake to show that anything in *The Rainbow* occurs as other than part of a coherent pattern. Shanks's point seems all the more egregious when it is seen that he is referring as an event 'dwelt on with no regard to the symmetry or substantiation of the story'[112] to the affair of Ursula and Skrebensky. This, one would have thought, might at once have satisfied the realistically minded critic as a study in adolescent psychology and have fulfilled the terms of the novel as a quest, symbolised by the Rainbow itself, for the union that existed between the

106

men and women of Tom Brangwen's forebears and that which he eventually achieved with his own wife, Lydia.

By and large, the literary historians and technologists are more grudging, but they are, on the whole, more discerning than the litterateurs and higher journalists. The differentiation can most easily be made in terms of preference. Neither liked *The Rainbow*, but whereas the litterateurs felt that Lawrence was a kind of highbrow Baedeker and voted for the travel-books, the academics preferred *Sons and Lovers* – mainly, it seemed, because it was a model of form.

For example, Elizabeth Drew[113] and Edward Lacon-Watson[114] could not understand Lawrence's later work at all and rested their testimony in his favour on *Sons and Lovers*. John Macy made the mistake of assessing the characters in terms of local application, and found Ursula's experience impoverished in comparison with that of her grandparents.[115] But the failure is not in Lawrence's dramatisation but in the society that he dramatises. The first story of the Brangwen family is more positive than the third because it embraces more of the central experience of life; the third story is an attack on a mechanised society. This, however, was found somewhat distressing by the critics: Mrs A. R. Marble thought *The Rainbow* not only sensual in portrayal but cynical in tone.[116]

Much the same tone was adopted by the more serious reviewers. To Gerald Gould in the *New Statesman* the book seemed dull, monotonous and pointless: 'The world which he presents to us in *The Rainbow* seems to consist almost entirely of fleshly people in paroxysms of emotion – largely sensual – which signify nothing.'[117] And the *Westminster Gazette* found the account of sexual awakening in three different generations repetitious: 'it is an analytical semi-psychologic investigation of sensuality, and in spite of its undeniable force and of the occasional glimpses of beauty which the author of *Sons and Lovers* is still able to show us, it is almost impossible to read it because of the sheer weight of its numbing monotony'.[118] Both the *Globe*[119] and the *World*[120] felt that it was a remarkable psychological study that, however, should not be allowed in the hands of youth of either sex. While the *Athenaeum*,[121] recognising the increasing discord between the principal actors and their setting, nevertheless felt that the book was too free in its treatment of sexual matters and exhibited tendencies that were decidedly unhealthy. Catherine Carswell, in the *Glasgow Herald*, realised that the purpose of this discord was to show that 'the modern heart was in a disastrous muddle where love between the sexes was concerned'; but felt that Lawrence had gone into 'revolting detail' and found no panacea in his 'gloating description' of the disease that afflicted the modern world.[122] What Mrs Carswell saw as a 'mannered idiom', 'a vicious rhythm' representing a falling-off from the days of *Sons and Lovers*,[123] the *Manchester Guardian* found to be obsessionalism and 'crazy iteration'.[124] The reviewer felt that Lawrence's treatment of sexual passion was narrowed and exaggerated; all the more so because it ran not in one individual but through three generations.[125] *Current Opinion* contented itself with referring to Lawrence's 'freedom in his treatment of sexual matters'.[126]

Indeed, it can safely be said that *The Rainbow* received only one favourable review, and that was in the *Evening Standard*, where it could hardly have had much effect. The critic said, courageously, 'the book is as indecent as life itself, and as poignant as death'. He did not agree with the idea of the book, even though he seemed to have understood it: 'Its people are tormented souls – tormented, perhaps, chiefly because they persist in striving to reach the spirit through the body, that one forlornest quest.' But he insisted that, in all the 'fleshy detail', there was no touch of prurience, and suggested that the book would offend only the 'gross of heart' who would not see 'the depths of the forest for the startling nakedness of the blazed trees'.[127] This is a remarkably apt characterization of the way in which the book was received by other reviewers and by the court. They objected to the incidentals because they were not aware of the perspective in which these incidentals were held.

With this exception *The Rainbow* received no appreciative comment in public until several years after its publication. The *Philadelphia Public Ledger*, indeed, had the courage to prefer it to *Sons and Lovers*; but what the critic was reviewing was a republication of *The Rainbow*, in 1924. The comment is worth quoting: 'Many of us will continue to find *The Rainbow* his most certain masterpiece, a thing no one else could have done, intricate in colour and rhythm like a profound dream. Most persons who shudder austerely at the 'sensual' scenes of *The Rainbow* will be found to confess (if you question them with a wise firmness) to never having read the book.'[128]

This is a great change from the accusations of sensuality and repetitiousness with which the book was belaboured when it first came out. In between, some well-meaning propaganda work had been done, mainly by young Americans, on Lawrence's behalf. One could hardly call these propagandists critics; rather they were disciples, concerned to expound what they would have termed Lawrence's 'philosophy'. Gilbert Cannan, an early defender, wrote in 1920: 'In

108

the pursuit of the logic of his genius . . . he was led to deal, like the poet and mystic that he is, with the subject of sex, and the result was *The Rainbow*, in which sex is symbolised and raised clear out of the region of actuality.'[129] Clearly Cannan had not absorbed the force of that originality – few books are more concretely 'actual' than *The Rainbow* – but he recognised that it existed. And in his comments on the reason why some of the most 'cultivated' readers found it obscene – because of the corruption that was in themselves – he did something to indicate the effect the original writer has on us; the quality of resistance, in fact.

This form of registering, while failing quite to understand, Lawrence's achievement may be seen in many of the early advocates of *The Rainbow*. After a survey of the earlier books, Louis Untermeyer said: 'finally in *The Rainbow*, possibly the most poetic and poignant novel of this decade, the dominant strain is given its fullest sweep'. The characters plunge 'with febrile energy and perplexed hunger toward some mystical consummation'.[130] Here, as in Cannan, there was a recognition that *The Rainbow* was more than a realistic tale. Lawrence himself, of course, was well aware of what he was doing; his famous comments in letters to Pinker[131] and Garnett[132] showed that. Less well known is his explanation of his way of working given in an interview with the American novelist H. J. Forman, who asked him why he didn't write more books like *Sons and Lovers*. Lawrence replied: 'That's what nearly everybody asks me . . . But I don't want to write more books like that. I write every book three times. By that I don't mean copying it and revising as I go along, but literally. After I finish the first draft I put it aside and write another. Then I put the second aside and write a third. The first draft is generally somewhat like *Sons and Lovers* . . .'[133]

In other words, Lawrence himself – as ever his own best critic – is saying that he had left the realistic novel, existing only at a narrative level, far behind him.

But, even now, there is surprisingly little criticism which takes into account the symbolism and dramatic effect of *The Rainbow* and subsequent novels. In Lawrence's own lifetime there was scarcely any which showed the faintest awareness of it. The earliest critic even to attempt to come to grips with his perceptions was Edwin Muir; who was far from liking all that he found in Lawrence, but who unarguably found much more than anyone else, at least until the publication, just after Lawrence's death, of Leavis's pamphlet *D. H. Lawrence*. Of Lawrence's descriptive faculty, Muir says not that it was 'beautiful' but that 'His landscapes are vivid, not because they are visually clear, but because they are intensely apprehended by all the senses together, as if there was between Mr Lawrence and nature an unspoken masonic understanding. They are peculiarly radiant and full, yet dreamlike, as if they were reflected not in the mind but in the blood.'[134]

Unfortunately, as this passage shows, Muir's prose wasn't quite equal to rendering all he appears to have felt, although he did cover himself by saying that 'with Mr Lawrence . . . we pass through a very vivid but rather vague experience . . . This out-and-in flowing communicates to everything a heightened life; the substance of experience is changed as if by alchemy. A communication has been established, a number of potencies have been released, and these alter everything.'[135] But Muir's example of this in action is far more clinching than his commentary. 'The horses which follow Ursula Brangwen over the wet field in *The Rainbow* give us the same feeling. *They are not visual entities merely, nor are they psychological ideas in Ursula's mind. They are instincts which have suddenly become articulate,* and which communicate with Ursula through the unconscious language of identification and repulsion – the two great forces which in their many forms Mr Lawrence has described again and again in his novels and poems.'[136] (my italics). Muir could have made his point even more formidably if he had said what the horses symbolise: the natural, breathing animal instinct that Ursula's society, for all its education, has left far behind it. Nevertheless, Muir's last sentence is especially pregnant. 'For this unconscious communication, all his characters strive; it is their fulfilment and the intellect has hardly any part in it.'[137] In other words, Muir is saying that Lawrence is *not*, like other novelists, concerned with the externals of living, but with the inner life which so rarely finds its way into words, and, when it does, is distorted out of all recognition to fall in with literary ideas of decorum.

Such a view may well seem less revolutionary now that *Wuthering Heights, Moby-Dick* and *Our Mutual Friend* are beginning to be read as dramatic poems; but it has yet to be demonstrated analytically from Lawrence's novels themselves. No wonder, then, that even the established senior novelists of Lawrence's time – successful realists themselves – would have little truck with *The Rainbow*.

Muir's point was taken up, a few years after he made it, by one of the earliest voices to speak for Lawrence from the Commonwealth. H. J. Davis, writing in the *Canadian Forum* in 1930, suggested that Lawrence was concerned with 'unconscious activity, dumb, dark, and terribly mysterious'.[138] Paul Rosenfeld, an American, had already written sympathetically of Lawrence's symbolic content at a time when it wasn't commonly realised that he had any. Rosenfeld's encomia were enthusiastic enough. 'The Rainbow, Lawrence's great successful venture in abstraction . . .' and '. . . Among the less strictly autobiographical novels, The Rainbow holds the foremost place.'[139] But it was early yet for detailed commentary by way of demonstration.

Similarly, Bonamy Dobrée pointed out that Lawrence was trying to give significance to physical experience, and that the emotional re-flexes accompanying it are his real problem. He has earned our grati-tude by insisting that Lawrence was primarily a dramatic poet, and by pointing the way in which the novel developed under his hands. 'His early work, such as Sons and Lovers, is frankly traditional, though tinged with genius . . . but a gradual change is perceptible through The Lost Girl, Aaron's Rod and his other books, to his last volumes. His characters are more and more becoming embodiments of ideas; the idea comes first, and has to be clothed in flesh and blood; but it cannot be too much insisted that his ideas are not purely intellectual ones.'[140] And Dobrée made a passing gesture in the direction of Lawrence's original-ity, saying that he was in the grand tradition of poetic novelists, such as Dickens and Emily Brontë, who see life as a whole rather than analyse it in order to comment upon individuals, and shared in their explosive vitality and concentrated power of making things actual.

Quite. And if critics had read Lawrence in the light of Emily Brontë, Dickens and Melville rather than in that of Wells, Bennett and Gals-worthy, a great deal of misunderstanding need never have occurred. They might still have found difficulty in explaining their perceptions, but they would not have found them so irrelevant to the business of living.

Another critic who has done much – in fact, most – to establish the nature of Lawrence's great middle-period novels is F. R. Leavis. He is understood to have discarded his earlier study of Lawrence from the canon of work he wishes to preserve; and yet one may, perhaps, draw upon it, if only to show the effect of Lawrence at the outset of a dis-tinguished critical career. No doubt Leavis would feel that his discussion of Lawrence's work in terms of his ideas was crude compared with what that work had to offer. However, it is interesting to see that Leavis's early comments on the originality of The Rainbow expressed clearly what is only suggested by Muir, and not indicated at all by Cannan or Rosenfeld. For example, Leavis spoke of Lawrence's 'sense of the mysterious intercourse of man with the world around him'. And it's interesting, also, to see that Leavis found The Rainbow far from easy. '*Sons and Lovers*, for all its poignant beauty, everyone I have discussed it with agrees with me in finding it difficult to get through. *The Rainbow* is a great deal more difficult.'[141]

No wonder, then, that Lawrence's work met with so much incomprehension. The impact seems to have been too great, too unexpected, to have been easily absorbed. The note Leavis insisted on is, however, the right one to suggest to a reader; certainly it is the one manifest in Leavis's own account of the book twenty-five years later. In the 1930 pamphlet, it appears as 'This drama of the inexplicit and almost inaccessible in human intercourse.'[142] The fact that Leavis should disapprove of his own early work on Lawrence shows, I think, the extraordinary difficulties that the early readers of Lawrence had to face.

We can understand, therefore, the extraordinary variety of response to the effect of the book. One would, by the same token, expect a wide divergence in interpretation. But this is not the case. Even the thrasonical Douglas seemed to realise that the book was about sexual relations in succeeding generations; and that, though it is the beginning of an interpretation, is not too misleading a summary. I do not think it is being unfair to say that what the more intelligent of the periodical reviews would have required was a family chronicle in the style of Arnold Bennett. The emotions worried them: it was not clearly seen that the idea of the book was one of successive degrees of sexual failure. Nobody pointed out the link-up between this and the opening up of the Brangwen country: while they remained isolated in their valley, they were so integrated as not to have individual consciousness. With the coming of the canal, we find an Alfred Brangwen marrying a girl from the next village. After the railway, strangers come in: Tom Brangwen's wife is a Polish refugee. Gradually, with the generations, the Brangwens look more and more out into the world, itself becoming more impersonal and industrialised; until Ursula, herself more educated, goes further out into the world than any of her family. But with the access of consciousness comes the consciousness of isolation; and we find her, in the end, coming up against the horses, themselves a living symbol of all she has lost; and, later, convalescent at home, once more looking out upon the Rainbow, a symbol of aspiration.

The latter part of this interpretation owes something to Frieda Lawrence, who without doubt was the most perceptive reader Lawrence had in his own lifetime. She never hesitated in her ascription to *The Rainbow* and *Women in Love* of the supremacy among Lawrence's novels. And she wrote in a letter to Cynthia Asquith: 'I think that the idea in *The Rainbow* is: *Love the ideal* as a background to these marriages which are really all failures to some extent. Hence the Rainbow between the ideal and these partial failures, because they are not complete failures. In the end the man fails Ursula because he has no ideal beyond the old existing state, it does not satisfy her nor him. For perfect love you don't only have two people, it must include a bigger universal connection. An *idea*, something outside themselves, and it is really against individualism.'[143] This letter is dated 1916. It stands alone in its time.

I think it can be shown that much of the comment which purports to refer to the artistry, or otherwise, of the book is irrelevant; and that most of the hostility which is relevant comes from a wholly inadequate conception of the novel as an art-form.

It is difficult, and not wholly desirable, to get free from the idea that a novel is primarily a way of telling a story. Yet such an idea militates severely at the present time against the publication of serious work in fiction, unless it rides in on a fashion of some kind. On the other hand, a novel clearly can best be identified by its appearance as a fiction, so that one would hardly like to deny the vast importance of plot. It enables some of the more fortunate novelists, like Melville and Conrad, and, in our own time, William Golding, to keep readers turning the pages through very suspense, whether they like what is being said or not.

Unfortunately, this effect is seldom possible except in novels of markedly brisk action, and such is not necessarily the most central subject-matter for literature nowadays. And so, too great a stress can be laid on the retailing of incident, as though this existed for its own sake; whereas plot has only a justification in so far as it is a function of the entire novel.

If the reader comes to *The Rainbow* expecting, in stock phrase, a good story well told, he is liable to be sorely disappointed. He will meet from the actual texture of the book a resistance such as he is normally conditioned to expect only from poetry. Furthermore, the criterion of realism – itself a very muffling convention – is likely to be outraged by some of the characters, dialogue and action. One accepts King Lear, at eighty-odd, with unflagging energy making speeches and rushing about the heath in a storm; just as one takes the remarkable combination of mad king, feigned madman and genuine fool. But, because *The Rainbow* appears to be a prose fiction, certain of its incidents are not so readily acceptable. What is required is, not so much acceptance of whatever the author puts forward by way of plot, as a heightened awareness – seeing the plot as only one dimension of a complex work, and conceding the possibility that a view limited to that one dimension may be a distortion of what *The Rainbow* has to offer.

It may quite reasonably be argued that the book is given to us under false colours; that it has more in common with Shakespeare than with Galsworthy, or even George Eliot. This may readily be conceded. How, after all, is a novel to manifest itself? It cannot be acted; it cannot be recited aloud, or taken in at a single sitting. How are we to experience it? Clearly it cannot be read as we read our morning newspapers. There is an anomaly in the very form, which undoubtedly heightens the amount of resistance it offers to the would-be reader.

But we employ a vast army of journalists, literary critics and academics to sift our creative effort for us. Surely it is their job to mediate between author and reader; to interpret and define the author's theme and procedure; to enlighten and persuade the bewildered or distrustful reader; to lessen, in brief, at once the resistance in the work and the resistance in its percipient? One cannot, however, look on the spectacle of Lawrence criticism and feel that this was done then; one cannot feel it is being done today. Journalists are primarily writing for newspapers who are interested primarily in gimmicks and personalities; critics are geared to recognise the averagely decent book and deflect sharply at anything unusual; academics are trained to categorise and show great caution in approaching the uncategorisable work of their contemporaries. The conclusion one draws is a depressing one: that an author of distinction has less chance than one who is second-rate of recognition in his own time.

Nevertheless, the resistance is not only in the audience but in the work. Pope, I have already said, appealed beyond a narrow circle; one reason was that he obviously wrote in a clear-cut tradition. The crucial example is Shakespeare who had all the luck: a vital tradition, a ready audience and a theatre in which his works could be staged.

The theatre, too, imposed on him certain economies: the work had to be clearly plotted, of a certain length; irrelevances, however beautiful, had to be ruthlessly excised. And this is not the only form of economy that literature has imposed upon its authors. Some of the most successful works have been comparatively small in scale and clearly defined in form; it is around them that one would expect to find most of a consensus. Yet, in practice, dissensions occur. What we must look to, then, is not so much a consensus of opinion, but a reconciliation of divergences.

114

CHAPTER SEVEN

Consensus and Reconciliation

The growth of critical activity in the present century has led to the submerged assumption that a poem can be expounded. A critic can certainly give some account of what he believes to be his response to a particular text. But this is very far from rehearsing all that is available to an interested reader. Considerations of space and time compel the critic to select his area of discussion carefully, and such selection is a personal matter which may give the impression of being the product of individual bias. Different aspects of different poems will seem to demand attention according to the moral and historical standpoint of different critics. Moreover, a critic is limited by the medium in which he writes; that of conceptual prose. He will necessarily have to enumerate separately what the poem, if successful, has fused together. The critic cannot, in fact, do more than semaphore what he perceives and hope that this will make his readers perceive it too. If he could do more, he would be rewriting the poem, or even seeking to replace it.

And yet differences of opinion among the critics may be more apparent than real. The question is not so much whether the critics produce different accounts of a given work as whether these accounts can be reconciled with each other when viewed in parallel and in relation to the text. Perhaps it is impossible to resolve all the possible accounts of a poem that can be given. But we should be able to demonstrate that the critics do not diverge wildly from each other when they select an approach to a complex work; for, of its very nature, such a work can say more, more subtly, than any analysis we can make of it.

It is worth pointing out that the *Ode on a Grecian Urn*, for example, has never been considered as anything but a masterpiece, and that the variations in the accounts that it has given rise to are not so bewildering as they have been made out to be. Superficially, indeed, opinions about the Ode seem to group themselves into two main categories. The traditional interpretation is that which considers the poem to be chiefly the expression of a view of art; for these critics the Urn is a perfect work which gives fixity to forms that in life would be fluid and impermanent. A second group of critics appreciates the Ode mainly as philosophical statement, and varies only in the extent to which it regards the Urn as a Platonic Idea. Both these groups of opinions, 'aesthetic' and 'philosophical', bring out an aspect of the Ode which is undoubtedly there: the Urn as Beauty, it may be, and the Urn as Truth. But there is a third group of opinions which includes both these aspects, as the Ode itself does. These critics feel that there is an element of paradox in the poem which leads to some kind of compromise, since the life of art and that of the world have each distinct limitations. The critics of this group vary in the extent to which they believe in the virtue of the compromise which art imposes on reality.

The differences between these categories of opinion are largely a matter of the degree of complexity which the critics attribute to the Urn. The philosophically inclined critic has to pay due regard to the fact that the transcendent vision conveyed by the Urn is unlikely to be sustained by human kind. And this leads us to a criticism of the Urn itself, and a recognition of the element of compromise in the poem, an element which, as we shall see, Keats makes into its characteristic strength. The critics of the first group, most of whom consider the Urn a simple thing of beauty, have some trouble in accommodating the last stanza of the poem into their general scheme. Those among them who regard the Urn as having a standpoint which is to be unequivocally approved, may, in their commentaries, over-elaborate what it stands for in order to allow for the ambivalence which has been pointed out by the third group of critics.

In practice, however, the poem seems to safeguard itself against misreading, on this issue as on others.[1] With the best will in the world, the 'aesthetic' critic is unlikely to be able to ignore the element of criticism in the 'beautiful' scenes presented by the Urn. The lover cannot kiss, the pipes may be sweeter but are unheard, the population of the now emptied little town has come to the sacrificial altar. It is not the poem, one would say, that is 'beautiful', but rather the Urn, with all the limitation of reality that the word would suggest.

The varying readings which the poem has attracted can be reconciled with each other to give some idea of a complex no single critique could convey. It is, as I said, the last stanza that has always appeared to give most trouble; and, undoubtedly, the final lines suffer if they are quoted out of context and without close reference to the poem.

116

> *O Attic shape! Fair attitude! with brede*
>   *Of marble men and maidens overwrought,*
> *With forest branches and the trodden weed;*
>   *Thou, silent form, dost tease us out of thought*
> *As doth eternity: Cold Pastoral!*
>   *When old age shall this generation waste,*
>   *Thou shalt remain, in midst of other woe*
> *Than ours, a friend to man, to whom thou say'st,*
>   *'Beauty is truth, truth beauty,' – that is all*
>   *Ye know on earth, and all ye need to know.*[2]

As one would expect, the critics whose attitude is not unlike that expressed in the final aphorism find it most lucid; and they belong to the first, aesthetic, group. For example, Robert Bridges finds the concluding lines 'very fine' as 'enouncing' the supremacy of ideal art over nature because of 'its unchanging expression of perfection'.[3] H. W. Garrod takes this further[4] and says that this suggests that there is nothing real but the beautiful; like Quiller-Couch,[5] he reads the poem as a sort of hymn to immortal art. The views may be seen to vary in emphasis and selection of detail, but not to diverge. What C. L. Finney,[6] a straight 'aesthetic' critic, calls an awakening in the last lines of the poem, Cleanth Brooks regards as a resolution.[7]

However, all these views could be more qualified in their approval of the Urn's teaching. A frequent over-simplification of the 'aesthetic' readings of this poem is that the Urn is too easily taken as something unequivocally to be admired. This is not a misreading, but Wilson Knight has noticed something of the necessity for criticism when he says that its assurance is not to be grasped until the mind is teased *out* of thought into some wider comprehension.[8]

The second group of critics has concentrated mainly on trying to define what this 'wider comprehension' may be. We shall take their definitions in decreasing order of the extent to which they regard the Urn as a Platonic Idea. Sir Maurice Bowra says that the Urn is speaking in the last lines for a unique experience of which it states the central essence: the discovery of beauty through the imagination is true in a sense that the conclusions of philosophy are not.[9] E. R. Wasserman agrees that the Urn does not communicate by thrusting a statement on the reader but by absorbing him into a participation in its essence.[10] And J. M. Murry accords with Wasserman in saying that the Urn is a way of entering a higher reality, and adds that it is a reality which can also illumine earth: the Urn has the property of sublimating our human weakness, if only for a short time.[11] Kenneth Burke, too, has said that great art can reconcile truth and beauty by taking the percipient to a level at which the earthly laws of contradiction no longer prevail.[12] This reading has obvious affinities with that of Bernard Blackstone, who treats the aphorism as a reconciliation of the opposed qualities of life and permanence.[13] There may be some question as to whether we can call the bourne in which this reconciliation takes place a true reality – that is, an ideal life seen without our human scales – or an identification of reality all about us; but the experience to which the critics are referring is clearly the same.

We shall consider the views of our third group of critics in ascending order of their belief in the virtue of the compromise which art imposes on reality. They are at one in feeling that too much fuss has been made about the last lines of the poem. William Empson suggests that these refer to the process of the artist digesting his sufferings and turning them into beauty; and a secondary reading is that receptivity to the outer life (truth) is what gives fullness to the inner life (beauty).[14] This latter relates to F. R. Leavis's interpretation, which indicates a measure of wish-fulfilment in the poem: truth, says Leavis, isn't really beauty, but the Urn can help us to feel it is. Like Empson, he sets limits to the application of the Urn's explicit advice as given in the aphorism: the 'pastoral' is 'cold' because its vision of a completely satisfying human life in an arrest of time is an illusion.[15] However, as E. C. Pettet says, the allusion has its own reality and represents the only truth we can know on this perplexing earth;[16] or, in the words of Kenneth Muir, the 'disagreeables' of life evaporate in the presence of the Urn.[17]

All these critics take the final aphorism to be an utterance of the Urn, and regard the Urn itself as a 'character', as something capable of being seen round, and, if necessary, criticised. It is no coincidence that critics such as Eliot[18] and Tate,[19] who identify the Urn's 'philosophy' with that of the poet, find the concluding lines tendentious: they assume a need to agree with an aphorism that, in context, is a dramatic utterance. But this is the only misreading that is likely to take place; and even this will only spoil the last couple of lines – by which time the poem has made its point, if it is going to make it at all.

Some critics, indeed, regard the poem as being a series of beautiful pictures;[20] but this last is not so much a misreading as an over-simplification. It will inadequately prepare the reader for the note of criticism in 'Cold Pastoral', and will make the final aphorism seem too explicit, not sufficiently placed in its dramatic context. Nevertheless, even with this reading, the poem remains valid.

118

It is true that any one of the accounts of the Ode I have cited may seem to be different from any other. But such variation is one that testifies to the impossibility of interpreting, once and for all, so complex a work of art as a great poem. Rather, we must be content to isolate the aspects which seem most relevant to the needs of the reader, and, in directing attention towards those aspects, hope that they will prove a way into the poem which will produce a response to it as a whole. Such variation, indeed, may be a timely reminder that the critic's work should be not pronouncement but discussion.

The important point to notice about the variation of opinion around a great poem is that each reading relates to the text; and that the readings themselves form a coherent pattern. It is certainly so in this case. To emphasise, as the 'aesthetic' critics do, the quality of the Urn as ideal art is at the same time to concede that the people on the Urn are limited in their very permanence. To stress, as the 'philosophic' group of critics do, the entry into a transcendent state of being is to admit that it cannot be sustained. And, as our third group of critics say, to the extent to which this aspiration is fulfilled, something of life is sacrificed. Only in a work of art can permanence and life be reconciled.

Critical discussion, then, tends to isolate aspects of a literary work. In a complete response, such aspects are fused; are experienced simultaneously. What Kenneth Muir says of the Ode on a Grecian Urn is true of any great poem: the artist's vision enables us, even if only fleetingly, to reconcile opposites and to see life whole.[21]

It is not necessary to agree with a poem in order to appreciate it; in practice a successful work has built-in safeguards against the moral or social predilection of the critic. Often this is a result of a species of dramatic ambivalence. Take Blake's philosophy, for instance: abstracted from his poems it is a system to which few would give serious credence. Yet the poems themselves command respect: whatever argument there might be about the philosophy of the Songs of Experience, there is no disagreement as to whether the songs themselves are worth appreciating. No conceptual framework could be so persuasive as their evocativeness; it seems to have an immediate effect on all the critics. And this is in spite of the very different attitudes they take up towards the concept of deity.

The Introduction to the Songs of Experience, for instance, functions between two poles: that of the Holy Word and of the Lapsed Soul.

119

Hear the voice of the Bard!
Who Present, Past, & Future, sees;
Whose ears have heard
The Holy Word
That walk'd among the ancient trees,

Calling the lapsed Soul,
And weeping in the evening dew;
That might controll
The starry pole,
And fallen, fallen light renew!

'O Earth, O Earth, return!
'Arise from out the dewy grass;
'Night is worn,
'And the morn
'Rises from the slumberous mass.

'Turn away no more;
'Why wilt thou turn away?
'The starry floor,
'The wat'ry shore,
'Is giv'n thee till the break of day.'[22]

Interpretations vary according to the amount of sympathy that critics have for the Lapsed Soul or lack of sympathy for the Holy Word. One could say that the Lapsed Soul is imprisoned in his material being and that the Holy Word is pleading for him back; or one could, at the other extreme, construe the poem as an attack on the Holy Word for the materialism with which He holds the Lapsed Soul in bondage. But moral predilections on the part of the critic need not impede his appreciation of the poem, for there is a real ambivalence in the presentation. This is recognised by F. R. Leavis, who finds it strange that God should be weeping and questions whether it would not be more suitable that the Soul should weep. The 'ancient trees', with their Druid associations, hardly suggest a Christian idea of God; though there is clearly a reference to the voice of God in the Garden calling Adam.[23] Perhaps, as Leavis himself suggests, one can make too sharp a distinction between God and Man.

Max Plowman takes it as being the Holy Word weeping;[24] he does so because of the close parallel with Genesis and its phrasing, but neither he nor Genesis can provide an answer for Leavis's question as to why the Holy Word should weep. F. W. Bateson, while accusing the God of the poem of being a 'jealous deity', is equally certain that it is the Holy Word that weeps;[25] and Stanley Gardner says that the Word is weeping because it is an imperfect God – not, that is, the true God of innocence.[26]

René Wellek, who agrees that it is the Holy Word who is calling the Lapsed Soul, says that it is the Lapsed Soul that is weeping in the evening dew – not God, but the Soul is weeping; presumably because it is being rebuked.[27] Kathleen Raine agrees that the Soul is weeping, but, in her reading, it is weeping for an entirely different reason: it has been reminded by the voice of the Bard of its former state.[28]

It is possible even to read this as the Bard weeping, if, like Margaret Rudd,[29] one takes the whole poem to be the Bard's lament. There is a remarkable complexity of effect here, but no confusion: the possibilities should be held by the reader, as they are by the poet, simultaneously present to the consciousness. In which case, the Holy Word is weeping at once for the resentment of the Soul against its bondage and for the bondage itself; the Soul weeps because it is aware of what it might be – a God, perhaps, who might control the starry pole; the Bard weeps for the lapse of man, and for his bondage too.

Oddly enough, Miss Rudd, who takes the Bard as weeping, sees the word 'Soul' as the subject of the phrase 'that might control'. 'There is still the enchanter's delight' (on the part of the Bard) 'in the soul's capacity to "control the starry pole".'[30] Wellek sees this as an apprehension of the Soul's potential power;[31] again, an apprehension on the part of the Bard. Miss Raine considers that the Soul has fallen and could, otherwise, have controlled the starry pole;[32] in other words, for her the control is not the Soul's potentiality but its former state.

But Gardner prefers to take the control as being that of the Holy Word;[33] he feels that it is a comment on God – He *could* control the starry pole, but He won't. Bateson, too, agrees with this idea of wilful passivity in God.[34]

Yet even here there need be no difficulty. If we regard the poem not as a simple statement but as a complex totality these ideas will all be seen to fit in with each other. The Soul has been made in such a way that it cannot realise its aspirations. It may aspire to control the starry pole, but is locked in a God-made material existence. The Holy Word could unlock it; He could, if He wished, control the starry pole. This may be the fault of the Holy Word or of the imprisoning materialism of the Lapsed Soul. The two spring from the same cause and are in nature closely associated. The Soul passionately resents this situation: it has the aspirations of a God, nor can the Holy Word fight the truth of those aspirations, though it may weep at them or at the impossibility of their realisation. The Holy Word tacitly admits and the Soul affirms that the starry pole ought to be controlled; but neither controls it. The Holy Word will not do it and the Soul cannot do it. However beautiful the world is, it is a prison.

The ambivalence of the last two stanzas is even more extraordinary than that of the first two. Whether they are spoken by the Holy Word or by the Bard is not very important. Although Wellek[35] and Gardner[36] agree with each other that the Bard is speaking, their interpretations of his words differ – they read them respectively as a call to aspiration and as a malign solace. Although Plowman[37] and Bateson[38] think that it is the Holy Word speaking, they differ similarly; Plowman is much nearer to Wellek in his interpretation than he is to Bateson, since he and Wellek consider it a benign call while Bateson, like Gardner, thinks it malevolent.

The words can indeed be read as a heart-cry – 'O Earth, O Earth, return' – or as an enticement. This is no more a weakness in the poem than the remainder of its ambiguities. The Holy Word is at once good and evil: He has created the Soul and He has limited it. The Soul is at once good and evil: it aspires to Godhead, and yet is limited by material creation. Probably the ultimate responsibility is that of the Holy Word: He could control His material creation, but does not. When it rebels against Him, He weeps and calls on it to return. But, even though the enticement may be there, it is meant genuinely. Bateson[39] and Foster Damon,[40] however, feel that what is offered is not enough; the 'starry floor' is a symbol of time and the 'wat'ry shore' of space – both limiting. This is true: all that is being offered is the world, beautifully evoked in the lines –

> *The starry floor,*
> *The wat'ry shore,*
> *Is giv'n thee till the break of day.*[41]

Wellek and Leavis had a controversy about these lines. Wellek claimed an exact symbolic connotation,[42] while Leavis claimed a direct evocative power.[43] But these two interpretations do not really diverge. The logic of the poem demands a limiting understanding of 'starry floor' and 'wat'ry shore'; just as in the very word 'beauty' there is an element of criticism. The rhythm, too, is rather more doubtful, less assertive and plangent, than it could be; and this serves a dramatic purpose. Coming after a crescendo of variations on the idea of 'turn' and 're-turn', the offer that is being made may not seem to cap what precedes

122

it. We do not get the climax that the rhythms, increasing in urgency as the repetitions develop, have led us to expect. So that even if we could not see that the aspiring Soul is imprisoned, we might feel that the gift of stars and water, though beautiful, should not be taken at too high a value.

From the Holy Word's point of view, this is the highest value He can allow the Soul. If He did more, and the Soul came to control the earth, the Soul, too, would be a God. This is why the poem can be so variously taken (and why such variations do not impede appreciation). Bateson limits himself when he refuses to see the poem in terms other than a view of the Holy Word as tyrant,[44] just as Margaret Rudd[45] and Foster Damon[46] limit themselves by not seeing that there are other things in the poem than the lament of the Holy Word, and that the lament of the Holy Word need not be taken at its face value. They are not exactly misunderstanding the poem, but they are presenting it as a smaller poem than in fact it is. Nevertheless, Bateson has an impressive point when he says that the poem is essentially *Paradise Lost*;[47] it is, indeed, *Paradise Lost* retold with all the implications that Milton's theology prevented him from stating but that his poetry suggested, often in opposition to that theology.

Man has a duty to God, but God has a duty to Man. The imagined relationship of creature to creator is full of difficulty. If one is right, the other must necessarily be wrong. Man has inborn aspirations; he has a soul; therefore he is overweening. God has made him; He is therefore responsible for him; He therefore is tyrannical. God could not allow Man power without abdicating His deity, or sharing it. Man cannot submit to God's law because he has too much of the divine in him. And the Lucifer suggestion of 'fallen light' implies that, in some sense, Man, as much as God, is responsible for his imprisonment. If Man aspired enough, he could shake off his bonds.

The poem can be taken as the Bard's presentation of his own attack on God, of an attack on Man by God, as an attack on Man by himself; as an exhortation to Man either to come to God or to rebel against him by either the Bard in both instances or in the former instance God; as the Bard's criticism of himself, or as the Bard's criticism of Man in the Bard's own shape.

This probably does not exhaust the possibilities. The poem is *for* God, because it creates superbly the natural universe He is giving Man, His heartbreak at Man's rejecting it (or at His wish to have even more), His yearning for Man. It is *against* God because it shows that the Soul has aspirations it cannot realise, that its lapse is probably the indulgence of these, that what is being offered is really bondage. It is *for* Man because he has a Soul and is therefore potentially a God but is not being allowed to fulfil his natural purpose by his own designer. It is *against* Man because it indicates a weakness in him that he cannot by his own efforts break out of his (material) prison.

So the ambivalence of the poem is more precise than any prose statement could be. When the reader is familiar with the poem, all these effects act upon him at once. In explication, however, the danger is that the critic may take sides without considering that the theme of the poem is the impossibility of taking sides in the issues involved.

The real test, however, is that in no individual interpretation can the poem be convicted of internal inconsistency; this is the way in which it protects itself against irrelevant connotations, and therefore a quite simple reading will – as we have seen – work. A further test might be that it is possible to relate all the interpretations to each other; the pattern is that of a divine paradox.

It seems not to be generally recognised that much literature is of this description. Comparatively few positive answers have been put forward by the poets; the positive, even of the greatest works, is implied characteristically through the dramatisation – not the mere reproduction – of questioning and disturbance. It is this very paradox that tends to arouse controversy: the virtue implied by its absence, the God-shaped blank in the world, the expression of the general in terms of sharp particulars. And the controversy almost always takes the shape of critics attempting to draw from a subtle complex a simple moral.

So many different readings of Wyatt's *They fle from me* have been put forward that we might suspect it to be a very bad poem indeed if our senses did not tell us that it is a very good one. Here, as with the poems by Keats and Blake, the readings are congruent with the poem and do not contradict each other. This does not mean that they are identical.

On the contrary. If we take the first line of the poem, we immediately find ourselves faced by a question.

They fle from me that sometyme did me seke.[48]

Well, who are *they*? Here are some of the answers that have been put forward.

An unstated number of women who have proved faithless to the poet. (Arthur K. Moore)[49]
Not only lost loves but lost powers of love. (Edward Lucie-Smith)[50]
Hangers-on, courtiers, princes' favourites. (S. F. Johnson)[51]

False friends, those who once enjoyed the poet's hospitality. (George Whiting)[52]
One particular mistress, now estranged. (E. E. Duncan-Jones,[53] F. W. Bateson)[54]
A woman seen in terms of wild beasts, creatures to be tamed. (Arnold Stein)[55]
A woman seen in terms of a falcon. (A. K. Moore)[56]
Doves, especially the doves of Venus. (F. Combellack)[57]
Birds of an earlier season, now migrated. (S. F. Johnson)[58]
Birds as a symbol of being forsaken. (J. D. Hainsworth)[59]
Birds, mice or rats which prisoners feed in their cells. (William Empson)[60]
Does, graceful, curious and skittish. (Leonard Dean)[61]
Deer (as in *Whoso list to hunt*). (F. W. Bateson)[62]

Perhaps we should confess ourselves bewildered in the face of this proliferation of readings. Here is ambiguity indeed; yet I think it can be shown to be defining, and not disruptive.

There is, it is true, nothing said explicitly in the poem about mistresses, flatterers, false friends, male or female; still less about wild animals, falcons, doves, deer or rats. Such details are supplied by the critics out of their own imaginations. What, however, I find very remarkable is that the details envisaged do not seem to interfere with an overall interpretation of the poem. Thus, whichever aspect of the question one attempts to answer, the *direction* of the poem is unaltered.

If the poem does not assert (say) a falcon, it does not prevent Arthur K. Moore from visualising one.[63] Arnold Stein, on the other hand, visualises a wild beast.[64] Yet both are difficult to manage; when tamed, the relationship is an uneasy one; both have a propensity for escaping, forgetting their skin-deep domestication, running wild again. Stein and Moore, then, can be shown to have much in common in their reading of the first stanza: they differ as to the kind of animal they have in mind, but both their kinds of animal are wild.

What of those who place more emphasis on the 'gentill, tame and meke' – Frederick Combellack, for example, with his doves[65] and Leonard Dean with his does?[66] Surely these are the opposite of wild beasts and falcons? But, in fact, there should be no difficulty in holding all these ideas simultaneously. There is a dual meaning of the word 'wild': wild in the sense of savage and to be tamed, and wild in the sense of shy and undomesticated and to be tamed! Wild, that is, as both falcons and doves are. We are all familiar with the usage in ordinary conversation. Here, impressively, it is acted out.

125

In all these interpretations one still gets the feeling that the rapport between hunter and hunted, tamer and tamed, is precarious. One still, too, sees that the creatures, once holding that rapport with the speaker, are fled. And this means more than the simple fact of deserting creatures. Such a real congruence of feeling, in spite of the surface differences of rationalisation, is what I mean by saying that a great poem safeguards itself against misreading.

The attempt to visualise what the poet left unvisualised is part of our imagist heritage. One does not have to agree with Professor Ryle, who erected his visual incapacity into a system,[67] to believe that a poem may exist through images, but never for them. We should be wise, therefore, to consider not the 'image' so much as its function in the poem. 'They' are not important as separate entities, poems in themselves, so much as for what they represent. This does not, of course, absolve the poet from creating the situation concretely on a literal level. 'They' are sufficiently there for the poetic effect, however, and this does not in the present case include a precise visual description. Rather the definition is all in the verbs, the actions – 'They *fle*', 'that sometyme did me *seke*', '*stalking*', 'they *put* themselves in daungere', 'to *take* bred at my hand' –

> . . . *and now they* raunge
> *Besely* seking *with a continual chaunge.*[68]

The fact that the speaker is being forsaken is, after all, the subject of the poem; rather, that is to say, than a consideration of what is forsaking him. And being forsaken is more real to the speaker than the identity of those who are forsaking.

More important than the specific metaphor is what it stands for. 'They' once sought out the speaker with some risk to themselves and partook of his bounty; now they are wild and are seeking restlessly. 'They' therefore can be taken as false friends, betraying courtiers, the loss of favour generally, the mistresses whom once the speaker could attract and who now 'range', and one particular mistress 'in special'. It is clear that there is no contradiction between these interpretations: they are reconciled in the poem's fusion of literal and metaphorical elements. To take the poem entirely metaphorically – the speaker forsaken by falcons, beasts, does or doves – would be to thin it out. Neither is it simply and literally a love poem: as the ensuing discussion will show, there is much more to the poem than a fall from a lover's grace; all the elements amount, surely, to a general sense of reversal – 'they fle from me that sometyme did me seke' – of which the second stanza is a particular instance. Everything that the speaker holds dear seems to have deserted him.

One should not take the poem, either, as simply a reversal of fortune. This was the usual interpretation in the days when Surrey was preferred to Wyatt – whose sexuality was played down in favour of allegory. To the nineteenth century Wyatt seemed a good deal closer to Gower than to Donne, as can be seen in a note on the second stanza of this poem by Wyatt's editor of 1816, G. F. Nott. 'Under the figure of a Lady offering to him unsolicited the tenderest mark of affection, he describes in a lively manner, his early good fortune and success in life.'[69] The sexuality which is apparent to modern critics is lost in allegorical distancing – which waters it down to 'affection' and 'success in life'.

Certainly the poem is about a reversal of fortune, but not quite in this way. It could be said that the poem's area of experience includes a reversal of love, but is not confined to it. To call it simply a love poem or simply a poem about fortune is not good enough. 'They fle from me' is not 'simply' about anything. No great poem is.

F. M. Padelford's gloss clearly derives from Nott: the poem 'personi-fies Fortune under the figure of a lady kissing her knight'.[70] Miss Foxwell closely followed this when she compared the poem with 'Ons methought Fortune me kyssed'.[71] However, the dangers of taking the poem too far away from immediate sexual experience are illus-trated by the note on *did me kysse* that Miss Foxwell supplied in her (1913) edition of Wyatt. 'The kiss was the ordinary form of salutation amongst the upper classes of Wyatt's day.'[72] Very possible; but not, I feel, 'in thin array after a pleasant guise', 'with naked fote stalking in my chamber' or 'in her arms long and smale'!

However, the concept of the Lady as Fortune, though it can be taken too far, is by no means an aberration of Wyatt's earlier editors, to be dispelled by the cold light of present-day criticism. In 1942 Lamson and Smith in their anthology of Tudor poetry glossed 'her' as 'Fortune's';[73] and, more recently still, George Whiting has supplied reasons for putting this interpretation forward: 'under the conventional mask of a love poem . . . Wyatt . . . describes his predicament in general, which was due to Fortune . . . In this poem "she" is Fortune, which had once favoured him (stanza two), has deserted him (stanza one), and is inconsistent and unfaithful, according to her nature (stanza three)'.[74]

Mr Whiting's is the most detailed explication of an allegorical read-ing that I have come across. Its faults are obvious enough: a playing down of the particularity of the second stanza, and a submerged assumption that the literal meaning of a poem is less important than its allegorical meaning. In fact, as will be shown in the course of discussion, in this poem both are equally important. Indeed, they are not so much held in relevant juxtaposition as indissolubly fused. So that the concrete instance of the general complaint can be taken as the subject of the poem; which, at the same time, clearly refers beyond itself to the complaint.

Let us, therefore, consider as a means of comparison the views of those who take the poem only on a literal plane; that is to say, who regard the Lady as being a particular lady, i.e. the speaker's mistress.

E. M. W. Tillyard, for example, is jocular about the Nott–Padelford–Foxwell line of interpretation, and draws attention to the title which the editor of Tottel's Miscellany gave this poem: 'The lover sheweth how he is forsaken of such as he sometime enjoyed.'[75] Dr Tillyard seems to be suggesting that, for a Tudor audience, the poem would exist solely on a literal plane. However, even this title seems to me to contain reverberant overtones. 'Forsaken', 'such', and, especially, 'enjoyed' can be taken on at least two levels; which would, in turn, indicate that the editor was a more perceptive critic than his emendations to the text would have led us to suppose.

Kenneth Muir goes further than Tillyard, and considers that the poem is about the time when Wyatt was happy in his love, contrasted with his present state. But he does suggest that there is a weight of generalisation in the poem when he describes it as being 'on woman's fickleness' (i.e. rather than the fickleness of one particular lady).[76]

Frederick Combellack, too, recognises a generality in the poem, but relates it to a particular happening. 'I should say the two stanzas' (i.e. 1 and 2) 'describe, metaphorically and literally, the same event, the visit of the lady to the poet's room.'[77] But a relevant question would be: Why, since the lady's visit is presented with such actuality, do we need a metaphorical lead into it? Obviously, the metaphors are doing more than grace a particular incident.

D. W. Harding has done well to emphasise the 'direct handling of experience in its real setting' which occurs in this poem. Direct personal statement is, indeed, the characteristic form of Wyatt's writing. But Harding also says that the love lament offered indirect expression to a range of feeling that might have arisen from quite other sources, such as the disappointments of Wyatt's diplomatic work, the fluctuations in the King's regard for him, and the hazards of his position as a courtier among intriguing rivals.[78] In other words, one could say that a statement of direct personal experience and a consideration of the reversal of fortune may not prove incompatible.

The Lady, then, is more than an incident in a poem: she means something beyond herself. This is suggested in the remarks of more than one critic who would support a literal reading of the poem. For example, Mrs Duncan-Jones writes: ' "Thanked be fortune" takes up the "continual change" of the first stanza: it was thanks to fortune rather than to heaven that things were once better than they are now, for fortune is the deity who presides over this changeable lady.'[79] If the lady is changeable, one might add, doesn't that tell us something about *ladies*? and about *change*? and about *Fortune*?

The possibility of accepting at one and the same time a literal and an allegorical reading has been put forward by a few critics. The right tone is set, I think, by Sir Edmund Chambers: 'Fortune, who rolls her ball and turns her wheel, has sometimes favoured him. One occasion he recalls in particular, for the sweetness of it.' And then he quotes, as particular instance of this general fact, the second stanza. Chambers concludes that success is a fleeting joy, since Fortune, who gives, will take away.[80]

The other side of it has been brought out by Hallett Smith who feels that the lady may be a representation of Fortune through her very particularity, and through her living up to what we would expect of Fortune, i.e. changeability. 'Perhaps there was an associative identification between Fortune as a lady and the lady of the love poem herself.'[81]

A composite reading would seem to be dictated by sheer logic. If Fortune is involved in the poet's change of fortune, then the lady's defection is at once an example of change and a lively personification of what Fortune does to you. Once more we are compelled to emphasise that there need be no contradiction between literal and metaphorical elements in the poem. Here, they may be seen to be reconciled in the fusion of the idea of Fortune in particular instance and Fortune in general; the lady herself and what she stands for.

How this is done is perhaps best indicated by J. D. Hainsworth, who says that the wider reference is only apparently submerged under the love story. 'The kiss can be taken as metaphorical, and the "she" who bestows it as Fortune, the medieval "goddess" whom the poet thanks at the beginning of the stanza.'[82] Perhaps one could quarrel with the implication here that there is a tension between the elements. I would make no separation between experience and convention in the actual poem, though I grant that the *material* of which it is composed may

129

have been disparate in character. It is a strength of the poem that such apparent opposites should have been brought indissolubly together. It is only a pity that the critics have been moved to place the emphasis on one aspect or the other, rather than, as Mr Hainsworth does in his explication, on the relation of Love and Fortune in the poem as a whole.

The superiority of this poem to Wyatt's lute songs is that, to a remarkable degree, the poet appears to be mastering his experience as the poem develops. The sense of desertion refers to more issues than that of one girl forsaking the speaker. Hence the ambiguous tone of the first lines – with, however, already an erotic undercurrent. The poem is about desertion in a very wide sense: desertion by friends, desertion by mistresses (and one in special), betrayal, downfall. It is prevented from falling into an inclusiveness so general as to be vague by the way in which the literal interacts with the metaphorical. The creatures of the opening lines are at once things which desert and symbols of desertion. And the latter, both in the general sense and as representatives of particular acts of desertion.

The same effect can be seen in the second stanza, when the poet begins to pull himself together by thinking about what *has* happened. The past is the only thing that hasn't been taken away from him. But the particular lady in this stanza is again a local example of Fortune in action. It might have been all right then, but we know (in the light of the first stanza) that it's not going to go on being all right! Moreover, this lady, with her kiss, is a little too much like a personification of Fortune herself to allow us to feel easy about it all. The very vividness and unlikelihood (since all have deserted) gives the incident an unreal dreamlike quality. The effect of the first stanza is summed up in the third – 'a strange fashion of forsaking'. One might ask '*Who* was forsaking *whom*?' The answer is, surely, that everyone was forsaking Wyatt.

This is a very impressive poem indeed, and it is my contention that the apparent divergences bear this out. They are themselves indications of how many areas of experience have been fused into this complex totality. The poem has attracted no major misreadings; although, as often happens in critical explication, a certain amount of over-simplification has taken place – as the views of Padelford and Foxwell on the one hand and those of Tillyard and Muir on the other only go to show.

Sometimes critics adopt the reverse procedure. There is often a temptation to do too much in the way of reading a poem. In the case of an inferior work, as we saw in a previous chapter, this will produce a private fiction. But, with major works, the most that happens is that a critic will labour hard and circuitously to establish what was staring him in the face all the time.

The reader of a poem that is worthwhile may use scholarship as an aid to understanding its connection with inferior work or with historical events. But scholarship can never do more than that; not, at least, with a poem worth reading. It is generally agreed that one of the tests of excellence is whether a poet can transcend the community for which he wrote. I have never understood why the corollary to this is not equally accepted: that we should read all poets as our contemporaries. There is, surely, no other way of reading them.

This last point is amply illustrated by the Herbert controversy. There is, so far as I am aware, only one Herbert controversy: for the most part, his path has been very peaceful – Herbert stands today in justly high estimation, in the annals of old and 'new' critics alike.

However, this happy state of affairs does not exist in relation to Herbert's most ambitious effort, *The Sacrifice*. There is a real divergence in the theory of how this should be read: I say the theory rather than the practice advisedly. The basic dichotomy is this: one school of thought considers that no reading is adequate unless it takes in all that most probably influenced the poem; the other would read the poem as we read the living verse of our own time. In the first camp are Rosemond Tuve[83] and Rosemary Freeman;[84] in the second, William Empson[85] and L. C. Knights.[86] In between are a number of critics who find no especial difficulty in coming to terms with both parties: Louis Martz[87] and Margaret Bottrall[88] come to mind – and such, indeed, will be the attitude of this particular enquiry.

Because, when one comes to look at the actual readings, they don't differ as much as the critical theories adduced from them. It is true that Professor Tuve approaches the poem by a very long way round, gathering an impressive array of miscellaneous information as she goes. While Professor Empson, with a simplicity irritating to scholars, takes the route direct. But there is surprisingly little divergence in their views of the poem, and both believe that it is a very great work.

This may seem oddly paradoxical. After all, everyone is persuaded that there is a controversy. And there have been several quite sharp exchanges on the issues we shall be discussing. Yet the consensus goes to show that scholarship does not necessarily get in the way of understanding a great poem. From this argument, indeed, it would seem that scholarship is not essential for the understanding of a work of literature. If it were, the work would hardly be a great one.

Professor Tuve reproaches Empson for an unscholarly approach,[89] but is herself for most of the time in agreement with his findings. If we look at general considerations first, we shall see that both critics agree as to the theme. Christ, says Professor Tuve, is at once the quiet sufferer of other people's actions and the omnipotent ruler of the universe;[90] or, as Empson more tersely puts it, at once scapegoat and tragic hero.[91] If we turn to the middle of the academic road for corroboration, we find Mrs Bottrall, for example, saying that the poem grasps the central paradox of Christianity; that the Man of Sorrows is indeed God.[92]

Of course, it is possible to argue, as Professor Tuve does,[93] that the paradox is as old as Christianity and that the poem is compounded of traditional elements. But these elements were present to all the religious poets of the seventeenth century, and yet only Herbert was able to write *The Sacrifice*. To that extent, however much the poem takes place within a tradition, it is a personal achievement.

One characteristically finds Professor Tuve seeking to play down Herbert's sharpness and originality, as in the following stanzas.

> *My crosse I bear myself, untill I faint:*
> *Then Simon bears it for me by constraint,*
> *The decreed burden of each mortall Saint:*
> *Was ever grief like mine?*
>
> *Oh all ye who pass by, behold and see;*
> *Man stole the fruit, but I must climb the tree;*
> *The tree of life to all, but only me:*
> *Was ever grief like mine?*[94]

It would not do to suggest that Professor Tuve's commentary on this is wholly mistaken; but it does proceed as though on the assumption that Herbert was unable to say anything unless ten previous authorities had already said it for him. Thus, Augustine's *Meditations*, the *Mass of Holy Cross*, the *Cursor Mundi*, the *Pomander of Prayer* of Thomas Becon, Bishop Bayly's *Practise of Pietie*, Ludolph's *Vita Christi*, Lancelot Andrewes's *Preces Privatae*, the *Speculum humanae salvationis*, Venantius Fortunatus's hymn *Pange lingua gloriosi* and *Crux Benedicta* are brought in by Professor Tuve with claims for their relevance.[95] One can't help hoping that Herbert had better things to do with his time than absorb all these. Professor Tuve, as if herself daunted by the list – must we read all this in order to understand Herbert? – considers that we need not think of the poet as knowing *all* these especial works.[96]

Which rather takes away from her credit in bringing them to our notice in the first place.

If, however, I continue to treat Professor Tuve's account of the poem with respect, it is because all this citation is only part of her procedure. Her commentaries on the poem are very useful; and, if we ignore most of the citation, amount to a searching, if incomplete, analysis of the poem's effect.

Thus she begins by saying that we are startled by the identification of the tree of sin with the tree of redemption.[97] Unfortunately it is this shock effect which Professor Tuve tries to muffle in her commentary. She brings up some heavy guns[98] to prove what Empson deduces from the poem itself:[99] that the Cross was made from the wood of the Forbidden Tree.

Why did Christ climb the tree? Empson points out that this gives Jesus a childlike quality: Eve could pluck the fruit while standing on the ground, but Jesus has to climb up to reach the point at which the sin began.[100] Professor Tuve is of the opinion that such a reading is not permissible since it has no liturgical counterpart.[101] But this is not the point: Herbert's material is what he made of it. To demonstrate her case, Professor Tuve should demolish Empson's reading within the terms of the poem: i.e. show where and in what ways he is misreading the lines.

But in practice, as apart from theory, Professor Tuve agrees with a good deal of this. She agrees that Christ in the metaphor used here seems a child;[102] but she makes this concession, not because of the plain sense of the poem, but because there is some medieval source for this – Seth finding Christ as a child in the tree. Empson, however, reached the same conclusion[103] by no process more elaborate than reading the poem –

Man stole the fruit, but I must climb the tree.[104]

Both critics agree that this implies Christ climbed the tree in order to expiate Adam's crime. They even agree that there is a suggestion here that Christ is climbing the tree to put the apple back,[105] though Professor Tuve claims, reasonably enough, that the latter is a subsidiary meaning.[106] But Empson sees that there is a typical Herbert conflict in the idea: 'He climbs the tree to repay what was stolen . . . but the phrase in itself implies rather that he is doing the stealing, that so far from sinless he is Prometheus and the criminal.'[107]

Yet even here the divergence is more apparent than real. Professor Tuve recognizes what Empson argues out,[108] that there is a paradox at the heart of the whole conception, since there is a close connection between the doing of a sin and the undoing of it.

What, then, is the issue between the critics? The basic point of the stanza would seem to be that Christ became guilty: this is not only expiation but also sin. The rather sinister implication is that one cannot take on a sin vicariously. Professor Tuve says that Christ becomes guilty as a matter of pre-ordained necessity;[109] Empson, that the idea of sin is tied in with the concept of Christ as child – the Son stealing from his Father's orchard.[110]

Paradox of this kind is always bound to produce what appear to be divergent readings. But if the idea of Christ expiating man's sin is held in mind throughout the apparent contrarieties, the critics will not seem to be in real disagreement. Professor Tuve emphasises the necessity of the expiation,[111] while Empson emphasises the attendant guilt.[112] But both these attitudes are found in the actual line, 'Man stole the fruit, but I must climb the tree'.[113]

Empson himself finds no difficulty in reconciling these possibilities; and a critical reading of the text, such as the one he has given us, is unlikely to bring in considerations unrelated to the poem, unless the poem itself is incoherent. One of the major discoveries of modern criticism in general, and of Richards and Empson in particular, is that a poem can bear more than one possible interpretation. So far from narrowing the possibilities of criticism into an orthodoxy, it seems to me that their approach has enormously enriched our conscious apprehension of literature. I am not suggesting that nobody before I. A. Richards was able to read a poem. But it is conceivable that any account then given of a poem would have fallen drastically short of the reader's experience.

In attempting to tie down a poem to one 'right' interpretation, critics like Professor Tuve seem to me to be ignoring the great advances that have been made. It is now, thanks to such analyses as Empson's account of *The Sacrifice*, far more possible to rationalise our response to literature than ever before. The reader need find no difficulty in holding several interpretations consciously in his mind and being aware of the way in which they interact.

It is true that, in pointing to one aspect of a poem, the critic may very well be influenced by considerations which he has not himself brought into conscious awareness. And perhaps the human mind is not capable of focusing upon all such considerations at once. But the attempt has to be made: a prerequisite for anyone with ambitions as a critic should be mastery of the greatest possible extent of awareness.

134

The individual interpretation may be valid, but will isolate only one facet of the poem's total effect upon a reader. By putting these interpretations in parallel we can arrive nearer to understanding the poem that occasioned them. Each individual interpretation will, of course, be a response personal to the individual reader; but, in a great poem, all these will add up to a total figure. In other words, by taking into account the facets isolated by various readers, it should be possible to approach very close to the poem as a whole; as, in fact, some sort of objective phenomenon. The reconciliation of attitudes in the poem will bring about a consensus of readings in the critics.

In discussing the general theme of Marvell's *The Garden* the critics fall into three main groups. Most of them regard the poem as a loss of paradise or innocence. Another group suggests that this is not just loss but some kind of ordering of experience or understanding. And the third group regards this mainly in terms of an increase or development of sensibility.

All these accounts have in common the idea that the Garden represents some kind of perfection, that the poet has retired to this (or is remembering it) as an act of contemplation, and that this increases his knowledge of the world. Any one of the accounts would be exclusive in the wrong sense of the word: perhaps as any one person's account of a poem must be. I shall attempt here a reconciliation of these views in an interpretation of the poem's general theme.

The Garden seems to include allusions to the Fall of Man and to women which link up with its attitude to society and labour. The poem begins with a final rejection of the lot of man: explicitly, giving up the symbols of success for their realities. But these symbols *are* in fact the realities – the oaks, palms and bays of a garden.

In the same way the poet describes the rejection of passion in very passionate terms, and puts forward a fantastic interpretation of straightforward myths in such a way as strongly to suggest the usual version. One's impelled to say that *obviously* Pan sped after Syrinx because she was a nymph, and the contention is backed up by emotive language – 'heat', 'retreat', 'chase', 'race', 'hunted'. Neither the Gods nor the poet can be detached. The rejection of women does not mean that one loses one's sexuality: on the contrary, the formal garden of the beginning later fairly burgeons with it. This is, of course, a contradiction of the earlier stanzas, but it is noticeable that the speaker is not quite certain whether he will find innocence and quiet in the garden, and suggests a possibility that these 'sacred plants' may not grow below – especially since they are personified as women. The curious – inquisitive – peach reaches itself *into* the hand of a fallen man, bringing about a fall into the material world. This is presented as an ardent wooing of the poet: a man in need of female companionship sees everything with a sensual bias, and the fall is presented as a sexual encounter. Whatever he has found in the garden, it is not innocence and quiet; or, at least, they are not the virgins Marvell takes them to be.

> *What wond'rous Life in this I lead!*
> *Ripe Apples drop about my head:*
> *The Luscious Clusters of the Vine*
> *Upon my Mouth do crush their Wine;*
> *The Nectaren and curious Peach,*
> *Into my hands themselves do reach;*
> *Stumbling on Melons, as I pass,*
> *Insnar'd with Flow'rs, I fall on Grass.*[114]

Any individual view of Marvell's Paradise is likely to be relevant; equally, any individual view is likely to be simpler than what that Paradise offers.

The interpretations of the critics differ according to the extent of guilt involved in Marvell's Paradise, and I shall take them in order of increasing attribution of guilt, from Kermode to Empson.

For Kermode, all is innocent. The sensuous appeal is as enchanting as the earthly Paradise and as innocent. 'The difference between this and a paradise containing a woman is that here a Fall is of light consequence, and without tragic significance.'[115] Kermode is near enough one current of thought in the poem to lose all sight of another. If the garden has all the enchantment of an earthly Paradise, it is debatable whether it can be innocent. The plants, as Kermode admits,[116] are most pressing in their attentions: there is everything to delight the sensual palate, though one would have to concede that the delight is fresh and genuine and not any more sinful than any other activity of fallen men. But this last is a necessary qualification: the Fall that is exhibited in this stanza is not of consequence to the protagonist who has lived to accept the pleasures and inducements of earth. It is, however, of heavy consequence when one considers what he has lost – the possibility of the repose which he sought in the garden. The garden is active, his being is active, his mind is active, the peace that he hoped for dissolves in these nutritious images. The garden, as Kermode says, cannot be a trap for virtue,[117] but this is human: the protagonist is a fallen man anyway, and has very little to lose. The point of the stanza is not just a presentation of Paradise, but a graphic illustration of the gap between the heaven we hope for and the garden we actually get.

Frank Bradbrook calls this stanza an impassioned and voluptuous wooing of the poet by nature. He points out that even though love has been explicitly rejected, all the emotions associated with love continue in the garden, and to this extent the poet is like the Gods; and, like the nymphs they pursue, nature is intensely active.[118] Miss M. C. Bradbrook and Miss Lloyd-Thomas suggest that this is an extension of the lines about the Gods: that metamorphosis is the answer to the decay of beauty and the triumph of time. 'In the garden life is perpetually renewed.'[119]

So far, to use the words of Milton Klonsky, the critics have held the protagonist guiltless of any 'corruptive action',[120] though they have been increasingly conscious of the canker in the rose-garden. With Klonsky, however, the question of sin comes in very strongly, though only in the last couplet: when he acts to assert his desires, then he is ensnared, stumbles and falls.[121] The built-in paradox which operates for Klonsky only in the last two lines moves for Lawrence Hyman as an ambivalence throughout the stanza. For Hyman, this is primarily a description of a happy garden state, but also has a strong undercurrent of sexual imagery.[122] So the stanza can be read in two ways: according to whether one envisages Paradise before Eve or Paradise after the Fall. The safety of this particular garden fall is, as A. H. King says, contrasted with the normal sin-associations of 'ensnar'd' and 'fall'.[123]

Other critics feel that the paradise is not a place of perfect innocence, even as a surface possibility, but rather, as Professor Røstvig says, a place for the re-ordering of one's senses, so that (two stanzas later) one may glimpse God in the garden.[124] Joseph Summers also sees this stanza as the presentation of paradise, but for him it is one irrevocably lost. However, this is not a matter for grief: 'The lost garden represents not measure but perfect fulfilment; its memory is an occasion for ecstasy.'[125] This view is not dissimilar to that of Professor Røstvig, but what is for her the poet's purification of his senses in order to attain a new intensity of vision,[126] is for Mr Summers a recollection of a vision irrevocably lost.[127]

It is, of course, possible to take exception to the way in which this paradise is presented: as Pierre Legouis reminds us,[128] it savours strongly of the earth. Ruth Wallerstein also emphasises the physical appeal of the garden, not as passion for its own sake, but as the delight of the sense in nature; a 'gathering image of Paradise'.[129] And yet Miss Wallerstein admits that there is something of violence in the stanza.[130]

And it is true that the very luxuriance of the garden suggests the fall: either because the laboured garden of the early stanzas has, of its own accord, proliferated, as Paradise did, or because the flowers and fruit are seductive, thrusting themselves on the protagonist of the poem.

This is put more explicitly even than this comment would suggest. So far from treating the stanza as a description of nature, Empson declares that Marvell has stepped back from overt conceits to a rich and intuitive use of Christian imagery. 'When people treat it as the one good "bit" of the poem one does not know whether they have recognised that the Alpha and Omega of the verse are the Apple and the Fall.'[131]

This is the crucial part of Empson's essay; not so much because it is the entire truth about the stanza as because it emphasises the facet that critics tend to leave out. It is at the other extreme from Kermode's reading: not only in opinion, for it is an over-simplification to term the Garden a place of innocence, but in its closely analytical approach. 'Melon, again, is the Greek for apple; "all flesh is *grass*", and its own *flowers* here are the snakes in it that stopped Eurydice. Mere grapes are at once the primitive and the innocent wine; the *nectar* of Eden, and yet the blood of sacrifice.'[132] All these eatable beauties give themselves generously, like a lover; and, like a lover, they ensnare the man in the garden; for Empson, this is the triumph of the attempt to impose a sexual interest upon nature.[133]

What has happened in the individual critiques is that aspects of the stanza have been exposed: the stanza is not about anything so simple as innocence or guilt, and Messrs Klonsky and Hyman have done well to recognise its ambivalence. There are three currents of thought running through. (a) The stated intention of the poem is that this should be a place of repose, and the fact that the vegetation is so active strongly suggests that even in the most favourable circumstances repose is not obtainable by man. (b) The stated intention of the poem is to do without woman, but the sensuality of the plants and the amorous nature of the imagery show us that this is not in the nature of man, either, because (c) man is so far fallen that every action re-enacts the Fall. Not the melon alone but all the other fruits, as Empson has shown,[134] are tempters, and tempters without any need of a snake. Under the most favourable circumstances, then, man will fall, as the first man did. And all these currents of thought lead us towards the great conclusion of the poem, that the garden can be at best a place of regeneration, but rest must be found in other worlds; that peace in this world can be found only in useful labour.

138

How well the skilful Gardner drew
Of flow'rs and herbes this Dial new;
Where from above the milder Sun
Does through a fragrant Zodiack run;
And, as it works, th' industrious Bee
Computes its time as well as we.
How could such sweet and wholesome Hours
Be reckon'd but with herbs and flow'rs!

The protagonist has returned to a garden which is, like that of the
first stanza, formal – not a burgeoning paradise of plants run wild. It
is this sense of order that is chiefly stressed by Frank Kermode, Jim
Corder and John Press. Other critics are more interested in the garden
of this stanza as a place of innocence, as though the Fall had never
taken place. But I shall concern myself initially with the former group
of critics.

Kermode seems not to sense any difference in the garden to which
the protagonist returns. 'In the last stanza the temperate quiet of the
garden is once more asserted, by way of conclusion . . . the time, for
us as for the bee . . . is sweet and rewarding; hours of innocence are
told by a dial of pure herbs and flowers.'[136]

Corder lays even more stress on the aspect of order which this
stanza reveals. 'The "happy garden state" is well-ordered in the
patterns of the formal garden', but this, for Corder, is a metaphor for
an order involving more than innocence.[137] This is an improvement
on Kermode's over-simple reading, but like Kermode, he seems to
have forgotten that the garden has not been like this throughout the
poem.

Press differs from these two critics in seeing the order and formality
of this last stanza as a development on the rest of the poem. 'Finally,
after the rapt vision of these stanzas, Marvell returns again to the
garden where Woman is excluded but where the industrious bee,
symbol of social order, computes Time which is itself dependent on
the living flowers woven into that sophisticated invention of man, the
floral sundial.'[138] But the garden is not the same as it was in the beginning, either: there were no symbols of order or of labour in the
garden of stanza 1: labour was excluded, left to the outside world.

The other critics are interested rather in the presence of God in the
garden, the relationship between innocence and the Fall. Professor
Røstvig goes so far as to subtitle the final stanza 'The Divine Hiero-
glyph';[139] and this, indeed, may be an indication of the poem's subtlety:

God so ordered the world (as the gardener ordered the garden) that man could find peace only *through* labour. Where one may differ from Professor Røstvig is in her implication that it is necessary to stay in this particular garden to find peace: it is now full of urban images, suggesting very strongly the presence of an outside world, or the need to return to it. It is true that, as Lawrence Hyman remarks, this scene, like the entire poem, can be read as a simple description of perfect innocence and peace. 'But if we look back at the opening stanza "the industrious Bee" recalls the "uncessant Labours" of men. The sundial, fragrant though it may be, measures the path of the sun (or the sun's shadow or shade) just as the "short and narrow-verged shade" of the trees. The bee, mortal as man, can do no more by its labours than to compute "its time".'[140] However, as Hyman says,[141] the poet does not rebel against this state of things, against labour and death, the consequences of sin. The contrast is between an ideal garden in which time is reckoned by flowers and the present garden where it is reckoned by labour.

This, again, suggests the central paradox of the poem: the search for rest which, because it *is* a search, repels that which it seeks; and the possibility of peace comes in only through the prosecution of that search. The activity of the sun and the bee, the very patterning of the garden, not wild but formal and produced by man's labours, reminds the protagonist that what in the first stanza he regarded as labours only to a material end may have a virtue in themselves. His labours are not, as he thought, a contrast to those of the herbs and flowers: they are as natural to him as growth is to them and are of the same kind. The garden is not a place of repose for the plants, but one where they are highly active. It is not the clock that counts their labours, nor any obviously attainable end; their life is an end in itself. Similarly, the labours of man may be an end in themselves: until, at least, they are ended themselves by a longer flight, to a world whose glimpse – by an effort as strenuous as any he has known in the outside world – the protagonist has, momentarily, attained.

He sought the garden because he was tired with his toils: however, work conducted with no eye to material advantage but in accordance with the demands of the task itself makes it not toilsome; no more than the growth of the flowers is toilsome to them. We are reminded of the world of labour because this is where the poet is returning. The garden is a place, not of rest, but of recuperation.

It will be seen that no one critic affords more than a partial view of the poem, though he may have a sense of the paradox on which it is built. The argument of the poem is one part of this paradox; the implicit direction of the imagery is another; and, it may be said, that juxtaposition and concurrence is a third sector of the total effect.

The Garden is not simply a poem about repose, or the Fall, or the act of contemplation, to take only three of the interpretations that assert themselves. It is not, any more than the other great poems we have discussed, simply about any one thing. Rather it combines within itself considerations of what possibilities of paradise are open to a fallen man. And it does this through the exercise of paradox to an extent unique in English poetry. It took the last, and perhaps the best, of the metaphysicals to write a poem in praise of labour with a setting which was a formal garden.

In the beginning of this chapter I said that a critic was limited by the exigencies of time and space, and by his medium, conceptual prose. To some extent we can get over this by doing what has been attempted here: surveying the reactions of not an individual solely, but of an audience; seeing whether we can reconcile their views into a consensus of readings. This is easier than it would appear when the work in question is a valuable one; indeed, the possibility of such a consensus is one possible test of value in literature. Such a procedure is also an enforcement of relevance: the omissions and simplifications that a personal predilection would allow are checked against the responses of other readers.

This is not to repose great trust in any individual response: there is no work so great that some critic has not misread it, somewhere, at some time. But his reading can be related to those of other critics; and it is for him to explain the reasons for his divergence away from the general consensus.

In practice, such a misreading will be more a matter of tone or emphasis, possibly of simplification; at least when a great work is under consideration. For it is a characteristic of such work that it imposes itself in something of the same way on different readers. One will judge the reading by the extent to which it relates to the text, and the work by the pattern of readings which it occasions.

Sometimes the work will be on so large a scale as to make terrifying demands upon the reader. Then we will find a tendency on the part of critics to assume a prepared position: to judge a work by preconceived standards rather than allow their possibilities of experience to be extended by it.

Even here, however, the work will safeguard itself against all but the most determined misreadings. There is no case in my experience when the pattern of variation among the critics has not been determined by the external stimulus of a work of art; a stimulus that is present to the extent that the work is effective. And this, in its turn, is ultimately determined by the value of what the artist has to offer.

CHAPTER EIGHT

Survival Values

No work of literature is a 'purely' aesthetic experience, divorced from any moral consideration. If it were, it could say anything and still be deemed valuable; that is to say, provided it said it well enough. But certain attitudes do not lend themselves to expression; literature is a social medium and cannot be distorted into anti-social attitudes without great loss of value. Efficacious expression, in other words, has a great deal to do with the quality of the attitudes expressed.

A valuable attitude is unlikely to exist as a simple 'positive'. Rather, the values of a work of literature are those which we need to assume in order to survive as human beings; and this is no simple matter. What is in question is not only survival as an individual but as a species; and, moreover, a species living socially. Since we balance uneasily between individual desires and social checks, such values tend to be complex. Certainly they cannot be expressed as straightforward moral directives.

Therefore a work of literature does not assert values; rather, it acts them out. The distinction is between the prepared position assumed by critics and the creation of an ethic which is that of survival itself. Such an ethic cannot pre-exist the work of literature; every writer has to create it, subject to the tradition in which he works, in his own terms. If this were not so, the writer could simply take over the directives of an existing religion and – so to speak – versify them. But, in practice, this is impossible. Indeed, so far from claiming that literature embodies religious values, I would suggest that religion itself is a precursor – an art for the simple-minded, using myth to the same end as literature uses fiction: to convey what, as human beings, we need to know.

Like a myth in its pristine state, before it is manhandled by theologians, a work of literature says more by implication than the critics can, for all their explicitness. Indeed, the effort to explicate forces criticism into gestures which are unnecessarily clumsy. Do you mean this or don't you? critics will demand of the author; but the author may at once mean and not mean. He is, after all, entitled to walk the

143

knife-edge between possibilities. Once we begin to summarise, to abstract, the conceptual links are liable to be our own.

In great works of literature, there is a surprising ethical caution, a tendency to keep on the borderline of explicit moral assertion. And often with such works, the critics have rushed in where the authors chose not to tread. For example, whether or not there is a Christian element in *King Lear* can be resolved by asking two questions: Does the play need to state its ethical concerns so plainly (not to say crudely)? and, Can the critic explicate those concerns without using language which assumes what no work of literature can afford – a prepared position?

King Lear is arguably the greatest work in English: its aesthetic value is virtually unquestioned, its moral value seems to be at one with its efficacy as a work of art. Yet it does not exist as a system of moral statements; rather it enacts before us an appalling paradox which is no less than that of the human condition. How can we reconcile the passions which drove man through and out of the jungle with his need to preserve a stable society? To me it is amazing what use Shakespeare makes of the raw material of human passions; particularly, incestuous desire and death-worship. Here, they are purified and intensified out of all recognition into the clarity and purpose of Lear's catastrophe. But even so clear an example can be misunderstood: interpreters have evaded the issue of *King Lear* for centuries. Given the facts of the play, they prefer to turn their eyes elsewhere.

In recent times it has been possible to do this simply by misreading: seeing, as Bradley did, the ecstatic swell of the last scene as pointing to a recovery or happy illusion.[1] Bradley's optimistic reading is novel, but the attitude it expresses is not new: the averting of eyes from the author's conclusion. This form of misreading was hardly possible to critics of an earlier age, mainly because they did not have at their disposal a critical prose capable of being manipulated with the ease of Bradley and his successors.

But the unsubtlety of earlier readers did not save them from a good deal of Bradleian wrong-headedness; in fact, it took forms which were a good deal more blatant. Either the Aristotelian unities were invoked as a corrective, with the same dogged faith as fellow-practitioners prescribed cupping and bleeding; or else the play was altered, simply and decisively. In either case, Shakespeare's resolution was avoided.

This evasiveness goes back to the opening of the theatres after the Restoration. A great deal had been lost in the interregnum; not least, the sense of tragedy. Evidently the audience was too much harrowed by Betterton's production of *King Lear* in 1663, for when he revived the play it was done with a happy ending written by Tate.[2] From then on, Tate's version held the stage, to be supplanted only by that of Garrick.[3] Yet a third version, by Colman,[4] seems never to have been staged; but, like the other two, it points to the basic problem. Quite evidently, the last scene of *King Lear* was too strong for eighteenth-century stomachs.

Tate's version was a rationalisation of much that was to be said concerning the deaths of Lear and Cordelia. Indeed, he ends with the line 'Truth and virtue shall at last succeed'[5] – substituting for Shakespeare's catastrophe a simple moral directive. Lear is restored to his kingdom; Cordelia married to Edgar; virtue reigns securely triumphant.

One can see why Tate's brisk evasion commanded the loyalty of actor-managers for a hundred years afterwards. The eighteenth century was worried by tragedy; it feared to be harrowed. The conflicts of the Civil War had been resolved; it was for peace at any price. Gildon[6] and Theobald[7] both found the ending disgusting and immoral: 'Cordelia and Lear ought to have survived . . . virtue ought to be rewarded . . .' In other words, the play was for them a violation of 'poetic justice'; and, for the most part, eighteenth-century critics, whatever their individual capabilities, carried on in this manner: Gentleman,[8] Taylor,[9] Mrs Griffith,[10] Lord Kames[11] – all these felt that Shakespeare had allowed innocence to suffer unnecessarily. And even men of the theatre, such as Murphy[12] and Davies,[13] who had got beyond the idea of poetic justice, still believed that what was fit for the study would outrage the sensibilities of the playgoer. No doubt they were going by the performance of Garrick in the leading role; but, by all accounts, he rendered it with needless realism.[14] Critics and actors alike were unable to see the possibility of other modes of presentation, An emasculated catastrophe was thought better, because less devastating, than the original.

But the fact that the Tate version should have aroused so much comment and defence through the eighteenth century shows an underlying uneasiness. This was clear in the dichotomy between Johnson's generalised approval of Tate and his specific horror at the death of Cordelia.[15] An unconscious romanticism seeped through the set and Augustan education. It seemed that critics were responding, in spite of themselves, to something that they did not want to admit.

Indeed, the reaction to Augustanism was well under way before Johnson produced his edition. It had been anticipated by Addison's attack on 'poetic justice' as a limiting concept,[16] and was seen mainly in the work of textual critics who necessarily had to pay close attention to the verse. Through the arguments of rival editors, a false neo-Augustanism was gradually replaced in favour of a reliance upon individual sensibility. In the comments of such editors as Capell,[17] Steevens,[18] Malone[19] and Eccles,[20] the characteristic Shakespearean density was seen and appreciated for the first time since the closure of the theatres a century earlier; the more so, since textual gloss tends to be a working out of ambiguities.

But, as with Johnson, the generalisations of these late eighteenth-century critics were less satisfactory than their specific points: though they were anything but Augustan, their attempts at wholesale interpretation prefigured a heaviness of reading characteristically post-Romantic. For example, Capell anticipated Bradley in suggesting that Lear imagined some motion of recovery in Cordelia's lips;[21] while Empson[22] and Stampfer[23] are foreshadowed by Warton[24] and Roderick,[25] who both believed Lear to be enfeebled at the end. In the main, though, the advance of criticism in the eighteenth century may be represented by a growing recognition of the inevitability of the final scenes of *King Lear*.

This recognition was brought to its highest reach by Coleridge, who defended Lear's death in terms of 'sad yet sweet consolation';[26] an aperçu which was softened to 'sympathy'[27] by Lamb and 'pathos'[28] by Hazlitt. Keats pointed to the distinction between fact and representation of fact:[29] the death of Cordelia, horrible as it would be in real life, is made meaningful in drama. The burden of interpretation in Romantic criticism is that the catastrophe is a merciful release from a world of suffering; and this is as far as rationalisation could go until the seminal work of Freud, Heilman and Danby in the twentieth century.

As all this would suggest, the Romantics had a truer understanding of the play than is commonly thought: the pressure from critics such as Coleridge[30] and Hazlitt,[31] and magazines such as *Blackwood's*[32] eventually brought about Kean's restoration of the last scene in the acting edition of the play.[33] The *New Monthly Magazine* wrote about the production in terms Lamb might have approved; it would seem that Kean's performance was quieter than would have been supposed, 'gentle yet intense'.[34] However, it would not be true to say that Kean was an early Bradleian: although he seems to have suggested the hope of reconciliation, the main line of his performance, according to his biographer, was heartbreak.[35] And this was transmuted into the elegiac interpretation of Macready – Forster speaks of his 'sublime touch of pathos over the dead body of the hanged Cordelia'.[36] There is certainly a community of vision at this period: Hudson's account of the death of Lear sounds almost like a description of Macready's performance,[37] while Continental critics such as Gervinus[38] spoke of Lear's final peace and gentleness.

But, as the nineteenth century wore on, there was less and less of this form of exaltation among the critics. One mode which the increasing pessimism took was the progressive denigration of Cordelia: Ulrici[39] and Oehlmann[40] felt her to be imprudent in defying her father. The Victorians evaded the question of how far the demands put upon Cordelia were legitimate; and so the Romantic sense of tragedy melted into a Victorian sense of pathos, and thence, by easy transition, into a *fin de siècle* gloom in which critics saw less and less reason for the tragic denouement. The play seemed more and more amoral – a Hardyesque universe pitted irrevocably against Lear and Cordelia. Clearly, if Victorian critics were to accept the play at all, they could do so only as proof of a nihilistic environment. As early as 1848 Birch had declared that Shakespeare had no moral standpoint:[41] his words are virtually interchangeable with those of Swinburne – for whom, thirty years later, *King Lear* seemed to stop at Act IV scene i, 'as flies to wanton boys . . .' 'Requital, redemption, amends, equity, expiation, pity and mercy are words without a meaning here.'[42] Given such a view, one wonders from where the play derives its value. There can be little doubt that this view set the seal on *King Lear*'s reputation as a drama of nihilism: Snider,[43] Jacox,[44] Lloyd,[45] Kreyssig,[46] ten Brink,[47] Dowden,[48] Moulton,[49] Wendell[50] – all, in their different ways, regard the play as a means of shattering Lear to pieces. In fact, there is clear evidence that *King Lear* was losing its hold over the imagination of readers: this can be localised in the artistic failure as a performance of Irving's Lear.[51] I think this loss was largely a matter of the decay of religion: critics had not yet seen the necessity of allowing the work of literature to create its own ethic. That it was not an artistic matter solely is shown by the really startling revival of interest in the play in the twentieth century.

Bradley certainly played an important part in this; what the nineteenth century was looking for, an interpretation that would fit in with preconceived morality, is roughly what Bradley put forward. He rescued the play from nihilism, certainly; but it may be felt that his terms were almost as dubious, positing a happy solution for Lear himself as a person.

One can understand Bradley's difficulty: clearly the description of the play by most of his immediate predecessors was totally out of step with their valuation – passive suffering in a chaotic universe can hardly make for great drama. But Bradley's deflection is no less great: to suggest a happy ending for Lear is to rewrite the play as effectively as Tate did.

So the theoretical question about how to read Shakespeare is quite irrelevant to the issue: Bradley was himself the main sponsor of the salvationist attitude to *King Lear* which his latter-day supporters seek to destroy. Bradley may be inferior to Wilson Knight as a guide to Shakespeare, but this is not a question of theory: Knight relies just as much on character-analysis as Bradley does on poetic symbolism. It is rather a matter of practice: Bradley is less a practical critic than Knight – has his eye, so to speak, too little on the text. Thus the real issue about *King Lear* is something of this sort: that the *play* is an aesthetic experience and makes its moral points in artistic terms; while the *critics*, committed to a form of analytical prose, cannot help rewriting the play into their own terminology, and, in so doing, alter it – explicating what the poet expressed.

The divergence about *King Lear* in modern times will be seen to be between the ideas of critics, not between varying ideas of the play. The controversies rest on a solid basis of agreement; and I do not propose to go into this. There is no need for detailed consideration of the Storm, the Fool, Gloucester's blindness, Lear's madness – about such issues the critics are agreed. This is, after all, the negative part of the play: bleak, troubled. Where the critics differ mainly is in their account of what, positively, the play puts forward: its values, in fact. Here, there are about a dozen points of divergence;[52] and nearly all of them turn on the dual difficulty of criticism. The critic has to assume a degree of explicitness in the play in order to explicate it; and he cannot help, in his explication, making explicit and less precise what the play implied with delicacy and precision. Statement is always less convincing than demonstration. The critics who are convinced by the play – and nearly all regard it as a masterpiece – fail to be convinced by each other's arguments.

Obviously the key to the play is the last speech of Lear. If the play is simply a spectacle of barbarism, it would express blank despair. If, on the other hand, the play is to be re-entitled 'The Salvation of Lear'[53] it will express hope. My aim is to show that these are too simple to be taken as alternatives; too limited to reflect the play's values. At the same time, an element of each of them is comprised in the complexity of the whole, and so will be present to any total appreciation.

I have identified five main areas of opinion among modern critics, varying according to the extent that they take Lear's death scene to be despairing. His death can be seen (a) as the ultimate reconciliation with Cordelia; (b) as a simply moral conclusion to the play; (c) as an illusion which saves Lear pain; (d) as a happy release from pain; and (e) as blank despair. Briefly, one would characterise these groups as being dominated by (a) Freud, (b) Campbell, (c) Bradley, (d) Knight and (e) Tolstoy. The first is the most complete interpretation; the three next deal with simplified aspects of the question (and I would contend that these are not contradictory); while only the fifth represents a disabling deflection and can be discounted as being partial, and, in the last analysis, negative.

Appreciation is not, in other words, as simple as these last critics would like to believe. Shakespeare was quite capable of ending a play on a sustained note of despair: consider, for example, the reaction of Othello when he discovers that Desdemona has been wrongfully killed. But is this what we find here?

> And my poor fool is hang'd: No, no, no life?
> Why should a dog, a horse, a rat have life
> And thou no breath at all? Thou'lt come no more,
> Never, never, never, never, never.
> Pray you undo this button. Thank you sir.
> Do you see this? Look on her. Look, her lips,
> Look there, look there.[54]

Surely this is highly ambiguous. The first phrase has been taken to refer to the Fool:[55] wrongly, I think, but certainly the undercurrent of reference is there – reference to loyalty, perhaps, and innocence, shared alike by the Fool and Cordelia. And then the second half of the line is not a statement but a question: 'no, no, no life?' Lear (as has been remarked)[56] is having immense difficulty in accepting the situation. The next few lines are usually taken as unequivocally despairing; and yet why *should* 'a dog, a horse, a rat have life / And thou no breath at all?' She *has* life, the inference is, but not here and not now, for 'Thou'lt come no more'. And therefore Lear will have to go to her. So the last lines can either mean (as Bradley and most modern critics have thought)[57] Cordelia is coming back to life, or that she is irrevocably dead. If we take the latter inference, though, we have to explain the curiously ecstatic tone of the whole passage. Why are we being asked to focus in this way – why should we 'look there'? Either reading of the passage makes for one interpretation: Lear thinks he is about to be reconciled to Cordelia – either because she is coming back to life and they will live together like Prospero and Miranda, Pericles and Marina, Leontes and Perdita; or else because she is dead and he will join her. This last reading has two possibilities, of course: it may be that there is an afterlife comparable to the romantic purgatory of Prospero's island; or else it may be that there is no afterlife, but even in that case Cordelia and Lear will meet and engage (as they could not do in life) in death.

It is this last point that is brought out by our first group of interpretations. These are primarily concerned with reconciliation and the key consideration here is that of Freud. Because Cordelia 'loves and is silent' she is associated with the dumbness of death. This is certainly true of her final appearance, in Lear's arms: she is, or appears to be, 'dead as earth'. Earth, of course, isn't really dead; it revives with the spring: again, the despair is qualified. Freud demonstrates parallels from folk-tales to show that, in stories about three sisters, very frequently the third is a silent woman, and that the silence is often associated with death. But this could also mean that the third daughter *is* death – 'the Goddess of Death . . . Death itself is nothing but a dead man'. Equally, according to Freud, this would explain Cordelia's stubbornness, since the third of the three Fates was death, and was also known as Atropos, the inexorable.[58]

This brings us to the other great theme of the play, the incest motive. Lear, in the first scene, chooses between his daughters: he divides his kingdom 'among his three daughters, in proportion to the amount of love that each of them expresses for him'. Because Cordelia does not speak, he fails to recognise her love which is so great that it cannot be expressed. Freud relates this to the story of Paris who had to choose between Hera, Athene and Aphrodite. 'We must not be led astray by the fact that Lear's choice is between three *daughters*; this may mean nothing more than that he has to be represented as an old man. An old man cannot very well choose between three women in any other way.'[59] Quite. And this is why Cordelia has to die. In her death, she is reconciled with Lear. Freud goes on to say that Lear is a dying man even at the outset of the play, yet he will not 'renounce the love of women', he insists on hearing how much he is loved. Again, it would seem that such love is not demonstrable. And Freud recalls the final entry of Cordelia in Lear's arms. 'Lear carries Cordelia's dead body on to the stage. Cordelia is dead. If we reverse the situation it becomes intelligible and familiar to us. She is the Death-goddess who, like the

Valkyrie in German mythology, carries away the dead hero from the battlefield. Eternal wisdom, clothed in the primeval myth, bids the old man renounce love, choose death and make friends with the necessity of dying.'[60]

But these need not be alternatives: Lear finds love in death, and it is only in death that he can find love. And just as Lear may be an old man in love with his daughter, so, in the tentative way in which he speaks to Cordelia (for instance, in the 'wheel of fire' speech), he may equally well be a child speaking to its mother. As Freud says of the last scene, 'What is represented here are the three inevitable relations which a man has with a woman – the woman who bears him, the woman who is his mate and the woman who destroys him; or that they are the three forms taken by the one figure of the mother in the course of a man's life – the mother herself, the beloved one who is chosen after her pattern, and lastly the Mother Earth who receives him once more. But it is in vain that an old man yearns for the love of woman as he had it first from his mother; the third of the Fates alone, the silent Goddess of Death, will take him into her arms.'[61] Here Freud is opening out his previous interpretation, rather usefully: Lear does not renounce love in dying into union with Cordelia.

It is this union that is emphasised by the remainder of the group of critics who belong to the general category seeing Lear's death as reconciliation. G. H. Clark bases his interpretation on the thesis that in death Cordelia and Lear are one,[62] and the point is brought out strongly by John Danby when he says that the earlier reconciliation scene could only be a temporary matter – 'Mutual forgiveness in a walled prison' is merely 'a virtuous ivory tower': only in the last plays do Lear and Cordelia find each other again and live happily ever after.[63] Yet what Danby also points out is that a good deal of the feeling here tends towards the last plays – and not just in Lear's part of the 'walled prison' scene, but also in the speeches of and about Cordelia after the storm.[64] One remembers the Gentleman's report of her, her nobility in the 'wheel of fire' scene, and her defiance of her sisters: this is anything but convalescence. So, too, in the detail of Lear's 'God's spies' speech, there is a positive force greatly in excess of the needs of the subject-matter: 'So we'll live / And pray and sing' – more action, perhaps, than is strictly called for. Thus, at the end of the play, the very speeches of Lear that deal with Cordelia dead are instinct with positive energy:

> Had I your tongues and eyes I'd use them so
> That Heaven's vault should crack.[65]

151

And again, there is a note of hope –

This feather stirs, she lives . . .[66]

The implication throughout is one of reconciliation as an aftermath and a justification of the great purgation Lear has undergone –

If it be so
It is a chance which does redeem all sorrows
That ever I have felt.[67]

It is this way in which survival values are affirmed even in the face of death. Critics of our last, Tolstoyan, group may counter that Cordelia does *not* live. The answer might be either that Lear thinks she does or that, if she doesn't, and he dies too, he is nevertheless reconciled with her in death. A bare plot-summary could not suggest this: but the tide of hope runs strong in the actual verse.

Cordelia, Cordelia, stay a little. Ha!
What is't thou say'st? Her voice was ever soft,
Gentle and low, an excellent thing in woman.[68]

The realisation of Cordelia's presence never drops for a moment: again, the fantasy world of the last plays that Danby refers to seems present here. But the important point is that it *is* fantasy: just as presentiment of afterlife, in default of any evidence, must be. All we have here is a question, and though the answer may be in the affirmative, as the positive quality of the verse would suggest, it can be no more than implication. To paraphrase Danby, the corrupt world will allow no terms to goodness.

It is Shakespeare's genius that he has raised incestuous passion to a pitch where it may be identified with goodness; and, in order to justify it, shows the world in its blackest colours. But the passion is only justifiable after the great purge of the madness and the storm, and then only possible in death, either in extinction or in afterlife. Which, the beholders cannot know. Their only evidence is in Lear's reaction. And he seems, as Robert Heilman puts it, to see life in Cordelia's death: 'the illuminating love that came to Gloucester in his blindness'.[69] Perhaps this is an illusion, so far as the spectators are concerned. But they cannot know what is the reality of Lear's illusion, if it is indeed one. He certainly seems to see something: otherwise why 'look there, look there'? But the spectators cannot tell whether it is a return to life, a vision of afterlife, or a focusing on death. And this is true, too, of 'that bourne' from which no traveller returns: as such, the death of Lear is a just representation of death itself.

But the accounts of the other critics in this first group show that this is not all. According to L. C. Knights we are, in this last scene, given a moment of truth: 'What our seeing has been directed towards is nothing less than *what man is* . . . What Lear touches in Cordelia . . . is, we are made to feel, the reality; and the values revealed so surely there are established in the face of the worst that can be known of man or Nature.'[70] Knights goes on to suggest that the point of the drama lies in this stripping away: the very worst that can happen to Lear has happened.[71] Knights makes the important distinction between what Lear sees and what we see: even if Lear's heart breaks at last – and Knights is one of the critics who is of the opinion that Lear died thinking Cordelia alive – this is part of a larger whole, involving Cordelia as well as Goneril and Regan. Lear's love for Cordelia is ground for self-affirming life and energy.[72]

It is to be regretted that Knights does not demonstrate this from an examination of the vivid qualities of the verse: it could readily be done. In fact, it is only by abstracting the plot from the total presentation that the critics of the very last group we shall consider have seen the play as frankly pessimistic, and so distorted its values out of all recognition.

Knights, like Heilman, is concerned with the truth revealed by the drama – what I have called survival values, in fact – rather than with an easy self-identification with any one of its characters.[73] The two critics are in something of a transitional position between Clark and Danby, who emphasise the aspiration towards unity in Lear and Cordelia, and the second group of critics we shall consider – those who take what seems to me a too simply Christian view of the drama. It is easy enough to read all the hope and vitality out of the lines once one gets far enough away from them; but, on the other hand, these qualities must not be emphasised at the expense of others. To do so would be to represent complex values as simple directives. And the play has a very bloody outcome: the question persists, was the suffering worthwhile – even as a lesson? But, as Knights insists, the 'questioning and disturbance', the absence of demonstrable truth, form 'an essential part of a meaning that lies not in a detachable moral but in the activity and wholeness of the imagination'.[74]

If there is a fault common to all the critics of the second group, to which we come now, it is that they tend to detach a moral from the total drama. Here, for example, is O. J. Campbell on the subject.

'Suddenly he makes the blessed discovery that Cordelia is not dead after all, that the breath of life still trembles on her lips . . . In the joy of this discovery, the old man's heart breaks in a spasm of ecstasy.'[75] Here Campbell would seem to be confusing Lear's personal vision with the total presentation of the play. But he goes on: 'For only to earth-bound intelligence is Lear pathetically deceived in thinking poor Cordelia alive. Those familiar with the pattern of the morality play realise that Lear has discovered in her unselfish God-like love the one companion who is willing to go with him through Death up to the throne of the Everlasting Judge. This knowledge enables Lear to meet Death in a state of rapture.'[76]

Previously I suggested that there was an ambiguity in the last scene held between the despair which some critics see in it and the unalloyed joy recognised by others. Here Campbell seems to be tipping the scales over in the latter direction: the questioning and disturbance (to use Knights's words) is a complex value: it will not admit of so simply positive a conclusion. God is not a character in *this* play. We cannot be *sure* that Lear will go with Cordelia before an everlasting judge. We cannot be sure that there is an afterlife for them, let alone what any judgment upon them in such an afterlife would be. All we have is what we are shown.

Yet, though Campbell's is an over-simple reading, it is natural for him to put the emphasis where he does. The verse is ecstatic, but its subject is Lear's contemplation, not the *subject* of Lear's contemplation. If Lear's is 'the heavenly joy of a redeemed soul', the redemption can only have taken place in the play, and this would mean sanctioning Lear's love for Cordelia. What we have is, however, no more than, at most, the implication of redemption.

Where Campbell follows Bradley[77] and R. W. Chambers[78] is in believing that Lear died in an ecstasy of joy.[79] Chambers suggests a parallel with the *Arcadia*;[80] and such a parallel would certainly be accurate with regard to the death of Gloucester. But it is by no means certain that Lear died in just the same way: at least, Shakespeare seems to have taken care not to describe the death of Lear with the same definition as he gave to that of Gloucester. This is not to deny that there is a kindred ecstasy in the final speeches of Lear; but it cannot be simply ascribed to joy at Cordelia's recovery. We cannot be sure whether Lear thinks she recovered or not. So to say Lear died 'in an ecstasy of joy' would seem to be even more simple a reading than Campbell's; and, like Campbell's, it averts attention away from the darker aspects of the drama. The drama is not, in other words, a straightforward appeal to sympathy or to horror: it is a delicate balance between those emotions, a complex pattern involving them.

Bradley has been blamed for the undilutedly joyful interpretation such critics as Campbell and Chambers put upon these lines, but he shows himself more aware than they are of the system of checks that runs throughout the play. His reading seen in context is far more qualified than that of his successors, and he belongs, as a result, to a third group of interpretations.

However, it was Bradley who started off the idea that Lear thought Cordelia was returning to life.[81] With one uninfluential exception,[82] no critic before him had put this idea on record: most critics afterwards – Knights,[83] Campbell,[84] Chambers,[85] Muir,[86] Spencer,[87] Barker[88] – have accepted his reading without question. Bradley was certainly wrong, in the sense that his interpretation of Lear's final ecstasy cannot be demonstrated from the text. And, naïvely, critics such as Miss Everett have assumed that the only other possibility is Lear's death from despair.[89] But this is to ignore the extraordinarily forceful character of Lear's speeches in the last scene. There is no collapse here: rather defiance and surprise. The fact that we cannot prove Lear's ecstasy refers to Cordelia's recovery does not mean that the ecstasy itself does not exist. Shakespeare implies a fantasy-world – in the 'wheel of fire' and 'God's spies' scenes no less than in this one – in which Lear and Cordelia can live together.[90] Where Bradley goes wrong is in not recognising consciously the extent to which this feeling is implied in the text.

> . . . *Thou art a soul in bliss, but I am bound*
> *Upon a wheel of fire that mine own tears*
> *Do scald, like molten lead . . .*[91]
>
> . . . *When thou dost ask me blessing, I'll kneel down*
> *And ask of thee forgiveness: so we'll live*
> *And pray, and sing . . .*[92]
>
> . . . *This feather stirs, she lives: if it be so*
> *It is a chance which does redeem all sorrows*
> *That ever I have felt.*[93]

Bradley certainly feels the force in the last scene, otherwise he would not have been so eager to invent a circumstance that the poet chose not to give us. This is clear from the terms in which he represents the situation: the first sentence is one which we can all agree with. 'And finally, though he is killed by an agony of pain, the agony in which he finally dies is not one of pain but of ecstasy.'[94] But the rest of his reading is less acceptable. It rests upon a gloss of Lear's final lines:

> *Do you see this? Look on her, look, her lips,*
> *Look there, look there!*[95]

And Bradley says of this: 'He is sure, at last, that she lives . . . To us, perhaps, the knowledge that he is deceived may bring a culmination of pain: but if it brings *only* that, I believe we are false to Shakespeare, and it seems almost beyond question that any actor is false to the text who does not attempt to express, in Lear's last accents and gestures and look, an unbearable *joy*.'[96]

Bradley recognises the joy, but also the accumulation of pain, and he shows up unoptimistically in recognising that all this is Lear's illusion. But one cannot take this as a total response to the play: it seems as though Bradley is attempting to impose an external morality on Shakespeare's ending. There is, after all, an irony which he does not mention in the tension between Lear and the onlookers (spectators on stage as well as off it): between what he sees and what they see. It seems that Bradley rests his case on the former; Miss Everett and the Tolstoyans generally opt for the latter.

But Barker is not one of these: he follows Bradley very closely, as indeed have all the actors since Bradley's time – Wolfit, Gielgud and Scofield[97] come most immediately to mind – in representing the end as a joyful one. Barker, though, emphasises even more than Bradley the fact that Lear is deceived – he says that the feather stirring on Cordelia's lips is a last mockery, for Lear is left with Cordelia's broken body in his arms. Even though it be with joy, his heart breaks; and, like Freud, Barker emphasises the way in which Cordelia images and sums up death: 'Dumb and dead, she that was never apt of speech.'[98]

The Bradleian stand may be faulted, then, in its specific interpretation, but not in its recognition of joy as a presence in even the darkest passages of the final scenes. What we may disagree with is the Bradleians' rationalisation of that joy.

The fourth group of critics is even more aware of the suffering and regards Lear's death as a release – the predominant attitude, as we have seen, of the Romantics. The critics of this group are certainly aware of the consummation visualised by Freud, the unity that Clark sees and the 'truth' maintained to be present by both Heilman and Knights; but they see it in terms of relinquishment of life. All the interpretations tend to the description of the play as the apotheosis of the death-wish.

Certainly this element is present in the play, but it is not present in isolation; if it were, the values of the play would amount to no more than a recommendation of death as the true solace of life. And certainly, death-wish is not so prevalent as Derek Traversi (for example) would have us believe. Like Bradley and Barker he emphasises the suffering, and regards the 'heaven' of the play as being an end to men. 'Lear, finally reconciled to his daughter, himself dies with his body in her arms, gaining in death the only relief conceivable in temporal terms from "the rack of this tough world", the course of which has proved so consistently indifferent to the spiritual intuitions which suffering itself has brought painfully to birth.'[99] Yet Traversi does not drain all the values from the play; he is no Tolstoyan. As well as suffering, he sees birth; and he is also aware of the purgative effect this must have on the beholders.

Wilson Knight, on the other hand, emphasises suffering *rather* than birth – 'the again gashed, impaled, quivering soul is more mercifully embalmed in death . . . there is peace merciful and profound and calm'.[100] But this is no more than the death-wish, for Knight says: 'It is utterly dependent for its serenity and tranquillity on the pain it ends . . . This is the absolute peace of death, of nothingness, when consciousness was late stretched, hideously drawn out beyond endurance on the rack of a life whose cruelty brings beauty to birth, whose beauty is its most agonising cruelty. Wherein shall we seek the revelation of *Lear* – in that deathless dream of love, or in this death?'[101]

The answer would seem to be, in both: bearing always in mind that the 'tranquillity' of the last scene is more than that of death, since Lear's questions are full of life images. Knight takes as alternatives two aspects of a synthesis; we may therefore feel that his view is too restrictedly gloomy.

And, for all his attempts to dissociate himself from 'the school of Knight', John Holloway seems very close to Knight's interpretation. He allows that Lear's heart breaks ('Break, heart, I prithee break') and that this is the culmination of an ordeal of torment renewed almost beyond belief ('Vex not his ghost, O, let him pass!').[102] But Holloway cannot be put among the Tolstoyans, because, like Traversi and Knight, he does recognise that there may be some admixture of joy with the grief: he admits Gloucester may be a parallel, but remarks that his death is not simply joyful but rather a paradoxical combination of joy and grief.[103] Although Holloway appears to disagree with Knight on the issue of Lear's death – he denies, for instance, that Lear dies into love[104] – he is at one with him in feeling that the death is primarily a fulfilment in terms of release. 'Union with Cordelia barely proves Lear's salvation: his salvation is what Kent says, release from a life of torment. But that union is the thing to which he rightly belongs.'[105]

In conceding this, Holloway has given away a good deal of his disagreement with our second, Salvationist, group of critics, and so shows the play to be more complex than some of his explicit statements would lead us to believe. Lear is certainly dying into some kind of union with Cordelia, even if it is only an illusion. To use Holloway's words, 'Conceivably Lear is meant to think for a moment that Cordelia is alive . . .';[106] but this, for Holloway, is just another irony in a series of disasters. So his rationalisation of the play tends to over-simplification, after all.[107] Which brings us to the complete sense of disaster shared by the fifth group of critics, those whom I have termed Tolstoyan; and here we have our first major deflection.[108]

Tolstoy found nothing in the play worth praising: he is troubled by its lack of realism, its lack of narrative logic, and by the violence it does to the expectations of the spectator.[109] These latter, however, appear to be geared to the historical novel; and, by such criteria, *Lear* would certainly fail. So far, then, Tolstoy's case is understandable, if mistaken. But his real assault comes when he considers the late scenes and finds them no more than 'awful ravings'.[110] Like his disciple in this line, Orwell,[111] he has extracted the meaning from the verse and so thinks that the suffering had no purpose at all, and that Lear is just as mad at the end as at the beginning. This would, of course, take all moral standpoint away from the play.

A writer of Tolstoy's stature may be allowed his economies. Possibly the great realist and psychologist would not have been either if he could have come to terms with poetic drama. But he has no credentials as an expositor of Shakespeare; and, as Orwell says,[112] the main interest in his essay is that it is written by Tolstoy.

Nevertheless, it is strange that so celebrated an *attack* on Shakespeare should come to the same conclusion as some of Shakespeare's defenders. It may suggest that the 'old' Shakespeare of, say, Barbara Everett[113] has very little to recommend him to a more civilised and humane audience. One respects Tolstoy because, on the evidence before him, he had the courage to attack: the academic critics in this group, working from very much the same evidence, tend to deprecate details, but, with the inertia of convention, to applaud the whole.

Given their excessively simplified modes of reading – like Tolstoy, they abstract the plot from the verse – it is difficult to see quite why they like the play. Possibly their rationalisation bears only a passing resemblance to their reaction; or represents a small sector of it. But it turns the play into a confused melodrama without direction or standpoint.

Let us take W. R. Keast, for instance. He completely ignores the fact that, in the last scene, Albany and the other spectators are living on a plane completely different from that of Lear, and that therefore their comments form a counterpoint to Lear's speeches, not a reinforcement of them. What is for Knight and Holloway a merciful sense of release – 'Break, heart, I prithee break' – is for Keast no more than a cry of despair.[114] The vitality and hope of the feather image completely escape him. Granted that Albany and Kent see an appearance of decay, this is contradicted at once by Lear's words and by his actions – he is strong enough to kill Cordelia's murderer and to bear her body on to the stage. What is missing from Keast's interpretation is not only a sense of tension but a sense of consolation – hence Kent's 'Break, heart' and 'Vex not his ghost' seem to him no more than 'general woe'.[115] Yet, without this consolation, the end of the play would be merely the torture of a vulnerable soul to no ascertainable purpose. Keast certainly recognises Lear's return to his former majesty of utterance, but, in the presence of the dead Cordelia, it seems to him no more than an irony: 'It is now joined to a deep awareness of his humanity as well, precisely when it is too late for him to achieve that which alone makes majesty, authority, even humanity, meaningful and valuable to him.'[116]

But even this is a recognition that Keast's reading is not altogether wrong: he realises, at least, that Lear's majesty is not for this world, though he has no sense of the possibility of Lear's reconciliation with Cordelia in death. Miss Everett does not seem even to sense this ethereal quality in the verse (except, perhaps, as irrelevant 'beauty').[117] Like Freud and Barker, she seems to believe that Cordelia is a summing-up of deadness; but, for her, in an artistic sense, this is curiously inert – imitative form, in fact. She sees no ambiguity in Lear's lines about Cordelia's lips: rather, 'It is natural enough that the central character of a poetic tragedy should finish by directing the attention, as it were, finally to the closed mouth of a dead human being, an image which presents most of what can be said about the physical limitations to an aspiring mind.'[118]

There is no sense of mystery here: no sense, either, that Cordelia is, in those last lines, taking Lear to her – or, as it may seem to Lear, coming back to him. We can't know which it is: in the end, it doesn't matter. Father and daughter are reconciled; the world is shut out. In that reconciliation inheres the value of the play.

Without it, we shall rest with the idea that the play is utterly pessimistic, depicting a chaotic universe. This certainly is the view of J. Stampfer: 'The deaths of Lear and Cordelia confront us like a raw fresh wound where our every instinct calls for healing and reconciliation.'[119] But Stampfer suppresses his instincts in favour of a reading which sees the end as unreconciled savagery and violence. He goes on to demonstrate the viciousness of the world of the play – without, however, demonstrating what he conceives to be its concomitant: that Lear fails to win through to an order in spite of it.[120] Like J. K. Walton,[121] he instances the hopeful speeches of Lear, but like him takes them to be delusion; and he goes farther than Walton in suggesting that, after them, Lear is mad.[122]

The limitation of this mode of reading can be seen in Stampfer's account of the line 'A plague upon you murderers, traitors all' – which he takes to be Lear's protest at Kent disturbing his contemplation of Cordelia.[123] It may be so; but this is rather included in a general denunciation of the world which has parted him from his daughter. But since Stampfer can find no hint of reconciliation in the play, it is no wonder that he takes only the negative side of Lear's lines and limits even that to specific aspects: this is 'a universe where dogs, horses and rats live, and Cordelias are butchered'.[124] Given this view, it is hard to see why Stampfer thinks the play worth discussion. Lear's purgation, for him, leads only to greater and greater misery: the drama plays upon 'the fear . . . that we inhabit an imbecile universe'.[125]

And this seems to be wholly Empson's view of the play – which, as he describes it, is completely demoralised. If Lear does think Cordelia alive, 'one could hardly take this as a consoling dogma . . . The final delusion of Lear is meant to be very sad, but in a way a mercy, as the characters tell us.'[126] For Empson, the play is just one disaster after another. 'I was trying to support the view of George Orwell, that the old man is "still cursing, still not understanding anything" at the end . . . The point is that the story knocks him off his perch; when Cordelia is hanged, he again wants revenge and kills the slave who was doing it.'[127]

The odd thing is that Empson thinks that this view makes for a better play: a sort of song for an unbreakable doll, it seems to me. It is certainly true that we should think worse of Lear if he continued to be a non-attached Yogi; but Danby has given excellent reasons[128] for

160

believing that, in fact, the *state* of being (though not necessarily the poetic aspirations) of the 'I will drink it' and 'Birds in a cage' scenes are rejected. But they are not rejected in favour of cunning and insanity. It is strange that Empson sees Lear as thinking that Cordelia is coming to life,[129] and yet turns this into something far more pessimistic than those critics who would reject that view. There is no evidence at all for Empson's contention that Lear has got on the wrong side of the next world as well as this one;[130] we simply don't know, and all we can do is hope: this seems to me the precise flavour of the verse in this scene.

No, no, no life?[131]

is a question, not of dogma.

And this is true, too, of our enquiry. We cannot, to put it crudely, know whether or not King Lear died smiling. At the end of the play we are in exactly the same position as the spectators on the stage. We can sense the tension between aspiration and apparent reality, between hope in the verse and despair in the plot. Most of the critics who have dealt with the play seem to me wrong in opting for one or the other of these possibilities: the values are more complex than that. In the beginning, I spoke of the play's 'ethical caution': and it is a fault of the criticism it has attracted that it has not exhibited a like tact.

On the other hand, the varying degrees of emphasis certainly expose different aspects of the drama; and though each reading may be termed a simplification, surprisingly few are completely off the point. Those that are seem to be at one in adopting a view of the play that would condemn it as a piece of nasty and irresponsible trifling: brutality for its own sake. But Shakespeare was adumbrating a morality far more delicate than that of his critics. He had an immensely difficult task, for he was implying a heaven without stating it: showing a possibility of reconciliation while conceding it to *be* impossible in life as we know it.

The haunting and romantic verse of Lear's last scenes with Cordelia seem to me instinct with this feeling. And by identifying Cordelia with death, Shakespeare dignifies the incest motif, just as he justifies it by denigrating the rest of the world. By making the world so bad, he makes Lear's impulses good. Even so, he cannot allow them to work in the world.

The values of a work of literature, then, are nothing like so straightforward as an ethical imperative. The pride, aggressiveness or lust of the tragic hero is assessed in the way in which it is presented before us;

the judgement is implicit in the manifestation. At the same time we are made to see that such passions are the force that drives the world; without them, society would be drained of energy, polite, static, febrile, conformist.

On the other hand, if these passions are allowed their fullest sway, they will act their way out into disaster; the individual desire, unchecked, can bring about the destruction of a society. The vitality of an impulse need be no recommendation. What is good for an unspecialised beast of the jungle will be bad for a closely knit community of social beings.

So the work of literature, like the world itself, strikes an uneasy balance between individual desire and social checks. For the tragic hero, his desires are real and therefore must be fulfilled; for the spectators they may be actively dangerous, and so must be checked.

The great tragedy adumbrates these desires in all their intensity; at the same time, it allows them to act themselves out and sets before us the resultant disasters. Yet even in disaster there is fulfilment: the catastrophe works backwards, implying a freedom impossible to this world, a freedom where desires may be given their full rein without, in the process, disrupting society. Over and over again, art enacts this tragic paradox: human passion surviving for ever, the fierce ardour of the wild beast stalking at large in a stable society.

And we, as the spectators, share in this sense of fulfilment. To take these passions at their face value, isolated as realistic detail, would be to lose all sense of dramatic context; rather we share in a morality enacted by an aesthetic experience. Our expectations are slaked in seeing a conclusion which is at once awful warning and completion of a logical cycle. Only in art can freedom and law be reconciled.

The great work, then, provides no simple panacea, no straightforward solution to the moral dilemma. It is the philosopher, not the artist, who legislates for mankind; the work of literature is not a system of precepts but a tragic example. It does not state its values but acts them out in such a way that they are judged through the very manner of enactment.

And so, because criticism is a branch of philosophy, we find the critic conceptualising this enactment and thus simplifying it. The individual view, however sensitive, is very limited. A full rationalisation of a work might be a consensus of all possible interpretations; even so, much would remain that could not be accounted for in rational terms.

How, then, are we to improve our mode of understanding? One

way is to recognise the character of critical divergence: to set individual views side by side, to note the pattern of variation, cause of divergence. In its turn, this would show beyond doubt that divergences are of different qualities; and a recognition of this would be a recognition of qualitative degrees of value and of communication in the different works considered.

In spite of modern developments, criticism is still a clumsy mode of judgement: it abstracts, simplifies, asserts; seeks, in fact, to replace the work of literature with something else that is hardly worth the having.

But once we recognise that no one man can hold all the answers, the onus is on us to compare his views with those of his peers. Clearly the way to do this is to trace a path through a complex of argument. The next step forward in criticism is one that would turn that activity from dogma into discussion.

A Group Approach to Criticism

Granted that criticism has made great strides in the present century, is there no further step to be taken? It would not do to be too complacent: the work of the great critics reflects primarily upon the past, and contemporary reviewing is at a woefully low ebb. Moreover, there is no safeguard against the extraordinary mistakes made by even the greatest critics – Leavis on Bottrall, for example, or Winters on Daryush.

Less spectacular, but equally urgent, is the need to correlate our interpretations. Over and over again a critic will rush into print the Final Interpretation of some overwhelming masterpiece that has been with us for ages – an action which suggests either that he has totally misunderstood his text or that he has simply isolated some aspect of it which chances never to have been rationalised before.

In practice, the variation in quality between modes of error – the distinction, for example, between misreading and over-simplification – has never been recognised. We are still taking all dissensions to be equal in degree. Therefore any progress in criticism will have to juxtapose differing interpretations more closely than ever before; must recognise and point out the difference in quality of such dissensions.

It is one thing for two critics to fall out over a misreadable text: each will be supplying his own fiction to eke out a private fantasy. It is quite another if two critics differ over a great work: each may be seeing a separate aspect, but the aspects will be congruent. Between these extremes there is a range of discussion which can best be typified in terms of quality; and such a typification can only take place through some form of discussion as group activity.

The closest criticism of our time probably took place in the practical criticism classes of F. R. Leavis. The results of some of these investigations have been written up in *Scrutiny*, notably in such articles as ' "Thought" and Emotional Quality' and 'Reality and Sincerity'. But it would have been fascinating to have some record of the actual discussion. As a former student of Leavis's, I can testify to an urgency, as well as a freedom of discussion, with which the classes of that great teacher have all too seldom been credited.

But to value Leavis highly as teacher and critic is not to follow him slavishly: rather one would regard him as having laid down the practical foundations on which subsequent critics can build.

Once graduated, I sought to take Leavis's approach into the modern sector. In 1955 I founded a creative writing group in London: its procedure was based very much on the practice of Leavis. All discussion derived from texts of poems or prose fictions, read by their authors, turn and turn about. These were duplicated and circulated the week before the work in question was to be read. This meant that members were able to acquaint themselves with the subject of discussion, and, with the text before them, could comment upon the poem or story and not upon something less relevant – the author's life, or philosophy, for instance. No effort was spared to find recruits for this Group. It was the reverse of a clique; the only criteria of entry were intelligence and seriousness. Such criteria are personal matters; mistakes, no doubt, were made. And yet it may be held that the truly serious, truly intelligent man will possess those qualities in such measure as to render them far from ambiguous.

There have been other gathering of writers before, from the Mermaid Tavern to G. S. Fraser's soirées in the fifties; none, I think, so selective in clientèle or so systematically devoted to close perusal and discussion of the text. At length, in 1963, the Oxford University Press published a selection from the work of this Group – called, modestly enough, *A Group Anthology*.

I cannot pretend that this compilation was favourably received. Publicity it certainly had; an embarrassing amount of attention was showered upon us, all the way from the fashion-mongering dithyrambs of *Time Magazine* to sharp little darts stuck into us by younger contemporaries at Oxford and Cambridge.

The interesting thing is that individual members of the Group had already been separately recognised: the central figures were Peter Redgrove, Peter Porter, Martin Bell, Edward Lucie-Smith, George MacBeth and myself; and every one of us has had his advocates at one time or another.

Why, then, was our anthology so savaged? I think this is a familiar case of response outrunning rationalisation. What the reviewers objected to was not so much the individual poems – many of which, rightly or wrongly, they had already acclaimed elsewhere – but the very idea, the enterprise, of a group. What they objected to was the conception of writers meeting regularly to discuss each other's work – indeed, they objected to the very nature of the discussion.

It is those who are unable to analyse who deprecate analysis. Once we have discredited close attention to the text, all sorts of anomalies can arise – biographical criticism, source-hunting, lionising, allusiveness, point-scoring – all of which make a critic's work so much more easy. But there is no substitute for critical analysis: the virtue lies not so much in the conclusion reached as in the reasons evinced for holding it. One may disagree with one's adversary, but at least one knows where he stands.

Critical analysis certainly exists in the work of the great critics; in, especially, that of Leavis and Empson and Winters. But there it is one man's analysis of his personal reaction to a text which, for various reasons, may not be available to him. Leavis, indeed, went a step further with his accounts of classwork – these I should regard as the most devastatingly original criticism of their period. But the Group went even further than that: bringing to bear the Leavisian awareness where it was most needed – on the work of our own time, our own work, before editors, publishers and reviewers had got hold of it. And we brought this awareness to bear not as individual statement, however well intentioned, but as active discussion. There was the additional check that all participants in discussion would be, at one time or another, contributors to the readings. This was a genuinely collaborative enterprise.

It is true that the Group always had a chairman, and that it was his job to set the area of discussion and to guide it relevantly. But he could not be more than *primus inter pares*; and was, at heated moments of debate, hardly so much as that. Contemporaries were talking to contemporaries, practitioners to fellow-practitioners; we had our differences, of course, but discussion for us was a means of sorting them out.

This gave rise to dissensions, some of which raised crucial points of critical theory. At their best our discussions had, I should say, the characteristics one would look for in progressive criticism: they juxtaposed sharply divergent reactions to a given text, and they defined the differing qualities of the dissensions embodied in them. I propose, in the remainder of this chapter, to quote four of these out of the many hours of discussion that have been preserved on tape. These four discussions all date from 1959, a period of the Group when discussion was at its most flexible.

We begin with highly subjective reactions arising out of an almost

166

totally incomprehensible poem: for the benefit of the author, who has done better work since, I should prefer this to remain anonymous.

MEETING BETWEEN STRANGERS

Across the room's thin silence broke
His words. Imploring her, his body willed
Response, commanding hers to speak,
Demanding from her what she felt to be
Impossible, the leap across their death,
A resurrected warmth in the chilled
Silence of tombs. He could offer nothing
But exchange of death for death in the sombre
Heat of the body's lust. He would annexe her body
Only to indulge in a ghastly rhumba for the dead
Against the sound of the living song in her head,
Which warned her not to compromise her freedom
For a love already cold.

      But she recalled
The sentimental moments and the passions
Their youth had shared – the swift, shy meetings,
And the trust between them, sureties of their loving –
And looking at him, she believed it almost possible
To sweep aside (as if they had been broken plates)
The fragmentary, scattered pieces of their life.
Then pity for the face that watched her come back
Limply from a world of jaded snapshots,
Turned her to him with a gesture of submission.

But only to find the aching flowers thrust out
In a thirst of sense and crushed against her,
Petals bruised and falling, and herself pursued
By fugitive scents that stabbed her down
Into the hollows of the temporal dead –
Till free of him at last, and able to creep
Into the vacant body, and armour, of sleep.

An individual critic may assert this poem to be impenetrable; but the discussion I shall quote now demonstrated this almost beyond question.

Lucie-Smith I must say I think this poem contains one very fine passage – the passage containing 'And looking at him she believed it was almost possible' down to 'submission'. This is the sort of writing

167

which I find very much alive, I must say. I don't think the poem sustains it, though.

McLAREN Well, I think the end is very fine, so we've got two passages between us.

LUCIE-SMITH I don't get the end – I don't see how the image works in the end. Perhaps you can explain it to me?

McLAREN I don't think it's a thing I can explain, it's just that I feel that this continual preoccupation of the poet's with words and their sound – which for me usually doesn't work – here seems at last to have worked properly. I do find that whereas I didn't at the beginning of it catch on to it properly – it didn't move me at all – the end did, and the image, although not easily to be explained, did seem to me effective – it did have what was presumably the right kind of effect.

LUCIE-SMITH No, I must say I find the last passage the failure of the poem. I think the opening is certainly explicable – I don't think it's as good as the passage I've pointed to, because I don't think it has quite the sharpness and definition and focus. But the last lines from 'but' to 'sleep' I find very difficult to construe, and I find them very confused in imagery – I mean to say, 'aching flowers', to take a simple example, creates all sorts of difficulties for me. It doesn't strike me as being a straightforward example of synaesthesia, as you get in Edith Sitwell, for example.

BELL I think it's a question of the sounds being pressed too much on you – you have 'aching', and 'vacant', in the last line – and I can see what the sound is doing, more or less, not necessarily in an abstract way, but a way in which language doesn't usually work.

McLAREN I suppose it's because I prefer poetry with images rather than poems which are not, because poems which are written in plain statement have to be very good indeed to be impressive, and I don't think that the statement of the beginning interests me particularly, and I don't think it is sufficiently well-constructed to evoke the proper response.

LUCIE-SMITH Yes, I mean to say you say blandly that you prefer poems written in images – well, I find great difficulty in finding any one complete image here. I mean to say they melt into each other at such a rate that I find it very difficult to find where I am – this is my difficulty . . .

McLAREN Well, there are only two – you've got 'flowers' and 'sense' and they're connected together.

LUCIE-SMITH Yes, but what are they doing, flowers and sense connected together? *How* are they connected? What are they *doing* with each other? How are they operating? I mean to say, to be bloody-minded, what *is* a hollow of the temporal dead?

McLAREN I think that *is* being a bit bloody-minded, Teddy.

LUCIE-SMITH   Well, what is it? Tell me! Define it for me!

McLAREN   Well, if it's a good image you don't define it. It's an image which I'm more or less prepared to let go – I don't know what it means, exactly, but I'm prepared to let it go.

MARGARET OWEN   Surely the 'aching flowers' passage connects back with the 'sentimental moments' earlier on in the poem, I should have thought.

LUCIE-SMITH   Yes, Peggy, granted that it's a simile for 'sentimental moments', well if it were developed again, so to speak, I wouldn't be complaining. But it's the fact that it – so to speak – that that line isn't hung on to. 'Only to find the aching flowers thrust out' is well enough by itself by reference backwards, but that when you go forwards that the difficulty arises, isn't it? 'In a thirst of sense' immediately creates a difficulty for me because it introduces a side-track, I think.

MARGARET OWEN   No, because that connects back again, I should have thought, to something earlier – 'exchange of death for death in the sombre / Heat of the body's lust'. I think it connects back there.

HOBSBAUM   I think that's right. I've been desperately trying to work out 'the hollows of the temporal dead'. I think it must refer to 'He could offer nothing / But exchange of death for death in the sombre / Heat of the body's lust'. If it doesn't, I can't imagine what it's all about. I think the 'aching flowers' may refer to the 'sentimental moments', but it's more likely to be her attempt to get into some kind of – I mean she yearns for some kind of contact with him, and this way she attempted to get into contact – whatever she put out – you see, these *feelers* – one would say, wouldn't one, in cant phrase? – were ruthlessly bashed back at her. In other words, she's crushed back, like that. (Banging his fists against each other.) I think that's what it means.

McLAREN   But actually they're put out by *him* and crushed against *her*.

HOBSBAUM   I think it should read 'But only to find *her* aching flowers thrust out / In a thirst of sense and crushed against her'.

McLAREN   No, I think it's about *him* trying to get into some kind of relationship with her. It then goes on to talk about her. And then we come back only to find that she has worked herself into an attitude of submission, only to find that, really, submission is not the right attitude; that what she was expecting with this gesture of submission was not what she got.

HOBSBAUM   So it's *his* aching flowers?

McLAREN   It's his aching flowers crushed against *her*.

HOBSBAUM   I can't see that, honestly I can't.

McLAREN   They can't be crushed against her at the same time as she's thrusting them out.

HOBSBAUM You see, if he isn't going to respond in that way – if he isn't going to, in other words, take up whatever gesture she's making towards him, that's a rebuff, you see, a rebuff back at her. Mind you, I think it's so ambiguous and obscure I wouldn't like to take that too far. I mean, I've just been working out in my mind while we've been talking a case for precisely the opposite of what I've been saying, and I think I could make one, which is rather upsetting. I think it is very obscure, and, quite frankly, although I can see that there's a good deal of feeling that comes over in spite of the extraordinarily turgid texture of this last passage –

MCLAREN Those were the grounds on which I defended it.

HOBSBAUM I can see what you're getting at, Robin, but I side with Teddy in so far as – if you can't really understand it, if it comes over almost in spite of itself, it's not very much of a success.

BELL It seems to me actually to come *through* the turgidity, not in spite of it, but through. It's rather like some early George Barker poems.

HOBSBAUM Well, you must admit, mustn't you, the ideas 'aching flowers' and 'thirst of sense' have a definite force in themselves, even though one can't quite find a meaning. That's the puzzling part about it.

HANNAH HOBSBAUM 'Hollows of the temporal dead' seemed to me to be quite clear – you're talking about death as a sort of waste – you don't know what you're going into – hollow in that sense – there's nothing. And 'temporal' because it's just sleep, isn't it? It's just a temporary thing. Is that it? That's how I took it anyway. I couldn't see what the difficulty was about understanding what the image meant.

LUCIE-SMITH Well, I must say, I think with this line you pays your money and you takes your choice.

HOBSBAUM There are too many alternative meanings for this line.

MCLAREN Well, in a sense you might say that's a very good thing on the Eliot principles of understanding poetry. Eliot once wrote more or less that you pays your money and you takes your choice. I mean that's what you do do, in fact. You don't abstract the meaning that the poet means, you abstract what you can from it. Of course, if you were conscious of four different meanings at once, then I agree with you that it's a failure.

HOBSBAUM Not exactly, no. I mean this is what Empson was trying to do in *Seven Types*, wasn't it? He was trying to say that – I think this much, that different areas of meaning in one given phrase can define each other – they can limit, in other words, the application of the phrase. But I think when you can think separately of four different things and at least two of them quite opposed – you see the kind of eternal death which goes on and on and another sense in which it could be just a metaphor for death as used previously, 'exchange of death for death in the sombre heat of the body's lust' – in other words, they compete, the opposed meanings – I can't see what's gained by that kind of ambiguity. I call it uncontrolled ambiguity.

ROSEMARY JOSEPH I must say this poem had a definite effect on me when I read it, you know, it did arouse an emotional response in me, but now that you've analysed it . . .

MARGARET OWEN It's something that happens to me very often.

HOBSBAUM Well, you know why, don't you? It's very often true that one reads an awful lot into a poem – that one re-creates the poem and rewrites the poem practically, often without realising it. I think that's the reason for the popularity of a good many people who just give a kind of vague indication of a poem on the page and you can build up a whole lot of things round it.

If the poem is not impenetrable, why do the readings of the Group diverge so wildly? Clearly Miss Owen and myself could not both have been right about 'aching flowers', the phrase we discussed; and my belief now, after this lapse of time, is that neither interpretation will hold: the phrase will simply not co-exist with its adjacent images. A similar divergence takes place around 'hollows of the temporal dead'. Individual readers may think that they have the meaning clear in their minds, but the phrase cannot take at one and the same time the various interpretations put upon it. Perhaps we should fall back upon a wholly subjective approach to the poem: when asked to define his reactions, one of our participants insisted that they were indefinable. But this makes one wonder why he bothered to come at all to a meeting which assumed, in fact, that texts were capable of being discussed. Or possibly one should argue that it is the poem that is indefinable; in which case the onus is on the proponent of such a view to demonstrate what makes this a viable mode of poetry.

Why, after all, publish such a poem? Given the fact that we would read into the text our own predilections, would it not be healthier to write poems of our own? A subjective mode of approach may make sense of the poem for one individual reader, but it would certainly get in his way when he came to read work which needed no such concession: Marvell's *Garden*, say, Herbert's *Sacrifice*, Blake's *Tyger*.

Our discussion concluded with a key theoretical point: that there are qualitative degrees of ambiguity, the worst of which is totally disruptive, and that the poem exhibits this latter in no small measure. Hence, I would say, in its turn, the low quality of the dissension: the divergences derive from frantic attempts on the part of individual readers to give the poem a sense and shape which the author was unable to bestow upon it. These attempts stem from different readers with different emotive predilections. Thus, in default of a stimulus from the poem, the reader will supply a referent of his own; and, being his own, it will not resemble that of another reader sufficiently to render the poem discussible. In a sense, the people at this meeting were not discussing the poem; they were each putting forward shadow-poems of their own, and, of course, failing to agree about them. Philosophically speaking, no discussion took place.

No doubt this poem, and the consequent dissension, is at an extreme; but it is an extreme of quality, not kind. There are many gradations in between before we reach a point at which divergences may be reconciled. For example, a poem may suggest an attitude without fully acting it out; this is common enough when the attitude suggested is an anti-social one. And whenever an author stops short of a complete meaning, for whatever reasons of taste or morality, there will not be wanting critics to complete his trajectory for him.

Martin Bell is the author of *Reasons for Refusal*, a classic poem which affirms the reality of the individual beyond his immediate physical circumstances. But he is also the author of *Manicure*, a poem which attempts to stand this attitude on its head; suggesting that we are the prisoners of our bodies and hinting – but only hinting – that our bodies make remarkably nasty prisons. Had he gone on to demonstrate this, the poem would have broken into its contingent bits, as the previous example did. Writing is a social matter: it is remarkably hard to use poetry as a means of asserting anti-social attitudes.

Obviously there is no attitude so anti-social that somebody has not held it at some time somewhere, but such a stance involves a built-in contradiction. Supposing one actually believes life to be revolting; wouldn't the honest way out be to commit suicide? Clearly Bell doesn't believe this: he is attempting a tactful verse exercise, trying to say the unsayable. But the text defeats itself, if not quite so whole-heartedly as explicit statement would.

MANICURE

Each finger-nail ugly again,
Must be clipped to a crisp moon.
Plain horny wedges,
A city's dirt under the edges,
Could sharpen to ten weapons,
Razors, flick-knives. Mustn't happen.
An urbane law

> (*Not nature red in tooth and claw*)
> *Says what nails are for:*
> *Combing the eye-brows neatly,*
> *Scratching oneself, discreetly,*
> *Squeezing blackheads, scraping corns from toes,*
> *And picking one's nose.*

There is an evasive quality here, of asserting and taking back one's assertion within the one poem. The evasiveness was brought out in the resultant discussion.

H. HOBSBAUM I think this poem is really in bad taste.

BELL It's meant to be, Hannah.

REDGROVE Yes, you see?

H. HOBSBAUM I don't see what it achieves apart from – as well as write this poem you might as well write about the most degrading things you can do, and degrade the human being as much as you can.

HAMPTON It states a matter-of-fact detail which goes in the centre into a suggested image and comes back to the matter-of-fact observation.

REDGROVE I don't take it so seriously as *that*.

HAMPTON I don't like the poem myself.

LUCIE-SMITH I think it's a jolly good poem. I think it's on a very relevant subject – the inescapable ugliness of physical being.

REDGROVE A civilised tone.

MACBETH It's a sort of literary exercise awfully like Graves in a way.

PORTER It *is* like Graves. But when one says that, what has one said? This is not a good poem because none of the dirt is moral dirt – it's all accidental dirt, isn't it? It's the dirt of scrap – all of these things – 'Human beings are trapped in their bodies and they can scratch themselves at that time, therefore, get used to it.'

HAMPTON They do grow these things after all, so why –?

REDGROVE The middle part surely images a beastliness underneath.

PORTER Yes, but it puts a 'not' in front of it. It's a rejection, a moral rejection.

REDGROVE You must do something deliberately to do that.

PORTER Rather a good poem, I think, Philip, in some ways?

HOBSBAUM I am amazed that so much praise . . . I think it's completely trivial. Why should one take an interest in this poem, actually, Peter, would you say?

PORTER Because he takes the common human function – clipping his nails or leaving them unclipped – and he uses that to show up a very big thing indeed, and it's all done in a very short space. It seems

173

to be nicely done in so far as one can talk about it technically, and it's the sort of short poem which has sufficient density to arouse you to think not outside of the words that are actually in the poem but to think relevantly to what the poem talks about and yet to extend what it's saying without necessarily introducing irrelevant gestures.

HOBSBAUM Well, quite frankly, I think that what is suggested is so much more important than what's actually presented that you can't help in reading this poem considering a great deal of what lies outside the poem. And therefore I take the poem rather as a kind of suggestion than as an achievement.

PORTER I think that's true, but I think there's nothing which lies outside the poem which hasn't got its fuse in the poem itself. I think the poem is a lot less trivial than you suggest.

REDGROVE I don't know why either of you go outside the poem for these suggestions. Isn't this the one example of keeping clean which can illustrate, as it were, the feeling about being clean and tidy and civilised, within reasonable bounds? He chooses the nails because this is the thing which illustrates this.

LUCIE-SMITH Well it makes a moral point as well. I think the same contrast is the physical squalor, which is inevitable, with the moral squalor, which isn't.

HOBSBAUM I'm sorry, but I think that's a tremendous statement – which may, in effect, be *implied* in the poem, but honestly – *moral* squalor?

H. HOBSBAUM Where's the moral point?

LUCIE-SMITH 'Could sharpen to ten weapons, razors, flick-knives. Mustn't happen.'

REDGROVE 'Mustn't happen.'

PORTER Why should otherwise the suggestion of the nails – since commonly only very few people fight with their nails – why should the nails be suggested as weapons were he not suggesting something outside?

HOBSBAUM I didn't take this as moral squalor, exactly. I took it more as being a relapse into some kind of savagery.

LUCIE-SMITH Well, surely the state of savagery is a state of moral squalor.

HOBSBAUM I don't think so at all. It's amoral rather than immoral.

PORTER Savages have a code of morality.

HOBSBAUM Well, then, Teddy's whole case falls to the ground. It just shows you, as soon as you start working out what the poem means, you've all got contradictory interpretations. It shows you how much of what you're saying is outside the poem.

LUCIE-SMITH Well, everyone's got contradictory interpretations of Hobbes, who runs to dozens of books . . .

PORTER But you could have contradictory interpretations about the greatest poet who ever lived, surely?

HOBSBAUM Not quite like this, Peter, no. I think the thing that makes a poem a poem at all is there would be some kind of agreement in, surely, what the poem's about and what it is and what it says.

HAMPTON I think there would be *some* kind of agreement, yes.

HOBSBAUM All the weight of the argument tends to rest on things which are more or less suggested in the poem and which extend out of it and run up this argument on the extensions, it seems to me, rather than what's in the poem. 'Moral squalor' and 'savagery' – there's a piece of basic disagreement for you right away.

There are two possible ways of taking this poem. Either one can, like Lucie-Smith and my wife, extend one set of its implications into a full statement against life; or one can, as Porter and Redgrove did, read into another set of implications a personal morality. In the first instance, one would read the poem from the last line back, ignoring carefully placed hints to the contrary; in the second instance, one erects these hints – 'mustn't happen' is one example – into an ethical enactment. Thus the poem can be read either as a case against physical being or a real concern in favour of it. It is, however, difficult to see how it can be both: Lucie-Smith and Redgrove both appear to like the poem, but their defence was couched in very different terms; and my wife, who shared Lucie-Smith's interpretation of the poem, did not share his favourable opinion of it. In little, this disruptive ambiguity may be seen in the divergence about the 'ten weapons' of the nails. Either the lengthening of the nails can be seen as primitive savagery or as decadent squalor; but there is no way in which it can be both.

One could certainly argue that this is a less chaotic poem than the first one, and this can be shown not only from the text but from the quality of the dissension arising out of it. Each of the two possible readings is consistent within itself; and given the reading, the images in the poem will be more or less congruent. But this is the congruence of evasion. What occurs is that the phrases inapposite to a given interpretation tactfully recede; as 'mustn't happen' receded for those who took the poem as a statement against life. However, this is only to say that such phrases are very lightly touched upon in the first place; they hardly amount to image or enactment, for an emphasis of this kind on the part of the poet would have brought about chaos.

So what we have here is a half-poem or ghost-poem; not an un-poem deriving from its readers' various imaginations, as in the first example, but one whose outlines are lightly suggested by its author relying upon a wholesale filling-in from his readers – which, of course, takes place. The theoretical point emerges that, once the readers, in discussion, started to work out what the poem meant, they ended up with contradictory interpretations; interpretations, moreover, that bore no relation to their valuation of the poem. And this is because the weight of argument was resting on things which were *suggested* in the poem and not *enacted* in it.

It may be felt that the whole discussion, together with the points arising out of it, seems too heavyweight for the poem by which it was occasioned; but I will venture to say that this is a point against the poem rather than the discussion.

An analogous dissension, rather higher in quality, came out of Lucie-Smith's *Rook-Shooting at Sunset* – which, for me, practically defines the phrase 'minor poem'.

ROOK-SHOOTING AT SUNSET

I see the farmer stand, back to the sun,
Half-sleeping birds in panic round his head,
A squat, phlegmatic man who aims his gun,
Fires, then saunters on with heavy tread.

The unkempt grass shows darker where he stood,
His echoing shots are drowned by the harsh cries
Amid the branches of the meagre wood
And he remains unconscious of my eyes.

Why do I stare? What is it holds me still
This broken cobweb tugging at my shoe?
I'll dream these shots tonight, and kill and kill
Birds that already stiffen in the dew.

Most people would take this to be a good poem because most people don't want to be deeply stirred by poetry; hence the current vogue for poems on innocuous subjects – small birds, furry beasts, life on the farm, and the like. Behind this poem stands, perhaps especially, Tennyson, a poet who skated very skilfully over the surface of life. And, on this level, the poem works: that is to say, it works as a description. Nobody could accuse Lucie-Smith of lacking eyes or ears; it is not what is *in* the poem that can be faulted, it is what is left out. And, challenged on this point, individual members of the Group sought to read into these attractive and innocuous lines a fear of death and thoughts about killing all their own.

HOBSBAUM Like George, I can't help feeling something is wrong which I don't think can be pointed to in local effects. I think one would have to take a rather broader view of it and try and tackle the poem as a whole. You see I don't really enter into this experience at all, it seems to me something which is presented, and much of the interest in it is in the *way* it's presented rather than in *what* is being presented. In other words, I can't exactly see why I should be interested in it. It doesn't seem to me to be anything that's particularly interesting in itself. I don't think that, however attractive you make an experience, unless you can give some kind of urgency or reason to make somebody who hasn't actually shared this experience interested, the poem is bound to remain a very limited thing.

PORTER The last two lines, Philip, do do that for you. This is a kind of unconscious prerecognition of one's own desire to destroy.

REDGROVE Yes, quite. I wish you could take that farther, your dissatisfaction with this, because it seems to me, at any rate, a common human experience, this feeling of tenderness and at the same time the wish to destroy that to which you feel tender.

HOBSBAUM You see now, this is the thing. While I can understand how you see that in the poem, and while I should imagine this must be the explicit intention of the poem, I just don't think enough is said about this feeling or enough of this feeling is given to us put in action to justify that kind of comment, that in fact this is a poem about the love of killing. I just don't think it is. To me it seems a descriptive poem in the sense that it describes a series of actions, possibly, or a pure action and something happening to someone as a result of that action. It does *not* go – explore, as I would say . . .

PORTER It doesn't give you the link, I agree, but it expects you to take the link.

REDGROVE To draw this conclusion – yes, fair enough.

HOBSBAUM If this is a poem about the love of killing, it should do rather more . . .

BELL No, no, it's not –

HOBSBAUM I'm not saying it is. I don't think it is. I think this is a descriptive poem and, as I say, I think that does imply a limitation.

MACBETH Exactly. I think its success is really due only to the first two stanzas, and there the description is very vivid, it's not just visual. One gets a sort of kinaesthetic quality in the 'fires' line and one gets the sounds – one gets all sorts of things. It's sensuously vivid, but the related experience leaves me absolutely cold. It doesn't convince me that that was why the poem was really written.

REDGROVE But you might draw a much vaster experience from the contrast of 'phlegmatic', 'aims his gun and fires', and '*saunters* off

177

with heavy tread' – but contrasted with the birds 'in panic round his head' and 'stiffening in the dew' – the casual thing.

MACBETH The thing is that eventually to me it seems all made up. It doesn't move me, it doesn't convince me about the repulsive thing.

PORTER The whole point, it seems to me, is conveyed in the tenses. To a certain extent what it's done – if you are not really going to kill people, then you can recreate in your own dreams killings that have been done ahead. You kill, in the last two lines, kill *and* kill, that is to say you keep killing in a dream birds that are already dead, and this seems to be the whole point of the poem is that seeing the act of death in life, you recreate it in your own dream as though you were killing those things which you already know from your preknowledge are dead. I took that to be the point of the poem.

MACBETH I don't take that. I think he's remembering experience, but instead of being the farmer who's killing the birds, it's he who's killing them.

HAMPTON I didn't get anything like that. I got it as a sort of resistance – reaction to the act of killing. One is horrified, terrified.

LUCIE-SMITH Surely the point is, I mean to say, it's this point that it's both an acceptance that you can identify with and a rejection.

BELL Actually, I think it's much more balanced than either Philip or George . . .

HOBSBAUM Oh, *I* didn't imply that there was a deeper meaning. I was questioning the fact that people had been reading this deeper meaning into it.

PORTER I quite flagrantly took a deeper meaning, yes.

BELL But what do you mean by a deeper meaning? It has been defined as a horror of one's own sympathy with the act of killing.

PORTER But there's no control in this. The last two lines emphasise that this is outside your control. What you dream is under no circumstances under the control of your conscious will, what you dream is entirely at the mercy of your subconscious.

HAMPTON Your subconscious may have a revulsion.

REDGROVE A sympathy with the sensuous act of killing.

HAMPTON It may be partly made up of sympathy and of antipathy – a revulsion to it. And the image comes out of that.

PORTER I took the poem to mean simply that the fact it's happened so often – it's happened in ordinary human life – that you come across something in your own life which you take no particular notice of – the idea that this poem actually recognises that you *do* take no notice of it – and later you dream the same circumstance in your own dream, the point about this poem is to take something, which, on the whole, even if you were appalled by it, you still know is outside your own control and then you dream it into your own life.

HOBSBAUM I think this rather proves Martin's point about there being an ambivalence of feeling in the poem. I still think that whether because the feeling tends to balance itself out or because, as I think, really it begins as a kind of – shall we say – an un-moral (meaning there's nothing particularly implied, at least at the beginning, or seems not to me) poem, and then becomes increasingly perhaps a more moral one, maybe because of that, but whatever it is I do think, you know, it's not quite either a poem about killing in the sense that any attitude is really given to us towards killing, nor is it really anything more, I would say, than is the sum of those first two stanzas. I don't find the third one does more than add a good many – I suppose – overtones – brings forward questions – but I think those rhetorical questions in those first two lines are largely because the poet hasn't himself made up his own mind.

LUCIE-SMITH That's the point of it.

BELL Don't you think there's something in 'Half-sleeping birds in panic round his head'?

HOBSBAUM Yes, now you've mentioned it I could see it. It didn't occur to me.

MACBETH I took that to be a brilliant descriptive line. I don't find it brought to a conclusion.

BELL I find the way the rhythm works in the first stanza implies a kind of moral judgement because it puts the physical movements so plainly – the kind of attitude the farmer has and the kind of thing it is – it's more than just being brilliantly descriptive. It's describing a kind of action.

HAMPTON And if there is an ambivalence, at last, is there any reason why there shouldn't be? Surely a poet can state –

HOBSBAUM Of course there's no reason why he shouldn't be ambivalent. All I'm saying is that really even the ambivalence itself I don't find terribly interesting, that's all. And I think much more would have to be done even with an ambivalent feeling about killing than is done here.

There was an evident consensus about the purely decorative qualities of this poem: at one level of discussion, clearly, the description will remain a description, with no reason for existing other than itself. This is no mean achievement, but it is not the way of major poetry. And any attempt on the part of a reader to take it in this latter way will involve some heavy reading-in. When done by reasonably sensitive people, this will weigh in upon the more ambivalent details. And it is around these that the crucial divergences have arisen.

For example, why did the poet kill the birds in his dream? To take only two divergent readings, Hampton's and Redgrove's, how can we reconcile, in the last stanza, horror at the act of killing and sympathy with that act? It might be argued that the feeling is ambivalent; but if there is an ambivalence here, it is a singularly restrained one. It would seem to depend on such half-formed images as 'broken cob-web' and the contradiction between the dream-killing and the birds already stiffening in the dew. Clearly the ambivalence is not acted out; indeed it is so tentative that it is best ignored. 'Why do I stare?' We don't need the poet's own testimony to be sure that he has no idea of the answer; why, then, should we supply it for him? Any such gesture on our part would take us right out of the poem.

Similarly, Redgrove and Bell read a moral weight into 'Half-sleeping birds in panic round his head' – the birds, they suggested, are being taken advantage of. But is there any enactment of this, as distinct from statement, in the poem? The verse is as measured as the farmer's tread, as deliberate as his aim; seems, in fact, very much on the side of the farmer. Any moral attitudes found in this line are those that its readers have put there. The poem does not move as a major work; it does not dramatise its moral contentions.

But it may work as a minor lyrical-descriptive poem; would work, perhaps, even better in this guise if it were deprived of its last stanza. And even as it stands, it is demonstrably a better poem than *Manicure*; at least it is coherent on a surface level, and the Group cohere in allowing its descriptive qualities. It is only when some go below the attractive surface that divergences arise. So the dissension, once more, is of a different quality: when dealing with the surface texture of minor art there is consensus; divergence occurs only when we seek to rationalise this into a morality. The poem should, in other words, be taken as a chipping from the studio which produced *Caravaggio Dying* – a poem which shows, as this does not, the way in which raw material can be given a moral purpose in art.

The dissensions about poems of major quality are of a different character entirely from those about minor poems. Here the trouble tends to be in the critic rather than the text: he is liable to extrapolate, to simplify. For example, Peter Porter has a poem, *A Christmas Recalled*, which most vividly evokes an Australian setting. The temptation is to stay with these evoked details, not to plumb below the surface. Conversely, one finds readers moralising away from the text; getting the moral but tending to deprecate the story. In the following poem, both are fused into a most impressive whole.

A CHRISTMAS RECALLED

The water pushed at its thin scud of oil
And knocked the musseled rocks, the opal broke,
Its skin of lights went out – the prawns were small
A foot down in the water jerking at
My glass bottle ; from the dock cranes smoke
Stood straight up, the gulls and cicadas noisily sat
On our huge summer, even the air was fat.

Summer was December and the water sounds
Of the presiding Harbour – ferries named
For Governors' ladies wallowed round
The river bends, past one haunted house, by
A thousand boatsheds, past the water games
Of spartan Girls Schools, regatta crowded bays,
Resting heavily at barnacled bituminous quays.

In this time I heard my uncle calling to my mother :
'Marion, I've made a new one, give it a try.'
I saw my face stretched in the cocktail shaker
When I wiped the condensation off ; we were
A drinking family and I would quietly lie
Eight years old drinking Schweppes in bed, their
Noise a secure lullaby, sipping at my fear.

But after eating too much one bloated day
When I broke three toys wantonly and clumsily
My uncle started to talk of the war, not the way
Men talk of the Last War but as prophets do
Of retribution : 'We've got about two or three
Years before the Japs come', and I ran to
The garden to cry – wars were not new

To any innocence, I thought of them
As I sat crying under the pepperina tree.
I thought too of death which was a word like 'When'
And not a thing like cat, so as they called
Me in for washing-up I looked to see
If they had painted what their talk foresaw
On their Christmas faces, the picture of a war.

HOBSBAUM Well, it is a simpler sort of thing than the first one, as Peter said. I think again what it does I feel it does most successfully. It seems to me a very usual thing to attempt to do – not, perhaps, a very hard thing – to try and recapture what it was to be a child and to be frightened by something which perhaps wouldn't frighten one in the same way, or, perhaps, not frighten one at all, if one was older. Here again, I feel it does gain a tremendous amount of weight by being in a particular place at a particular time, by being so definitely in this climate at this period with this particular set-up – much more than, I think, often happens when people try to recall a state of mind in rather abstract words, summarising as they would do when they are adults.

LUCIE-SMITH Surely, Philip, there's a bit more to this poem than that. This strikes me as being a poem which is, I think, very successful. But its main interest is that Peter's poems have always had moral preoccupations and this poem has a strongly moral preoccupation simply in a way we're not used to him presenting it – it doesn't really strike me as being more than *superficially* a poem of recollection, it strikes me as a poem about the badness of war, in fact, i.e., surely the point of the poem is that they should – you know, that people talk casually about wars and don't mean it, and I mean to say that this is wrong, which of course it *is* wrong when one thinks of it.

HOBSBAUM Well, you're rather seeing the poem without the child's sensibility which seems to me the essential thing in the poem.

LUCIE-SMITH I mean to say, surely, if there's a point in the poem it is that – you know, the point's made ironically because it's seen through a child's sensibility, i.e. you know, that adults passing the whole thing off, as you can imagine them doing, and yet the child's sensibility is the true one in this case, it's closer to –

HOBSBAUM It won't work on this interpretation because you've got the uncle talking about the war as prophets do of retribution. It's not quite like that, I think you've oversimplified it. They aren't *always* passing the war off casually, are they?

ROBERTS Surely isn't one of the shocks in the last two or three lines possibly – or maybe I'm just getting the meaning wrong – but it suggests to me that the child when he hears these grown-ups talking about war expects that they should look very different from their ordinary everyday selves – he's somehow shocked by the idea that these friendly people – these men – should suddenly be talking in these awful prophetic, presumably rather fierce and frightening, terms.

LUCIE-SMITH The point is that people enjoy prophesying doom.

HOBSBAUM Yes, well of course the child's quite right.

ROBERTS It should be a different person who's doing it.

HOBSBAUM Well, not so much as that, I should say, as that they're

182

resuming their Christmas faces, their ordinary way of going on, after this little bout of prophecy, and just carry on as before.

BELL   The point about the poem surely is that this is not just a child's memories, it's an extraordinary intelligent child who saw enough at the time which imprinted itself upon his whole life, and which he continues to interpret – like 'I saw my face stretched on the cocktail shaker'. You see, that's not only a child's memories, it's a child taking account of his environment and noting something about it at the time and still remembering it. To bring up just the phrase 'just a child's memories' seems to me a little weak for this.

HOBSBAUM   I mean, the child's memories of the child's perceptions, if you like that better, and granted, of course, obviously, that this is no ordinary sensibility.

SMITH   Isn't Teddy right, Philip, in suggesting that this poem makes an effect which is much greater than the sum of any parts, it distils something, it recaptures something – it's a very intangible business?

PORTER   May I just say – seeing the harbour of Sydney – it's meant to have some kind of that quality that Sydney would. I remember seeing Sydney, I suppose.

BELL   In a sense in this impulse he sees his future life embedded ready to come out. I mean there's a sense of heredity here and family relations belonging to a society, there's a whole train of events in which he's bound up.

SMITH   There's an awful lot about the way human beings behave and the way they sit in their landscapes . . .

LUCIE-SMITH   The heredity point, of course, is made quite specifically, isn't it? 'I wiped the condensation off', 'we were a drinking family', and so on, you know? But, you know, I do think the point about the moral slant is a valid one. I don't think Peter's changed his spots.

HOBSBAUM   No, but one isn't given undiluted moral – the point I was trying clumsily to make was that a good deal has been done – not particularly by Peter, I think – in just giving us conclusions without showing us how those conclusions were built up and what happened to bring about this particular state of mind, you see.

LUCIE-SMITH   Yes, well surely, I mean to say it's the usual thing – it isn't the smart poem which draws the moral in the verse at the end, but in a sense the poem *is* the moral, you know.

HOBSBAUM   The moral *is* in the poem. Absolutely.

All this took place some years ago, and I am sorry to have to convict my younger self of gross literalism. But evidently the weight of adverse opinion caused me to shift my ground – I think, now, in the right direction. Looking back, it was the extreme persuasiveness of the surface details that led me to believe that the poem was 'simply' about an Australian childhood. As the discussion shows, it is about that; and, as

Lucie-Smith says, about adult irresponsibility; and, as Roberts says, a child's disillusionment; and, *pace* Bell, about its effects upon his adult sensibility; there is, too, a distinct sense of heredity and social relationships in what amounts to a very fine poem indeed.

A synthesis of these views would be a critique of the poem. Thus one could say that the Australian childhood so vividly evoked is far more than that. An atmosphere of complacency is suggested in the images of life just going through pre-ordained motions. It's mostly done in the verbs – the ferry boats 'wallowed', the 'regatta-crowded' quays were 'resting heavily' –

> *From the dock cranes smoke*
> *Stood straight up, the gulls and cicadas sat*
> *Noisily on our huge summer . . .*

This does not occur in the poem because it is 'good imagery', nor even because it happened to be that way. For the adults are complacent, too; witness their pursuits and talk. But the child senses flaws in the apparently prevailing calm – for example, he sees his distorted image in the cocktail shaker. A child's sensitivity to atmosphere demands to be allayed by the certainties of grown-ups; but Christmas is a time when these behave as foolishly as children, and with less reason. Talking like a prophet about retribution may be no more than a mischievous game for adults, though it is much more than that for children; and these adults have reduced themselves to worse than children, since they have debased their natural fear of death to a childish concept, not grasped emotionally. The irony is that this reduction awakens adult fear in the child.

This is, then, a poem about the eye of childhood and the deadening sophistication of middle age; about a willed complacency, disturbed in spite of itself by foreboding, which it therefore debases; about the approach of war, the fear of war, and war itself. It is in this way far more than a personal experience. Porter's poetry seldom does one thing at a time, and its complexity of effect is liable to make one question the validity of any single account it gives rise to.

The critic might well despair of giving any idea of the attitudes fused into this dramatic complex if he had not the advantage of hearing the views of his fellows and the opportunity of pitting his reading against theirs. Such a procedure will necessarily expose to rational understanding more and more aspects of the whole; it seems to me the way in which criticism will necessarily develop; and certainly some such approach is behind the undertaking of this whole book.

184

The approach might be called meta- or para-criticism; that is to say the comparison and evaluation of different accounts of a given text. The point of the operation, though, is not the assessment of critics, but the assessment of the work that they are discussing. Moreover, the assessor himself cannot abdicate responsibility: he may act as chairman of the discussion, as I did in the dissensions we have just examined, but he must also hold a view of his own; his own sensibility must be down there in the wrangles of the critics, just as it must also hold some kind of balance, as fair-mindedly as possible, when he comes to give his final account of those wrangles.

My basic procedure, in this chapter and in the book at large, has been to find a text which has caused a fair amount of dissension; to locate within that text the main points of divergence among the critics; and, at each point, to map out a pattern of variation. The next task was to ascertain the cause of variation, and from each cause to draw a point of critical theory. And some such procedure, it seems to me, must be at the heart of any real development in literary criticism.

I should hardly like to inflict on younger contemporaries the nine years of labour that have gone into this book; a good deal of this could be circumvented if we kept accurate records of what goes on in group discussion. The faults of such discussion are obvious – a tendency to *ad hoc* formulations, to verbal clumsiness, to simplified stands. But all of these are, equally, through the exigencies of discussion, open to challenge; and challenge, moreover, on the spot, at the moment of enunciation. It is no accident that many of our best critics have been good teachers; and that, as some of them freely admit, their best work has come out of animated discussion in class and seminar.

Critical magazines might bear this in mind. Obviously a lively seminar is not always available, but to a great extent this lack can be compensated for by opening up the columns as a critical forum and encouraging debate. No book, either, should be tackled by one reviewer; at least two reviews should be printed, and any serious differences compounded in later issues. No reader is so naïve as to suppose any one view to be finally authoritative; clearly the more he is exposed to divergence among the critics, the more he is likely to gain some personal grip on the work in question – either because he sees possibilities in the text he had never previously envisaged, or because he sees interpretations that diverge widely and so has to make some sort of a judgement between them.

In any case, any critic putting forward his own view would be none the worse for taking into account the views of his fellows; none the worse, either, for considering the reasons for his divergence from them. So that even if my envisaged Critical Forum does not come to pass, at least we should have critics who are prepared to argue with their colleagues rather than pronounce over them, or, worse still, evade the issues.

Criticism, then, as a mode of discussion, not dogma, is called for. And the closer the discussion to the text, the more precisely can we account for our opinions. We know of the psychological attitudes, the raw material, the personal experience, the literary tradition, the social mores, all of which condition the making of a poem; but they are not the poem itself. Poems are basically – not attitudes, images, ideas – but words; at least the words are all we have to point to.

The mistake has been, at one extreme, to consider a poem away from its expression in words; at the other, I will admit, to take the individual words in isolation from the context that is embodied in them. Put another way, one could say that a poem is an artefact to make one reader feel much the same way as another reader; and presumably, though not demonstrably, the same way as the writer himself.

Therefore we should discuss how the artefact is made up: to analyse it is not to destroy but to understand. And, since literature is a form of verbal communication, all considerations of value are tied up with what is being communicated, and how. So, although criticism cannot be solely a matter of words – what, after all, do the words stand for? – it must concern itself with words; how, in this or that instance, the language worked, how one word conditioned another.

Unfortunately, this, like other theoretical considerations, is a province shirked by the literary critic proper; no doubt because he so seldom finds himself arguing fundamental points of principle with his peers. And the problem is given over to those who are less practically concerned in the field; who expand into larger and larger considerations of Language, to the impoverishment of their sense of language as deployed in particular instances. The linguist, the psychologist, the philosopher and even the mathematician – all have their say about language, and all aggregate communication into their respective specialisms.

I have already suggested that practical criticism will find it necessary to juxtapose different interpretations; I have also said that it should recognise differences of quality in different dissensions. But even this will be of little avail unless our practice has a sound theoretical base. Valuation should not take place in the void; it should be recognised that all valuation is bound up with what must be our next advance, a development in our views of communication in language.

CHAPTER TEN

A Critique of Linguistic Theory

To produce a viable theory of language is to confute, if one is not to avoid, the myriad theories that already exist. For each specialism lays claim to a monopoly of wisdom upon this subject.

Imagine a symposium with some such title as 'Communication in Words'; suppose it to take place between, let us say, a physiologist, a linguist, a psychologist, a mathematician, a philosopher and a literary theorist. It is doubtful whether such specialists could arrive at an agreed definition, let alone any sort of general consensus in the field. The exact analogy would be that of the blind men who went to see the elephant.[1] One, you may remember, seized the tail and said the creature was very like a rope; another, resting against its leg, remarked that it was like a tree; yet a third felt its side and compared it with a wall; while the one who made contact with the trunk found the elephant to be very like a snake. All were right, according to their limited experience of the creature, and yet clearly each individual is wrong. Now language is such an elephant.

This comes out clearly in the numerous theories about how language originated in society. The pioneer theories, as characterised by the nineteenth-century historian of language Max Müller[2] are simple enough. One theory presupposes a natural connection between words and the things they stand for; another regards speech as beginning in onomatopoeia; a third supposes speech to originate with involuntary interjections; while a fourth derives it from sound associated with communal physical effort. Later theories propose speech to be founded in gesture;[3] while Darwin, as against all preceding and most subsequent theory, refused to see any difference in kind between the speech of man and the cries of animals.[4] Perhaps the most comprehensive theory about the origin of speech is that of Diamond, who takes the verb to be central to all primitive languages and finds that it is then used characteristically in the imperative; *cut, break, crush, strike* are among the earliest meanings of which we find traces in language.[5]

But what of more highly developed usages? It is evident that the proportion of verbs to other parts of speech decreases as a language develops, and this, in its turn, marks the increase of conceptualisation as society becomes more complex. There is a close connection between language and thought; to name an object is to select it for attention,[6] and, as language develops, it enables us to describe and analyse more and more features of the human world.[7]

But a study of the origins and even of the development of language need do little to tell us how it works at the present time. The natural thing to do is to turn to the physiologists; they, after all, can explain something of how language originates in the make-up of the human individual. Yet, when one comes to examine their writings on the subject, they are seen to be concerned mainly with the study of aphasia. It seems odd that, to get an idea of the physical basis of language, one should have to study it when it breaks down. Hughlings Jackson, in his pioneer work in this sector, stressed again and again the close relation between conception and language, speech and physical motion; 'a person has not mind and speech, any more than he has speech *and* movements of articulation'.[8] On the contrary, he goes on to say, it is from the use of a word that we judge its proportionate value. Thus, any enquiry into the origin of speech in the nervous system should take into account the nature of the thing said.

We know a certain amount about the purely physical aspects of speech. In his decisive study of speech disorders, Russell Brain points out that the co-ordination of articulatory muscles derives from specific sectors of the brain; in particular, fibres passing from the lower part of the left frontal lobe into the corresponding region of the right hemisphere by the corpus callosum.[9] Electrical stimulation of the cerebral cortex may produce either a positive effect, vocalisation, or a negative one; namely, interference with speech in progress.[10] This would suggest that brain lesions can only affect speech by disturbing the physiological processes which underly it.[11] So far we are on the purely physical plane.

But the process of speaking is a process of recognising a total pattern, since words can only be used sensibly by someone understanding their meaning.[12] This process of recognition involves the activity of physiological organisations which Russell Brain has termed 'schemas'; 'learning to speak depends upon the establishment of a schema initially for each phoneme'.[13] The schema is the means by which a large number of variable stimuli elicit much the same response; the wide range of heard sounds is systematised and selected by the cerebral cortex. This is a neural activity whereby the unconscious comparison of incoming impulses against a schema leads to conscious recognition. In much the same way, the word-schemas regulate the expression of a word either in uttered speech or in writing.

But one may question whether this theory holds good for units larger than a single word; total acts of communication, in fact. Just as a word is an organisation of a more complex order than a phoneme, so a sentence is an organisation of a more complex order than a word.[14] What happens later modifies the significance of that which has already been heard, so that the earlier parts of a sentence must be held in suspension until the later parts determine their meaning. An unvarying response may indeed be elicited by a single word like 'dog' or 'cat', but it is response at a very low level. A legitimate question with such an example might well be '*Whose* cat?' or 'What *kind* of dog?' – to be answered only by a more complex form of utterance – which in its turn would determine more precisely the reaction of the percipient. Therefore utterances vary in quality, from simple words through queries and sentences up to the most complex verbal structures: tragedies, let us say, or epic poems. Such matters are not to be explained in terms of neurological signal and response.

Moreover, to describe speech as a physiological function is to limit its scope. Such a description may give us some idea of how a given utterance arose, but it would not tell us what made the utterance meaningful or how it imposed itself on its auditor. The physiologist could not tell us how a poem communicates with the person responding to it. Yet this could be the most meaningful utterance of all. It would seem, then, that we would do better to examine the structure and behaviour of language.

But are we any better off with the linguists? They, after all, observe language in its various forms, chronicle its development, describe its behaviour. But what is the use of a concern with language as a general function? Surely we should study specific acts of language; particular communications, in fact. It is their love of the general and disregard for the particular that leads so many linguists to discursiveness and abstraction.

Much of their difficulty lies in the insistence of the founder of linguistics, de Saussure, on its status as an exact science.[15] This, among other things, leads to a needless multiplication of categories: semantics, historical linguistics, structural linguistics, stylistics, etymology, philology and the like. The distinctions between these various areas of study will not be easily drawn by the layman.

The quasi-scientific claims of linguistic studies lead, too, to sterile wrangles about facts that have no more than a pseudo-status. It may make sense for physicists to argue about the smallest indivisible particle of matter; it seems absurd for linguists to quarrel about the smallest particle of language.[16]

At first sight, the field of linguistics seems nothing but a host of competing factions. But one may distinguish a dominant train of thought, and this is one that attempts to describe the action of language without reference either to its meaning or to the social context by which it is conditioned.

It would seem to be impossible to discuss language without an interest in what the language under discussion is saying. Yet the seeds of this neglect are inherent in de Saussure's pioneer formulation: 'the true and unique object of linguistics is language studied in and for itself'.[17] This would seem to put paid to any idea of communication in words. For de Saussure and his school it appears that language is no more than a limited number of elements or phonemes that can be called up by a corresponding number of written symbols.[18] According to this view, the word in itself is arbitrary: what is a tree in English can be called *arbor* in Latin and there is no reason for preferring the one to the other.[19] For de Saussure, language is not substance but form.[20] And these forms are studied in abstraction from context, whether linguistic or social.[21] And so on, and so on.

It is surprising how little the Saussurean school of linguistics has modified the preconceptions of its founder. We find Sapir differentiating between language and thought, and so recognising the meaning of words only as part of the process of association. 'Tempest', for example, has a softer glamour than 'storm' because of its association in the mind of the reader with Shakespeare's play.[22] Here, once more, we have words studied in and for themselves, and language considered apart from context. Here, too, the context ignored is a social as well as linguistic one. 'Nor can I believe,' he goes on, 'that culture and language are causally related. Culture may be defined as *what* a society does and thinks. Language is a particular *how* of thought.'[23] One would have considered that the 'what' and 'how' could have been conjoined in literature, thus providing at once a linguistic *and* a social context. But Sapir has an answer for this, too. He compares language as the medium of literature to marble, the medium of sculpture.[24] However, given any particular instance, the analogy will break down; since one sculptor need not handle his material in anything like the same manner as another. In fact, behind Sapir's theory of linguistics is a very simple aesthetic fallacy. It can be localised in his comparison of language with a garment or with a prepared groove or road.[25] This is the Form–Content Distinction, which I have dealt with elsewhere.[26] And it may be argued that so mechanistic a view of language as that propounded by de Saussure and his successors was pretty well bound to lead its proponents into the more simple-minded of the cultural impasses open to them.

These impasses are not only aesthetic but scientific ones, and they can be severely hampering. Bloomfield, for example, evinces a theory that is very near Behaviourism. Meaning seems to him to be an internal process, individual to each person, and therefore not ascertainable. 'The mental processes or internal bodily processes of other people are known to each one of us only from speech-utterances and other observable actions.'[27] The inference here is that such 'observable actions' as language cannot be used for communicating mental processes. This is to ignore the stimulus that can be given by major works of literature – a stimulus that is likely to provoke a similar response in different people. But it is doubtful if Bloomfield would discriminate among the qualities of various stimuli. Certainly he seems not to recognise any superiority in the great writer's use of language. 'The individual features in which the language of the great writer differs from the ordinary speech of his time and place interest the linguist no more than do the individual features of any other person's speech and much less than do the features that are common to all speakers.'[28] In this way, linguistics regards all communications, meaningful and less meaningful, as equally valid, since all are capable of being described at the level of language-behaviour. But this is a very low level: it reduces the most varied utterances to a generalised plasm which may be called the Lowest Common Multiple of speech. It might well be argued that a mode of description which would fit all known utterance is hardly worth embarking upon in the first place.

The methods of linguistics, as one of its leading exponents has admitted,[29] strive towards those of natural science. But the results must necessarily be very different. Language does not exist as a generalised ideal; it exists in terms of particularities. And a study that reduces those particularities to a system is liable to find itself without adequate means of differentiation.[30] Linguistics evades criteria of value; it simplifies specific operations of a language into a set of rules.[31] Such rules may, indeed, fit the gross stock of utterance, but they will hardly tell us much about the statement that transcends the conventions of its time.

There have, indeed, been attempts within the Saussurean framework to be closely analytical. The Dynamic Philology of Zipf was a

192

simple statistical system, measuring such matters as the length of words and their frequency of occurrence.[32] While Chomsky's Transformation Theory uses algebraic symbols as a way of characterising different forms of sentences, and differentiating between forms that are ostensibly similar.[33] This, however, is still differentiation without discrimination: Chomsky has described the transformational side of the language process as though it was the whole story.

But is it possible for linguistics to supply a more adequate account of language procedures? Recent dissidents from the Saussurean approach[34] do not seem to have done more than multiply existing categories. Perhaps the most advanced gestures in this field have been made by M. A. K. Halliday. His differentiations at first might seem a good deal more subtle than those of other linguistic systems. For example, it is possible for him to distinguish two sentences of equivalent structure by pointing to differences between individual sections.[35] But Halliday is gravely hampered by having at his disposal no unit of language larger than a sentence.[36] Thus he has difficulty in describing sentences as wholes and prefers rather to break them down. However, the units into which he breaks them are hardly original ones: we have met terms like 'subject', 'predicator', 'complement' and 'adjunct' before,[37] and they suggest little beyond external structure. What we want are finer discriminations, and it is here that Halliday's system fails us. He has, indeed, a scale of differentiation that he calls 'delicacy'; that is to say, depth of detail in description. For example, 'all the ten houses on the riverside' has the same primary structure as 'the finest old houses on the riverside'. But a more delicate statement of the modifier ('all the ten', 'the finest old') shows distinct secondary structures. He describes the distinction between the two sentences quoted as DaDbO and DbO respectively, where D = deictic and O = ordinal. But this is a clumsy mode of differentiation, and Halliday himself admits the scale of delicacy is by no means a satisfactory instrument as yet.[38] However, he sees an improvement coming about through statistical work in grammar. This might, indeed, make the quantitative distinctions more precise, but it would not turn them into distinctions of quality. There is therefore a gap between what Halliday says he is doing and what he really does. Clearly we would all welcome an analysis in depth of specific acts of communication. But is this, in fact, what we are given? His system might well differentiate between equivalent structures, but this would not tell us much about their meaning. It is, for example, doubtful whether Halliday could offer a close analysis of a poem so as to bring out its value; and, without this ultimate reach of discrimination, of what use is his approach to language? Linguistic acts vary in efficacy: it is no good describing the average if we are unable to describe the excellent. A discussion of language can only proceed relevantly by way of specific evaluations. So, in spite of all Halliday's efforts in the field, we are still too near the mechanistic conception of language as phenomenon set apart from the social world. And it would be my contention that this concept is inherent in the study of linguistics.

It must be by now apparent that what I am objecting to is not a theory of language alone but a whole mode of discussion of language. There is a basic and ill-concealed assumption in linguistic studies that language operates homogeneously. As John Lotz most unfortunately put it, 'language serves as the vehicle of abstract thought, exalted mysticism, and poetic inspiration – but it is used as well in the ravings of a maniac and the mutterings of a drunkard'.[39] One would have thought rather that language was being *misused* in such utterances as the latter. The 'science' that cannot discriminate between the language of King Lear and that of Poor Tom hardly deserves even to be ignored.

As we saw in the formulations of Bloomfield, linguistic 'science' has strong leanings towards Behaviourism. This is not surprising, since it chooses to lump specific instances of speech together as operations of a general system. And, just as many linguists observe language without a thought for its meaning and value, so the Behaviourist examines the activity of mankind in a laboratory, and therefore sees only a pattern abstracted from context.

Psychology would claim to have travelled far from such antecedents: of all studies, it has proved itself most adept in jettisoning its pioneers. J. B. Watson, for example, is a perpetual embarrassment to his successors; and no wonder. What is one to make of a theorist who denies the presence of meaning in behaviour? 'We watch what the animal or human being is doing. He means what he does. It is foolish to ask him while he is acting what he is meaning. His action is the meaning. Hence exhaust the concept of action and we have exhausted the concept of meaning.'[40]

But, in that case, what meaning have these sentences, the ones I have just quoted? It is just possible that Watson himself would say that they *have* none, in which case we must assume that they exist for their own sake and not to impart information to us. If this is so, our one concern is why they were written at all. Watson himself can hardly put a high value on his work: he refers to himself in passing as a complex of reacting systems.[41] This is hardly likely to predispose those

194

with a higher opinion of themselves in favour of his judgement. There can be no doubt that Watson is denying the presence of the individual, in himself no less than in others; in speech, as in all other activities. This would make nonsense of the greatest work man has produced; it would reduce the language of Shakespeare to counters rearranged by a chance process signifying nothing.

Watson is not dead: his disciple, Skinner, still figures on book-lists and committed himself to a proposition no less startling – that we should reject any formulation of language in terms of meaning. Thus he says that a thirsty man asking for a drink of water no more uses the word 'water' than, in taking the offered glass, he uses a reach![42]

We must agree with Skinner that the word 'water' conditions the next action, the taking of the glass. But it would not have been a glass that was offered if the word had been misunderstood; and it is certain that the urgency of the context, linguistic as well as social, would have had a good deal to do with the promptitude of the relief.

However, as this example will suggest, Skinner is not interested in context: his basic particle is what he calls a unit of behaviour. And so he divides up the language according to a system of his own. The *mand*, for example, is Skinner's name for an imperative of some kind – demand, command, etc.[43] The *tact* is that unit of behaviour which makes contact with the outside world – a referent, no less.[44]

Such terms grossly over-simplify the operation of language. Surely it is obvious that an act of communication, in order to succeed in eliciting a response, must be efficacious? And if the communication is enacted before us, whether it be a request or a poem, it should be possible to analyse the nature of its efficacy. Skinner writes as though we were all spectators at a dumb-show; seeing actions but not hearing the words that bring them about. In fact, however, behaviour need not be as meaningless as the Behaviourists maintain if we examine with sufficient closeness that which provokes it.

Clearly Skinner is wrong on three counts: in depriving language of meaning, in seeking to compartmentalise it into units, and in choosing units of such clumsiness that we can only marvel at his claim to have achieved a method of functional analysis.[45] Given the terms he uses, no close approach is possible to the verbal stimulus; especially if it be the complex stimulus of a work of art. At his very best, however, when struggling with the more positive kinds of ambiguity,[46] Skinner does succeed in doing much more awkwardly what is already to be found in the work of the literary critics. The difference is that Empson and Graves describe particular effects; Skinner seeks to bundle them into his pre-existing system.

Given this mode of study, it is difficult to see how any useful theory could be developed. If one must talk about language in general terms, it is best discussed as an aggregative process, a balancing against each other of disparities, rather than a compartmentalising process of division.

Certainly language cannot be studied statistically in terms of its external effect upon subjects of an experiment. The immediately post-Watson school of gadgeteers 'measured' speech in terms of physiological indices – speech-movements,[47] muscle potentials,[48] salivary reactions,[49] galvanic skin responses,[50] and the like. Later on, studies in transference sought to take language into areas of learning,[51] and experiments in perception and association attempted to analyse the effect upon the percipient of signs as stimuli.[52]

Osgood, Suci and Tannenbaum set themselves up against all this, and claimed to be attacking associative methods.[53] But it cannot be said that their own experiments marked a new beginning. They extracted definitions of particular words from their subjects, but no subject was left to his own devices and no word was supplied with a context. Thus they put before a subject the word 'father' and supplied him with a string of alternatives designed to fine down his response to that word – 'happy' or 'sad', for example, 'slow' or 'fast', 'hard' or 'soft'.[54] But the very fact of putting forward an alternative biases the subject in a certain direction. When asked whether father is hard or soft, one is being directed into the assumption that he is necessarily one or the other. Osgood and his associates give an account of their experiments that suggests their lists of alternatives were not arrived at lightly;[55] but they still were arrived at, and still the subject is acted upon by preconceptions neither in him nor necessarily in the word. Obviously it would be difficult to elicit a useful definition from the subject simply by putting the word before him; but this, again, is an indication that the words should not be taken out of a context if they are to retain a meaning. It might be argued that the very neutrality of a word out of context might serve as a way of testing subjective reactions of individual subjects. In which case the Osgood, Suci and Tannenbaum experiment might be termed a more sophisticated form of associative process, but hardly what its inventors claimed it to be – a means of semantic differentiation.

Not only content but quality of response would be an issue in any such enquiry. But the categories suggested by Pool,[56] for instance, for measuring the intensity of the attitude expressed by the subject – repetition of words, hesitation of speech, etc. – differ from those of Osgood only by having a greater flexibility of comparison. The foundations of psychology were not very well laid, and it is difficult to erect a satisfactory argument upon them. At the same time, they stretch so far that psychologists seem unable to escape.

Reviewing recent studies in the subject, Leonard Krasner remarked that they nearly all followed the Skinnerian paradigm: the dependent variables are the speaker's verbal behaviour and the independent variables are generalised conditioned reinforces intended to bring verbal behaviour under the control of the examiner.[57]

But what use is a study systematised in this way? Surely it is obvious that the most interesting patterns of speech take place in circumstances which are under no examiner's control. That is to say, they take place in the environment of the speaker himself. Abolish this in favour of laboratory conditions, and language will be generalised and abstracted out of all recognition. The kind of item which can be presented on an index card is meaningful only for the purposes of very limited experiment, and to ask participants in such an experiment whether such items are 'true' or 'false' is to reduce the complexity and potential of linguistic communication to the status of a parlour game.[58] It might be argued that one has to start the study of language somewhere. To which one would be compelled to reply that no study can start with falsification of its premises.

No wonder, then, that attempts to develop the restricting hypotheses of Behaviourism have resulted in variations on an old theme; either that, or the study has turned itself into something else entirely as in the transitional area known as psycholinguistics.

The more precise psycholinguists and their allied theoreticians are in describing the function of language, the less regard they seem to pay its meaning. The result is that one feels the whole time that they are imposing upon the flux of actuality a stereotype of their own. In so far as it develops away from Behaviourism, psychology aspires towards the state of pure mathematics.

G. A. Miller felt that communicative behaviour was necessarily variable and so was best discussed in statistical terms.[59] Once this was done, the amount of regularity he found was astonishing: 'one's own verbal behaviour follows statistical rules with considerable orderliness.'[60] It seems to have escaped him that his methods of observation have imposed their own orderliness upon that which he is observing. Indeed, he is following the psycholinguistic tendency to discuss a language as though it were a code. Once one begins thinking in these terms, the *how* of communication becomes far more important than the *what* of what is being communicated. Cherry remarks that the information content, so called, of signals is not a commodity but rather a property;[61] that is to say, the use or truth of the information is secondary to the task of getting it across more clearly.[62] Bar-Hillel and Carnap make the same point when they suggest that information theory as practised nowadays is not interested in the content of the symbols whose information it measures.[63] Thus, what has come to be called the theory of communication describes information mainly in terms of the statistical rarity of signals from an observed source.[64]

Clearly the term communication is being misused here. It is irresponsible for theorists in this sector to aggregate the word to their procedure. If they were right in this usage, we should be compelled to regard communication as no more than a ratio of signal to noise. Language may seem imponderable compared with the mathematics required to convey it, but this is only to say that the discussion of content is more difficult than the discussion of the means by which it is conveyed. In theory, the two should never be separated.

But in practice the tendency is to try and work out an ideal language which will get rid of the ambiguity and complexity of speech as we have it.[65] Various hypotheses have been expressed as to how such a language would work. Some logicians have tried to abstract language from specific human situations;[66] statistical psychologists reduce patterns of events to counting systems;[67] mathematicians synthesise language-data processing systems such as automatic 'translators',[68] 'decision-making' programmes for answering business correspondence,[69] and the like.

This, however, is the use of language at a very low level: the assemblage and re-assemblage of building blocks, no less.[70] Or, as one mathematician put it, 'our model of language is fully analogous to the perfect gas of thermo-dynamics'.[71]

A whole symposium was devoted to this question of artificial languages.[72] There is no doubt about their practical application; what one objects to is the way in which their inventors tend to discuss them as improvements on an existing norm. To find a linguistic equivalent for the existing input mechanisms of computers;[73] to propose a geometric model for item definition;[74] or to devise, for a computer system, a 'simplified and rigidly structured language'[75] – these are not problems in communication. Rather they are techniques to reduce the human factor in certain technical processes. The confusion comes in the analogy so often made between computers and brains. In spite of the extraordinary claims that have been made for these instruments,[76] computers are not brains, nor anything like them. They cannot determine their own instructions, interpret complex situations outside themselves or think intuitively.[77] Therefore, whatever the artificial language is that they are using, it corresponds only superficially with natural language. There are no simple one-to-one relationships in English;[78] nor can each word be tied down to a simple definition.[79] This is what gives the language its life. When we enter the world of the computer, we leave the sentient, breathing response of the human being behind. It would be as well if the communication theorists, so called, remembered that.

The ultimate reach in artificial languages is the notation of pure mathematics. Many people regard it as superior to any other language.[80] Words, they say, are clumsy, indefinable, referential. Whereas numbers convey much information in a compact form and expose new possibilities by being convertible to many other forms.[81]

Bertrand Russell defined mathematics as the science of number.[82] This gives us at once the strength and the limitation of mathematics as a form of communication. Its economy and consistency of expression, clarity of sequence, provides a high degree of assurance that the argument put forward is valid.[83] But, by the same token, all emotive qualities are absent; suggestion is minimal. No matter what intuition went into the process, all we are left with is its bare bones.

There are not wanting those who would seek to drain emotion from language in the hope of moving nearer to 'reason'. But this, again, is an arid ideal. One could, presumably, reduce a poem to algebraic symbols denoting its logical procedures; however, no one but a madman would imagine the end-product to have much to do with the poem. Even in logical argument, so termed, this is true: that there is an element of persuasion in the choice of the very words used, and that those words are not the clothing of the argument but the argument itself. At best, mathematics could be its skeleton.

Another limitation of mathematics as a language is that it is general; that is to say, it deals with classes of facts, not particulars.[84] Thus what seems to be a particular in mathematics is in fact a conceptual model, depending for its efficacy on mirroring the general behaviour of members of a given class.[85] It has been argued that classification is the most fundamental objective in mathematics; that it studies properties of sets that remain invariant under certain specified groups of transformations.[86] But though this may be a property of one specialised code, it is not a property of natural language. In speaking, we are concerned to point to the individual event; locate, one may say, the individual rather than the average.

Above and beyond all, mathematics is limited by being quantitative. This means that it takes no account of the value of any given situation or process. It describes without judging. One of the more unfortunate aberrations brought about by its currently high prestige is the assumption that these characteristics can be passed on to natural language. But in practice it is virtually impossible to frame a sentence which does not carry some evaluative weight; so natural language, when inclined towards mathematics, acquires only a limitation which cannot be put to use and sacrifices some of its own essential attributes.

The whole question is exhaustively discussed in Whitehead and Russell's *Principia Mathematica*. 'The symbols for classes, like those for descriptions, are, in our system, incomplete symbols: their *uses* are defined, but they themselves are not assumed to mean anything at all ... These classes, so far as we produce them, are clearly symbolic or linguistic conveniences, not genuine objects as their members are if they are individuals.'[87]

Here, then, we have an artificial language whose 'words' exist not as entities but in terms of relationships, one with another. This might be said of natural language seen from some points of view, but what separates mathematics off is that its 'words' have no direct reference to a world outside themselves. As Gottlob Frege remarked, 'It is possible for a mathematician to perform quite lengthy calculations without understanding by his symbols anything intuitable, or with which we could be sensibly acquainted ... We realise perfectly that other symbols could have been arranged to stand for the same things.'[88] Number, therefore, is a property abstracted from external objects and cannot be applied to events and ideas without distortion of meaning.[89] This is not to denigrate the concept of number; merely to show that, just as it has its uses, it has its limitations.

Mathematics, then, abstracts from given situations and tells us their norm, their statistical average; generalises them into a logical pattern. While poetry, let us say, focuses upon one of those given situations, defines its particulars, specifies what gives it its significance. Mathematics posits the universal in terms of an individual formula; poetry dramatises the universal by getting to the bottom of one of its particular instances. It is a great fault of the theorists that they talk about the particulars of language in such a way as to make them sound very much like the generalities and abstractions of mathematics.

This is nowhere more marked than in the dealings of philosophers with the concept of communication in art. Here we have a whole area of study known as Semiotics, or the Signification Theory. Perhaps, as Mrs Hungerland suggested,[90] it arose out of the Instrumentalist account of aesthetic experience as equilibrium. The chief proponent of this theory, Charles Morris, looks upon the work of art as sign, rather as a map may be said to signify a tract of country.[91] But there is some question as to what it is denoting: is it a psychological process on the part of the artist, an Ideal Work, or an Idea? We are told that the work of art as sign denotes any object which has a selection of the properties of that work. But this would suggest that the more complete the selection, the more successful the sign; in other words, the work of art is at its best when it denotes itself.[92] Would we not, in short, be better off with the terrain rather than with the map by which it is signified?

Obviously not, since Morris argues elsewhere that iconicity is not a criterion in works of art – though, at the same time, he suggests that value is inherent in them.[93] Signs can be stimuli at the level of Pavlov's bells,[94] or they can be the whole complex of a language.[95] It is difficult, faced with such elasticity of application, to see what use the term 'sign' is; other than to say, what we knew already, that a work of art is that which it signifies.

Perhaps the real use of the theory is to draw attention to the fact that art formalises the raw material with which it deals.[96] This was argued out laboriously by Albert Gehring, an early exponent of the Signification Theory, when trying to make a distinction between symbol and representation in music.[97] Something of the same sort was indicated by Wittgenstein, who suggested that a sign was a picture in the sense that it symbolises something other than itself. In other words, one would be able to undetstand the sign if one knew the vocabulary to which it belonged.[98]

This is the basis for Suzanne Langer's theory of semblances: 'art is the creation of forms symbolic of human feeling'.[99] The grammar of artistic vision, she says, develops from the expression of vital rhythms. It would seem, then, that art is an elaborate code. But none of the Signification Theorists have worked this out beyond its simplest terms – a musical score as sign of a musical work,[100] a fixed line as sign of motion,[101] for instance. So it would seem that what works of art have in common is only a lowest common denominator of denotation. Beyond that, each is an individual, and this theory of aesthetics leaves us no wiser than we were: we still have to find what is signified by the work of art as sign.

The trouble here is that 'sign' aggregates all too readily to the mathematical concept of number as symbol; and such a concept does not fit the cumulative effect which is the characteristic property of language. As an antidote, proponents of affectivity in particular have laid down a special definition for language as used in the arts. Unfortunately it separates the language of the arts off not only from mathematics, which would be a good thing, but from referential truth generally.

The ancients were not much troubled by this problem; our concern seems to have developed as a result of the practical study of language set in motion by such distinguished anti-grammarians as Jespersen, Vendryes and Stern.[102] The last-named, by way of emphasising the experiential qualities of language, draws a distinction between the configurational significance of phrases as opposed to the individual meaning of words.[103] This kind of distinction gave rise to the Independence Theory, whereby emotive language is taken to be separable from referential and factual uses.

Russell pointed out that words do more than demonstrate the facts denoted by them,[104] while Ogden and Richards relate the affective use of language to all functions beyond the plainly factual. The distinction is between the emotive use of words to evoke attitudes, as in poetry, and the referential use of words as statement, as in science. On the one hand is a concern with the character of the attitudes aroused; on the other, a concern with the correctness of the facts retailed.[105] Behind the distinction is Bergson's differentiation of virtual from actual knowledge;[106] and, in practice, it is difficult to keep affective theories of language away from this sort of mysticism. Ogden and Richards seem to require literature to give up its efforts to convey knowledge or referential truth in favour of an intuitive recording of experience.[107] That is to say, literature should be untranslatable; possibly unparaphrasable. This led Richards to his theory of 'pseudo-statements', where he argued that poetry only seemed to convey facts, or conveyed facts that were to be understood only in a special, emotive way.[108] A similar formulation may be found in Yvor Winters, but he – wisely I think – used it as a means of indicating an unsatisfactory kind of poetry.[109]

What Jespersen and Vendryes, among others, were to Richards, later anti-grammarians such as Hayakawa and Lee seem to have been to a more recent theorist of this school, C. L. Stevenson. Lee differentiates the intensional orientation of language towards fiction and myth from the extensional orientation towards fact.[110] Hayakawa makes a similar distinction between affective truth, which may mean no more than our agreement with the sentiments expressed, and scientific truth.[111] While Stevenson himself takes emotive language as an entity quite distinct from descriptive language: the words that convey emotion are not the ones that would best describe it. According to Stevenson, emotive words have been shaped by experience towards stimulating or disposing the percipient towards specific reactions; and this mode of experience must be differentiated from cognitive meaning, which is the disposition of a sign to convey knowledge in the light of which one acts.[112]

The main weakness of this theory of language, as with the aesthetic theory of affectivity generally, is the extreme sharpness of differentiation. It takes no account of the factual content of literature; none, either, of the persuasive element in conceptual prose. It has, too, a submerged bias against the supposed fairy-tales of literature in favour of the practicalities of science. Most disturbing of all, within the boundaries of art itself, the Independence Theory favours a kind of bodiless bird-song or lyricism at the expense of the referential elements of literature.

Yet this distinction between the affective and referential modes of language has been embraced by many theorists: 'impression' – 'expression' (Jespersen),[113] 'implication' – 'entailment' (Strawson),[114] 'connotation' – 'designation' (Beardsley),[115] 'pictorial thinking' – 'empirical thinking' (Aldrich),[116] 'secondary meaning' – 'primary meaning' (Abercrombie),[117] 'emotional-conative' – 'conceptual' (Greene),[118] 'interinanimation' – 'independence' (Richards),[119] 'association' – 'meaning' (Sparrow),[120] 'obliquity' – 'directness' (Tillyard),[121] 'implication' – 'sense' and 'ambiguity' – 'statement' (Empson).[122]

Stevenson counselled us against using affective terminology as a universal dustbin for non-descriptive uses of language,[123] but, with some uninfluential exceptions,[124] his advice has not been heeded. In a wide area of theory[125] it can be said that the two modes of speech are now identified with the arts and the sciences respectively. We now have an emphasis on form in artistic discourse and on content in scientific discourse. Obviously, in practice, the two cannot be mutually exclusive. Yet the Independence Theory attempts to make us look at one element to the exclusion of others; perhaps even to make a distinction within the work, where no such distinction exists.

One would like to be able to say that theorists of literature have cleared the matter up, but in practice they are mesmerised by the Independence Theory. Characteristically, they are evasive about the assumption upon which their criticism rests. But, when they commit themselves to a theory of language, the main point at issue is how far poetry is a separate mode of speech.

Speaking from the scientific side, Max Eastman contrasts the communication of knowledge in 'practical language' with poetry,[126] which he claims as a form of incantation making more sense in primitive society than at the present time.[127] Even within the art of poetry itself, Eastman differentiates between 'intellectualist' and 'hypnotic' poetry, and condemns the twentieth century for returning to primitivism by letting the 'hypnotic' mode gain ascendancy.[128] More and more of the referential matter available to Lucretius and even to Donne is being lost to poetry. According to Eastman, the only way for poetry back to truth is for it to irradiate the work of scientists, conceptual analysts, and the like.[129] In other words, the true habitat of poetry is the scientific paper! This is a bold, if misguided, attempt to close up the gap posited by the Independence Theory between a 'poetic' and 'referential' meaning. It could, as a solution, only make sense if such a gap existed.

Still, this is a mistake very popular among the theorists. Technically, Christine Brook-Rose is on the other side from Eastman, speaking on behalf of the litterateurs, and yet she makes very much the same distinction. Speaking of symbolism, she says: 'The literal fact or scene may have symbolic meaning . . . but this is achieved by the connotation that words and even syntax have acquired in a civilisation or period, and not by means of the metaphoric relation of words to each other.'[130] This is a distinction which, for her, takes place within the field of poetry, but clearly Miss Brook-Rose feels that the symbolic usages tend out of poetry and into prose. Once more we have the distinction in the use of language: for Miss Brook-Rose, poetry is characteristically metaphorical, and in moving towards symbolism it becomes referential and prosaic. So, while in effect attacking Eastman's stand, Miss Brook-Rose succumbs to it: the anti-litterateur and the litterateur alike recognise a distinction between the language of poetry and that of prose; and, significantly enough, they recognise it in terms of referential weight.

Donald Davie claims this distinction as being an aberration deriving from Bergson via Hulme; in which, if we consider the genesis of the Independence Theory, he is almost certainly right.[131] He feels that it is possible to use the syntactical forms of prose in poetry. But, when this is done, the apparent identity of form masks a totally different function.[132] Yet he, too, is unable to escape from the Independence Theory: the more he seeks to show how poetry can include prose-elements, the more he finds himself insisting on a distinction in terms of reference.[133] He speaks, for example, of syntax like music, where the poem is an aesthetic whole existing for its own sake, as distinct from objective syntax, syntax following a form of action in the world at large.[134] The crucial question, of course, is whether these qualities can be combined; but this problem, which should have been the core of the enquiry, is treated perfunctorily at the end of his book.[135]

There are theorists who have attempted to synthesise the two halves of the Independence Theory in critical terms: a distinguished example is Winifred Nowottny. The logic of ordinary discourse is merely the ground-plan of poetry, she says:[136] the language is at full stretch in a poem and so contains more than speech proper.[137] Unfortunately Mrs Nowottny's metaphor gives away part of her case: an affective theorist, she tends to take quantity in lieu of quality. Or, alternatively, she seems to regard 'poetry' as a kind of overlay on the ground-plan of prose. That is to say, her particular analyses are less sensitive than her theories would seem to require. For example, she falls victim to an appallingly obscure poem by Dylan Thomas, *There Was a Saviour*, and after thirty pages of hammering its meaning out[138] comes to the conclusion that the poem seems opaque because it has abandoned the language of ordinary men.[139] So, however she attempts to unite in theory the two uses of language envisaged by the Independence Theory, 'poetic' and 'referential', in practice she abandons reference gladly in order to make special rules for poetic form.[140]

The fact of the matter is not that in some way poetic language works upon a ground-plan of referential truth; still less that it rejects reference altogether. Rather the poet's language may be held to work at such a degree of precision as to render the referential elements with greater force than a prosaic usage would allow. In other words, the poet communicates his meaning more clearly, concretely, definitely.

So we are back at the word communication again; back with the very idea of language. It is plain that the experts we called into our symposium won't help us very much. Let us briefly recapitulate. It may help to hold in mind a particular text: Blake's Introduction to *Milton*, say.[141] Now here is a superlatively fine act of communication: what would the specialists find to say about it?

The physiologist, presumably, would be concerned with the neurological operations that give rise to the poem: his would be a kind of submerged intentionalism, dealing with the very physical basis out of which the poem arose. There are still psychiatrists who regard Blake as a psychotic granted intervals of lucidity between his delusions.[142] But this is to be so clinical as to exclude all possibility of human interest.

The linguist would look at the poem as a pattern of language behaviour. The fact that it was more valuable than the Prophetic Book it precedes, let alone than the revivalist ravings of the late seventeenth century,[143] would seem to him irrelevant. So, too, would the meaning. It would rather be the order and length of phrases, the structural make-up of the sentence, that would interest him. In lieu of analysis we would have that last substitute for criticism: description without discrimination.

Psychologist, next: your Behaviourist would take the poem as phenomenon; might even claim that not enough was known about Blake's background for the text to be interpretable. Alternatively, he might treat the poem as mild experiment. If he was interested in the author, he could point to symbolism indicative of sexual stress in the young poet at a time of crisis. If interested in the response of percipients, he could attach a questionnaire to the poem and find what, given the questions he asked, his 'subjects' made of it. At best, as with Skinner, he might attempt to chart the influence of the poem's multiple variables upon individual behaviour.[144] But this has already been done, far more delicately, by the literary critics. All the psychologist can do is to substitute for that delicacy a non-analytical, non-evaluative form of literary criticism.

Applied mathematicians would be concerned with little more than the poem's suitability for transmission; and this they would term 'communication theory'. While pure mathematicians might siphon off all that makes the poem meaningful – its resonance, its feeling – in attempting to translate it into a tidier form of language.

Philosophers would be no more helpful. Signification Theorists would find the surface of the poem a sign for something evinced below it, and would thereafter speak of the sign and not the meaning. While theorists of affectivity would claim that the factual content of the poem was something distinct from any lyrical appeal it might have: its truths to be taken on a special, 'poetic' level.

And literary theorists, to whom in our bewilderment we should be able to turn for enlightenment, might condemn the poem as incantation or praise it as incantation, but in either case would be reducing it to an entity divorced from the practical concerns of life. Like all the others we have listened to, these theorists seem to be saying something irrelevant to the issue.

The blind men and the Elephant! Perhaps the answer is that we can see no Elephant, only elephants of varying size, shape and market value, and all in more or less active motion.

Yet the species 'elephant' is something that they all have in common. And, if that is true, then any useful theory about them could only come from the observation of particulars. One could go further and say that the value of the theory would depend on the value of the particulars observed.

Too much time is spent on examining utterances that are meaningless; such utterances can teach us nothing. What we should be examining is the nature of valuable communications: or, as we call them, works of art. Ultimately our theory of language must be a theory of communication must be a theory of value. Interpretation and evaluation are one and the same thing; with one qualification – that you can only interpret a valuable work.

Search, then, the utterances of critics on great works and it may be possible to see the effects of meaningful language at close quarters. It may be, to change the metaphor slightly, that we shall only succeed in adding one more elephant to the zoo. But at least it will be a live one, and we shall have the opportunity of observing it in action.

CHAPTER ELEVEN

A Theory of Communication

Existing linguistic theories fail for four reasons. First, because they consider language apart from meaning. Second, because they take no account of the value of the communication conveyed. Third, because they consider words out of linguistic context. And fourth, because they pay no regard to the social implications of that context.

Any viable theory of language must be at once semantic, evaluative, contextual and socially oriented. Otherwise it will fail to explain that which most needs explanation, the meaning and value of major communicative acts.

All criticism, whatever its explicit avowals, tends towards evaluation. In a work of great value, interpretation and evaluation are the same process. There is no instance of which I am aware when a difference of evaluation has not at its root a difference of interpretation.

Thus, when we say how good a specific poem is, we are also committing ourselves to a judgement of what it is about. Similarly, the very act of interpretation commits us to a view that there is something in the work which can be interpreted. Whatever our aesthetic hypotheses, the process of discussion presupposes that we think works of literature can be discussed.

Not all works of literature are equally discussible; the quality of our criticism depends on the quality of the work we criticise.

But this begs one crucial question: on what, in its turn, does this quality depend? What of the efficacy of expression? Granted, as practitioners would say, that poems are written with blood rather than words, still it would seem that the words are all we have to point to. These, after all, are the means by which the work manifests itself. Obviously the work is more than the printed marks upon the page, but it is from those marks that it must be recreated. And one may gather from that metaphor something of the process involved. If we use metaphors of birth and life to signify approval of the work, this may indicate that the work does not consist of disparate parts but is rather an organic whole. Thus, when we employ words such as 'vivid', 'coherent', 'alive' as evaluative terms, we are saying something crucial about the way in which language can be positively used.

Philosophers have suggested that knowledge is increasingly stratified into specialisms too complex to be apprehended by a single human mind, and that therefore we are losing the ability to define that which we know. One young aspirant some years ago instanced the fact that no definition of life has survived criticism.[1]

What was worrying this theorist, and philosophers generally, is their idea of language. Clearly a non-contextual, non-organicist theory will lose definition in a maze of definitions. There is no way of tying down a word to one given meaning. Any such attempt misconceives what words are and how we use them.

Any dictionary will provide a range of possible meanings for any single word, and even that will not account for the innumerable associations and gradations of emphasis. How, then, do we find it possible to understand one another? Surely there must be some way of limiting a given word's area of association?

There most certainly is; but in order to show how this happens we must lose the elementary misconception of the word as unit of language. The unit of language is not the word, nor the sentence, nor yet the paragraph.

Take the word 'mill'. As a noun alone, it can be an apparatus worked by steam, electricity, water or wind for grinding grain; it can be the structure containing such apparatus; it can be machinery for manufacturing paper, cotton or wool, or, again, the factory housing it; it can be a grinder for rendering down such substances as pepper or coffee; it can be an instrument of punishment for prisoners; a cant term among boxers for a prize fight; a slang term for any sort of hard time – and all this is only in its guise as a noun. As other parts of speech, 'mill' is capable of taking on dozens of additional meanings.

This is not all. If you say 'the mill has gone on half time' you may awaken gloomy echoes of the Hungry Thirties. If, on the other hand, you say 'There's trouble down at t' mill', all you are likely to do is to remind us of *The Crowthers of Bankdam* and other meaty family chronicles. Yet the word 'mill' refers to the same structure in both sentences.

Thus, even when limited to one 'meaning', a word can have a range of associations. In practice, however, a word can be limited and so defined into some sort of precision; and this is effected by its context.

True, the usual sort of context does not define the word so sharply as to render misunderstanding impossible. For example, someone who has heard 'there's trouble down at t' mill' used as a recurring cliché in the novels of Thomas Armstrong and Phyllis Bentley, and in the films made from them, will find it more ridiculous than someone who has not.

However, it is possible for words to be arranged in such a way that they work on one another to limit their respective ranges of association and so cohere into their own, defined, context. Let us look once more at Blake's Introduction to *Milton* –

> *And did the Countenance Divine*
> *Shine forth upon our clouded hills?*
> *And was Jerusalem builded here*
> *Among these dark Satanic Mills?*[2]

The last three words, in particular, have given rise to quite a number of interpretations. F. W. Bateson identified 'dark Satanic Mills' with the altars of the churches; indeed, with religion in general.[3] W. W. Robson, on the other hand, said that they were textile mills.[4] Bateson replied that in 1805, when the poem was written, there were no such things.[5] Robson suggested that, whatever was in Blake's mind in 1805, in the mind of the modern reader 'dark Satanic Mills' was irrevocably associated with the Industrial Revolution.[6] And J. Bronowski said that Blake probably *meant* the Industrial Revolution: an engraver would be hard hit before most trades were affected, and, in any case, the future development of industry could be foreseen by anyone who was not a political innocent.[7] While John Bayley found the shock of the phrase so immediate that agreement on exact interpretation was unnecessary.[8]

Without going as far as that, one could certainly claim the interpretations are not so disparate as the diverging critics would like them to be. Albion 'eyeless in Gaza at the mill with slaves' is, as Empson suggested, co-present in 'dark Satanic Mills' with the Industrial North.[9] Not just with the Industrial North, either. Blake has caused the associations of 'mills' with routine, labour and punishment to be concentrated into a predominance in his poem. Each of the critics whose interpretation I have cited seems to be putting forward some version of humanity in bondage. The critics may differ as to what the mechanisms of bondage are: whether they are the mills of (a false) God, organised religion, textile factories, materialist industrialism, the Newtonian universe; but these are all manifestations of what Blake was indicting in his poem. We see not one manifestation of humanity's bondage, but any and every manifestation. The poem defies any single interpretation because it is more, not less, subtle and defined than any interpretation could be. The poem, not the individual word, is the unit of language.

We should certainly have to admit that a paragraph limits word associations more than a sentence does. But in a successful work of literature the words qualify each other into a totality that is more precise, because at once more subtle and complex, than a paragraph. Words cannot be, as individuals, defined, because they are the instruments of definition.

Our young philosopher has said that, with all existing knowledge, we still couldn't define life.[10] This need not surprise us: 'life', even as a word out of context, is harder to handle than 'mill'. What we mean by the *word* can't be defined; but it can, in a sense, be recreated. I could offer this –

> *daffodils*
> *That come before the swallow dares, and take*
> *The winds of March with beauty . . .*[11]

or this –

> *To bend with apples the moss'd cottage trees,*
> *And fill all fruit with ripeness to the core . . .*[12]

or this –

> *See, banks and brakes*
> *Now, leaved how thick! laced they are again*
> *With fretty chervil, look, and fresh wind shakes*
> *Them . . .*[13]

or this –

> *It's June.*
> *Everything's come out in flush and white,*
> *In ruff and sun, and tall green shoots*
> *Hard with their sap . . .*[14]

My first-year class in practical criticism could analyse any of these to show the life in them. But does any of these passages amount to a definition? Rather we should say that the poet has created a response to life precise enough to awaken a correspondence in us, his audience. And that is as near a definition of life as the nature of language will allow us to get. Definition, in other words, lies not in statement but in demonstration.

I have been, by inference, deprecating the precision of a conceptual use of words. The alert reader may notice that I appear to have denied my own case even in the act of presenting it, since I am arguing against the possibility of argument. Certainly I think that discursive prose, like conversational speech, is not a precise form of communication. Understanding depends too much on good-will; one will be understood by those who want to understand – but they'll have to meet the argument half-way. Even then one has the pitiable spectacle of philosophic disciples contradicting each other on the precise import of the message conveyed by their master. Any two interpretations of Bentham or of Wittgenstein diverge widely from each other.[15] Perhaps the limitations of conceptual prose account for differing schools of philosophy.

What I have called a creative use of language, on the other hand, creates a context so actual that it imposes itself on readers of widely differing temperaments in something of the same way. And only inexperience – in living as well as reading – will prevent our responding to a genuine work of literature. The precise use of language is that which defines a situation; and that, in its turn, is found only in the work of the great writers.

Evaluative words, again. And they are unavoidable if we are to take into account the factor ignored by most linguists: the different degrees of efficacy shown in different acts of communication. But we can make our prose more precise by backing statement with example, by analysing the example chosen, and by drawing from that analysis a theoretic inference; this is the quadripartite procedure I should like to see adopted in critical theory.

So far it may be felt that my argument has been confined too much to a verbal level; as though the distinction between one work and another was a matter of *writing*. But what does this writing involve? Not merely a just use of words, surely. Granted the work exists on the page as words, nevertheless the language itself must be shaped and driven by a controlling impulse. What this impulse may be we cannot know, and it is a waste of time trying to find out; but we can certainly define its effect upon us, and we can use the response of our contemporaries as a check upon that effect.

Here we must turn not only to major poets but to major critics. If we consider the reaction of readers such as Leavis and Murry to a work such as *Antony and Cleopatra* and relate their response to our own, we shall approach as closely to an idea of language in action as conceptual prose will permit.

One has to get rid, first of all, of the idea that factual explanation is in some way more truthful than poetry. This is best done by considering the raw material from which *Antony and Cleopatra* is made; most notably, North's translation of Plutarch. There is nothing positively *wrong* with either Plutarch or North: the former is detailed, anecdotal, as reasonably accurate as a layman would require, while the latter writes a prose of exceptional vivacity. Let us examine it.

Therefore when she was sent unto by divers letters, both from Antonius himself, and also from his friends, she made so light of it and mocked Antonius so much, that she disdained to set forward otherwise, but to take her barge in the river of Cydnus; the poop whereof was gold, the sails of purple, and the oars of silver, which kept stroke in rowing after the sound of the musicke of flutes, howboys, citherns, viols, and such other instruments as they played upon in the barge. And now for the person of herself: she was laid under a pavilion of cloth of gold of tissue, apparelled and attired like the goddess Venus commonly drawn in picture: and hard by her, on either hand of her, pretty fair boys apparelled as painters do set forth god Cupid, with little fans in their hands, with the which they fanned wind upon her. Her Ladies and gentlewomen also, the fairest of them were apparelled like the nymphs Nereids (which are the mermaids of the waters) and like the Graces, some steering the helm, others tending the tackle and ropes of the barge, out of the which there came a wonderful passing sweet savour of perfumes, that perfumed the wharf's side, pestered with innumerable multitudes of people. Some of them followed the barge all alongst the river-side: others also ran out of the city to see her coming in. So that in the end there ran such multitudes of people one after another to see her, that Antonius was left post alone in the market-place in his Imperial seat to give audience: and there went a rumour in the people's mouths, that the goddess Venus was come to play with the god Bacchus, for the general good of all ASIA.[16]

All well so far: it is when we compare it with the verse which derives from this passage that we realise how little is actually focused in North's prose. This is what Shakespeare made of his raw material.

> ENO. *I will tell you.*
> *The barge she sat in, like a burnish'd throne,*
> *Burn'd on the water. The poop was beaten gold;*
> *Purple the sails, and so perfumed that*
> *The winds were love-sick with them; the oars were silver,*
> *Which to the tune of flutes kept stroke, and made*

> The water which they beat to follow faster,
> As amorous of their strokes. For her own person,
> It beggar'd all description. She did lie
> In her pavilion, cloth-of-gold, of tissue,
> O'erpicturing that Venus where we see
> The fancy out-work nature. On each side her
> Stood pretty dimpled boys, like smiling Cupids,
> With divers-colour'd fans, whose wind did seem
> To glow the delicate cheeks which they did cool,
> And what they undid did.
>
> AGR. O, rare for Antony.
>
> ENO. Her gentlewomen, like the Nereides,
> So many mermaids, tended her i' th' eyes,
> And made their bends adornings. At the helm
> A seeming mermaid steers. The silken tackle
> Swell with the touches of those flower-soft hands
> That yarely frame the office. From the barge
> A strange invisible perfume hits the sense
> Of the adjacent wharfs. The city cast
> Her people out upon her; and Antony,
> Enthron'd i' th' market-place, did sit alone,
> Whistling to th' air; which, but for vacancy
> Had gone to gaze on Cleopatra too,
> And made a gap in nature.[17]

We can do little better than cite Leavis's fine analysis of this latter passage. Where North and Plutarch have 'some steering the helm, others tending the tackle and ropes of the barge', Shakespeare renders the same action thus:

> At the helm
> A seeming mermaid steers. The silken tackle
> Swell with the touches of those flower-soft hands
> That yarely frame the office . . .[18]

And Leavis points out that the tactual imagery of the second sentence gains its strength from the contrast between the hard and energetic associations of 'tackle' and the sensuous adjective 'silken' – 'hands take hold of the cordage, and it seems impossible to dissociate "swell" from the tactual effect'.[19] One could go further than this and say that all the phrases are linked up and indeed subsumed in a sexual metaphor – the 'tackle' is at first limp and silken, but swells under the touch

214

of the 'flower-soft' hands: in little, a recapitulation of what happens to Antony under the enchantment of Cleopatra.

In comparison, North and Plutarch give us facts devoid of meaning – one gentlewoman did this, another did that – with no cohesion among those facts and no organic relationship with the rest of the action.

In Shakespeare we have the precise use of language which is an essential characteristic of the great writer. This language is not a matter of the individually well-chosen word – both North and Shakespeare use the word 'tackle' – but rather the way in which the words act upon each other and so create a total context. 'Tackle' is, literally, the cordage controlling the sails; by extension, the sails that mysteriously swell out of that cordage; it is there to be tackled, it *is* tackled (by the flower-soft hands); and, indeed, swells under this impulsion into what Leavis has termed a masculine hardness. The situation is recreated in all its solidity; it is unmistakable.

Poetry of this order always exhibits a density of language: call it concentration, ambiguity, paradox, tension or what you will – provided you grant also that the ambiguity is controlled, defining rather than disruptive. For the different meanings of the word 'tackle' pull in the same direction; irrelevant connotations are kept out. Moreover, though in one sense the exclusion of irrelevance limits the individual word, at the same time this limitation enables it to work upon other words, similarly limited, and to condition them – itself at the same time being conditioned – into a composite whole. And it is this whole which is the unit of language.

The whole is defined by its aesthetic boundaries. When the quality of the poetry deteriorates, the work finishes, no matter what its formal limits are. Thus *The Prelude* consists of a dozen or so live passages[20] blocked off from each other by a quantity of explanatory material – needless, because the passages are self-supporting poems. Similarly, *Paradise Lost* exists in fragments, each defined by the quality of the poetry it embodies. When the poetry ceases, so does the work: we cannot respond to that which fails to communicate with us.

But the creative limits of the very greatest works coincide with their formal limits; and this is the case with *Antony and Cleopatra*. The great work is itself a verbal unit: the context defined by its aesthetic boundaries. One should not take the individual speech we have considered out of its dramatic context. On the contrary, the remarkable fact about this description, so called, is its organic relationship with the rest of the play. Notice, for example, the moral point it raises about the use Cleopatra makes of Antony – controlled, as he is, by her flower-soft touch. Much the same issue is embodied in the curious paradox of the cupids: their fans *glowed* the delicate cheeks which they seemed to cool – 'and what they undid did'. This latter phrase looks backward to Philo's great opening speech when Antony's whole course of action is set before us, and in much the same terms –

> *His captain's heart*
> *Which in the scuffles of great fights hath burst*
> *The buckles on his breast, reneges all temper,*
> *And is become the bellows and the fan*
> *To cool a gipsy's lust . . .*[21]

A bellows has as much chance of *cooling* the flames of a fire as Antony had of satisfying Cleopatra. The energy of these images, and those of the Enobarbus speech, fight against the logical condemnation of the lovers' waywardness. Thus the tension is not only in the images – the power exerted over masculinity by femininity, the paradox of the bellows attempting to cool the flames – but in the contradiction between what is said and the way in which the speaker says it. While explicitly criticising Antony's conduct, Philo renders it in glowing colours. This contradiction is fruitful, for Antony is possessed of a force which is anti-social and disruptive but which may not be denied. Once more in Shakespeare we find the essential conflict between social check and individual desire. And once more the resolution takes place outside the play, mirrored in dramatic context only by implication.

For it is beyond even Shakespeare to picture a social context where the interests of male and female are identical, where duty and love can be reconciled. But he can imply, as in *King Lear*, an other-world where such resolution could conceivably take place. And, characteristically, he does this in Cleopatra's death-scene –

> *If she first meet the curled Antony*
> *He'll make demand of her and spend that kiss*
> *Which is my heaven to have . . .*[22]

Her *heaven* to have – this is a passion which, so far as we are concerned, can only burn itself out; but it burns itself out of this world into some hypothetical existence where Antony not only lives but is, once more, 'barbered ten times o'er' to greet her, provided she does not delay over-long in dying. And, as Murry remarks in his fine account of this scene,[23] the image of dying is done in terms of love and motherhood –

216

> *If thou and nature can so gently part*
> *The stroke of death is as a lover's pinch*
> *Which hurts, and is desired . . .*

> *Dost thou not see my baby at my breast*
> *That sucks the nurse asleep . . .*[24]

And even in that last image there is the density characteristic of great poetry: the nurse is asleep as she is being sucked, but also it is the sucking that is putting her to sleep. Only in that dream of an afterlife can Cleopatra call Antony 'husband':[25] there is no way in this world that she can deny duty and term the politic Caesar 'ass unpolicied'[26] – a phrase gently echoed by Charmian when she says

> *Now boast thee death in thy possession lies*
> *A lass unparallelled . . .*[27]

So one can point to verbal correspondences, verbal density, and, throughout, a sensuous immediacy of realisation, at once selective and dramatic; and point to this in all the more conviction having North in mind as basic comparison – North who has none of these things. What Shakespeare has done is to draw from a situation only suggested by his raw material the relevant dramatic and social implications. One points to the words, but in so doing indicates their reaction upon one another; indicates, in fact, what the words are doing.

It is not too much to say that, by this concentration of purpose, we know great poetry. One cannot lay down prescriptive rules, but, at the same time, it is possible to point out that works which are often considered to be different from one another nevertheless use language in something of the same way. Let us take an instance apparently at the other extreme from *Antony and Cleopatra*. It is a commonplace to say that Johnson totally failed to understand Shakespeare's use of language; and even Leavis has insisted on the generalising and abstract tendency of *The Vanity of Human Wishes*.[28] Yet is the language so un-Shakespearian? Leavis's own example would hardly seem to advance his case.

> *Unnumber'd suppliants crowd Preferment's gate*
> *Athirst for wealth and burning to be great;*
> *Delusive Fortune hears th' incessant call,*
> *They mount, they shine, evaporate, and fall . . .*[29]

Athirst goes along with *burning*; and there is no need for Johnson to specify the shooting star or firework image implied in the verbs of that last line. The fact that the suppliants are unnumbered suggests that Preferment will prefer none of them; their very brightness indicates the frenetic quality of their life, the inevitability of their early extinction. Thus Johnson and Shakespeare, different as they are, share certain properties of language that we can conveniently refer to as cohesion, density, concreteness. And, this being so, is it too much to say that we are likely to find these properties in the works of other poets also?

Poets as different as Wyatt, Herbert, Marvell, Blake, Wordsworth, Shelley, Keats and Whitman all have this much in common: that their best work enacts rather than states, demonstrates rather than conceptualises; that the individual words react upon each other so that we are provided with a fusion of disparate experience rather than the A + B + C reasoning of conceptual prose. When Shakespeare considers a topic, all manner of associated images rush in upon his language and so create, in highly dramatic terms, the feel and presence of the situation. I am not doing anything so coarse in grain as drawing the distinction of the Independence Theorists between poetic and referential uses of language. All verbal communication is necessarily referential, but some isolates and links up the key references to the world to which the verbal communication refers. The presence of a persuasive element even in the most conceptual prose suggests that all communication tends towards this form of dramatic concentration; but only certain communicative acts achieve it. Shakespeare's superiority over North and Plutarch is a superiority of reference; and the superiority is in the quality, not the quantity, of the information conveyed.

Conceptual prose, be it history, biography or criticism, is a more or less successful creative impulse; at its best, as in 'our excellent and indispensable eighteenth century',[30] it arrives astonishingly near its goal. The greatest philosopher in the language, the greatest historian, the greatest critic, the greatest political theorist, the greatest biographer – all may be held to have inhabited that period, which nevertheless totally lacked the central forms of literature, epic and tragedy, and so, for all its virtues, must be accounted something of a failure in the history of civilisation. The fourteenth century could offer very little in the way of conceptual thought in English, but consider what it produced in the way of creative literature – *The Canterbury Tales, Piers Plowman, Gawain and the Green Knight*. Verbal communication, that is to say, at its highest reach.

If, then, we seek to characterise language, we must characterise

218

literature; and, words being what they are, it is easier to cite examples in action than to philosophise around individual communicative acts.

Nevertheless, conceptual prose – the prose of our discourse – has its exigencies, and my reader is certainly entitled to an attempt at generalisation. The theory implied in what has gone before should satisfy the conditions ignored by proponents in other fields of activity. That is to say, it should take account of the meaning, value and context of the linguistic act.

Words cannot be considered separately. They are not separate units but part of a whole. This whole is created by the various parts working upon one another: a process of mutual and aggregative definition. But it is the whole that is defined, not the individual word.

Thus, like 'mill', 'dark' has a range of possible meanings. One can play upon them by instancing one phrase, such as 'a dark tunnel', and showing how the word acts quite differently in another, such as 'a dark man'. If one went on, it would be possible to limit the range of association of the word still further; as in 'I walked down a dark tunnel', for instance. But in limiting the individual word one is rendering the act of communication more precise – 'I walked down a dark tunnel because I had no spirit with which to meet the day' would be a case in point. And one could still further play upon the various aspects of 'dark' by changing individual words and so altering the context. Thus the sentences 'I *wandered* down a dark tunnel' or 'I *staggered* down a dark tunnel' are different, as verbal wholes, from the original 'I *walked* . . .'

But how far is this a total act of communication? It certainly lacks the immediate force we experience in

O dark, dark, dark, amid the blaze of noon[31]

or

O dark dark dark. They all go into the dark . . .[32]

It is therefore reasonable to suggest that the original example is, by comparison, incomplete: why, after all, was the 'I' of the sentence going down a tunnel? Further, one could suggest that the language is working at lower pressure than in the lines of verse, from Milton and Eliot respectively, which we cited by way of contrast.

But are even these lines total acts of communication? Certainly they cannot be taken as self-substantive poems. Behind the line from Milton is the tragic situation of Samson, 'eyeless in Gaza at the mill with slaves'.[33] Behind the line from Eliot is the presence of *Four Quartets* – that spiritual autobiography with the poet –

219

in the middle way, having had twenty years –
Twenty years largely wasted, the years of l'entre deux guerres –
Trying to learn to use words . . .[34]

And if we say, as we must, that there are flaws in both poems, we are in fact saying that the whole is not a perfect whole, that it carries a certain amount of waste matter. And the more it carries, the more deadness the reader must seek to revitalise, adding to the poem something of his own personal substance; until the time comes when the poem is wholly his, not to be shared on equal terms with any other reader; what I have called, in fact, a misreadable poem.

Between the supremacy of *Lear* and *Antony* and the inadequacies of modern obscurantists comes the bulk of our literature. And, in so far as it is valuable and precise, it will be found to be using language in something of the same way; organically, that is to say, and contextually. The effect, as I have said, is that of a situation created so forcefully that different readers experience something of the same reaction to it. And perhaps it would be impossible to create the situation with this degree of force if the raw material from which it is drawn were all of a kind. The greatest literature seems to be a reconciliation of apparent disparities.

For example, the great poets seem to share something of the same moral problem: the relationship between 'I ought' and 'I want', one could call it. The 'life' passages I cited earlier on all have in common a certain phallic and procreative aspiration –

> . . . take
> *The winds of March with beauty* . . .
> . . . fill *all fruit with ripeness to the* core . . .
> . . . *banks and brakes*
> *Now,* leaved *how thick* . . .
> . . . *tall green shoots*
> Hard *with their sap* . . .[35]

And each and every one of the speakers is regretting his bondage to a social norm paled off from the fecundity of nature. So this mode of language – that of the great writers – goes along with a highly characteristic theme; that seen, particularly, in Blake's escape from the mill in which the human spirit is ground and punished. It is poignant that his chariot of fire is found only in the clouds: Cleopatra, too, had to leave the baser elements of earth behind – 'I am fire and air' – in order to meet her curled Antony.

We cannot separate words from meanings, literature from morality, communication from context, poetry from reference; nor should we try. Literature is a series of answers to the reiterated question 'How? how? how?'. Blake is answering, in his own way, the cry of post-lapsarian man: 'how did I get here? how does it feel? how do I come to be so unhappy? how do I free myself from this bondage?'

Ultimately all the great writers can offer us is death: Piers takes his people off on a pilgrimage, Keats's swallows leave when the winter comes, Pope buries his failing civilisation in darkness, and Shakespeare's characters meet in death as they could never do in life. The greatest literature operates, in other words, morally as well as verbally between two poles: dramatises the tension between the social check and the individual desire.

Enough is presented to work upon the reader and so to allow for comment. The dramatised situation, whatever its latent disparities, is subject to analysis. Strictly speaking, what we are doing is not so much analysing the work as its effect upon ourselves. But since we share a common humanity with our fellows, if the work has done its job its effect on one reader should not be eccentrically different from its effect upon another. The divergences that seem to take place are largely a result of the selectivity imposed by the limitations of the medium in which we couch our analysis. This can be shown by relating apparently divergent views to each other and back to the text.

There are, of course, exceptions to this generalisation. Any reader can have an off day or a quirk of temperament that prevents him responding to a particular work. But again, this can be demonstrated by an appeal to the experience of other readers. And of course there are levels below which the reader may fail to respond: one cannot expect even the greatest masterpiece to evoke much response in a child or a cretin or a man from Mars. But these are barriers of circumstance, and can readily be shown to be so. There are, too, barriers of time: possibly Johnson or Coleridge would see aspects of Shakespeare more pressing to them than they would be to us in our present circumstances. But it can be said that readers of a certain ability should experience something of the same reaction to a given work if it is successful.

Of a certain ability – I can see that difficulties might be raised by this. But in practice it is possible to define a point below which one starts to lose respect for the opinion of one's fellows. One can demonstrate, by citing the reasons offered for judgement, when the professor becomes ossified, the young academic pusillanimous, the reviewer idle, the journalist superficial, the layman torpid, the student childish, the public at large quiescent.

The same is true of a change in circumstance. We can agree that, if the Bomb fell, there might be precious little of Shakespeare left. And supposing a few persons survived, grubbing for roots, it is unlikely that they would have the repose of spirit necessary for an appreciation of *Timon of Athens*.

We can grant, then, that literature is subject to circumstance. But this does not matter provided we are able to characterise the circumstances that would bring about disability of judgement. And to an extraordinary extent the greatest works are able to circumvent such disability.

Let me put it this way. Literature is like a mountain surrounded by the sea. Social and linguistic cataclysms engulf the lower reaches, and works which delighted readers of their own time are lost for ever beneath the waves. The tide sometimes uncovers the middle slopes, and a Donne or Crabbe is exposed to view. But the topmost crags seem to weather through: often, indeed, enhanced by linguistic changes, certainly dominating future ages, revealing to successive generations of readers new aspects of themselves. So that, in disagreeing with Johnson or Coleridge, we find that we are exploring new aspects of *Lear* or *Antony*.

On one level we can say that the power of feeling behind such works makes for their endurance. This is, too, a matter of our needs: they show us so much which is germane to the human condition that we can forget them only at our peril. On another level, we can say that the power of feeling is at one with the power of language: such works concentrate into themselves much which was verbally alive in their period and so survive to the present day. By the same token, our present day is to a great extent conditioned by the influence of those particular works.

Certainly, while the human individual and his social circumstances remain fairly constant, the conditions which operate with regard to language will remain constant also. Conceptualise as we will, one example is worth all our individual propositions. And what is a great work of literature but the most trenchant example of all?

So, when the individual act of criticism is superseded, the works which it discusses will remain: kept alive by their force of feeling, sense of conflict, and by the verbal interplay of paradox and ambiguity in which such feeling and conflict is expressed; kept alive, too, by our continuing need for such things. For what the critical theorist talks about these works actually do. The moral that the theorist draws from their action is what they themselves – more precisely – enact. So at best the theorist is saying something like this: 'Here are my findings – relate them back to the work, are they right, do you think?' Such, at least, has been my own approach to this most difficult of all subjects. Yet all I can do is point the way. It is for the reader to take it.

Notes

1 THE PERSONAL RESPONSE

1 R. P. Blackmur, *Language as Gesture* (1954) p. 316.
2 Yvor Winters, *In Defence of Reason* (1960) p. 22.
3 Hart Crane, *Collected Poems*, ed. Waldo Frank (1938) pp. 104–5.
4 Blackmur, op. cit. p. 310.
5 Ibid. pp. 309, 314.
6 Winters, op. cit. p. 598.
7 Ibid. p. 592.
8 Crane, op. cit. p. 37.
9 Winters, op. cit. p. 592.
10 Blackmur, op. cit. pp. 308, 311, 312.
11 Ibid. p. 34.
12 Emily Dickinson, *Poems*, ed. Thomas Johnson (1955) p. 568.
13 Blackmur, op. cit. p. 36.
14 Ibid. pp. 36–7.
15 Ibid. p. 37.
16 Ibid.
17 See Blackmur, op. cit. p. 48.
18 Winters, op. cit. pp. 289, 293.
19 Ibid. p. 289.
20 Ibid. pp. 297–8.
21 As quoted by Winters (pp. 295–6) from *Poems* (1890). The original text may be found, punctuated very differently, in *Poems* (1955) p. 185.
22 Winters, op. cit. p. 297.
23 Ibid.
24 Wallace Stevens, *Collected Poems* (1955) p. 55.
25 Blackmur, op. cit.p. 224.
26 Stevens, op. cit. p. 392.
27 Ibid.
28 Winters, op. cit. p. 69.
29 Blackmur, op. cit. p. 249.
30 Ibid. p. 243.
31 Winters, op. cit. p. 458.
32 Blackmur, op. cit. pp. 243, 244, 248.
33 Winters, op. cit. pp. 439–40.
34 Blackmur, op. cit. pp. 247–8.
35 Ibid. pp. 248–9.
36 Ibid. p. 248.
37 Stevens, op. cit. p. 41.

38 Winters, op. cit. p. 443.
39 Blackmur, op. cit. pp. 249, 436.
40 Winters, op. cit. p. 431.
41 Blackmur, op. cit. p. 236.
42 Stevens, op. cit. pp. 66–7.
43 Winters, op. cit. p. 433.
44 Blackmur, op. cit. p. 236.
45 Ibid. p. 447.
46 Winters, op. cit. p. 447.
47 Blackmur, op. cit. pp. 236–7.
48 Winters, op. cit. p. 447.
49 Randall Jarrell, *Poetry and the Age* (1955) p. 128.
50 A. Alvarez, *The Shaping Spirit* (1958) p. 138.

2 THE APPRECIATION OF MINOR ART

1 All quotations from D. W. Harding on James Gould Cozzens come from his article, 'The Limits of Conscience', in *Spectator*, cc (1958) 491. All quotations from Angus Wilson on this same author come from 'Back to Galsworthy', in *Observer*, 13 April 1958.
2 James Gould Cozzens, *By Love Possessed* (1958) p. 185.
3 Ibid. p. 566.
4 Arthur Mizener, *The Far Side of Paradise* (1951) p. 242.
5 Maxwell Geismar, *The Last of the Provincials* (1947) p. 331.
6 J. W. Aldridge, *After the Lost Generation* (1959) p. 52.
7 Dan Jacobson, 'F. Scott Fitzgerald', in *Encounter*, xiv (1960) 72–3.
8 John Farrelly, 'Scott Fitzgerald', in *Scrutiny*, xviii (1952) 270–1.
9 John Chamberlain in *New York Times*, 13 April 1934. And see the extended version of this article, in *Scott Fitzgerald*, ed. A. Kazin (1951) p. 98.
10 Andrews Wanning, 'Fitzgerald and his Brethren', in *Partisan Review*, xii (1945) 549.
11 Arthur Mizener, 'Poet of Borrowed Time', in *Eighteen from Princeton*, ed. Willard Thorp (1946) p. 349.
12 D. W. Harding, 'Mechanisms of Misery', in *Scrutiny*, iii (1934) 317. See also *Scrutiny*, xviii (1952) 172.
13 Farrelly, op. cit. p. 270.
14 Mizener, *The Far Side of Paradise*, p. 250.
15 Jacobson, op. cit. p. 72.
16 Scott Fitzgerald, *Tender is the Night* (1939) p. 26.
17 Jacobson, op. cit. p. 72.
18 Farrelly, op. cit. p. 268.
19 Geismar, op. cit. p. 329.
20 Mizener, *The Far Side of Paradise*, p. 242.
21 Jacobson, op. cit. p. 72.
22 Scott Fitzgerald, op. cit. pp. 26–7.
23 Jacobson, op. cit. p. 72.
24 Ibid.
25 Geismar, op. cit. p. 329.

26 Farrelly, op. cit. p. 268.
27 Aldridge, op. cit. p. 52. Mizener, *The Far Side of Paradise*, p. 42.
28 C. Hartley Grattan, first published in 1934 in the *Modern Monthly*; reprinted in *Scott Fitzgerald*, ed. A. Kazin, p. 107.
29 D. W. Harding, 'Scott Fitzgerald', in *Scrutiny*, XVIII (1951-2) 170.
30 Scott Fitzgerald, *The Great Gatsby* (1926) p. 216.
31 Mizener, *The Far Side of Paradise*, p. 174.
32 Farrelly, op. cit. p. 270.
33 Scott Fitzgerald, op. cit. p. 10.
34 Ibid. p. 21.
35 Ibid.
36 William Troy, 'Scott Fitzgerald – The Authority of Failure': first published in 1945 in *Accent*; reprinted in *Scott Fitzgerald*, ed. A. Kazin, see p. 189. Mizener, 'Poet of Borrowed Time', in *Eighteen from Princeton* ed. W. Thorp, p. 346.
37 Scott Fitzgerald, op. cit. p. 144.
38 Mizener, 'Poet of Borrowed Time', in *Eighteen from Princeton*, ed. W. Thorp, p. 346.
39 Marius Bewley, *The Eccentric Design* (1959) p. 279.
40 Alfred Kazin, 'An American Confession', in *Scott Fitzgerald*, ed. A. Kazin, p. 177.
41 Farrelly, op. cit. p. 269.
42 Lionel Trilling, *The Liberal Imagination* (1951) p. 251. Bewley, op. cit. pp. 281, 283, 287.
43 Scott Fitzgerald, op. cit. pp. 26, 112-13, 218.
44 Bewley, op. cit. p. 281.
45 Alfred Kazin, *On Native Grounds* (1942) p. 322.
46 Aldridge, op. cit. p. 50.
47 Mizener, *The Far Side of Paradise*, p. 178.
48 Bewley, op. cit. p. 281.
49 Ibid. pp. 280-1.
50 Farrelly, op. cit. p. 269.
51 Mizener, *The Far Side of Paradise*, p. 176.
52 Harding, in *Scrutiny*, XVIII (1952) 170.
53 Trilling, op. cit. pp. 247-8.
54 Farrelly, op. cit. p. 268.
55 Wanning, op. cit. p. 548.
56 Ibid.
57 Kazin, op. cit. p. 321.
58 Ibid.
59 Aldridge, op. cit. p. 49.
60 Farrelly, op. cit. p. 269.
61 Geismar, op. cit. p. 317. And see Scott Fitzgerald, op. cit. p. 118.
62 Scott Fitzgerald, op. cit. p. 47.
63 Bewley, op. cit. p. 274.
64 H. L. Mencken, 'The Great Gatsby: first printed in the *Baltimore Evening Sun*, 3 May 1925; reprinted in *Scott Fitzgerald*, ed. A. Kazin, p. 89.
65 Charles Weir, Jr, 'An Invite with Gilded Edges': first printed in the *Virginia Quarterly Review* in 1944; reprinted in *Scott Fitzgerald*, ed. A. Kazin; see pp. 136-7.
66 Trilling, op. cit. p. 253.
67 Farrelly, op. cit. p. 270.

3 THE CONCEPT OF AVAILABILITY

1 See Kenneth Muir, *Milton* (1955) p. 3, and E. M. W. Tillyard, *Milton* (1930) p. 355 – 'For the last two hundred years Milton has been allowed, in spite of suppressed murmurs, a secure position on an eminent pedestal.' But the murmurs have not been altogether suppressed, except in the summaries of modern critics. See also J. Thorpe, *Milton Criticism* (1951) and J. H. Hanford, *A Milton Handbook* (1939), where such names as Leavis, Murry and Eliot fail to appear.

2 John Dryden, Preface to *Sylvae* (1685) p. xxviii. See also the 'Apology for Heroic Poetry' (Preface to *The State of Innocence*, 1677) pp. ix ff (and see Nathaniel Lee's commendatory verses, ibid. p. vii); Dedication prefixed to the *Satires of Juvenal* (1693) pp. viii–ix.

3 John Dennis, *The Grounds of Criticism in Poetry* (1704) pp. 53–4. See also Dennis's Preface to his translation of Ovid's *Passions of Byblis* (1692) p. 4. For other contemporary doubts about Milton's language see Richard Leigh, *The Transproser Rehears'd* (1673) pp. 41–3; reprinted in W. R. Parker, *Milton's Contemporary Reputation* (1940), where the attribution to Leigh is also made. And, a little later, Alexander Pope, in his Postscript to the *Odyssey* (1726) II 278–9.

4 Joseph Addison, in *Spectator*, no. CCCLXIX. See also no. CCXCVII.

5 Richard Bentley (ed.) *Paradise Lost* (1732). See esp. his emendations to I 74; III 117, 161, 228; IV 181; VI 652.

6 Samuel Johnson, 'Life of Milton', in *The Lives of the English Poets* (1779) II 214–21, etc.

7 S. T. Coleridge, Lecture on Milton (1818), in *Miscellaneous Criticism*, ed. T. M. Raysor (1938) pp. 163–4.

8 John Keats, *Letters*, ed. M. Buxton Forman (1947) no. 156, p. 425 (17–27 Sept. 1819). See also *Letters*, no. 145, p. 373 (24 Aug. 1819), no. 151, p. 384 (21 Sept. 1819): 'English ought to be kept up'.

9 Ezra Pound, *Literary Essays*, ed. T. S. Eliot (1954) pp. 216–17, 237–8, 247. T. S. Eliot, 'A Note on the Verse of John Milton', in *Essays and Studies by Members of the English Association* (1936). See also Eliot's essays on the Metaphysical Poets (1921), on Marvell (1921), on Dryden (1921) and on Blake (1920); all reprinted in *Selected Essays* (1932).

10 Johnson, op. cit. pp. 121–2.

11 William Blake, *The Marriage of Heaven and Hell* (n.d.: but Geoffrey Keynes suggests 1790 – see *A Bibliography of William Blake* (1921) p. 107) p. 6.

12 P. B. Shelley, 'A Defence of Poetry', in *Literary Criticism*, ed. J. Shawcross (1909) p. 145.

13 e.g. William Hazlitt, 'Of Shakespeare and Milton', in *Lectures on the English Poets* (1818) pp. 124–31, esp. p. 128. W S. Landor, 'Southey and Landor', in *Works* (1846) II 60, 61; reprinted in *Complete Works*, ed. T. Earle Welby (1927) V 238, 242. John Keble, 'Sacred Poetry', in *Quarterly Review*, XXXII (1825) 229; reprinted in *English Critical Essays*, 19th Century, ed. E. D. Jones (1916) p. 218.

14 Walter Bagehot, 'John Milton', in *National Review*, IX (1859) 180–1, see generally pp. 176ff; reprinted in *Literary Studies*, ed. R. H. Hutton (1879) I 212. See also ibid. pp. 206ff.

15 Mark Pattison, *Milton* (1879) esp. pp. 199–200. Matthew Arnold, 'A French Critic on Milton', in *Mixed Essays* (1879) esp. pp. 261, 272. And see Edmond

Scherer, 'Milton et le *Paradise perdu*', in *Études sur la littérature contemporarie* (1876) esp. pp. 151ff. *Selections*, trans. G. Saintsbury (1891), see pp. 120ff.

16 A. J. A. Waldock, *Paradise Lost and its Critics* (1947) ch. 1.

17 C. S. Lewis, *A Preface to Paradise Lost* (1942) pp. 70, 121ff.

18 B. Rajan, *Milton and the Seventeenth Century Reader* (1947) p. 85.

19 J. Middleton Murry, *Heaven and Earth* (1938) p. 164.

20 Douglas Bush, *Paradise Lost in Our Time* (1945) p. 47.

21 *Paradise Lost*, XII 401–35. Thus the Atonement is a spiritual act for Lewis (op. cit. pp. 88–9), but not for Saurat (*Milton, Man and Thinker* (1925) pp. 174ff) or Murry op. cit. p. 164). Nor are Saurat and Murry in agreement with each other: for Saurat the Atonement is rational and therefore good (op. cit. p. 177); for Murry it is rational and therefore bad (op. cit. p. 164). There is not even agreement about its presence in the poem: it does not occur as an action for Bush (op. cit. ch. 2), but rather as a basic fact running throughout the poem; while for Rajan it does not seem to be there at all (op. cit. pp. 85ff).

22 Walter Raleigh, *Milton* (1900) pp. 162–3.

23 Muir, op. cit. p. 131.

24 David Daiches, *Milton* (1957) p. 212.

25 Edwin Greenlaw, 'A Better Teacher than Aquinas', in *Studies in Philology*, XIV (1917) esp. pp. 200ff.

26 Bush, op. cit. p. 79.

27 Tillyard, *Milton*, p. 237.

28 E. M. W. Tillyard, *The Miltonic Setting* (1938) pp. 70–1.

29 Cleanth Brooks, 'Milton and Critical Re-estimates', in *PMLA* LXVI (1951) 104.

30 Tillyard, *Milton*, p. 237; Greenlaw, op. cit. p. 215.

31 Raleigh, op. cit. pp. 133ff.

32 Lewis, op. cit. chapters 11 and 12.

33 Addison, in *Spectator*, no. CCXCVII.

34 Landor, op. cit. II 60.

35 C. M. Bowra, *From Virgil to Milton* (1945) pp. 230–2.

36 Saurat, op. cit. p. 220.

37 Daiches, op. cit. p. 185.

38 Lewis, op. cit. chapters 6 and 7.

39 H. J. C. Grierson, *Criticism and Creation* (1949) pp. 41–2.

40 John S. Diekhoff, *Milton's Paradise Lost* (1946) p. 8.

41 E. E. Stoll, *From Shakespeare to Joyce* (1944) p. 430.

42 Arnold Stein, *Answerable Style* (1953) p. 123.

43 Ibid.

44 Ibid.

45 Ibid.

46 Lewis, op. cit. p. 125.

47 Muir, op. cit. p. 160.

48 Bush, op. cit. p. 86.

49 Tillyard, *Milton*, p. 256.

50 F. T. Prince, 'On the Last Two Books of Paradise Lost', in *Essays and Studies by Members of the English Association*, ed. B. Willey (1958).

51 *Paradise Lost*, XII 469.

52 See Prince, op. cit. p. 42. He compares Milton's method not only with that of

Henry James ('the dramatized consciousness'), but with that of T. S. Eliot (Tiresias – 'what Adam sees, in fact, is the substance of the poem').

53 Lewis, op. cit. p. 109.
54 Stein, op. cit. pp. 33–4; and see p. 30.
55 Muir, op. cit. p. 152.
56 Waldock, op. cit. pp. 110–11. And see *Paradise Lost*, vi 348–9.
57 Stein, op. cit. pp. 31–2.
58 Muir, op. cit. p. 152.
59 Stein, op. cit. p. 24.
60 Grierson, *Milton and Wordsworth* (1937) p. 116.
61 Tillyard, *Milton*, p. 170.
62 Hanford, op. cit. pp. 205–7.
63 Lewis, op. cit. pp. 48–9. ('*Of course*, the trees have golden fruit. We always knew they would.')
64 Stein, op. cit. pp. 54, 68.
65 Bush, op. cit. p. 17, and see also his *English Literature in the Earlier Seventeenth Century* (1945) p. 387.
66 Diekhoff, op. cit. p. 94. Tillyard, *Milton*, p. 282.
67 Basil Willey, *Seventeenth Century Background* (1934) pp. 247–8. John Erskine, 'The Theme of Death in *Paradise Lost*', in *PMLA* xxxii (1917) 581.
68 Paul Elmer More, 'The Theme of *Paradise Lost*', in *Shelburne Essays 4th Series* (1906) pp. 239–53, esp. p. 244. Daiches, op. cit. p. 187.
69 William Empson, *Some Versions of Pastoral* (1935) pp. 186–7.
70 Cleanth Brooks and J. E. Hardy, *Poems of Mr John Milton* (1957) pp. 273ff.
71 Robert Martin Adams, *Ikon: John Milton and his modern critics* (1955) p. 127.
72 F. R. Leavis, *Revaluation* (1936) p. 50.
73 *Paradise Lost*, iv 218–20.
74 Daiches, op. cit. p. 176.
75 Bush, op. cit. pp. 94–5.
76 Daiches, op. cit. p. 176.
77 Lewis, op. cit. pp. 49–50.
78 Empson, op. cit. p. 186.
79 *Paradise Lost*, iv 288–90.
80 Raleigh, op. cit. pp. 222–3.
81 Lewis, op. cit. p. 50.
82 Leavis, *Revaluation*, p. 64.
83 Waldock, op. cit. pp. 92–6.
84 Muir, op. cit. p. 147.
85 T. S. Eliot, British Academy Lecture on *Milton* (1947) p. 11.
86 F. R. Leavis, 'Mr Eliot and Milton', in *The Common Pursuit* (1952) p. 20.
87 Daiches, op. cit. p. 175. J. B. Broadbent, 'Milton's Hell', in *ELH* xxi (1954) 169–70.
88 *Paradise Lost*, i 670–3; see also 60–3, 209–10, 227–9, 561–3 and 670ff, generally.
89 Stein, op. cit. esp. pp. 43–5.
90 *Paradise Lost*, ii 458–60.
91 Lewis, op. cit. p. 55. And see Bush, op. cit. pp. 96–7.
92 T. De Quincey, 'Milton', in *Blackwood's Magazine*, xlvi (1839) 778–9; rep. *Works*, ed. D. Masson (1889–90) pp. 103–4.
93 Rajan, op. cit. p. 124.

94 *Paradise Lost*, I 192–210.

95 T. S. Eliot, *Milton* (1947) pp. 15–16.

96 Leavis, *The Common Pursuit*, p. 22.

97 Eliot, *Milton* (1947) pp. 14–15.

98 Leavis, *The Common Pursuit*, p. 22.

99 T. S. Eliot' *Milton* (1947) p. 15.

100 For example, Christopher Ricks (*Milton's Grand Style* (1963) p. 6) claims a traditional identification between Satan and Leviathan. But even if he were correct, it is up to the poet to render the identification inevitable; to recreate it in his own terms. Has this been done here? If the poet has not done the work, he cannot expect 'tradition' to do it for him.

101 James Whaler, 'The Miltonic Simile', in *PMLA* XLVI (1931) 1034.

102 *Paradise Lost*, II 629–43.

103 Empson, op. cit. p. 171.

104 Ibid.

105 Adams, op. cit. p. 122.

106 Whaler, loc. cit. p. 1055.

107 Waldock, op. cit. p. 141.

108 *Paradise Lost*, IV 977–87.

109 Tillyard, *Studies in Milton* (1951) p. 63.

110 Empson, op. cit. p. 172.

111 Geoffrey Hartman, 'Milton's Counterplot', in *ELH* XXV (1958) 11.

112 John Peter, *A Critique of Paradise Lost* (1960) p. 57.

113 Whaler, loc. cit. p. 1057.

114 Waldock, op. cit. p. 142.

115 Ibid.

116 Tillyard, *Studies in Milton*, p. 64.

117 Empson, op. cit. p. 172.

118 Zachary Pearce, *A Review of the Text of Paradise Lost* (1732) pp. 66–7, 148.

119 Waldock, op. cit. p. 143.

120 Rajan, op. cit. pp. 52–3, 124.

121 Tillyard, *Studies in Milton*, p. 63; Empson, op. cit. pp. 171–2.

122 *Paradise Lost*, I 299–313.

123 John Peter, 'Reflections on the Milton Controversy', in *Scrutiny*, XIX (1952) 12.

124 Broadbent, op. cit. p. 184.

125 Daiches, op. cit. p. 161.

126 Muir, op. cit. p. 139.

127 Ibid.

128 Broadbent, op. cit. p. 184.

129 Daiches, op. cit. p. 162.

130 Peter, op. cit. p. 12.

131 Charles Williams, *Introduction to the English Poems of John Milton* (1940) pp. xxvii ff.

132 Lewis, op. cit. p. 40.

133 L. A. Cormican, in *Penguin Guide to Literature*, ed. B. Ford, III 176–9.

134 Daiches, op. cit. pp. 157–8.

135 Lewis, op. cit. pp. 44–5.

136 Bush, op. cit. pp. 70–1.

137 E. E. Stoll, *From Shakespeare to Joyce* (1944) ch. 2, and esp. p. 32.

138 Muir, op. cit. p. 147.

139 Leavis, *The Common Pursuit*, pp. 18–19.
140 Leavis, *Revaluation*, pp. 45–6, 63.
141 Empson, *Seven Types of Ambiguity* (1930) pp. 15–16; *Some Versions of Pastoral*, pp. 173–4.
142 Waldock, op. cit. pp. 36–7.
143 Brooks and Hardy, op. cit. pp. 275–7.
144 *Paradise Lost*, XII 624–9. e.g. Tillyard, *Milton*, pp. 256, 117; Peter, op. cit. p. 11; Daiches, op. cit. p. 214; Prince, op. cit. p. 46; Erskine, op. cit. p. 581; Stoll, op. cit. pp. 430, 434; Bush, *English Literature in the Earlier Seventeenth Century*, p. 411.
145 Grierson, *Milton and Wordsworth*, pp. 106–16. Lewis, op. cit. ch. 11.
146 Waldock, op. cit. pp. 197–206.
147 Lewis, op. cit. p. 130. Leavis, *Revaluation*, pp. 46ff. Douglas Bush, op. cit. 'Paradise Lost in Our Time', pp. 95ff.
148 e.g. Leavis, Empson, Waldock, Stoll, Cormican, Peter, Brooks and Hardy. And see Wilson Knight's very interesting essay in *The Burning Oracle* (1939).
149 e.g. C. S. Lewis, *The Allegory of Love* (1936) p. 44. Graham Hough, *A Preface to the Faerie Queene* (1962) pp. 100ff. Northrop Frye. *The Anatomy of Criticism* (1957) p. 91.
150 R. S. Crane and William Empson might just as well be reading two different novels when they come to consider *Tom Jones* as a whole. Thus Crane takes the plot to be a straight unfolding of events (*Critics and Criticism* (1952) pp. 632ff) while for Empson it is the working out of a double irony (*Kenyon Review*, XX (1958) 218ff). For Crane, Tom is unambiguously 'a naturally good man' (p. 623), but for Empson his implied goodness is undermined at every turn by the author's explicit assertions that the hero is doing wrong (p. 218). Interestingly enough, the book allows each of these critics to indulge his idiosyncrasies to the top of their bent: a firmer text would have required more disciplined handling on the part of the commentators.

James Joyce affords similar opportunities for fun and games among the critics. Is *Ulysses* a genial book, as William York Tindall says (*James Joyce* (1950) 125), or does it exhibit an aloofness bordering on neutrality (David Daiches, *The Novel and the Modern World* (1939) pp. 108, 137–8)? Does the end of the book indicate Bloom's inability to come to grips with the world (Douglas Knight, 'The Reading of *Ulysses*', in *ELH* XIX (1952) p. 64) or is it rather a paean of affirmation (Stuart Gilbert, *James Joyce's 'Ulysses'*, (1930) p. 394)?

There are more works of this nature than the critics seem to realise. A number of specific sections work, and this serves to give the idea of a whole; but the wholeness is only illusion. This is, perhaps, especially the case with the showpieces of modern experimentalism – in addition to *Ulysses*, Pound's *Cantos* and Eliot's *Waste Land*. The point could readily be demonstrated through a comparison of critical commentaries. Such works as these deliberately strive for a fragmentation which characterises literature of the past that, like *Paradise Lost*, has deteriorated through the action of time without disintegrating into total obscurity.

4 MISREADABLE POEMS AND MISREAD POEMS

1 Mrs L. Redford, in *Observer*, 7 Oct. 1951.
2 Richard Perry, ibid. 14 Oct. 1951.

231

3 John Sparrow, *Sense and Poetry* (1934) p. 81. (He, by the way, considers 'Emily' to be red.) And see *Observer*, 11 Nov. 1951.

4 Edith Sitwell, in *Observer*, 7 Oct. 1951.

5 Maurice Wollman (ed.), *Modern Poetry 1922–34* (1935) p. viii. And see Josephine Malone, in *Observer*, 28 Oct. 1951, and also ibid., 11 Nov. 1951.

6 Philip Toynbee, in *Observer*, 30 Sept. 1951.

7 Joyce Montague, ibid. 21 Oct. 1951.

8 Exhaustive researches have failed to turn this up, from Miss Sitwell's work or that of any other poet. She herself refers to it in the *Observer*, 28 Oct. 1951.

9 See Sacheverell Sitwell, *The Dance of the Quick and the Dead* (1936) p. 28.

10 Kingsley Amis, in *Essays in Criticism*, II (1952) 342.

11 Montague, loc. cit.

12 E. H. Gombrich, in *Observer*, 18 Nov. 1951.

13 John Tutin, ibid.

14 Helen Walters, ibid. 25 Nov. 1951. Geoffrey Nokes, in *Essays in Criticism*, II (1952) 339, 340, 341.

15 F. F. McIntyre, in *Observer*, 21 Oct. 1951.

16 Montague, loc. cit.

17 Gombrich, loc. cit. And see Chaucer, 'Knight's Tale', lines 177–80.

18 Tutin, loc. cit. also 25 Nov. 1951. But see Walters, loc. cit.; T. E. Hendrie, ibid. 2 Dec. 1951.

19 N. Young, ibid. 2 Dec. 1951; Nokes, loc. cit. p. 339.

20 McIntyre, loc. cit.

21 Edith Sitwell, in *Observer*, 7 Oct. 1951; and Introduction to the Penguin *Selected Poems* (1952) p. xxxi, reprinted in her *Collected Poems* (1957) p. xxxiv.

22 Amis, loc. cit. p. 344.

23 W. E. Shewell-Cooper, *The Complete Gardener* (1950) pp. 136–7, 168, 180, 615.

24 Quite a substantial account in *Essays in Criticism*, II (1952) 338ff.

25 Edith Sitwell, 'Spring'. First printed in *Bucolic Comedies* (1923) p. 12; reprinted in *Collected Poems* (1957) p. 14.

26 *Bucolic Comedies*, pp. 12–13; *Collected Poems*, pp. 14–15.

27 Nokes, loc. cit. pp. 341–2; Amis, loc. cit. pp. 342–3.

28 I base this remark on a highly intelligent comment by one of the contributors to the *Observer* controversy, M. Harrison, 21 Oct. 1951. More fun and games were had in the *Spectator*; see esp. vol. 192, pp. 47, 96, 123, 147, 203, 230 and 290.

29 Northern Ireland General Certificate of Education, 'A'-level, July 1963.

30 Sidney Keyes, *The Cruel Solstice* (1943) pp. 40–1; reprinted in *Collected Poems* (1945) p. 48.

31 Roy Fuller, in *London Magazine*, II (1955) 83.

32 W. S. Graham, *The Nightfishing* (1955) pp. 22–3.

33 Fuller, loc. cit. p. 83.

34 G. S. Fraser, in *London Magazine*, II (1955) 68–9.

35 J. A. Stephens, 'The "I am" of W. S. Graham' (c. 1961). This paper has not yet been published

36 Ibid.

37 Fraser, loc. cit. pp. 68–9.

38 Stephens, op. cit.

39 Fraser, loc. cit. pp. 68–9.

40 In one of my adult education classes, held under the auspices of the South Yorkshire W.E.A., in 1960–1. One student thought *The Nightfishing* was a religious poem about martyrdom. Another took it to be a poem about the soul bleeding in the world in which it was fixed and tested by suffering. Yet another interpretation was a sort of sea-story, about a whaler haunted by some past encounter with a monster of the deep. All these interpretations relate far more to the personalities of the people concerned than to the text with which they were confronted. In all innocence they were trying to comprehend the incomprehensible. The only way in which this could be done was by producing material of their own and bending the enigmatic language of the poem to suit that material.

41 Graham, op. cit. p. 28. And see Fuller, loc. cit. p. 83.

42 Graham, op. cit. p. 19. And see G. S. Fraser, in *New Statesman*, 19 March 1955.

43 Graham, op. cit. p. 22.

44 See *Wheel of Fire* (1930) pp. 80ff. Surely one of the great essays of our century.

45 P. B. Shelley, *Poetical Works*, ed. Thomas Hutchinson (1952) p. 667.

46 F. R. Leavis, *Revaluation* (1936) pp. 217–18.

47 Allen Tate, *On the Limits of Poetry* (1948) p. 126.

48 Milton Wilson, *Shelley's Later Poetry* (1959) p. 27.

49 F. A. Pottle, 'The Case of Shelley', in *PMLA* LXVII (1952) 607.

50 Shelley, op. cit. p. 667.

51 Leavis, op. cit. p. 218.

52 Shelley, op. cit. p. 668.

53 Leavis, op. cit. p. 219.

54 Pottle, op. cit. pp. 607–8 n.

55 Wilson, op. cit. p. 28.

56 René Wellek, 'Literary Criticism and Philosophy', in *Scrutiny*, V (1937) 381.

57 Shelley, op. cit. p. 668.

58 Leavis, op. cit. p. 220.

59 Wellek, op. cit. p. 382.

60 Pottle, op. cit. p. 608 n.

61 Wilson, op. cit. pp. 28–9.

62 Tate, op. cit. p. 126.

63 Shelley, *Ode to the West Wind* (in *Poetical Works*, ed. T. Hutchinson (1952) pp. 577 ff).

64 F. W. Bateson, *English Poetry: a critical introduction* (1950) p. 213n.

65 Shelley, op. cit. lines 63–4.

66 Neville Rogers, *Shelley at Work* (1956) p. 227.

67 G. Wilson Knight, *The Starlit Dome* (1941) p. 200.

68 F. A. Lea, *Shelley and the Romantic Revolution* (1945) p. 155.

69 Shelley, op. cit. lines 5–8.

70 Ralph Houston, 'Shelley and the Principle of Association', in *Essays in Criticism*, III (1953) 57.

71 Bateson, op. cit. p. 214n.

72 Shelley, *Poetical Works*, ed. Hutchinson, p. 668. Neville Rogers (op. cit. p. 50) points out that this line derives from one by Calderón – 'cuna y sepulcro en un botón hallaron' (they found a cradle and a sepulchre in a bud). But the necessary linkage provided by 'botón' is missing from the Shelley line.

73 Shelley, *Ode to the West Wind*, lines 9–12.

74 Houston, op. cit. p. 57.
75 Bateson, op. cit. p. 214n.
76 W. Milgate, 'Reading Shelley', in *Essays in Criticism*, IV (1954) 90.
77 Shelley, op. cit. lines 14–15.
78 Leavis, op. cit. p. 205.
79 See, for instance, Lea, op. cit. p. 155.
80 Shelley, op. cit. line 14.
81 Wellek, op. cit. 380.
82 D. W. Harding, 'Shelley's Poetry', in *Penguin Guide to Literature*, ed. Boris Ford, V (1957) 212.
83 R. H. Fogle, *The Imagery of Keats and Shelley* (1949) pp. 265–6.
84 Rogers, op. cit. p. 227.
85 Leavis, op. cit. p. 205.
86 Shelley, *Ode to the West Wind*, line 13.
87 Wellek, op. cit. p. 380.
88 Harding, op. cit. p. 212.
89 Yvor Winters, *In Defence of Reason* (1960) p. 369.
90 Rogers, op. cit. p. 225.
91 Lea, op. cit. p. 152.
92 Pottle, op. cit. p. 606.
93 Knight, op. cit. p. 200.
94 Bateson, op. cit. p. 215.
95 Kathleen Raine, 'Who Made the Tyger?' in *Encounter*, II (1954) 43.
96 Stanley Gardner, *Infinity on the Anvil* (1954) p. 128 (but see the whole argument, pp. 123–8).
97 Hazard Adams, *Blake and Yeats: the contrary vision* (1955) p. 238.
98 David V. Erdman, *Blake: prophet against empire* (1954) p. 180.
99 F. W. Bateson (ed.) *Selected Poems of William Blake* (1957) p. 117.
100 Damon quotes this as being written on a painting in the Tate Gallery. See S. Foster Damon, *William Blake* (1924) p. 277.
101 Damon, op. cit. p. 277.
102 Margaret Rudd, *The Divided Image* (1953) p. 91.
103 Ibid.
104 Raine, op. cit. p. 44.
105 William Blake, *Complete Writings*, ed. Geoffrey Keynes (1966) p. 115.
106 Raine, op. cit. pp. 44–5.
107 Hermes Trismegistus, *The Divine Pymander*, trans. John Everard (1650) book II, paras. 12–14, pp. 17–18, and ed. W. Wynn Westcott (1894) p. 23. This gets rather mauled in Miss Raine's transcription; esp. para. 14 which is paraphrased most unacceptably to suit her case. See Raine, op. cit. p. 46.
108 Raine, op. cit. p. 47.
109 Ibid. p. 48.
110 Ibid. pp. 48–9.
111 Ibid. p. 48.

5 THE PRINCIPLE OF THE ROVING CRITERION

1 Henry James, in *Nation*, I (1865) 787; reprinted in *House of Fiction*, ed. Leon Edel (1957) pp. 253–4.

2 Hippolyte Taine, *Histoire de la littérature anglaise* (1864) IV 48–51; trans. H. van Laun (1871) pp. 357–8.

3 Walter Bagehot, 'Charles Dickens', in *National Review*, VII (1858) 462–3, 464–5, 476–7; reprinted in *Literary Studies*, ed. R. H. Hutton (1879) pp. 189–90, 192–3, 207–8, etc.

4 G. H. Lewes, 'Dickens in Relation to Criticism', in *Fortnightly Review*, XVII (1872) 148–9, 150–1. And see George Saintsbury, *The English Novel* (1913) pp. 226–9, and his *Corrected Impressions* (1895) pp. 120–2, 131–3, for a preference for *Pickwick Papers* over *Our Mutual Friend*.

5 George Santayana, *Soliloquies in London and England* (1922) pp. 62–3, 66–7, 72–3.

6 F. R. Leavis, *The Great Tradition* (1948) p. 19.

7 R. C. Churchill, 'Dickens, Drama and Tradition', in *Scrutiny*, X (1942) 366, revised for the *Penguin Guide to Literature*, ed. Boris Ford (1958) VI, esp. 139–40.

8 K. J. Fielding, *Charles Dickens: a critical introduction* (1958) p. 185.

9 Jack Lindsay, *Charles Dickens* (1950) p. 380.

10 Henry James, loc. cit. p. 787; reprinted in *House of Fiction*, ed. Edel, p. 256.

11 Fielding, op. cit. p. 186.

12 George Orwell, 'Charles Dickens', in *Inside the Whale* (1940) p. 49.

13 Ibid.

14 G. K. Chesterton, *Charles Dickens* (1906) p. 235.

15 Edmund Wilson, 'Dickens: the two Scrooges' (1939), in *The Wound and the Bow* (1941) p. 79.

16 Humphry House, *The Dickens World* (1941) p. 162.

17 Monroe Engel, *The Maturity of Dickens* (1959) p. 137.

18 J. Hillis Miller, *Charles Dickens: the world of his novels* (1958) p. 300.

19 Wilson, op. cit. p. 80.

20 Edgar Johnson, *Charles Dickens: his tragedy and triumph* (1953) p. 1035.

21 Engel, op. cit. p. 143.

22 Miller, op. cit. pp. 323–4.

23 Lindsay, op. cit. p. 383.

24 *Our Mutual Friend* (1865) book IV, ch. 6; first edition, vol. II, p. 209.

25 Chesterton, op. cit. p. 188.

26 House, op. cit. p. 162.

27 Engel, op. cit. pp. 143–4.

28 Miller, op. cit. pp. 282, 315, 324.

29 Henry James, op. cit. p. 787; reprinted in *House of Fiction*, ed. Edel, p. 255.

30 Ibid.

31 Orwell, op. cit. p. 16.

32 Fielding, op. cit. p. 190.

33 George Gissing, *Charles Dickens: a critical study* (1898) p. 79.

34 *Our Mutual Friend*, book II, ch. 15; vol. II, p. 131.

35 Miller, op. cit. p. 282.

36 *Our Mutual Friend*, book III, ch. 5; vol. II, p. 34.

37 Ibid. book I, ch. 2; vol. I, p. 10.

38 Lindsay, op. cit. p. 382.

39 House, op. cit. p. 169.

40 *Our Mutual Friend*, book I, ch. 5; vol. I, p. 35.

41 Ibid. book I, ch. 15.

42 Gissing, op. cit. p. 79.

43 Chesterton, op. cit. p. 135.

44 House, op. cit. p. 169.

45 Miller, op. cit. p. 305.

46 Lindsay, op. cit. p. 382.

47 *Our Mutual Friend*, book II, ch. 15; vol. II, p. 135.

48 Fielding, op. cit. p. 189.

49 Ibid.

50 Ibid.

51 Lindsay, op. cit. pp. 384–5.

52 Orwell, op. cit. p. 13.

53 Miller, op. cit. p. 327.

54 *Our Mutual Friend*, book IV, ch. 13; vol. II, p. 274.

55 Lewes, op. cit. pp. 146ff.

56 Gissing, op. cit. p. 59; and surely he has Lewes in mind when he speaks of the 'man of letters' shaking his head at Dickens (p. 125), but see pp. 245–53 generally. And see Lewes, op. cit. pp. 148–9.

57 George H. Ford, *Dickens and his Readers* (1955) p. 253.

58 Engel, op. cit. p. 132. Miller, op. cit. p. 311. And see *Our Mutual Friend*, book I, ch. 12; vol. I, p. 109.

59 House, op. cit. pp. 166ff.

60 Engel, op. cit. p. 133.

61 Miller, op. cit. p. 294.

62 Johnson, op. cit. p. 294.

63 Lindsay, op. cit. p. 381.

64 Miller, op. cit. pp. 295–6.

65 *Our Mutual Friend*, book III, ch. 13; vol. II, p. 288.

66 Miller, op. cit. p. 295.

67 Engel, op. cit. p. 165.

68 Miller, op. cit. pp. 309–10. And see *Our Mutual Friend*, book I, ch. 11; vol. I, p. 99.

69 Miller, op. cit. pp. 312–13.

70 Wilson, op. cit. p. 83.

71 Ibid.

72 Johnson, op. cit. p. 1044.

73 Miller, op. cit. pp. 316ff.

74 Engel, op. cit. p. 142.

75 Ibid. p. 140.

76 Lindsay, op. cit. p. 384.

77 Johnson, op. cit. p. 1044.

78 Miller, op. cit. pp. 318ff.

79 Engel, op. cit. pp. 138–9.

80 *Our Mutual Friend*, book I, ch. 3; vol. I, p. 24.

81 See Henry James, loc. cit. p. 287, and Monroe Engel's courageous but misguided defence of Wegg, op. cit. pp. 135, 136, 141 ('curious but not really whimsical'). Betty Higden has been defended by Fielding, op. cit. p. 185, and by Lindsay, op. cit. p. 382. The other key divergences are analysed in the text.

82 See *Scrutiny*, XIV (1947) 185ff, for the first use of this term in an essay on *Hard Times* by F. R. Leavis which more or less defines it. The second essay in the series (*Scrutiny*, XIV (1947)) was by G. D. Klingopulos and was on *Wuthering*

Heights. The series, continued mainly by Leavis and concentrating on Lawrence, went on for some years.

83 Frances Jeffrey, 'Crabbe's Poems', in *Edinburgh Review*, XII (1808) 133.
84 *Lyrical Ballads* (1798) p. ii – 'The majority of the following poems are to be considered as experiments'.
85 *Lyrical Ballads*, 2nd ed. (1800) II 14.
86 Jeffrey, op. cit. pp. 135–6.
87 Reprinted in *The Prelude*, ed. E. de Selincourt and H. Darbishire (1959) appendix, pp. 639–40.
88 *Lyrical Ballads* (1800) p. 14.
89 Charlotte Brontë, Preface to the second edition of *Wuthering Heights* (1850) p. xxiii.
90 *Atlas*, XXIII (1848) 59 – 'a creature in whom every evil passion seems to have reached a gigantic excess'. The reviewer finds *Agnes Grey* 'nore agreeable'.
91 *Examiner* (8 Jan. 1848) p. 21 – 'He is an incarnation of evil qualities . . . it is with difficulty that we can prevail upon ourselves to believe in the appearance of such a phenomenon so near our own dwellings as the summit of a Lancashire or Yorkshire moor.'
92 *Quarterly Review*, LXXXIV (1848) 175.
93 William W. Kinsley, *Views on Vexed Questions* (1881) p. 316. True, on the republication of the book a rather more suitable response was drawn from G. H. Lewes (*Leader*, 1 953). But there is every evidence that he was divided in his mind between 'the coarseness apparently of violent and uncultivated men' and 'the extraordinary power of vigorous delineation'. Indeed, he grants the book its power, using the word three times in a fairly short review. However, his attitude may be summed up thus: 'One cannot dine off condiments, nor sup off horrors without an indigestion.'
94 *Tait's Edinburgh Magazine*, XV (1848) 138ff.
95 Charlotte Brontë, op. cit. p. xxii.
96 *Spectator*, XXIV 1026 – 'Ahab, indeed, is a melodramatic exaggeration.'
97 *Albion*, X (1851) 561. Like the *Spectator*, this reviewer terms Ahab a monomaniac.
98 W. Harrison Ainsworth (for attribution, see Hugh W. Hetherington, 'Early Reviews of Moby-Dick', in *Moby-Dick Centennial Essays*, ed. Tyrus Hillway and L. S. Mansfield (1953) p. 114) *New Monthly Magazine*, XCVIII 308.
99 *Spectator*, loc. cit. – 'greatly assisted by various chapters of a bookmaking kind'.
100 *Atlas*, XXVIII (1851) 697 – 'we might get over a volume smoothly enough . . . delighted with the descriptive powers . . . when suddenly the sluice would be lifted, the torrent would burst forth, and for a score of chapters . . . we would wade wearily through a waste of satirical or quasi-philosophical rhapsody'. And see *Peterson's Magazine*, Jan. and Feb. 1852, where the feeling is that, if the work had been compressed one half and all the 'transcendental' chapters omitted, it would have been the best sea story in the language.
101 *Examiner*, Nov. 1851, p. 709 – 'We cannot say that we recognise in this writer any advance on the admirable qualities displayed in his earlier books – we do not see that he even greatly cares to put forth the strength of which he has shown himself undoubtedly possessed.' And see the *Democratic Review*, Jan. and Feb. 1852.
102 See advertisements in the *New York Evening Post*, 27 and 28 Aug. 1852; 3 and 6

Sept. 1852. See also Melville's obituary in the *New York Tribune*, LI 29 Sept. 1851 – 'He won considerable fame as an author by the publication of a book in 1847 entitled *Typee* . . . This was his best work . . .' I am well aware that Hugh W. Hetherington ('Early Reviews of Moby-Dick', in *Moby-Dick Centennial Essays*, ed. Hillway and Mansfield, pp. 89ff) begins by suggesting that the hostility towards Melville in his own time has been exaggerated by twentieth-century commentators. Nevertheless he himself suggests (on p. 93) that Melville never recovered from the 'terrific blows' of his adverse reception. And it would take more than Hetherington or his predecessor in this line. John C. McCloskey ('Moby Dick and the Reviewers', in *Philological Quarterly*, XXV (1946) 1ff) to balance the scattered appreciative comments against the exasperated hostility and amazing violence of (say) the *Examiner*, loc. cit. and the *New Monthly Magazine*, loc. cit.

103 *Literary Gazette*, 6 Dec. 1851, p. 841.

104 *Atlas*, loc. cit. And see *New York Evangelist*, 20 Nov. 1851.

105 *New York Commercial Advertiser*, LIV (28 Nov. 1851) – 'There are few readers who will not be at first repulsed by its eccentricity . . . the science of cetology is pleasantly interwoven with this legend.' And see the *Examiner*, loc. cit. – 'It contains more about the whale . . . than we should have supposed possible to be poured out of "one small head".' But *in toto* the book is condemned as an extravaganza.

106 Horace Greeley (attribution by Hetherington, loc. cit. p. 103), *New York Daily Tribune*, XI (22 Nov. 1851) – 'We have occasional touches of the subtle mysticism which is carried to such an inconvenient excess in *Mardi*, but . . . we always safely alight from the excursion through mid-air upon the solid deck of the whaler.' But see *Southern Quarterly Review*, Jan.–Feb. 1852. And the *Athenaeum* (25 Oct. 1851) had not one word to say in favour of (p. 1112) 'this ill-com-pounded mixture of romance and matter-of-fact . . . this wild book . . . (p. 1113) this absurd book . . .' etc.

107 Yvor Winters, *In Defence of Reason* (1960) p. 201.

108 D. H. Lawrence, *Studies in Classic American Literature* (1924) p. 160.

109 Winters, op. cit. p. 211.

110 Lawrence, op. cit. p. 160.

111 Charles Eliot Norton, in *Putnam's Monthly*, VI (Sept. 1855) 323.

112 In a private letter written to Whitman on 21 July 1855, which the latter pub-lished in the *New York Daily Tribune*, XV (10 Oct. 1855).

113 R. W. Griswold, in *Criterion*, 10 Nov. 1855. For attribution, see Bliss Perry, *Walt Whitman* (1906) p. 100n. It may well be Griswold, for the latter in his stupendous compilation *The Poets and Poetry of America* (17th edition, 1856) exhibits no ordinary measure of bad taste. Vast selections of Whittier and Holmes may have influenced later anthologists; not so, forgotten figures like the mock-Elizabethan Charles Fenno Hoffman or the orient-mesmerised Bayard Taylor. This is a debased palate: its reaction to Whitman need not surprise us.

114 *Boston Intelligencer*, 3 May 1856.

115 *Critic*, XV (1 April 1856) 171.

116 *New York Criterion*, 10 Nov. 1855.

117 *New York Times*, 1855; reprinted in *Leaves of Grass Imprints* (1860) p. 23.

118 *Critic*, loc. cit. p. 171 – 'We, who are not prudish, emphatically declare that the

man who wrote p. 79 of the *Leaves of Grass* deserves nothing so richly as the public-executioner's whip.'

119 Walt Whitman, *Leaves of Grass* (1855) p. 79.

120 *Criterion*, loc. cit. – 'We trust no one will require further evidence – for, indeed, we do not believe there is a newspaper so vile that would print confirmatory extracts.'

121 *Women in Love* (1920) p. 343 (i.e. ch. xxiii). And see Whitman, op. cit. p. 79.

122 Loc cit. p. 171.

123 *Leader*, vii (7 June 1856) p. 547 – 'like the measured prose of Mr Martin Farquhar Tupper's *Proverbial Philosophy*'.

124 Loc. cit. p. 321.

125 Whitman, op. cit. p. 79.

126 Very typical is the review of *Men and Women* in the *Athenaeum* (17 Nov. 1855) pp. 1327–8. The reviewer recognises incidental bits of lyrical detail, but fails to grasp the poems as dramatic wholes. More intelligent is George Brimley (for attribution, see the *Browning Society's Papers*, 1881–4, *Bibliography of Browning* by F. J. Furnivall, p. 92) in *Fraser's Magazine*, liii (Jan. 1856) 105–16, esp. p. 114. But, though he prefers monologue to lyrical fragment, he sees Browning's genius as essentially prosaic – that of 'a fine biographer or essayist'.

127 A representative example is J. C. Squire's review of *The Waste Land*, in *London Mercury*, viii (1923) 655–6 – 'a grunt would serve equally well'. And see F. L. Lucas, in *New Statesman*, 3 Nov. 1923.

128 Ivor Brown, in *Observer* (9 Sept. 1951) – 'All he needs is to keep his Muse at least lightly tethered to the plausible and credible.' And see his 'Children of the Mist', ibid. 16 Sept. 1951, which helped to spark off the very different Sitwell controversy. (And see correspondence following – ibid. 16, 23 and 30 Sept. 1951.) Harold Hobson, in *Sunday Times* (9 Sept. 1951) – 'Young writers are constantly being urged to abandon the tea-cup-and-conversation drama for something more momentous, and Mr Whiting's gallant effort to do so makes one wonder if the advice is always wise . . . He is incapable of looking at an ordinary man walking down Regent Street, and seeing him as an ordinary man walking down Regent Street. He seems to have been born without a sense of normality . . .' etc., *ad nauseam*. *The Times* (6 Sept. 1951) – 'a badness that must be called indescribable . . . This piece . . . is fantasy plunging portentously in a sea so dark and wide and stormy that the shores of reality are rarely glimpsed.' A week later, the same critic refers deferentially to J. B. Priestley as a playwright who had never been afraid to be original; he also discusses Terence Rattigan with respect (loc. cit. 11 Sept. 1951). In a subsequent letter (12 Sept. 1951) it was two men of the theatre, Tyrone Guthrie and Peter Brook, who came to the rescue of this play – just as three men of the theatre, Peter Ustinov, Christopher Fry and Alec Clunes, had originally discovered it. An analogous case is that of James Forsyth.

129 e.g. Frank Kermode, in *Spectator*, ccii (1959) 628 – 'superior doggerel' (but see letter from two poets, Edward Lucie-Smith and Peter Porter, ibid. p. 702). Charles Tomlinson (*Listen*, iii (1960) 26ff) found in this volume 'inadequacies of tone' and a disabling immaturity – 'the rich and splendidly controlled rhetoric of, say, 'The Quaker Graveyard at Nantucket', has gone overboard . . . one can scarcely build a poetic on such a scaffolding'. Donald Davie (*Granta*, lxiv, 17 Oct. 1959) termed the book 'monstrous folly', 'coy exhibitionism' and

added 'This is no break-through for the rest of us . . .' Dr Davie spoke for himself. In fact, it showed a generation of writers younger than Kermode, Tomlinson and Davie how to be nakedly honest in the language of ordinary domestic conversation. My last phrase is taken from one of the few favourable reviews *Life Studies* received – which I commissioned from Edward Lucie-Smith for *Gemini*, II (1959) 57ff. It is interesting to note that Lucie-Smith quotes with approval a passage beginning 'All night I've held your hand' (*Life Studies* (1959) p. 59), which is unequivocally condemned by both Tomlinson and Davie.

6 RESISTANCE

1 See Maynard Mack's edition of the *Essay on Man* (1950), Introduction, pp. xvff.
2 Samuel Johnson, 'Life of Pope' (*Lives of the English Poets*, 1779–81).
3 *Observer*, 29 Jan. 1911.
4 *Saturday Review*, 13 May 1911. And see the *Evening Standard*, 30 Jan. 1911, which said that *The White Peacock*'s realism was extremely individual and could hardly be more vivid; and Violet Hunt, in the *Daily Chronicle*, 10 Feb. 1911, applauded its coarse and lusty passion and exuberance.
5 Frederic Tabor Cooper, in *Bookman*, XXXIII (1911) 195.
6 Henry Savage, in *Academy*, 18 March 1911.
7 F. M. Hueffer, in *English Review*, VIII (1911) 356–7. And see the *Scotsman*, 9 Feb. 1911, which considered the plot very simple and took the book to be mainly a record of the common round of life in an English rural district. See also the *Daily Mail*, 3 Feb. 1911, which agreed that the strength of the book was in its 'wonderfully detailed' background rather than in its theme. The *Manchester Guardian*, 8 Feb. 1911, praised the sensitivity of Lawrence's impressions while deprecating his lack of selectivity; while, for the *Birmingham Daily Post* (3 Feb. 1911) a 'healthy open-air tone' redeemed what was, after all, rather a 'disjointed tale'. The *Sheffield Daily Telegraph* (11 May 1911) indeed considered the plot incoherent, but nevertheless felt that the book was saved by its 'able nature sketches'; the *Morning Post* (9 Feb. 1911) said that the book would be remembered for the 'lyrical charm' of its descriptive passages; while the *Nottingham Guardian Journal* (21 Feb. 1911) passed over Lawrence's vulgar attempts at romance to descant upon his minute and vivid description of English rural life.
8 *Athenaeum*, 25 Feb. 1911. (Very emphatic about the novel being written by a woman.)
9 *Yorkshire Post*, 15 Feb. 1911.
10 *Times Literary Supplement*, 26 Jan. 1911. And see the *Glasgow Herald*, 18 March 1911 – which failed even to see the point of the book's title ('but it has a peculiar flavour, not altogether agreeable, of its own').
11 Robert Lynd, in *Daily News*, 14 Feb. 1911.
12 Stuart Sherman, *Critical Woodcuts* (1926) p. 24.
13 F. R. Leavis, *D. H. Lawrence* (1930) p. 6.
14 Edward Shanks, 'D. H. Lawrence: some characteristics', in *London Mercury*, VIII (1923) 68.
15 Bonamy Dobrée, *The Lamp and the Lute* (1929) p. 87.

16 *The White Peacock* (1911) pp. 237–42.

17 Ibid. p. 238.

18 Ibid. pp. 89–91.

19 *Times Literary Supplement*, loc. cit.

20 *Saturday Review*, loc. cit.

21 J. W. Cunliffe, *English Literature During the Last Half-Century* (1919) p. 292.

22 *The White Peacock*, pp. 89, 90.

23 For example, W. L. George (*A Novelist on the Novel* (1918) pp. 94–5) suggested that the author's talent was lyrical – a vision of nature in relation to himself rather than a realisation of man; and Edward Garnett (*Friday Nights* (1922) p. 153) while acknowledging the poetry of Lawrence's impressions of nature, at the same time deprecated their unchastened vivacity.

24 The more adverse critics – J. M. Murry, for instance (*Son of Woman* (1931) pp. 22–3), found both the strength and the weakness of the book in its authenticity; as Joseph Collins (*The Doctor Looks at Literature* (1923) p. 263) said, Lawrence's main concern is the photographic description of rustic scenes; even though this left the book open to the criticism of A. R. Marble (*A Study of the Modern Novel* (1928) p. 159) that it was poetic in description but defective in structure.

25 *New York Times*, 17 Nov. 1912.

26 *Evening Standard*, 12 June 1912. The *Westminster Gazette*, 8 June 1912, felt that the experiences of these characters were the point of the novel, though the reviewer conceded that Lawrence's curiosity is detailed and his touch sometimes over-heavy. It was the nakedness of the experience that distressed the *Birmingham Daily Post* (12 July 1912); in the *English Review*, XI (1912) 661, Hueffer, too, found the lovers almost terrible in their sensitiveness of reflexion; and 'B.S.' in the *Manchester Guardian* of 12 June 1912 felt there was something inartistic in the absorption with which Lawrence followed every moment of their lives.

27 *Morning Post*, 17 June 1912.

28 'A.W.C.L.', *Sheffield Daily Telegraph*, 4 July 1912.

29 Much of the feeling of the book seemed extraneous to the action. The *Saturday Review* (22 June 1912) instanced Siegmund glorying over his body in the sea, like an artist taking credit for a piece of work not his own (and see the *Sheffield Daily Telegraph*, loc. cit.) while the *Athenaeum* (1 June 1912) objected to his being credited at thirty-eight with the ecstatic passions of youth.

30 'A Reprehensible Jaunt', in *Nottingham Guardian* (Literary Supplement) 2 July 1912.

31 *Daily News*, 21 June 1912.

32 There are exceptions to this. Edward Shanks (loc. cit. pp. 66–7) alone felt that *The Trespasser* was, structurally, an improvement on Lawrence's first novel. Edward Garnett (op. cit. p. 154), on the other hand, considered that the artist's intensity of perception was at variance with an occasional commonness of tone.

33 Leavis, op. cit. p. 6. Or, as Joseph Collins (op. cit. p. 264) more crudely put it, Lawrence had at once an impassioned apprehension of nature and a great capacity for describing the feelings of commonplace people.

34 George, op. cit. p. 97.

35 John Arrow, *J. C. Squire v. D. H. Lawrence* (1930) p. 7.

36 Murry, op. cit. p. 57.

37 Hueffer (loc. cit. p. 661) instances the beginning of chapter VIII, 'The way home lay across country . . .' (*The Trespasser*, 1912, pp. 67ff); the *Morning Post* (loc. cit.), Helena's sensations when seabathing (*The Trespasser*, pp. 69–70); the *Manchester Guardian* (loc. cit.), the views from the boat and the train on the lovers' journey back to London (*The Trespasser*, pp. 176ff); the *Westminster Gazette* (loc. cit.), *Birmingham Post* (loc. cit.) and *Saturday Review* (loc. cit.) Siegmund's return to his wife and family (*The Trespasser*, pp. 196–202); and the *Athenaeum* (loc. cit. p. 614) the finding of his body after he has committed suicide (*The Trespasser*, pp. 252–7).

38 On Alan Sillitoe, Stan Barstow and Stanley Middleton (see esp. *Harris's Requiem*) in particular.

39 Catherine Carswell, in *Glasgow Herald*, 3 July 1913. And see advertisement for the book, in the *Daily Mail*, 18 July 1913.

40 *Evening Standard*, 24 June 1913.

41 *New York Times*, 21 Sept. 1913.

42 *Independent*, 9 Oct. 1913.

43 *Sunday Times*, 1 June 1913.

44 Hugh Walpole, in *Blue Review*, I (1913) 192.

45 *Saturday Review*, 21 June 1913. The reviewer gives as one example the scene in *Sons and Lovers* where Paul holds the hem of Miriam's dress against the wind. 'No man could have invented this piece of description at the factory or the desk.'

46 Douglas Goldring, *Reputations* (1920) p. 71.

47 Garnett, op. cit. p. 154.

48 Marble, op. cit. p. 159.

49 Cunliffe, op. cit. p. 293.

50 Dorothy Brewster and Angus Burrell, *Dead Reckonings in Fiction* (1924) p. 224.

51 J. M. Manly and Edith Rickert, *Contemporary British Literature* (1922) p. 98.

52 Paul Rosenfeld, *Men Seen* (1925) p. 59.

53 Stephen Potter, *D. H. Lawrence* (1930) pp. 46–7.

54 H. J. Seligmann, *D. H. Lawrence: an American interpretation* (1924) pp. 1, 5–6.

55 Murry, op. cit. p. 23.

56 Leavis, op. cit. p. 7.

57 Hubert Bland, in *New Statesman*, 5 July 1913.

58 F. M. Hueffer, in *English Review*, XV (1913) 157.

59 Hubert Bland, loc. cit. ('I do not feel that Mr Lawrence thought out his end from the beginning . . .')

60 Darrell Figgis, in *The Nineteenth Century, and after*, LXXIV (1913) 802.

61 *Athenaeum*, 21 June 1913.

62 Harold Massingham, in *Daily Chronicle*, 17 June 1913.

63 *Yorkshire Post*, 23 July 1913. *Daily Telegraph*, 18 June 1913. *Times Literary Supplement*, 12 June 1913. *Irish Times*, 4 July 1913. *Observer*, 8 June 1913. *Outlook*, 6 June 1913.

64 *Nation*, XIII (1913) 577 (but see p. 563).

65 *Manchester Guardian*, 2 July 1913.

66 *Westminster Gazette*, 14 June 1913.

67 Henry Savage, in *Academy*, 28 June 1913.

68 Ibid.

69 Shanks, op. cit. p. 70.

70 Dobrée, op. cit. p. 102.

71 John Macy, *The Critical Game* (1922) pp. 331–2.
72 George, op. cit. pp. 95–6.
73 Collins, op. cit. p. 261.
74 Robert Lynd, in *Daily News*, 7 June 1913.
75 Harvey Wickham, *The Impuritans* (1929) p. 261.
76 Murry, op. cit. p. 29.
77 Collins, op. cit. p. 261.
78 Cunliffe, op. cit. p. 293.
79 Murry, op. cit. p. 29.
80 *Daily Telegraph*, loc. cit.
81 *Sunday Times*, loc. cit.; *English Review*, loc. cit.; *Yorkshire Post*, loc. cit.; *Times Literary Supplement*, loc. cit. The *Independent* (loc. cit.), the *Westminster Gazette* (loc. cit.), and the *Irish Times* (loc. cit.), together with Harvey Wickham (op. cit. pp. 260–1), all suggested that Mrs Morel found recompense in the adoration of her sons; Henry Savage (loc. cit.) and J. W. Cunliffe (op. cit.) went so far as to say that Paul took his place as a realised character only in terms of her affection for him. The *Outlook* (loc. cit.), however, saw nothing in her case except misery and torture.
82 The real hint of criticism comes with the *Evening Standard* (loc. cit.) which saw Mrs Morel as being plucky but also bitter-sweet and even sharp in tone, while the *Nation* (loc. cit. p. 577) admitted that we did not always love her. While the *New York Times* (loc. cit.) conceded that her nobility might in itself have helped her husband on his downward path; and it is the *New Statesman* (loc. cit.) in particular that accuses her of a failure in understanding. There was something of the shrew in her temperament, agreed the *Saturday Review* (loc. cit.), and the *Manchester Guardian* (loc. cit.) found her sometimes downright disagreeable.
83 Collins, op. cit. p. 261.
84 Shanks, op. cit. p. 70.
85 Murry, op. cit. p. 29.
86 Seligmann, op. cit., p. 5.
87 Goldring, op. cit. p. 70.
88 See *Daily Express*, 15 Nov. 1915; *Sunday Times*, 14 Nov. 1915; *Daily Telegraph*, 15 Nov. 1915.
89 See *Daily Express*, loc. cit.; *Sunday Times*, loc. cit.; *Daily Telegraph*, loc. cit.
90 See *The Times*, 15 Nov. 1915; *Morning Post*, 15 Nov. 1915; *Daily Express*, loc. cit.; *Observer*, 14 Nov. 1915.
91 See *Morning Post*, loc. cit.; *Daily Telegraph*, loc. cit. Sir John Dickinson, from newspaper accounts of his various promotions, had a reputation for patience and leniency, as well he might have since, for twenty-three years before going to Bow Street, he was metropolitan police magistrate at the Thames Court, Arbour Street, East Stepney, dealing mainly with seamen's offences. How, then, did he come to conduct this 'trial' in such an arbitrary fashion? Part of the explanation is, I think, to be found in the fact that his only son had been killed in the front line a month before the trial. He would hardly be in a mood to appreciate a book which spoke contemptuously of 'wooden soldiers'. Hence a natural, but extremely unfortunate, critical deflection. Several of Lawrence's friends felt that resentment at the anti-war stand of the book was the unexpressed undercurrent behind much of the hostility

it aroused. See, for instance, Gilbert Cannan, in *New York Tribune*, 10 Jan. 1920.

92 See *The Times*, loc. cit.; *Morning Post*, loc. cit.; *Daily Express*, loc. cit.; *Daily Telegraph*, loc. cit.; *Observer*, loc. cit.; *Sunday Times*, loc. cit.

93 James Douglas, in *Star*, 22 Oct. 1915. The language Douglas used in this review is remarkable for its unbridled violence. 'There is no doubt that a book like this has no right to exist . . . The subtlety of phrase is enormous, but it is used to express the unspeakable and to hint at the unutterable . . . A thing like *The Rainbow* has no right to exist in the world of war. It is a greater menace to public health than any of the epidemic diseases which we pay our medical officers to fight inch by inch wheresoever they appear. They destroy the body, but it destroys the soul . . . Life is infinitely more precious than literature. It has got to go on climbing up and up, and if literature strives to drag it down to the uttermost depth, then literature must be hacked off the limbs of life . . .' etc. The interesting thing is that Douglas's indignation is so great that he is unable to get near enough the text to discuss it.

94 Clement Shorter, in *Sphere*, LXIII (23 Oct. 1915) – 'The whole book is an orgie [*sic*.] of sexiness.' Shorter's tone is more moderate than that of Douglas and Lynd, and he does imply that he would not have the book censored. Yet his review was perhaps the one most instrumental in bringing about *The Rainbow's* seizure. It is odd that the President of the Brontë Society should have been so squeamish about the passions exhibited in Lawrence.

95 *The Rainbow* (1915) ch. XII.

96 Ibid.

97 Ibid.

98 Ibid.

99 Ibid.

100 Ibid.

101 *Daily News*, 15 Oct. 1915. This whole review, like that of Douglas, is written in a tone of violent abuse. 'It is mainly a prolix account of three generations of sexual crises . . . His men and women are cattle who chronically suffer from the staggers . . . for the most part the book is windy, tedious, and even in its excitement nauseating . . . it seems to me largely a monotonous wilderness of phallicism . . .' etc. Robert Lynd, like James Douglas, was an Ulsterman; there could be a tie-up there. He graduated in English from Queen's University, Belfast, under the totally undistinguished aegis of Professor H. M. McMullen. He later became Literary Editor of the *Daily News*. But he was possessed of hardly any taste – we find him reviewing favourably six weeks later (*Daily News*, 16 Nov. 1915) a mild pseudo-realist novel about schools called *Soul of a Teacher* (by Roger Wray). Unlike Ursula, the hero of Wray's book is providentially saved from the upper and nether millstones by being left a legacy. For a further instance of Lynd's lack of taste, see his enthusiastic review of Wells's *Boon*, in the *Daily News*, 3 May 1915. But there may be another reason for Lynd's critical deflection regarding *The Rainbow*. Ernest Weekley, Frieda Lawrence's first husband, was a regular reviewer of books in language studies in Lynd's columns (see, for instance, *Daily News*, 28 April and 11 Oct. 1915). It may be that editor and contributor knew each other and shared some feelings about Frieda's defection (James Douglas, too, was an occasional contributor – see *Daily News*, 14 Oct. 1915). But this is only surmise. And in any case deflection of this nature is a symptom, not a disease.

102 G. W. de Tunzelmann, in *Athenaeum*, 20 Nov. 1915. Here, again, is a case where one could point to a possible cause of deflection, though this is not the whole story of resistance against the book. De Tunzelmann was, in reality, von Tunzelmann, and appears to have been pathologically afraid, at a time of anti-German feeling, of having his antecedents found out. Hence his opposition to 'German' psychology, as represented by the school of Freud, and so his attack on *The Rainbow*, as evincing the school's tenets in action.

103 Collins, op. cit. p. 261.

104 George, op. cit. p. 101.

105 Cunliffe, op. cit. p. 294.

106 *Nation*, 20 Nov. 1915.

107 John Galsworthy, MS Letter to J. B. Pinker, Autumn 1915, Lazarus Collection (Item 87, Lawrence Exhibition Catalogue, University of Nottingham, 1960). I owe this reference to Dr Keith Sagar, who has now published the letter in his invaluable *Art of D. H. Lawrence* (1967).

108 Obituary of D. H. Lawrence, *Evening Standard*, 10 April 1930.

109 Sir Ernest Hodder-Williams (interview): *New York Tribune*, 3 Jan. 1920.

110 J. C. Squire, *New Statesman*, 20 Nov. 1915.

111 J. B. Priestley, in *London Mercury*, VIII (1923) 98 (He was reviewing, rather ineptly, the volume containing 'The Ladybird', 'The Fox' and 'The Captain's Doll'.)

112 Edward Shanks, op. cit. p. 67.

113 Elizabeth Drew, *The Modern Novel* (1926) pp. 81–2.

114 Edward Lacon-Watson, *Lectures to Living Authors* (1925) p. 154.

115 John Macy, *The Critical Game* (1922) pp. 329–30.

116 Marble, op. cit. p. 159.

117 Gerald Gould, in *New Statesman*, 23 Oct. 1915. The review is full of the smart touches with which prolonged reading of the *New Statesman* has familiarised us, e.g., 'the most improper thing about it is the punctuation'.

118 *Westminster Gazette*, 9 Oct. 1915. Like a number of other reviews of *The Rainbow*, this is full of digressions and shows a marked reluctance to get to grips with the text. The reviewer appears to think that Lawrence is telling an identical story three times over.

119 *Globe*, 5 Oct. 1915. ('The author's frankness is amazing, and he seems to forget that lack of reticence is not the greatest thing in literary art.')

120 *World*, 26 Oct. 1915. ('It cannot be called a pleasant book ... the lower impulse of passion dominating, in each crisis as it arises, the pronounced religious side and all social conventions.')

121 *Athenaeum*, 13 Nov. 1915. (Though the reviewer takes the discord to be a defect in the book.)

122 Catherine Carswell, in *Glasgow Herald*, 4 Nov. 1915.

123 Ibid. About Anna and Will she says: 'We are introduced with what most people will find revolting detail to a passion fruitful in a sense but bitter and terrifying at the core, where the modern poison is at its disintegrating work.' Mrs Carswell in her book *The Savage Pilgrimage* (1932: pp. 38, 40) allowed her readers to infer that her review was a favourable one. As these extracts show, it was not. Her son as recently as 1959 wrote to the *New Statesman* (May 9) to put forward his mother as one of Lawrence's defenders. But in this instance he was wrong. Mrs Carswell was indeed sacked from the *Glasgow Herald*, but

not for reviewing Lawrence's novel favourably; she was sacked for reviewing it at all.

124 'H.M.S.', in *Manchester Guardian*, 28 Oct. 1915. I am indebted to Mr F. B. Singleton, Librarian of the *Guardian*, for the information that this review was by Mrs H. M. Swanwick. See Kingsley Martin, *Father Figures* (1966) p. 171.

125 Ibid.

126 *Current Opinion*, Feb. 1916.

127 *Evening Standard*, 21 Oct. 1915. Possibly by Arnold Bennett. Lawrence always maintained that Bennett had stood by him. Could this review be what he was referring to?

128 *Philadelphia Public Ledger*, 9 Nov. 1924.

129 Gilbert Cannan, in *New York Tribune*, 10 Jan. 1920.

130 Louis Untermeyer, in *New Republic*, 11 Aug. 1920.

131 16 Dec. 1915. See *Collected Letters*, ed. H. T. Moore (1962) p. 399.

132 5 June 1914. See *Collected Letters*, ed. H. T. Moore (1962) pp. 281–2.

133 H. J. Forman, 'With D. H. Lawrence in Sicily' (interview with D. H. Lawrence), in *New York Times Book Review and Magazine*, 27 Aug. 1922. The whole interview takes one nearer to the *personality* of Lawrence than anything else that has been written about him.

134 Edwin Muir, in *Nation and Athenaeum*, 4 July 1925.

135 Ibid.

136 Ibid.

137 Ibid. And also 'We remember the scenes in his novels, we forget the names of his men and women. We should not know any of them if we were to meet them in the street, as we should know Anna Karenina, or Crevel, or even Soames Forsyte . . . They are not men and women; they are male and female . . . Thus character in Mr Lawrence's novels is always melting into instinct, and human nature into nature pure and simple.' Etc.

138 H. J. Davis, in *Canadian Forum*, x (Feb. 1930) 163.

139 Paul Rosenfeld, ibid. (see note 52) pp. 55, 59.

140 Dobrée, op. cit. (see note 15) pp. 102–3.

141 F. R. Leavis, *D. H. Lawrence* (1930) p. 8.

142 Ibid.

143 Frieda Lawrence, Letter to Lady Cynthia Asquith, 1916 (in *Memoirs and Correspondence*, ed. Tedlock, 1961).

7 CONSENSUS AND RECONCILIATION

1 For instance, the nature of the 'unheard melodies' of stanza 2; the fusion of mortal with immortal in the 'happy love' of stanza 3; and, especially, the sacrifice presented to us in stanza 4.

2 *Ode on a Grecian Urn*, in *Poetical Works*, ed. H. W. Garrod (1958) p. 262. But I have inserted the inverted commas that appear in the 1820 volume, since they seem to me vital for the understanding of the poem. See Alvin Whitley, 'The Message of the Grecian Urn', in *Keats–Shelley Memorial Association Bulletin*, IV (1953).

3 Robert Bridges, *John Keats* (1895) p. 58.

4 H. W. Garrod, *Keats* (1926) pp. 105–7.

5 A. C. Quiller-Couch, *On the Art of Reading* (1920), pp. 91–3. It is true that some critics have balked at the conclusion of the poem, but that is because they have taken it out of context. Eliot, for instance (*Selected Essays* (1932) p. 256) found 'beauty is truth, truth beauty' no more than a statement of equivalence; and Allen Tate (*On the Limits of Poetry* (1948) pp. 179–80) regarded it as a violation of the set limits of the poem – 'truth is *not* beauty, since even art itself cannot do more with death than preserve it, and the beauty frozen on the urn is dead since it cannot move'. The answer to this is given in the readings of our third group of critics, but one could anticipate by suggesting that the poem is an attempt to reconcile within its form the opposition which Tate has, justly, recognised. After all, the poet makes these inanimate figures live in the vitality with which he presents and recreates them. What Bridges (op. cit.) and Garrod (op. cit.) regard as a recovery, and Eliot (loc. cit.) and Tate (loc. cit.) as, in some sort, a betrayal is, of course, both; the final lines answer the earlier questions of the poem. Cleanth Brooks manages, to some extent, to reconcile these views (*The Well-Wrought Urn* (1947) pp. 149–50). Though the people on the Urn have been presented by the poet as a rich and breathing world, nevertheless he has never forgotten that they are part of an artefact. The recognition becomes explicit in the last stanza: 'Cold pastoral' sums up the paradox. The Urn will continue to say what it has always said, that truth is the imaginative perception of sacrifice (see p. 148) – and *that*, as opposed to the disorganised facts of history, is beauty (pp. 150–1).

6 C. L. Finney, *The Evolution of Keats's Poetry* (1936) p. 644. He compares the 'artistic beauty' of the Urn with the 'natural beauty' of the nightingale. Both illumine reality rather than deaden it.

7 Cleanth Brooks, op. cit. pp. 149–52, esp. p. 151 – 'It is a speech in character and supported by a dramatic context'.

8 G. Wilson Knight, *The Starlit Dome* (1941) p. 296.

9 C. M. Bowra, *The Romantic Imagination* (1950) pp. 146–8.

10 Earl R. Wasserman, *The Finer Tone* (1953) p. 57.

11 John Middleton Murry, *Studies in Keats, New and Old* (1939) p. 81.

12 Kenneth Burke, *A Grammar of Motives* (1945) p. 462. And see Marius Bewley, *The Complex Fate* (1952) p. 233.

13 Bernard Blackstone, *The Consecrated Urn* (1959) pp. 340–1. His actual terms are 'living truth' and 'brute fact'.

14 William Empson, *The Structure of Complex Words* (1951) pp. 372–3.

15 F. R. Leavis, *Revaluation* (1936) p. 254.

16 E. C. Pettet, *On the Poetry of Keats* (1957) p. 346.

17 Kenneth Muir, ed., *John Keats* (1958) p. 70. (And see *Letters*, ed. M. B. Forman, p. 71, no. 32, 21 Dec. 1817.)

18 Eliot, op. cit. p. 556. And see note 5.

19 Tate, op. cit. pp. 179–80. And see his very imagistic view of Keats's verse on p. 181 – 'the pictorial method' he calls it. And also see note 5.

20 A tendency in this direction is inherent in those who hold what I termed the 'aesthetic' view of the poem – Robert Bridges, op. cit. p. 58; A. C. Quiller-Couch, op. cit. pp. 91–3; C. L. Finney, op. cit. pp. 639–41. And see Sidney Colvin, *Keats* (1887) p. 173 – 'the arrest of life as though it were an infliction in the sphere of reality'; D. G. James, *Three Odes of Keats* (1952) p. 17.

21 Muir, op. cit. p. 70.

22 *Poetical Works*, ed. Geoffrey Keynes (1966) p. 210.

23 Leavis, op. cit. pp. 141, 142.

24 Max Plowman, *An Introduction to the Study of Blake* (1927) p. 167.

25 F. W. Bateson, *Selected Poems of William Blake* (1957) p. 113.

26 Stanley Gardner, *Infinity on the Anvil* (1954) pp. 118–19.

27 René Wellek, 'Literary Criticism and Philosophy', in *Scrutiny*, v (1937) 377.

28 Kathleen Raine, 'The Lapsed Soul', in *The Divine Vision*, ed. V. de Sola Pinto (1957) p. 52.

29 Margaret Rudd, *The Divided Image* (1953) p. 84.

30 Ibid.

31 Wellek, ibid. p. 377.

32 Raine, op. cit. p. 62.

33 Gardner, op. cit. p. 118.

34 Bateson, op. cit. p. 113.

35 Wellek, op. cit. p. 377

36 Gardner, op. cit. p. 118.

37 Plowman, op. cit. p. 167.

38 Bateson, op. cit. p. 113.

39 Ibid.

40 S. Foster Damon, *William Blake: his philosophy and symbols* (1924) p. 274.

41 Introduction to the *Songs of Experience*, in *Poetical Works*, ed. G. Keynes (1966) pp. 210, 18–20.

42 Wellek, op. cit. p. 377.

43 F. R. Leavis, 'Literary Criticism and Philosophy', in *Scrutiny*, vi (1937) 65.

44 Bateson, op. cit. p. 113.

45 Rudd, op. cit. pp. 84–6.

46 Damon, op. cit. p. 274.

47 Bateson, op. cit. p. 113.

48 *They fle from me*, in *Collected Poems*, ed. Kenneth Muir (1949) p. 28, line 1.

49 Arthur K. Moore, 'The Design of Wyatt's *They fle from me*', in *Anglia*, LXXI (1952) 103.

50 Edward Lucie-Smith. In conversation, in 1961.

51 S. F. Johnson, in *Explicator*, XI (1953).

52 George Whiting, in *Essays in Criticism*, x (1960) 221.

53 E. E. Duncan-Jones, in *Explicator*, XII (1953–4).

54 F. W. Bateson, *English Poetry: a critical introduction* (1950) p. 143.

55 Arnold Stein, 'Wyatt's *They Flee from Me*', in *Sewanee Review*, LXVII (1959) 32–4.

56 Moore, op. cit. pp. 104–5.

57 Frederick Combellack, in *Explicator*, VII (1949) 36.

58 Johnson, op. cit.

59 J. D. Hainsworth, in *Essays in Criticism*, VII (1957) 92ff.

60 William Empson. In an MS note written in 1961 upon the first draft of this enquiry into the criticism of Wyatt's poetry; and in conversation subsequently.

61 Leonard Dean, ed., *Renaissance Poetry, English Masterpieces III*, 2nd ed. (1950) p. 3.

62 Bateson, op. cit. pp. 140ff.

63 Moore, op. cit. p. 105.

64 Stein, op. cit. p. 33.

65 Combellack, op. cit. p. 36.

66 Dean, op. cit. p. 3.

67 Gilbert Ryle, *Concept of Mind* (1949) ch. VII, esp. pp. 210–22.

68 *Collected Poems*, ed. K. Muir (1949) p. 28, lines 6–7.

69 G. F. Nott (ed.), *Works of Howard and Wyatt* (1816) II 546.

70 F. M. Padelford (ed.), *Early Sixteenth Century Lyrics* (1907) p. xxxv.

71 A. K. Foxwell, *A Study of Sir Thomas Wyatt* (1911) p. 105.

72 A. K. Foxwell (ed.), *The Poems of Sir Thomas Wiat* (1913) II 81.

73 Roy Lamson and Hallett Smith, *The Golden Hind* (1942).

74 Whiting, op. cit. pp. 220–1.

75 E. M. W. Tillyard (ed.), *The Poetry of Sir Thomas Wyatt* (1928) p. 156. And see Tottel's *Miscellany* (1557) folio 23.

76 Kenneth Muir (ed.), *Collected Poems of Thomas Wyatt* (1949) p. xxv.

77 Combellack, op. cit.

78 D. W. Harding, *A Guide to English Literature*, ed. Boris Ford, I (1954) 199, 206–7.

79 Duncan-Jones, op. cit.

80 E. K. Chambers, *Sir Thomas Wyatt and other studies* (1933), p. 126.

81 Hallett Smith, 'The Art of Sir Thomas Wyatt', in *Huntingdon Library Quarterly*, IX (1946) 351.

82 Hainsworth, op. cit. p. 93.

83 Rosemond Tuve, *A Reading of George Herbert* (1952) pp. 23–5.

84 Rosemary Freeman, *English Emblem Books* (1948).

85 William Empson, *Seven Types of Ambiguity* (1930) pp. 286–95.

86 L. C. Knights, *Explorations* (1946). And see his review of *George Herbert*, by Joseph Summers, *Sewanee Review*, LXIII (1955).

87 Louis Martz, *The Poetry of Meditation* (1954).

88 Margaret Bottrall, *George Herbert* (1954). And see also Robert Montgomery, 'The Province of Allegory in George Herbert', in *Texas Studies in Literature and Language*, I (1959); Douglas Brown, ed., *Selected Poems of George Herbert* (1960).

89 Tuve, op. cit., e.g. p. 25.

90 Ibid. p. 49.

91 Empson, op. cit. p. 294.

92 Bottrall, op. cit. p. 90. And see F. E. Hutchinson (ed.), *The Works of George Herbert* (1941) p. 485.

93 Tuve, op. cit. pp. 32ff, esp. 40–3. But see Brown, op. cit. p. 147; Martz, op. cit. pp. 93, 95.

94 *The Sacrifice*, in *Works*, ed. F. E. Hutchinson (1941) p. 33, lines 197–200.

95 Tuve, op. cit. pp. 81ff. But see L. C. Knights, in *Sewanee Review*, LXIII (1955) 483.

96 Tuve, op. cit. p. 90.

97 Ibid. p. 85.

98 Ibid. p. 83. E.g. Byrd's *Songs of Sundry Natures* (1589), Southwell's *Christ's Return out of Egypt*, Verstegan's *Lullaby*, Middleton's *Marriage of the Old and New Testament*, Honorius's *Commentary on the Song of Songs* (1618), Guillaume de Deguileville's *Pèlerinage de l'âme*, etc.

99 Empson, op. cit. p. 294.

100 Ibid. p. 232.

101 Tuve, op. cit. p. 31.

102 Ibid. p. 90 (and see p. 89).

103 Empson, op. cit. p. 294.

104 *The Sacrifice*, in *Works*, ed. Hutchinson (1941) p. 33, line 202.

105 Tuve, op. cit. p. 86; Empson, op. cit. p. 294.

106 Tuve, op. cit. p. 86 – qualified approval: the tradition *in a sense* carries this meaning.

107 Empson, op. cit. p. 294.

108 Tuve, op. cit. p. 90.

109 Ibid. p. 84 (and see pp. 82–3).

110 Empson, op. cit. p. 294.

111 Tuve, op. cit. pp. 82ff.

112 Empson, op. cit. p. 194.

113 Line 102. However, Professor Tuve's regard for tradition and ritual does sometimes betray her into recognising only part of what the poem has to offer. Take, for example, the final stanza:

> *But now I die; now all is finished.*
> *My wo, man's weal: and now I bow my head.*
> *Only let others say, when I am dead*
> *Never was grief like mine.* (249–52)

Professor Tuve compares this superb ending with Lydgate's poem:

> 'When I gave peace thou madst debate,
> I do thee weal, why do'st me wo?'

(quoted, op. cit. p. 46). But though Herbert may be (as Professor Tuve puts it – op. cit. p. 46) working in the same tradition, the brevity of his phrasing points to a far greater measure of identification between God and man. I should hardly, for example, call the bouncy rhythm and obvious interrogation of Lydgate's poem a vehicle for what Professor Tuve terms 'brief and biting contrasts' (op. cit. p. 46); her phrase would have been more appropriate to Herbert.

And this approach – from Lydgate onward, so to speak – leads Professor Tuve to take a simple and straightforward interpretation of Herbert's stanza: 'All is finished – and well finished, if man will but return this love' (op. cit. p. 46n). This interpretation is certainly a sound one, but it does not exclude the possibility of an ironic complement; particularly since Empson has seen another possibility.

It is true that the primary meaning recognised by Professor Tuve is the main interpretation Empson puts forward; that, after the death of Christ mankind will admit that his was the supreme grief (op. cit. p. 289). But Empson also sees that the last lines can be taken as a threat, directed from the Cross at mankind –

> *Only let others say, when I am dead,*
> *Never was grief like mine.*

> *(The Sacrifice,* 251–2)

in which case it is these others who are crying out about their grief; a grief which exceeds even that of Christ in agony: 'only let my torturers say, never was grief like theirs' (Empson, op. cit. p. 289).

This is, perhaps, the most far-reaching paradox yet. Professor Tuve objects to the interpretation as suggesting a spiteful irony in the speaker (Tuve, op. cit. p. 41). But there is nothing here that has not already been suggested, if not completely spelled out, in previous paradoxes. And, coming at the end of the poem as it does, this particular paradox reinforces and concentrates the earlier suggestion: that the Redeemer is also a judge.

114 Andrew Marvell, *Poems and Letters*, ed. H. M. Margoliouth (1952) p. 49, *The Garden*, lines 33–40.
115 Frank Kermode, 'The Argument of Marvell's *Garden*', in *Essays in Criticism*, II (1952) 235.
116 Ibid.
117 Ibid. p. 235.
118 Frank Bradbrook, 'The Poetry of Andrew Marvell', in *Penguin Guide to English Literature*, ed. Boris Ford, III (1956) 200.
119 M. C. Bradbrook and M. G. Lloyd-Thomas, *Andrew Marvell* (1940) p. 61.
120 Milton Klonsky, 'A Guide through the *Garden*', in *Sewanee Review*, LVIII (1950) 22.
121 Ibid.
122 Laurence Hyman, 'Marvell's *Garden*', in *Journal of English Literary History*, XXV (1958) 18.
123 A. H. King, 'Some Notes on Andrew Marvell's *Garden*', in *English Studies*, XX (1938) 120.
124 M.-S. Røstvig, *The Happy Man* (1954) pp. 259, 261.
125 Joseph Summers, 'Marvell's "Nature",' in *Journal of English Literary History*, XX (1953) 124.
126 Røstvig, op. cit. pp. 261, 262.
127 Summers, op. cit. p. 124 (he compares the Garden with Eden and the Hesperides).
128 Pierre Legouis, *André Marvell, poète, puritain, patriote* (1928) p. 93 – 'Il jouit en gourmet autant qu'en poète de la société des pommes, des grappes de la vigne, du brugnon, de la pêche et des melons.'
129 Ruth Wallerstein, *Studies in Seventeenth Century Poetic* (1950) p. 328.
130 Ibid.
131 William Empson, *Some Versions of Pastoral* (1935) p. 131.
132 Ibid. p. 132.
133 Ibid.
134 Ibid.
135 Marvell, op. cit. lines 65–72.
136 Kermode, op. cit. p. 241.
137 Jim Corder, 'Marvell and Nature', in *Notes and Queries*, CCIV (1959) 60–1. And see Joan Jenkins, unpublished Master's Thesis, 'The Place of Andrew Marvell in Seventeenth-Century Poetry' (Texas Christian University, Fort Worth, U.S.A., 1956).
138 John Press, *Andrew Marvell* (1958) p. 28.
139 Røstvig, op. cit. p. 261.
140 Hyman, op. cit. p. 22.
141 Ibid.

8 SURVIVAL VALUES

1 A. C. Bradley, *Shakespearian Tragedy* (1904) p. 291.
2 Nahum Tate, *King Lear* (1681): see esp. pp. 62ff. And see *Roscius Anglicanus* by John Downes (1708), p. 33, and Thomas Davies's *Dramatic Miscellanies* (1783) II 260.
3 David Garrick, *King Lear* (1786).
4 George Colman, *King Lear* (1768). The main distinction between Garrick and

Colman is that the former follows Tate in having Cordelia marry Edgar, while the latter omits the love interest altogether. Yet another version was the German adaptation by F. L. Schröder (1778), also with a happy ending. This was anatomised by George Moir in *Blackwood's Magazine*, xxxvii (1835) 242.

5 Tate, op. cit. p. 67. Tate brings about his happy conclusion quite briskly. Lear is discovered with his head on Cordelia's lap (p. 62). We are shown what Shakespeare only refers to: the Captain's intrusion upon the prisoners and Lear's striking down of the assassins. But here, of course, the assassination is unsuccessful (p. 64). The *deus ex machine* turns out to be Edgar – 'Death! Hell! Ye Vultures hold your impious hands' (p. 63) – who comes in with Albany and rescues the hapless prisoners (p. 64). A scroll is discovered testifying to the wickedness of Goneril (p. 65), and Albany resigns her part in the kingdom back to Lear (p. 65), who confers his sovereignty upon Cordelia and both upon Edgar (p. 66). Gloucester is not allowed to die – 'thou hast Business yet for Life' (p. 66) – but Lear and Kent decide to retire to 'some close Cell' to pass their time 'In calm Reflection on our Fortunes past' (p. 67). As Edgar remarks, 'peace spreads her balmy wings' (p. 67), and the play ends with virtue securely triumphant.

6 Charles Gildon, 'An Essay on the Art and Progress of the Stage in France, Rome and England', prefixed to the 1710 edition of the *Works of Shakespeare*, ed. Nicholas Rowe, vii 406. Gildon began more humanely than this effort would suggest, as the friend of Dryden and opponent of Rymer. See his *Reflections on Mr Rymer's Short View of Tragedy and an Attempt at a Vindication of Shakespeare* (1694). Contained in *Miscellaneous Letters and Essays on Several Subjects* (1694) pp. 64ff.

7 Lewis Theobald, in the *Censor*, no. 10 (2 May 1717) p. 72. See also his edition of the *Works of Shakespeare*, v (1733) 217.

8 Francis Gentleman, *The Dramatic Censor*, i (1770) 376–7. This arises out of a comparison between the Tate and Colman versions of *King Lear* (op. cit. pp. 352ff).

9 Edward Taylor (of Steeple-Aston, Oxfordshire), *Cursory Remarks on Tragedy, on Shakespeare, etc.* (1774) pp. 45–7. The pamphlet was published anonymously; see D. Nicol Smith, *Eighteenth Century Essays on Shakespeare* (1903) p. xxi, for the attribution.

10 Elizabeth Griffith, *The Morality of Shakespeare's Drama Illustrated* (1775) p. 351.

11 Lord Kames, *The Elements of Criticism* (1762) iii 233 (he feels that the causes of Cordelia's misfortune are by no means so evident as to exclude the gloomy notion of chance). And see Charlotte Lennox, *Shakespeare Illustrated* (1754) iii 290–1; Elizabeth Montague, *An Essay on the Genius and Writings of Shakespeare* (1770) p. 35.

12 Arthur Murphy, *The Gray's Inn Journal*, ii (1756) 222 – 'it would be too much to see this actually performed on the stage'. And see ibid. ii (1756) 73.

13 Davies, op. cit. ii, 260–6 – 'Were you to produce that subject on the stage, in action, none but a heart of marble could sustain it.'

14 See Theophilus Cibber, *Two Dissertations upon the Theatre, etc.* (*Dissertations upon Theatrical Subjects,* 2nd Dissertation, 1756), p. 41 – 'Can this be properly expressed by the whindling of an old fribbling nykin when reconciled to his naughty cocky?' (and see p. 35, p. 36). Admittedly Cibber was prejudiced, but his words may not seem so harsh if one recollects the anecdote retailed by Murphy

(*Life of Garrick* (1801) I 27–30) of the way in which Garrick derived his action, during the more stressful parts of *King Lear*: by imitating the horrified gestures of a man who had accidentally dropped his baby daughter from an upper window on to the flagstones below. As against this form of needless realism, Cibber affirms the dignity of Garrick's rival, Spranger Barry.

15 Samuel Johnson, *The Plays of Shakespeare*, VI (1765) 159. And see F. R. Leavis, 'Johnson as Critic', in *Scrutiny*, XII (1944) 193, 198.

16 Joseph Addison, in the *Spectator*, no. 40 (16 April 1711) – 'a ridiculous Doctrine in Modern Criticism, that they are obliged to an equal Distribution of Rewards and Punishment, and an impartial Execution of Poetical Justice'.

17 Edward Capell, *Notes and Various Readings to Shakespeare*, I (1780) 188–9.

18 George Steevens, *The Plays of William Shakespeare* (1773) ed. Johnson and Steevens, IX 485, 487.

19 Edmund Malone, *The Plays and Poems of William Shakespeare*, VIII (1790) 686–7.

20 Isaac Ambrose Eccles, *The Plays of Lear and Cymbeline* (1794) I 438 (a sensitive commentary), pp. 440, 446, 447 – ('perhaps he points to the pale colour of the lips in death'). See also John Monck Mason, *Comments on the Last Edition of Shakespeare's Plays* (1785 – i.e. the one by Steevens) pp. 357–8; and Appendix, pp. 59–60; and Preface (n.p.) – 'there is perhaps no species of publication whatever more likely to produce diversity of opinion than verbal criticisms . . .' See, as well, Samuel Henley (replying to Mason on the subject of 'the promised end'). Cited by Isaac Ambrose Eccles, op. cit. I 435–6.

21 Capell, op. cit. p. 189 (on the grounds that some actual convulsive appearance might occur in a recently dead body).

22 William Empson, 'Correspondence on *King Lear*', in *Critical Quarterly*, III (1961) 67.

23 J. Stampfer, 'The Catharsis in *King Lear*', in *Shakespeare Survey* XIII (1960) 1–2.

24 Joseph Warton, in the *Adventurer*, no. 122 (1754) p. 311 (but he gives considerable attention to the verse, as evidence in his remarks on 'Pray you, undo this button', ibid. p. 312).

25 Richard Roderick, *Remarks on Shakespeare*. Contained in *The Canons of Criticism* by Thomas Edwards, 6th ed. (1758) p. 236. Again, this forerunner of romanticism has many shrewd remarks about texture: see his comments on the range of emotion displayed by the play (ibid. p. 235). See also William Richardson, *Essays on Shakespeare's Dramatic Characters* (1784) esp. p. 82; J. G. von Herder, *Von Deutscher Art und Kunst* (1773) pp. 95–6 – which shows that there were critics well before Schlegel (*Lectures on Dramatic Art* (1811) vol. II, ii, p. 168 translated by John Black (1815) II 208) and his disciple Franz Horn (*Shakespeare's Schauspiele* (1823) I 196ff), who could defend the play against charges of arbitrariness (*pace* Kames, Griffith, Montague, *et al.*) As these notes (1–25) suggest, Kenneth Muir is quite wrong in asserting that the eighteenth-century neglected this play – Introduction to the New Arden *King Lear* (1961) p. xlv.

26 S. T. Coleridge, *Shakespearian Criticism*, ed. T. M. Raysor (1930) I 66.

27 Charles Lamb, 'On Garrick and Acting', in *Reflector*, II (1812) 309. It is often assumed that Lamb, in his strictures against *King Lear* in performance, was basing his remarks upon an actual production. It may be so; but the only recorded piece of theatrical criticism Lamb wrote on this subject is a study of the King Lear of William Cooke – whom, however, he reproaches as not being vigorous enough. See 'Cooke as Lear', in *Morning Post*, 9 Jan. 1802.

28 William Hazlitt, *Characters of Shakespeare's Plays* (1817) 174–5.

29 John Keats, *Letters*, ed. M. Buxton Forman (1947), Letter 32 (21 Dec. 1817) p. 71.

30 Coleridge, op. cit. II 219 – 'a vindication of the melancholy catastrophe'.

31 William Hazlitt, in *London Magazine*, June 1820, p. 686; reprinted in *Dramatic Essays* (1895) p. 208. The attribution is made by F. W. Hawkins, *Life of Kean* (1869) II 212.

32 *Blackwood's Magazine*, V (1819) 228–9. Laurence Irving attributes this review to John Doran (see *Life of Henry Irving* (1951) p. 550), but I doubt whether Doran, though admittedly precocious, would have been reviewing for *Blackwood's* at the age of twelve. Irving's attribution is the result of a too careless reading of Hawkins's *Life of Kean*, where Doran's opinion of 1864 (see note 35, below) and the *Blackwood's* review are brought, rather clumsily, into juxtaposition.

33 This claim for the influence of the critics is specifically made by F. W. Hawkins, op. cit. II 212. Kean's acting text was still very imperfect (see *New Monthly Magazine*, IX, 1823, p. 108: the Fool was not restored until the Macready production of 1838).

34 *New Monthly Magazine*, loc. cit.

35 Hawkins, op. cit. II 214. See also John Doran, *Their Majesties' Servants* (1864) II 556, 559.

36 John Forster, in *Examiner*, 4 Feb. 1838, reprinted in *Dramatic Essays* (1896) p. 54. Macready's performance seems to have been more woman-centred than that of Kean. Cordelia's prolonged absence is an important consideration of the play that may be taken (like Macready's performance) as a transition between Romantic and Victorian sensibility; namely, that of Anna Jameson in *Characteristics of Women*, II (1832). See esp. pp. 106–8 – 'sighing and groaning his life away over the lifeless form of Cordelia'.

37 H. N. Hudson, *Lectures on Shakespeare*, II (1848) 278.

38 G. Gervinus, *Shakespeare* (1862) pp. 212ff, trans. F. E. Bunnet (1863), pp. 237–8.

39 Hermann Ulrici, *Ueber Shakespeare's Dramatische Kunst* (1839), pp. 211, 237–8, trans. A. J. W. Morrison (1846) pp. 197–8 (but see also p. 204).

40 W. Oehlmann, 'Cordelia as a Tragic Character', in *Jahrbuch der Deutschen Shakespeare-Gesellschaft*, II (1867) 124–31, esp. 126.

41 W. J. Birch, *An Enquiry into the Philosophy and Religion of Shakespeare* (1848), pp. 427–9. But it was still possible for 'Cosmopolite' (1862, see *Shakespeare: Was He a Christian?* p. 5) to argue the exact opposite.

42 A. C. Swinburne, *A Study of Shakespeare* (1880) pp. 171–2.

43 Denton J. Snider, *The Shakespearian Drama* (1887) pp. 200ff.

44 Francis Jacox, *Shakespeare Diversions* (1875) pp. 278ff. And see George Moir (a follower of Schlegel), 'Shakespeare in Germany', Part 1, in *Blackwood's Magazine*, XXXVII (1835) 245.

45 S. W. Singer and W. W. Lloyd, *Dramatic Works of William Shakespeare*, IX (1856) 530 (an essay by Lloyd).

46 F. Kreyssig, *Vorlesungen über Shakespeare* (1874) pp. 106–7.

47 Bernhard ten Brink, *Five Lectures on Shakespeare* (1893) pp. 155–6, trans. by Julia Franklin (1895) pp. 239–40.

48 Edmund Dowden, *Shakespeare: his mind and art* (1875) p. 267.

49 R. G. Moulton, *Shakespeare as a Dramatic Artist* (1885) p. 215. Moulton was a close follower of Swinburne – he even uses Swinburne's image of the arch (op. cit. p. 172) as an integral part of his criticism.

50 Barrett Wendell, *William Shakespeare* (1894) p. 301. And see Mary Preston, *Studies in Shakespeare* (1869) p. 62; J. C. Bucknill, *The Psychology of Shakespeare* (1859) pp. 183ff.

51 A good account of this is given by W. Graham Robertson in his autobiography, *Time Was* (1931) pp. 167–8. Apparently Irving retrieved his interpretation to some extent by the fifth night. See also Laurence Irving, *Henry Irving* (1951) p. 551.

52 I put them in the form of questions. For example: Is the play Christian? What are the gods so often invoked in it? What was involved in Lear relinquishing his power? In what sense was he a 'ruined piece of nature'? What does the attitude of Cordelia mean? *Was* Lear a 'very foolish fond old man'? What is meant by the very last words of the play? etc. With the central question before us, the critics in these instances have answered such questions as these already: thus making one feel that perhaps answers weren't needed in the first place. However, as in the main line of enquiry explored here, consideration of these issues would undoubtedly show that the critics' quarrels are with each other, not with the play.

53 See the article by O. J. Campbell, in *Journal of English Literary History*, x (1948).

54 *King Lear*, v iii 305–11.

55 See the famous comment by Joshua Reynolds quoted in *Shakespeare's Plays*, ed. Johnson and Steevens (1785) ix 607; *Plays and Poems of William Shakespeare*, viii (1790), ed. Edmund Malone, pp. 685–6. And see John Forster, 'The Restoration of Shakespeare's *Lear* to the Stage', in *Examiner*, 4 Feb. 1838.

56 Stampfer, op. cit. (see note 23) pp. 1ff.

57 e.g. Knights, Campbell, Chambers, Muir, Spencer, Barker. See notes 83–8.

58 Sigmund Freud, 'The Theme of the Three Caskets', first published in *Imago*, ii (1913). In *Works*, xxi 294ff, esp. 296.

59 Ibid. pp. 292–3.

60 Ibid. p. 301.

61 Ibid.

62 G. H. Clark, 'The Catastrophe in *King Lear*', in *Queen's Quarterly*, xli (1934) 380.

63 John Danby, *Shakespeare's Doctrine of Nature* (1949) p. 194.

64 Ibid. p. 195.

65 *King Lear*, v iii 258–9.

66 Ibid. line 265.

67 Ibid. lines 265–7.

68 Ibid. lines 271–3.

69 R. B. Heilman, *This Great Stage* (1958) p. 55.

70 L. C. Knights, *Some Shakespearian Themes* (1959) p. 117.

71 Ibid. p. 118.

72 Ibid.

73 I am conscious of not having done justice to Heilman here. He seems to me perhaps the most valuable commentator upon Shakespeare since Wilson Knight. See, particularly, his analysis of the clothes imagery in *King Lear* (op. cit. pp. 67ff).

74 Knights, op. cit. p. 116.

75 O. J. Campbell, 'The Salvation of Lear', in *Journal of English Literary History*, xv (1948) 107.

76 Ibid.

77 Bradley, op. cit. p. 291.
78 R. W. Chambers, *King Lear* (1940) p. 44.
79 Campbell, op. cit., p. 107.
80 Chambers, op. cit. p. 45. Gerald Smith, 'A Note on the Death of King Lear', in *Modern Language Notes*, LXX (1955) 403–4f, cites a parallel – between a pseudo-scientific work of 1597, called *Problems of Aristotle,* and *Antonio's Revenge* (Marston) on one hand, and this latter work and *King Lear* on the other; and comes to much the same conclusion as Campbell. Such a 'parallel' proves nothing unless its conclusions can be demonstrated from the text of the prime subject of discussion. If such conclusions cannot be demonstrated, then they are irrelevant and unnecessary.

   An intermediate position between the second group of critics and Bradley is taken by Huntington Brown ('Enter the Shakespearian Tragic Hero', in *Essays in Criticism*, III (1953) 292–3) and Kenneth Muir ('Correspondence on *King Lear*', in *Critical Quarterly*, III (1961) 68); and see also Muir's introduction to his Arden Edition (1961) p. lix. Both emphasise a development in Lear's drama towards an advance in understanding. And see Mark van Doren, *Shakespeare* (1941) p. 250 – 'two old men who learned too much too late'; Theodore Spencer, *Shakespeare and the Nature of Man* (1943) p. 152 – this last suggests that it is Lear's discovery that life is good that kills him.
81 Bradley, op. cit. p. 291.
82 Capell, op. cit. (see note 17) p. 189.
83 Knights, op. cit. p. 118.
84 Campbell, op. cit. p. 107.
85 Chambers, op. cit. p. 44.
86 Muir, op. cit. p. 68 (and see the Arden introduction).
87 Spencer, op. cit. p. 152.
88 Harley Granville-Barker, *Prefaces to Shakespeare,* First series (1927) p. 185.
89 Barbara Everett, 'The New King Lear', in *Critical Quarterly*, II (1960) 329ff.
90 See Danby, op. cit. p. 195.
91 *King Lear*, IV vii 45–7.
92 Ibid. v iii 10–12.
93 Ibid. v iii 265–7.
94 Bradley, op. cit. p. 291.
95 *King Lear*, v iii 310–11.
96 Bradley, op. cit. p. 291.
97 The last-named is thought to have grounded his performance upon the interpretation of Jan Kott. But this incredibly vulgar book (*Shakespeare Our Contemporary* (1964) pp. 101ff) does not specify the nature of Lear's end; nor very much else.
98 Granville-Barker, op. cit. pp. 154, 185.
99 D. A. Traversi, '*King Lear*', in *Scrutiny*, XIX (1953) 230.
100 G. Wilson Knight, *The Wheel of Fire* (1930) p. 223.
101 Ibid. pp. 223–4.
102 John Holloway, *The Story of the Night* (1961) p. 90.
103 Ibid.
104 Ibid.
105 Ibid. p. 94.
106 Ibid. p. 90.

107 Like E. E. Stoll (*Art and Artifice in Shakespeare* (1933) p. 143) Holloway feels that tragedy has sway (op. cit. p. 90). And Stoll will not even allow Lear a momentary illusion (op. cit. p. 143).

108 I ought to say that some critics hold a transitional position halfway between the modified gloom of Knight and Holloway and the complete sense of disaster shared by the critics whom I have termed Tolstoyan. The main distinction to be observed is that J. K. Walton ('Lear's Last Speech', in *Shakespeare Survey*, XIII (1960) 16–17) and Emrys Jones ('Correspondence on *King Lear*', in *Critical Quarterly*, III (1961) 73) feel that the play ends in unalloyed gloom, but still have a sense of purgation – the catastrophe isn't merely pessimistic. Nevertheless their view seems to be a simplified reading. For example, Walton cites Lear's attempts to prove Cordelia alive as Shakespeare's way of emphasising her deadness, and Jones quotes Kent's 'all's cheerless, dark and deadly' out of context when Kent is trying to bring Lear back to his senses. A former colleague of mine, M. P. MacDiarmid, in conversation in 1963 took this to mean that Lear is mad, but it would seem to suggest rather that he is focused in some direction quite different from that of his interlocutors. Lear is concerned solely with Cordelia: hence it could be said, in answer to Mr Walton, that Lear himself instances images of life throughout the scene in refusing to believe in Cordelia's death.

109 Leo Tolstoy on 'Shakespeare and the Drama' (trans. V. Tchertkoff), in *Fortnightly Review*, LXXXVI (Dec. 1906) p. 967.

110 Ibid. p. 980.

111 George Orwell, *Shooting an Elephant* (1950): see esp. pp. 41, 46, 47, 51, 52, 53.

112 Ibid. p. 56.

113 Everett, op. cit. p. 339 – she suggests that the question of whether Shakespeare was right in turning his raw material into a moral act is too hard to answer, but it cannot be answered by turning *King Lear* into a morality play.

114 W. R. Keast, 'Imagery and Meaning in the Interpretation of *King Lear*', in *Modern Philology*, XLVII (1949) 63.

115 Ibid.

116 Ibid.

117 Everett, op. cit. p. 332.

118 Ibid. p. 337.

119 J. Stampfer, 'The Catharsis in *King Lear*', in *Shakespeare Survey*, XIII (1960) 1.

120 Ibid. pp. 1, 2.

121 Walton, op. cit. p. 14.

122 Stampfer, op. cit. p. 2.

123 Ibid.

124 Ibid. p. 4.

125 Ibid.

126 W. Empson, 'Correspondence on *King Lear*', in *Critical Quarterly*, III (1961) 67.

127 Ibid.

128 Danby, op. cit. p. 194.

129 Empson, op. cit. p. 67.

130 W. Empson, *The Structure of Complex Words* (1951) p. 155.

131 *King Lear*, V iii 305.

1 John G. Saxe, *The Blind Men and the Elephant. Clever Stories of Many Nations* (1865) pp. 61–4.

2 Max Müller, *Lectures on the Science of Language* (1861): see esp. pp. 344ff.

3 W. Wundt, *Völkerpsychologie* (1904). See esp. book 1, sections 1–6, pp. 37ff. Leonard Bloomfield, *An Introduction to the Study of Language* (1914) p. 5.

4 Charles Darwin, *The Descent of Man* (1871) pp. 58ff.

5 A. S. Diamond, *The History and Origin of Language* (1959) p. 264. This is true only of Indo-European languages. Some primitive societies have, in the European sense, no verbs at all. The origin of language is a topic largely avoided by modern linguists, through sheer paucity of evidence.

6 Ernst Cassirer, *An Essay on Man* (2nd printing, 1945) pp. 122–3.

7 G. A. de Laguna, *Speech: its Function and Development* (1927) pp. 191ff.

8 John Hughlings Jackson, *Selected Writings*, ed. J. Taylor (1931–2) 84. And see vol. I, p. 82; vol. II, pp. 156–7, 160, 166, 198ff, 210.

9 Russell Brain, *Speech Disorders* (1961) p. 54.

10 W. Penfield and L. Roberts, *Speech and Brain Mechanisms* (1959) pp. 119ff.

11 Brain, op. cit. p. 56.

12 Jackson, op. cit. II, 160.

13 Russell Brain, *Perspectives in Neuropsychiatry*, ed. D. Richter (1950) pp. 127ff, and *Speech Disorders* (1961) pp. 57ff.

14 Brain, *Speech Disorders*, p. 79.

15 F. de Saussure, *Course in General Linguistics* (1915, trans. W. Baskin, 1960), esp. pp. 1, 79.

16 e.g. de Saussure, op. cit. p. 106; E. Sapir, *Language* (1921) pp. 24ff; Leonard Bloomfield, *The Study of Language* (1933) pp. 74ff; J. R. Firth, *Papers in Linguistics* (1957) pp. 180ff; Stephen Ullmann, *Semantics* (1962) pp. 22ff; Z. Harris, *Methods of Structural Linguistics* (1951) pp. 23ff; C. F. Hockett, *A Course in Modern Linguistics* (1958) pp. 166ff.

17 F. de Saussure, op. cit. p. 232.

18 Ibid. p. 15.

19 Ibid. pp. 65ff.

20 Ibid. pp. 113, 122.

21 Ibid. p. 106.

22 Edward Sapir, *Language* (1921) pp. 14, 41.

23 Ibid. p. 233. J. R. Firth and B. L. Whorf show much greater awareness of the relationship between society and language than this. But their work is a hybrid of linguistics and anthropology, and seems to me better as it approaches the latter and recedes from the former. This is only to reinforce my original tenet, that linguistics, as a mode of describing and evaluating acts of language, is no use to a reader at all.

24 Ibid. pp. 237ff.

25 Ibid. pp. 236, 14.

26 See my article 'Current Aesthetic Fallacies', in *British Journal of Aesthetics*, VII (1967) 117–18.

27 Leonard Bloomfield, *The Study of Language* (1933) pp. 142ff.

28 Ibid. p. 22.

29 Ibid. p. 509.

30 See Louis Helmsjev, *Prologomena to a Theory of Language*, trans. F. J. Whitfield (1953) p. 5 (and see p. 49 for the inevitable Form-Content Distinction). And see also C. F. Hockett, *A Course in Modern Linguistics* (1958) p. 564, etc.

31 Z. Harris, *Methods in Structural Linguistics* (1951) pp. 366–7.

32 G. K. Zipf, *The Psycho-Biology of Language* (1935) pp. 21ff.

33 Noam Chomsky, *Syntactic Structures* (1957) e.g. pp. 3ff; see also ch. 4.

34 M. A. K. Halliday, 'Categories of the Theory of Grammar', *Word*, XVII (1961) 279–80.

35 Ibid. p. 258.

36 Ibid. p. 253.

37 Ibid. p. 257.

38 Ibid. pp. 258, 267.

39 John Lotz, 'Linguistic Symbols Make Man', in *Psycholinguistics*, ed. S. Saporta (1961) p. 14.

40 J. B. Watson, 'Is Thinking Merely the Action of Language Mechanisms?' in *Brit. J. Psychol.* XI (1920) 103.

41 Ibid. p. 94.

42 B. F. Skinner, *Verbal Behavior* (1957) p. 10.

43 Ibid. pp. 35ff.

44 Ibid. pp. 81ff.

45 Ibid. pp. 1ff.

46 Ibid. pp. 239–40.

47 A. M. Thorson, 'The Relation of Tongue Movements to Internal Speech', in *J. exp. Psychol.* VIII (1923) 1–32.

48 E. Jacobson, 'Electrophysiology of Mental Activities', in *Am. J. Psychol.* XLIV (1932) 677–94. L. W. Max, 'An Experimental Study of the Motor Theory of Consciousness', sections III and IV, in *J. Comp. Psychol.* XIX (1935) 469–86; XXIV (1937) 301–44.

49 G. H. S. Razran, 'Salivating and Thinking in Different Languages', in *Psychol.* I (1935–6) 145–51.

50 Molly Mason, 'Changes in the Galvanic Skin Response Accompanying Changes of Meaning during Oral Repetition', in *J. gen. Psychol.* XXV (1941) 353–401. W. E. Bingham, Jr, 'A Study of the Relations Which the Galvanic Skin Response and Sensory Reference bear to Judgments of the Meaningfulness, Significance and Importance of 72 Words', in *J. Psychol.* XVI (1943) 21–34.

51 C. N. Cofer and J. P. Foley, 'Mediated Generalization and the Interpretation of Verbal Behaviour. I. Prologomena.' in *Psychological Review*, XLIX (1942) 513–40. C. E. Osgood, 'Meaningful Similarity and Interference in Learning', in *J. exp. Psych.* XXXVI (1946) 277–301; 'An Investigation into the Causes of Retroactive Interference', in *J. exp. Psychol.* XXXVIII (1945) 132–54.

52 L. Carmichael, H. P. Hogan and A. A. Walter, 'An Experimental Study of the Effect of Language upon the Reproduction of Visually Perceived Forms', in *J. exp. Psychol.* XV (1932) 73–86. D. C. McClelland and J. W. Atkinson, 'The Projective Expression of Needs: I. The Effect of Different Intensities of the Hunger Drive on Perception', in *J. Psychol.* XXV (1948) 205–22. L. Postman and J. S. Bruner, 'Perception under Stress', in *Psychol. Rev.* LV (1948) 314–24. J. S. Bruner and C. C. Goodman, 'Value and Need as Organizing Factors in Perception', in *J. abnorm. Psychol.* XLII (1947) 33–4. L. Postman, J. S. Bruner and E. McGinnies, 'Personal Values as Selected Factors in Perception', in *J. abnorm. soc. Psychol.* XLIII (1948) 142–54. R. M. Dorcus, 'Habitual Word Associations to

Colours as a Possible Factor in Advertising', in *J. appl. Psychol.* xvi (1932) 277–87. T. F. Karwoski, F. W. Gramlich and P. Arnott, 'Psychological Studies in Semantics, I. Free Association Reactions to Words, Drawings and Objects', in *J. soc. Psychol.* xx (1944) 233–47. W. A. Bousfield, 'The Relationship Between Mood and Affectively Toned Associates', in *J. gen. Psychol.* XLII (1950) 67–85. J. P. Foley, Jr. and Z. L. Macmillan, 'Mediated Generalization and the Interpretation of Verbal Behaviour: (v) "Free Association" as Related to Differences in Professional Training', in *J. exp. Psychol.* xxxiii (1943) 299–310. D. Howes and C. E. Osgood, 'On the Combination of Associative Probabilities in Linguistic Contexts', in *Am. J. Psychol.* lxvii (1954) 241–58.

53 C. Osgood, G. Suci and P. Tannenbaum, *The Measurement of Meaning* (2nd printing, 1958) pp. 9ff, 18ff.

54 Ibid. pp. 26–7.

55 Ibid. pp. 31ff, esp. p. 33. For instance, forty names were taken from the Kent-Rosanoff list of stimulus words for free association and those were read in fairly rapid succession to a group of approximately 200 undergraduate students who were instructed to write down after each stimulus noun the first descriptive adjective that occurred to them. The data was then analysed for the frequency of occurrence of all adjectives. Twenty concepts were selected.

56 I. de Sola Pool, *Trends in Content Analysis* (1959) pp. 189–233, reprinted in *Psycholinguistics*, ed. Saporta, pp. 303–4, 309–10, 318ff.

57 Leonard Krasner, 'Studies of the Conditioning of Verbal Behaviour', in *Psychological Bulletin*, lv (1958) 148–170, reprinted in *Psycholinguistics*, ed. Saporta: see esp. p. 75 of latter.

58 I was thinking particularly of Anne M. Nuthmann, 'Conditioning of a Response Class on a Personality Test', in *J. abnorm. soc. Psychol.* liv (1957) 19–23. But really my strictures apply generally to experimental psychology as at present practised. See, for instance, any of the following: I. G. Sarason, 'Interrelations among Individual Difference Variable, Behaviour in Psychotherapy, and Verbal Conditioning'. Paper read at West. Psychol. An., Eugene, Oreg., May 1957; D. M. McNair, 'Reinforcement of Verbal Behaviour', in *J. exp. Psychol.* liii (1957) 40–6; M. C. Cushing, 'Affective Components of the Response Class as a Factor in Verbal Conditioning', in *Dissertation Abstr.* xvii (1957) 2313. Examples could be multiplied.

59 G. A. Miller, *Language and Communication* (1951) p. 9.

60 Ibid. p. 95.

61 E. C. Cherry, *On Human Communication* (1957) pp. 7, 9.

62 Ibid. p. 226.

63 Yehoshua Bar-Hillel and Rudolf Carnap, 'Semantic Information', in *Communication Theory*, ed. Willis Jackson (1953) p. 503.

64 E. C. Cherry, op. cit. p. 226. And see Claude Shannon and Warren Weaver, *A Mathematical Theory of Communication* (1949) passim.

65 See E. C. Cherry, op. cit. p. 242.

66 Y. Bar-Hillel and R. Carnap, op. cit. p. 510.

67 H. Zemanek, H. Kretz, A. J. Angyan, 'A Model for Neurophysical Functions'. in *Information Theory*, ed. Cherry (1961).

68 Paul Garvin, 'The Definitional Model of Language', in Garvin, *Natural Language and the Computer* (1963) p. 21.

69 D. G. Hays, 'Basic Principles and Technical Variations in Sentence-Structure Determination', in *Information Theory*, Cherry (1961) p. 367.

70 But see Bloomfield's analogy, in *Language*, p. 33; see *Language* (1914) p. 90.

71 Benoit Mandelbrôt, 'An Informational Theory of the Statistical Structures of Language', in *Communication Theory*, ed. Willis Jackson, p. 498.

72 *Natural Language and the Computer*, ed. Paul Garvin.

73 Paul Garvin, 'A Linguist's View of Language Data-Processing', in *Natural Language and the Computer*, ed. Garvin, pp. 84ff.

74 R. M. Hayes, 'Mathematical Models for Information Retrieval', ibid. pp. 287ff.

75 L. E. Travis, 'Analytic Information Retrieval', ibid. esp. pp. 344–5.

76 See Norbert Wiener, *Cybernetics* (1961) pp. 146ff, 197.

77 E. C. Berkeley, *Giant Brains* (1949) pp. 7–8.

78 Solomon W. Golomb, 'A Mathematical Theory of Discrete Classification', in *Information Theory*, ed. Cherry (1961) p. 420.

79 In a BBC/TV Brains Trust, round about 1960, Bernard Williams suggested that the ultimate task of the philosopher was the construction of an ideal dictionary.

80 See, for instance, Berkeley, op. cit. pp. 209ff. W. Karush, 'On the Use of Mathematics in Behavioural Research', in *Natural Language and the Computer*, ed. Garvin, pp. 73ff.

81 Karush, ibid.

82 Bertrand Russell, *Introduction to Mathematical Philosophy* (1919) p. 195.

83 Karush, op. cit. p. 74. And see Kenneth F. Iverson, 'Description of Finite Sequential Processes', in *Information Theory*, ed. Cherry, p. 447.

84 Zemanek, Kretz and Angyan, op. cit. p. 270.

85 Golomb, op. cit. p. 404.

86 Felix Klein, *Erlangerprogramm*. See Golomb, op. cit. p. 404.

87 A. N. Whitehead and Bertrand Russell, *Principia Mathematica* (1910) I, e.g. pp. 75ff.

88 Gottlob Frege, *The Foundations of Arithmetic* (1884), trans. J. L. Austin (1950) p. 22c.

89 G. Frege, op. cit. p. 31c.

90 Isabel Hungerland, 'Iconic Signs and Expressiveness', in *Journal of Aesthetics and Art Criticism*, III (1943); reprinted in *The Problems of Aesthetics*, ed. E. Vivas and M. Krieger (1963) p. 234.

91 Charles Morris, 'Esthetics and the Theory of Signs', in *Journal of Unified Science*, VIII (1939).

92 Ibid. p. 136.

93 Charles Morris, 'Science, Art and Technology', in *Kenyon Review*, I (1939), reprinted in *The Problems of Aesthetics*, ed. Vivas and Krieger, p. 110.

94 *Signs, Language and Behaviour* (1946) p. 10.

95 'Science, Art and Technology', loc. cit. p. 106.

96 See Hungerland, op. cit. p. 232.

97 Albert Gehring, *The Basis of Musical Pleasure* (1910) ch. IV, esp. p. 81, see also app. D, pp. 136ff.

98 L. von Wittgenstein, *Tractatus Logicophilosophicus* (1922), 3.5, 4, 4.001, 4.01, 4.012.

99 Suzanne Langer, *Feeling and Form* (1953) pp. 48, 62.

100 Wittgenstein, op. cit. 4.012.

101 Suzanne Langer, op. cit. p. 66.

102 C. K. Ogden and I. A. Richards, *The Meaning of Meaning* (1923) pp. 261, 394, 409. And see O. Jespersen, *The Growth and Structure of the English Language* (1905); *The Philosophy of Grammar* (1924); J. Vendryes, *Le Langage* (1921) trans. P. Radin (1925) esp. pp. 136–9. Their precursors are Ch.-A. Séchehaye, *Programme et Méthode de la linguistique théorique* (1908); Ch. Bally, 'L'Etude systematique des moyens d'expression', in *Neueren Sprachen*, XIX (1911); G. von der Gabelantz, *Die Sprachwissenschaft*, 2nd ed. (1901) – 'Language is not used by man merely to express something but to express himself'. See book I, chapter 1.

103 Gustaf Stern, *Meaning and Change of Meaning* (1931) p. 23 (and see p. 155), p. 147.

104 Bertrand Russell, *The Analysis of Mind* (1921) pp. 200, 209, 211.

105 Ogden and Richard, op. cit. pp. 149, 257, 372.

106 Henri Bergson, *La Perception du changement* (1911) p. 12 – 'connaissance virtuelle, connaissance actuelle'. And see note 131.

107 Ogden and Richards, op. cit. pp. 271, 363.

108 I. A. Richards *Science and Poetry* (1926) pp. 56, 58.

109 Yvor Winters, *In Defence of Reason* (1960) pp. 40ff.

110 Irving J. Lee, *Language Habits in Human Affairs* (1941) p. 148.

111 S. J. Hayakawa, *Language in Thought and Action* (1949, rep. 1952) p. 130.

112 C. L. Stevenson, *Ethics and Language* (1944) pp. 37–46, 64–7.

113 O. Jespersen, *The Philosophy of Grammar* (1924) p. 309.

114 P. F. Strawson, *Introduction to Logical Theory* (1952) p. 48.

115 Monroe Beardsley, *Thinking Straight* (1950) pp. 125ff, 147–8.

116 Virgil Aldrich, 'Pictorial Meaning and Picture Thinking', in *Kenyon Review*, V (1943) esp. pp. 410, 412.

117 Lascelles Abercrombie, *The Theory of Poetry* (1924) p. 125. See also p. 119 ('experience' – 'thought'), p. 121 ('value' – 'meaning').

118 T. M. Greene, *The Arts and the Art of Criticism* (1947) pp. 99ff, 103.

119 I. A. Richards, *The Philosophy of Rhetoric* (1936) pp. 48ff.

120 John Sparrow, *Sense and Poetry* (1934) pp. 1, 10, 12–13.

121 E. M. W. Tillyard, *Poetry, Direct and Oblique* (rev. ed. 1945) p. 10.

122 W. Empson, *The Structure of Complex Words* (1951) pp. 15ff; *Seven Types of Ambiguity* (1930) pp. 1–2.

123 C. L. Stevenson, op. cit. pp. 76, 79.

124 e.g. W. B. Stanford, *Ambiguity in Greek Literature* (1939) pp. 70ff; Abraham Kaplan and Ernest Kris, 'Esthetic Ambiguity', in *Phil. and Phen. Res.* VIII (1948) 416ff; Philip Wheelwright, *The Burning Fountain* (1954) p. 61. I do not mean to malign the arguments put forward by these theorists; merely to deplore the fact that they have not been attended to.

125 e.g. Kenneth Burke, *The Philosophy of Literary Form* (1941) pp. 140, 143; Max Rieser, 'The Language of Poetic and of Scientific Thought', in *J. Phil.* XL (1943) 421–2, 424, etc.

126 Max Eastman, *The Literary Mind* (1931) pp. 90–1.

127 Ibid. p. 80.

128 Ibid. pp. 178–9.

129 Ibid. p. 255.

130 Christine Brook-Rose, *A Grammar of Metaphor* (1958) pp. 287–8.

131 Donald Davie, *Articulate Energy* (1955) pp. 2–3. And see note 106.

132 Ibid. p. 23.

133 Ibid. pp. 79ff.

134 Ibid. pp. 85ff.

135 Ibid. p. 164, and see pp. 161ff.

136 Winifred Nowottny, *The Language Poets Use* (1962) pp. 82–3.

137 Ibid. p. 123.

138 Ibid. pp. 188ff.

139 Ibid. p. 219.

140 Ibid. p. 221.

141 Nonesuch edition (1932) pp. 464–5.

142 J. C. Coleman, *Abnormal Psychology and Modern Life* (1950) takes a stand towards creative writing rather like this.

143 See, for instance, the broadsheet quoted by F. R. Leavis in *The Common Pursuit* (1952) p. 205.

144 B. F. Skinner, *Verbal Behaviour*, pp. 227ff, esp. 239–43.

11 A THEORY OF COMMUNICATION

1 Bob Shaw, 'A Concept of Universal Indefinability', in *Arrows*, no. 74 (Winter 1959).

2 William Blake, Introduction to 'Milton', in *Poetry and Prose of William Blake*, ed. Geoffrey Keynes, 3rd ed. (1932) pp. 464–5.

3 F. W. Bateson, *English Poetry: a critical introduction* (1950) p. 8.

4 W. W. Robson, in *Essays in Criticism*, II (1952) 112–13.

5 F. W. Bateson, in *Essays in Criticism*, II (1952) 107.

6 W. W. Robson, in *Essays in Criticism*, loc. cit.

7 J. Bronowski, *The Man without a Mask* (1943) p. 130. And see W. Empson, in *Essays in Criticism*, III (1953) 116–17.

8 John Bayley, in *Essays in Criticism*, II (1952) 455–60.

9 W. Empson, in *Essays in Criticism*, III (1953) 116–17. Elementary versions of this theory have been adumbrated (see Stephen Ullmann, *Semantics* (1962) pp. 48–9 for some useful references; also L. B. Salomon, *Semantics and Common Sense* (1966) p. 50). But none of them has been applied with any great effect to literature. Similarly, the literary critics rest their cases upon very crude assumptions about language. It seems to me tragic that 'literature' and 'language' have gone their separate ways throughout the twentieth century. The only moment when the two 'aspects' cohere is in the final paragraph of Richards's chapter XXI of *Principles of Literary Criticism* – 'The effect of a word varies with the other words among which it is placed'. But Richards has not demonstrated this: hence the need for my whole enquiry.

10 Shaw, op. cit.

11 Shakespeare, *Winter's Tale*, IV iv 118–20.

12 Keats, *To Autumn*, lines 5–6.

13 G. M. Hopkins, *Thou art indeed just, Lord* . . . lines 9–12.

14 Peter Redgrove, *Memorial*, lines 19–22. See *The Collector* (1960) pp. 40–1.

15 See, for instance, the gap between Erik Stenius (Wittgenstein's *Tractatus* (1960) pp. 140ff) and David Favrholdt (*An Interpretation and Critique of Wittgenstein's Tractatus* (1961) pp. 68ff) for a divergence on Wittgenstein's problem of the false sentence. And see James Mill, *Government*, reprinted in *Political Tracts* (1821) pp. 4–5; John Stuart Mill, *Utilitarianism* (1863) pp. 8ff (and see pp. 47–9); George

Grote, *Fragments on Ethical Subjects* (1876) pp. 72ff. These diverge on Bentham's 'greatest happiness' principle. See Jeremy Bentham, *Principles of Judicial Procedure*, in *Works*, ed. John Bowring (1843) II 13.

16 Thomas North, *Plutarch's Lives of the Noble Grecians and Romans* (1579) pp. 981-2.
17 Shakespeare, *Antony and Cleopatra*, II ii 194-222.
18 Ibid. lines 212-15.
19 F. R. Leavis, '*Antony and Cleopatra* and *All for Love*', in *Scrutiny*, v (1936) p. 164.
20 e.g. *The Prelude* (1805), I 1-94, 271-350, 372-427, 452-89; IV 400-504; v 389-422; VI 553-72; XI 279-316; XIII 1-65. *Paradise Lost*, on the other hand, is perhaps best read as books I, II, IV, IX, and the *conclusion* of book XII; bearing in mind, however, that all except the last carry an expendable amount of waste matter. See Chapter Three, passim.
21 *Antony and Cleopatra*, I i 6-10.
22 Ibid. v ii 299-301.
23 J. M. Murry, *The Problem of Style* (1922) pp. 36ff.
24 *Antony and Cleopatra*, v ii 292-4, 307-8.
25 Ibid. line 285.
26 Ibid. lines 305-6.
27 Ibid. lines 313-4.
28 F. R. Leavis, *Revaluation*, p. 118.
29 Samuel Johnson, *Vanity of Human Wishes*, lines 73-6.
30 Matthew Arnold, 'Study of Poetry', in *Essays in Criticism*, 2nd Series (1888) p. 40.
31 Milton, *Samson Agonistes*, line 80.
32 T. S. Eliot, *East Coker*, III 1.
33 Milton, op. cit. line 41.
34 Eliot, op. cit. v 1-3.
35 See notes 11-14.

Index

265

Hendrie, T. E., 51
Henley, Samuel, 253
Herbert, George, 131–4, 171, 218, 249, 250
Herder, J. G. von, 253
Hetherington, Hugh W., 237, 238
Hillway, Tyrus, 237, 238
Hobbes, Thomas, 174
Hobsbaum, Hannah, 170, 173–5
Hobsbaum, Philip, 165, 169–71, 173–5, 177–9, 182–3, 192
Hobson, Harold, 89, 239
Hockett, C. F., 191, 192
Hodder-Williams, Sir Ernest, 106
Hoffman, Charles Fenno, 238
Hogan, H. P., 196
Holloway, John, 157–8, 257
Holmes, O. W., 88, 238
Holtby, Winifred, 101
Honorius, Augustodunensis, 133
Hopkins, Gerard Manley, 211, 220
Horn, Franz, 253
Hough, Graham, 48
House, D., 196
House, Humphry, 75, 76, 78, 80
Houston, Ralph, 63, 64
Hudson, H. N., 147
Hueffer, F. M., 92, 94, 95, 97, 241, 242
Hulme, T. E., 204
Hume, David, 218
Hungerland, Isabel, 201
Hunt, Violet, 240
Hutchinson, F. E., 249
Hutchinson, Thomas, 233
Hutton, R. H., 227, 235
Hyman, Lawrence, 137, 138, 140

Irving, Henry, 147, 255
Irving, Laurence, 254, 255
Iverson, Kenneth F., 261

Jackson, John Hughlings, 189
Jackson, Willis, 260
Jacobson, Dan, 22, 23, 24, 27
Jacobson, E., 196
Jacox, Francis, 147
James, D. G., 118, 247
James, Henry, 74, 76, 77, 79, 80, 81, 229, 236
Jameson, Anna, 254

Jarrell, **Randall**, 13
Jefferies, Richard, 101
Jeffrey, Francis, 82, 83, 84
Jenkins, Joan, 251
Jespersen, Otto, 202, 203
Johnson, Edgar, 75, 80, 81
Johnson, Samuel, 32, 33, 91, 145, 217, 218, 221, 222
Johnson, S. F., 124, 125
Johnson, Thomas, 224
Jones, E. D., 227
Jones, Emrys, 257
Joseph, Rosemary, 171
Joyce, James, 231
Juvenal, 227

Kames, Lord, 145, 252, 253
Kaplan, Abraham, 203, 262
Karwoski, T. F., 196
Karush, W., 199
Kazin, Alfred, 25, 28
Kean, Edmund, 146, 254
Keast, W. R., 159
Keats, John, 32, 115–19, 124, 211, 218, 220, 221, 227, 246, 247
Keble, John, 32
Kermode, Frank, 89, 136, 138, 139, 239, 240
Keyes, Sidney, 53–5, 66
Keynes, Geoffrey, 227, 234
King, A. H., 137
Kingopulos, G. D., 236
Kinsley, William W., 85
Klein, Felix, 199
Klonsky, Milton, 137, 138
Knight, Douglas, 231
Knight, G. Wilson, 58, 62, 66, 79, 80, 117, 148, 149, 157, 231, 257
Knights, L. C., 131, 149, 153, 155, 156, 249
Kott, Jan, 256
Krasner, Leonard, 197
Kretz, H., 198, 199
Kreyssig, F., 147
Krieger, Murray, 261
Kris, Ernest, 203, 262

L., A. W. C., 94
Lacon-Watson, Edward, 107
Laguna, G. A. de, 189

Lamb, Charles, 146, 253
Lamson, Roy, 127
Landor, W. S., 32, 34
Langer, Suzanne, 201
Langland, William, 218, 221
Laun, H. van, 235
Lawrence, D. H., 82, 87, 88, 90–114, 237, 240, 241, 242, 243, 244, 245, 246
Lawrence, Frieda, 112, 244
Lea, F. A., 63, 64, 66
Leavis, F. R., 37, 38, 39, 40, 41, 46, 47, 58, 59, 60, 64, 65, 74, 82, 91, 92, 94, 97, 102, 109, 111, 112, 118, 120, 122, 164, 165, 166, 206, 212, 214, 227, 236, 237, 253, 263
Lee, Irving J., 202–3
Lee, Nathaniel, 227
Legouis, Pierre, 137, 251
Leigh, Richard, 227
Lennox, Charlotte, 252
Lewes, G. H., 74, 79, 236, 237
Lewis, C. S., 33, 34, 35, 36, 37, 38, 39, 46, 47, 48, 228, 229
Lindsay, Jack, 74, 75, 76, 78, 80, 81, 236
Lloyd, W. W., 147
Lloyd-Thomas, M. G., 137
Longfellow, H. W., 88
Lotz, John, 194
Lowell, J. R., 88
Lowell, Robert, 89, 239–40
Lucas, F. L., 89, 239
Lucie-Smith, Edward, 124, 165, 167–71, 173–4, 175, 176–80, 182–4, 239–40
Lucretius, 204
Lydgate, John, 250
Lynd, Robert, 92, 94, 99, 104, 244

MacBeth, George, 165, 173, 177–9
McClelland, D. C., 196
McCloskey, John C., 238
MacDiarmid, M. P., 257
McGinnies, E., 196
McIntyre, F. F., 51
McLaren, Robin, 168–71
MacMillan, Z. L., 196
McMullen, H. M., 244
McNair, D. M., 260
Macready, W. C., 147, 254
Macy, John, 99, 107

Malone, Edmund, 146
Malone, Josephine, 232
Mandelbrôt, Benoit, 198
Manly, J. M., 97
Mansfield, L. S., 237, 238
Marble, A. R., 93, 96, 107, 241
Margoliouth, H. M., 251
Marston, John, 256
Martin, Kingsley, 246
Martz, Louis, 131, 249
Marvell, Andrew, 5, 135–41, 171, 218, 251
Masefield, John, 89
Mason, John Monck, 253
Mason, Molly, 196
Massingham, Harold, 98
Masson, David, 229
Maupassant, Guy de, 93
Max, L. W., 196
Melville, Herman, 82, 86–7, 89, 90, 91, 110, 111, 113, 237, 238
Mencken, H. L., 29
Methuen, Sir Algernon, 102, 103
Middleton, Stanley, 95
Middleton, Richard, 133
Milgate, W., 64
Mill, James, 212, 263
Mill, John Stuart, 212, 263
Miller, G. A., 197
Miller, J. Hillis, 75, 76, 78, 79, 80, 81
Milton, John, 31–48, 123, 219, 227, 228–9, 230, 264
Mizener, Arthur, 21, 22, 23, 24, 25, 27
Moir, George, 252, 254
Montague, Elizabeth, 252, 253
Montague, Joyce, 51
Montgomery, Robert, 249
Moore, Arthur K., 124, 125
Moore, Thomas, 85
More, Paul Elmer, 37
Morris, Charles, 201
Morrison, A. J. W., 254
Mosheim, J. L. von, 69
Moulton, R. G., 147, 254
Muir, Edwin, 102, 109, 110, 111, 246
Muir, Kenneth, 33, 35, 36, 39, 45, 46, 118, 119, 128, 130, 149, 155, 253, 256
Müller, Max, 188
Murdoch, Iris, 90

Wasserman, E. R., 117
Watson, J. B., 194–5, 196
Weaver, Warren, 260
Weekley, Ernest, 244
Weir, Charles, 29
Welby, T. Earle, 227
Wellek, René, 60, 64, 65, 121, 122
Wells, H. G., 93, 106, 111, 244
Wendell, Barrett, 147
Westcott, W. Wynn, 234
Whaler, James, 41, 42, 43
Wheelwright, Philip, 203, 262
Whitehead, A. N., 200
Whitfield, F. J., 192
Whiting, George, 125, 127
Whiting, John, 89, 239
Whitley, Alvin, 246
Whitman, Walt, 87–91, 218, 238, 239
Whittier, J. G., 238
Whorf, B. L., 258
Wickham, Harvey, 99, 101, 243
Wiener, Norbert, 199

Willey, Basil, 37, 228
Williams, Bernard, 261
Williams, Charles, 46
Williams, Helen Maria, 85
Wilson, Angus, 15–17, 20, 90
Wilson, Edmund, 75, 76, 79, 81, 82
Wilson, Milton, 59, 60
Winters, Yvor, 1–13, 66, 87, 164, 166, 202
Wittgenstein, L. von, 201, 212, 263
Wolfit, Donald, 156
Wollman, Maurice, 50
Wordsworth, William, 13, 82–5, 89, 90, 91, 215, 218, 237, 264,
Wray, Roger, 244
Wundt, W., 188
Wyatt, Sir Thomas, 124–30, 218

Young, N., 51

Zemanek, H., 198, 199
Zipf, G. K., 192
Zola, Émile, 93